The Origins of Russian Literary Theory

SRLT

NORTHWESTERN UNIVERSITY PRESS
Studies in Russian Literature and Theory

SERIES EDITORS
Caryl Emerson
Gary Saul Morson
William Mills Todd III
Andrew Wachtel
Justin Weir

The Origins of Russian Literary Theory

Folklore, Philology, Form

Jessica Merrill

NORTHWESTERN UNIVERSITY PRESS / EVANSTON, ILLINOIS

Northwestern University Press
www.nupress.northwestern.edu

Studies of the Harriman Institute
Columbia University

The Harriman Institute, Columbia University, sponsors the Studies of the Harriman
Institute in the belief that their publication contributes to scholarly research and
public understanding. In this way the Institute, while not necessarily endorsing
their conclusions, is pleased to make available the results of some of the research
conducted under its auspices.

Printed in the United States of America

10 9 8 7 6 5 4 3 2 1

Library of Congress Cataloging-in-Publication Data

Nawmes: Merrill, Jessica E., author.
Title: The origins of Russian literary theory : folklore, philology, form / Jessica
    Merrill.
Other titles: Studies in Russian literature and theory.
Description: Evanston, Illinois : Northwestern University Press, 2022. | Series:
    Northwestern University Press Studies in Russian literature and theory |
    Includes bibliographical references and index.
Identifiers: LCCN 2022000292 | ISBN 9780810144903 (paperback) |
    ISBN 9780810144910 (cloth) | ISBN 9780810144927 (ebook)
Subjects: LCSH: Formalism (Literary analysis)—History. | Russian literature—
    History and criticism—Theory, etc. | BISAC: LITERARY CRITICISM / Russian
    & Former Soviet Union | LITERARY CRITICISM / European / Eastern (see
    also Russian & Former Soviet Union)
Classification: LCC PN98.F6 M47 2022 | DDC 801.950947—dc23/eng/20220105
LC record available at https://lccn.loc.gov/2022000292

Contents

Acknowledgments

This book has been profoundly shaped by the generous help of colleagues, by inspirational working groups, and by critical institutional funding. The final shape of the manuscript owes much to the expert advice of Galin Tihanov, who patiently read multiple drafts of the book. I also owe a huge thanks to Ilya Kliger for his probing questions and observations, and for general advice along the way. I am much indebted to Peter Steiner and Igor Pil'shchikov for their numerous valuable suggestions and corrections on draft chapters. Igor Pil'shchikov also provided invaluable aid in making the archive of the Moscow Linguistic Circle much more easily accessible to me. I want to thank Gabriella Safran for her careful reading of an early draft, and her encouragement in the revision process. An important thank-you is owed to Kevin Platt and the members of the Penn History Kruzhok for their incisive feedback on a draft of the introduction in spring 2019.

My thinking on the legacy of Russian Formalism has been deeply informed by a number of collaborative scholarly groups. First among these is the Historical Poetics Working Group. In particular, my participation in two important conferences organized by Boris Maslov, in 2015 and 2016, had a considerable impact on my understanding of the nineteenth-century origins of modern literary theory. I want to thank all the members of this group for their continued help and inspiration. I am also indebted to the Archaists and Innovators working group, organized by Serguei Oushakine and Mark Lipovetsky in 2018, for their shared enthusiasm for rethinking the legacy of Viktor Shklovsky. A formative influence was a yearlong seminar on Formalisms in 2012–13, hosted by the Center for Cultural Analysis at Rutgers University. I want to thank its directors, Jonathan Kramnick and Jonah Siegel, and the Fellows for introducing me to debates in English on the concept of form and new formalisms. Finally, I would not have been able to write this book without a Mellon Fellowship of Scholars in the Humanities at Stanford University. This gave me the time and resources to conduct new research, and the opportunity to discuss my ideas with a group of inspiring colleagues led by R. Lanier Anderson and J. P. Daughton.

Acknowledgments

The seed for this book was planted when I was a graduate student in the Slavic Languages and Literatures Department at UC Berkeley. My first forays into the fields of literary theory, philology, and folklore were expertly guided by Harsha Ram, Alan Timberlake, Viktor Zhivov, and Ronelle Alexander. Even as I undertook to write a new book after the PhD, the lessons I learned from my dissertation advisor, Irina Paperno, have proven to be continually relevant, and needed. I want to thank her again here for her peerless mentorship over the years.

The completion of this book was made possible by the all-around support I have received from Columbia University. I want to thank Ronald Meyer, and acknowledge the generosity of the Harriman Institute in the form of two Faculty Publication Grants. Junior Faculty Development and Chamberlain leaves from Columbia in 2019–20 gave me time to complete a final round of revisions. Most importantly, my colleagues in the Slavic Languages Department have been a continual source of support and encouragement. Very special thanks are reserved for Kirsten Painter for her expert editing and huge help with manuscript preparation, and to Irina Finkelshtein for her no less heroic work deciphering and transcribing archival materials. I am also deeply grateful for all of the work of my editors at Northwestern University Press, and to Jessica Hinds-Bond for the index. My research has also been supported by the Russian Science Foundation, project number 16-18-10250.

Note on the Text

We are following a modified Library of Congress transliteration system in this volume. To make the body of the main text more readable to a general audience, first and last names ending in -*ii* have been changed to -*y,* such as Anatoly or Shklovsky rather than Anatolii or Shklovskii. We have also, for the sake of readability, collapsed -*iia* endings to -*ia.* For the same reason, names beginning with *iu-* or *ia-,* such as Iurii and Iazykov, have been changed to Yury and Yazykov. Names are given in their standard English form when one exists. Bibliographic references, including the notes, follow the standard Library of Congress transliteration system. Unless otherwise noted, the author is responsible for the translations offered in this text.

The Origins of Russian Literary Theory

The Philological Paradigm

THE TERM "THEORY" as used in literary studies encompasses a broad spectrum of overlapping intellectual traditions. Some of these are overtly defined by a shared philosophical commitment—for example, Freudian, Marxist, or postcolonial theory. Others can be defined by a shared theory of language or set of interpretive procedures—for example, New Criticism, Russian Formalism, or deconstruction. However, despite the breadth of the field, (French) structuralism and post-structuralism clearly hold a central place in the history of modern literary theory. These movements, dominant in the 1960s and 1970s, constituted a peak moment for literary theory; they were internationally influential not only in literary studies, but across the humanities and social sciences more broadly. As a result, earlier movements—particularly Russian Formalism and Czech structuralism (active from the 1910s to the 1940s)—are often understood as precursors to post–World War II structuralism. The broader contours of this book affirm the basic truth of this accepted genealogy.

However, my rationale for writing a new intellectual history of modern literary theory has been spurred by evidence that this history is not strictly linear. The end point for my narrative is a resurgence of interest in the study of literary form, which has been growing since the turn of the twenty-first century. This momentum is manifested in movements such as new formalism, historical poetics, quantitative formalism, and cognitive poetics. These diverse approaches often call for a "return to form," along with efforts to reconsider the conceptual framework for its study. This scholarship can be situated within the broader phenomenon that Julie Orlemanski has described as the "turn against the linguistic turn."[1] She cites historian Michael Roth's evocative 2007 description of this latest turn as a sea change felt across the humanities:

> For the last decade or so, recognition has been spreading that the linguistic turn that had motivated much advanced work in the humanities is over. The massive tide of language that connected analytic philosophy with pragmatism,

anthropology with social history, philosophy of science with deconstruction, has receded; we are now able to look across the sand to see what might be worth salvaging before the next waves of theory and research begin to pound the shore.[2]

The "linguistic turn," for this book, refers to the extension of Ferdinand de Saussure's linguistic theory as a kind of "Ur-logic" that supported analogies between "the organization of language, texts, cognition, and society."[3] The waning of the structuralist and post-structuralist paradigm is a central factor in the rise of novel approaches to the concept of form within literary studies. What is being sought, apparently, is a concept of form, and a rationale for studying literary form, that does not presuppose a structuralist philosophy of language. (For a brief explication of the latter, see the appendix.)

This book seeks to contribute to this process by explicating the assumptions underlying the pre- or non-structuralist branches of Russian Formalist literary theory. I will refer to these branches as "lost" directions in literary theory, because they are largely unstudied. In order to make them visible and coherent we need to reconstruct a forgotten philosophy of language, one that traced the origins and evolution of patterns in language usage to their extralinguistic sources. These sources varied: in the mid-nineteenth century, philologists drew on universal logics to explain regularities, and referred to philosophies of history (e.g., a Hegelian philosophy of history as a directional process) to explain language change. As I will show, the Russian Formalists initially assumed that psychological laws were the ultimate source of verbal form, and that social factors (e.g., population contact, movement) caused its persistence or change over time. This mode of thinking about language, which I will refer to as the "philological paradigm," differed from the structuralist philosophy of language. The latter insisted that the source of formal linguistic patterns, and the explanation for their evolution over time, is in the structure of language itself. This central difference, between language-extrinsic and language-intrinsic explanatory logic, has extensive ramifications for the concept of verbal form, and for the relationship between form and cultural history.

My approach to reconstructing this lost philosophy of language is intellectual-historical. I seek to explain the history of ideas by situating them in relation to academic, scholarly, and cultural institutions. My analysis, and often the novelty of my arguments, relies on archival research in the institutional archives of the Moscow Linguistic Circle and the Prague Linguistic Circle, as well as the personal archives of Roman Jakobson, Viktor Shklovsky, and others. The most important of these sources, for this book, is the archive of the Moscow Linguistic Circle (MLC).[4] Its contents, including minutes of

bimonthly meetings held between 1918 and 1923, allow for a more historically contextualized understanding of the early years of the movement.[5]

I use these sources to reconstruct lost paths within the intellectual genealogy that begins with the Russian Formalists and culminates with post-
structuralism. These are the branches of Formalism, developed in the late
1910s and early 1920s, which structuralist and post-structuralist accounts
often discount as "inadequacies" which were fortunately "eliminated in the
second phase of formalism."[6] I have sought to take these abandoned paths
seriously, to explain their presuppositions and goals, and to present them
as potentially useful for developing Formalist approaches to literary studies
today. I do this by locating a starting point for the history of literary theory
earlier in time. While most histories of the field begin with the 1910s, I begin
in the mid-nineteenth century. In chapter 1, I argue that in order to reconstruct the philosophy of language which informed Russian Formalist theory,
we have to look to Romantic language philosophies and comparative philology. This allows us to see how Russian philologists drew on these traditions
in an original move to develop a "theory of verbal art" (*teoriia slovesnosti*)
that inspired the Russian Formalists to improve on their work.

After 1900, this book treats institutions and individuals more typically covered in the existing scholarship on Russian Formalism: Alexander
Veselovsky and Alexander (Oleksandr) Potebnia; the Formalist societies
OPOIAZ (the Society for the Study of Poetic Language) and the MLC; the
Prague Linguistic Circle; and the collaboration between Roman Jakobson
and Claude Lévi-Strauss in the 1940s and 1950s. This, in its broad contours,
is a familiar trajectory. However, because my aim is not to trace a single genealogy, but to call attention to forgotten ideas which have remained largely
unstudied, the central parts of this book—chapters 2, 3, and 4—all describe
the same period: the mid-1910s and early 1920s. Chapter 2 calls attention
to the social and political motivations for the OPOIAZ study of poetics in
the revolutionary period, and recovers an unacknowledged, antibourgeois,
Formalist theory of authorship. These motivations become more visible
when the Formalist movement is presented as the successor to the philological paradigm. Chapter 3 illustrates the psychological underpinnings of
Shklovsky's narrative theory, and chapter 4 examines the pre-structuralist,
sociolinguistic poetics of Jakobson and the MLC. By shifting our focus to
seemingly marginal, theoretical detours, I recontextualize some of the Formalists' more famous ideas—for example, the declaration of the autonomy
of art, the meaning of defamiliarization (*ostranenie*), and the concept of
poetic language—which have come to seem self-evident. Chapter 5 describes the emergence of structuralism: rather than present post–World
War II structuralism as a culmination of earlier movements formed in Rus-

sia and in Czechoslovakia, I stress the differences between the structuralist literary theory which emerged in the 1950s (which was rooted in information theory) and the earlier work based on the historical study of natural languages. The book's conclusion jumps from the 1960s to the twenty-first century, drawing connections between the lost paths of the 1910s and 1920s and the formalisms that are in development today.

The arguments in this book are made possible by a wealth of existing scholarship on Russian Formalism and Czech structuralism. To recuperate lost branches of theory presupposes an existing, established narrative which overlooks these branches. The foundational scholarship on these movements was published primarily in the 1970s. Some of the most important monographs include those by Victor Erlich (1965), Fredric Jameson (1972), Aage Hansen-Löve (1978), Peter Steiner (1984), and Jurij Striedter (1989).[7] These books generally take an ahistorical approach to their subject matter; the movements are explained in terms of their internal logic, which connects different thinkers. Steiner's *Russian Formalism: A Metapoetics*, for example, organizes Formalist theory into four conceptual tropes. More recent scholarship, including this book, takes a contextualizing, historical approach—seeking to explain Formalism and structuralism as products of a historical moment and milieu. Exemplary of this second wave of scholarship are works by Ilona Svetlikova (2005), Galin Tihanov (2004, 2019), and Jan Levchenko (2012).[8] While this second wave of contextualizing work often complements the internal accounts, the two approaches can also produce divergent interpretations of Formalist theory. This book argues that contextualizing Russian Formalism in the linguistic philosophy of the Formalists' contemporaries and teachers, that is, as informed by the philological paradigm, allows for a new understanding of some of their central ideas.

This divergence emerges in part from the fact that the first wave of scholarship on Russian Formalism often explained Formalism through the lens of structuralism.[9] Even while scholars admit the difficulty of subsuming the diverse Formalist thinkers and schools under a single paradigm, there is a general tendency in the scholarship from the 1960s to the 1980s to privilege Formalist ideas that appear compatible with structuralism. Erlich articulates this with an explicit value judgment: "Russian formalism *at its best* was or tended to be Structuralism."[10] Generally speaking, scholars adopt two (often overlapping) strategies to confine Formalism within a structuralist lens: they explain it using a teleological narrative, as evolving in the direction of structuralism; or they treat it ("at its best") as equivalent to structuralism, a narrative of conflation. Striedter's book exemplifies the first approach. Striedter accounts for differences between Russian Formalism and structuralism as "stages" of development. In his words, his book describes "a single and coherent method which evolved in clearly distinguished stages"; these are labeled "early Formalism," "late Formalism/early Prague Structuralism," and "Prague Structuralism." What allows Striedter to treat this history as one of stadial evolution is his view that "during its entire existence Russian Formalism was closely allied with the budding discipline of structural linguistics."[11] While I do not want to dispute that Formalist theory was always in a state of "evolution," something that the Formalists themselves stressed, I am calling attention to the tendency, in the reception of Formalism after the 1960s, to see the movement as a progression toward the achievement of structuralism.[12]

In contrast to the discourse of phases or stages, Jameson conflates Formalism and structuralism as two "projections" of the ideas of Ferdinand de Saussure. He playfully suggests that "French Structuralism is related to Russian Formalism . . . as crossed cousins within an endogamous kinship system. Both ultimately derive from Saussure's foundational distinction between *langue* and *parole* . . . but they exploit it in different ways."[13] The English-language reception of Formalism shows a stronger tendency toward conflation, likely encouraged by the delayed introduction of the movement, contemporaneously with structuralism in 1960s. (I will return to this point at the end of this introduction.) By situating Russian Formalism in an intellectual history that is not structuralist, this book seeks to counter overly reductive interpretations of the movement which derive from the teleological and the conflating narratives established in the 1970s.

Significantly, even within the first wave of scholarship on Formalism, there was no consensus as to the movement's relationship to structuralism. Steiner contrasts Russian Formalism and Czech structuralism on the basis of their epistemologies: Formalism idealized "facts" and strove for "pure knowledge: knowledge devoid of any external presuppositions," while the structuralists grounded their theory in an "epistemological stance" deriving from an "awareness of a system."[14] Building on this claim, Steiner describes Russian Formalism as a "pre-paradigm" or "inter-paradigm" state of science, a movement defined by "conceptual disunity."[15] This opposition between Russian Formalism and Czech structuralism informs his 1984 monograph, which concludes that Russian Formalism was "not the sum total of its theories . . . but a *polemos*, a struggle among contradictory and incompatible views."[16] Unlike the teleological and conflating narratives, Steiner stresses the fundamental differences between structuralism and Formalism. Of the accounts summarized here, I find Steiner's description of Russian Formalism as a "*polemos*" most compelling. I agree with his conclusions that efforts to "pin down the identity" of the movement as a whole are futile, and that the movement's methodological and epistemological "pluralism" truly raises the question of whether a single label—Russian Formalism—is "worthwhile to retain . . . at all."[17] However, my analysis diverges from Steiner's conclusions.

This book will show that there was a non-structuralist, and yet coherent, conceptual paradigm that informed the emergence of Russian Formalism. I will be referring to this as the "philological paradigm." My work builds on the scholarship of colleagues in Russia, such as Svetlikova, Levchenko, and Ilya Kalinin, as well as others in the United States and Europe who view Russian Formalism as a response to turn-of-the-century artistic, philosophical, and political thought. My approach is particularly close to that of Ilona Svetlikova's 2005 monograph, in which she demonstrates the importance of European psychologism to the emergence of Russian Formalism. I share her ambition "to understand the Formal School as a part of a particular intellectual whole; to connect the scholarly work of its members with a particular tradition and a particular scholarly context."[18] My work is also crucially informed by that of Galin Tihanov, who has helped to establish the broader historical context for Formalism. His seminal 2004 essay "Why Did Modern Literary Theory Originate in Central and Eastern Europe?" identifies a cluster of philosophical, ideological, and cultural factors as the necessary conditions for the emergence of modern literary theory. My book, like Svetlikova's and Tihanov's work, seeks to identify the critical aspects of the intellectual context which enabled the emergence of Russian Formalism. However, the context that I describe is broader than Svetlikova's and narrower than Tihanov's.

My thinking has also been impacted by the recent work of Boris Maslov and Ilya Kliger on the legacy of Alexander Veselovsky. In separate articles, and in a collected volume, *Persistent Forms: Explorations in Historical Poetics* (2015), they have called attention to Veselovsky's work in the field he described as "historical poetics" (*istoricheskaia poetika*). Their scholarship not only seeks to demonstrate Veselovsky's largely unacknowledged importance to the emergence of modern literary theory, but also to present his work as a resource for twenty-first-century literary studies. I share their commitment to rethinking the history of theory as a means of spurring creative and productive new scholarship.[19] In this book, I attempt to strike a balance between historicizing Russian Formalist theory with regard to the intellectual context of the early twentieth century, and highlighting aspects of this theory that are consonant with movements in the twenty-first century. As I discuss in the conclusion, one point of commonality is in grounding the concept of "form" in relation to cognitive principles and mechanisms that are not specific to language. Another shared feature is in the perceived relevance of literary forms to sociopolitical concerns. Ultimately, however, my goal is to clarify the Formalists' conceptual presuppositions so that others may judge the utility of these ideas for themselves.

THE PHILOLOGICAL PARADIGM

It is to be stressed that in using the adjective "philological" I am not suggest-ing that every aspect of philological study is evoked by the term "philological paradigm." In this section I will outline which aspects of philological study were relevant for the "philological paradigm." Philology, as a term used with-out a descriptive adjective, is often defined as the study of texts. As Saussure put it, "philology seeks primarily to establish, interpret, and comment upon texts."[20] Or as Sheldon Pollock more recently has argued, "philology is, or should be, the discipline of making sense of texts. It is . . . the theory of textuality as well as the history of textualized meaning."[21] These definitions refer to a scholarly tradition, also called textual studies, which is often traced to Friedrich August Wolf, Friedrich Wilhelm Ritschl, and Karl Lachmann. This is *not* the philological tradition that I am discussing here. Instead, my argument is about *comparative* philology, a distinct branch of study, traced to the work of German and Danish scholars such as Franz Bopp, Rasmus Rask, and Jacob Grimm, who established a method and techniques for the comparative study of Indo-European grammatical structures and lexica in the 1810s and 1820s.

In introducing the philological paradigm, I will first describe the method that these scholars adhered to. I will then turn to the philosophy of language that informed the paradigm and shaped scholars' thinking about the nature and limits of their object of study. In Russian, the method that defines the philological paradigm is often referred to as the "comparative-historical method" (*sravnitel'no-istoricheskii metod*). It was inspired by the tradition of comparative Indo-European grammar study established by Franz Bopp and others, which was then extended to the study of mythology by Jacob Grimm. In Russia, Fyodor Buslaev (1818–1897), a highly influen-tial professor of Russian literature at Moscow University, insisted on adher-ence to the comparative method for academic philological studies. Buslaev was, like Grimm, a scholar of grammar and mythology as well as oral tradi-tions (folklore). His students, Alexander Veselovsky (1838–1906) and Alex-ander Potebnia (1835–1891), proposed extending this method to the study of written literature.

Locating the beginnings of modern literary theory in the mid-nineteenth century allows for a reinterpretation of the view that literary theory emerged as part of a "linguistic turn" which occurred with Saussurean, structuralist linguistics in the 1920s. The turn to linguistics (philology) as a model for a theory of literature was actually urged decades earlier. In an 1870 introduc-tory lecture to a course on the "History of World Literature" ("Vseobshchei istorii literatury"), Veselovsky enthusiastically promoted the comparative his-torical method for literary study:

It is well known what a revolution the application of the comparative method has wrought in the study, and in the value of the results obtained, in the field of linguistics. The method has also recently been introduced in the areas of mythology, folk poetry, the so-called migratory legends . . . the successes of linguistics on this path give hope that in the areas of both historical and literary phenomena we may also expect, if not identical, at least approximately exact results.[22]

The rhetoric here is remarkably similar to later pronouncements by theorists such as Jakobson, Roland Barthes, or Claude Lévi-Strauss, claiming that adopting the latest, cutting-edge linguistic theories would allow for analogous progress in the field of literary studies (see chapter 5).

The comparative historical method is based on the process of inductive inference. As Dan Hunter explains: "Induction is, generally, the process of taking a number of specific instances, classifying them into categories according to relevant attributes and outcomes, and deriving a broadly applicable rule from them. That is, we take a number of isolated experiences and attempt to explain them by a general rule that covers all the instances examined."[23] In Veselovsky's words, the scholar begins with a "series of facts" taken from "historical and social life" and begins to look for repeating relationships within a "series," and to compare these to relationships observed in "parallel series of similar facts" for verification. Successive verification allows the scholar to posit principles, and then to confirm cause and effect, and finally to move from generalizations to "laws."[24]

Though Veselovsky does not give a particular example of the comparative historical method, we can supply one from the study of sound change. The method was applied in this field by observing patterns in the formal differences between cognate words. Rasmus Rask wrote that "if there is found between two languages agreement in the forms of indispensable words to such an extent that rules of letter changes can be discovered for passing from one to the other, then there is a basic relationship between the two languages."[25] In Grimm's most famous work, in which he compared the words for "daughters"—*thugatere* (Greek), *daughters* (Gothic), *töchter* (Old High German)—he observed that the Greek consonant sound "Th" regularly became "D" and "T" in successive changes in the history of Germanic languages.[26] Successive comparisons (e.g., of the words for "two") reveal a principled, regular pattern, which has become known as "Grimm's law."

Thus, the goal of comparative philological studies was to elucidate a rule or law that governs a category of linguistic phenomena. In the nineteenth century, this work was subsumed within a larger preoccupation with questions of historical sequence. The rules derived from comparison were,

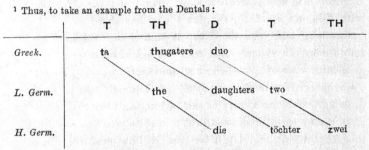

	T	TH	D	T	TH
Greek.	ta	thugatere	duo		
L. Germ.		the	daughters	two	
H. Germ.			die	töchter	zwei

[1] Thus, to take an example from the Dentals:

It will be seen that the High Germ. is always a stage in advance of Low Germ., and this a stage in advance of Greek, Latin, Sanskrit, &c. The Germ. *z* is sounded *ts*; and *s*, like *h*, is a breathing.—TRANS.

Comparative pronunciation chart from Jacob Grimm, *Teutonic Mythology*, 3: xxi. Originally published 1882–1888.

as a result, applied historical developments, but importantly, these were not understood to be absolute or exceptionless.

As Robins and others have pointed out, "the very term 'Grimm's law' is an anachronism; he did not make technical use of the word law to describe what he referred to as sound shift [*Lautverschiebung*]; and in a much quoted passage he remarked: 'The sound shift is a general tendency; it is not followed in every case.'"[27] The anachronism here derives from projecting later expectations onto nineteenth-century comparative philology. Scholars of nineteenth-century linguistics have suggested that developments beginning around 1870 represented an important shift in terms of the rationale for comparative studies. The earlier (pre-1870) rationale is described as reconstructing earlier language states for their own sake, a process which referred to logic (rather than the formal properties of words, such as phonology) as a means of explanation. The later rationale understands comparative reconstruction as "a means for lengthening the history of a language and consequently providing better evidence to account for existing forms."[28] While it is difficult to generalize about all of nineteenth-century linguistics, scholars have suggested that it was not until later in the century that comparative philologists began to prioritize formal explanations for language change. Analyzing comparative linguistics before the 1870s, Paul Kiparsky has argued that although comparativists such as Bopp were capable of highly sophisticated thinking about phonology, their reconstructions proceeded on the basis of semantic analysis, preferring this kind of argumentation over phonological data, even when it was known.[29] Sound shifts, such as the "general tendency" described by Grimm, did not have to be exceptionless "laws" because the history of language was not understood to be exclusively determined by the intrinsic constraints of its formal structure.

Even philologists who argued that language history *is* determined by "inalterable laws" did not always locate the source of these laws in the formal structure of language. For instance, August Schleicher famously argued that language is properly understood as an "organism." Although Schleicher's studies focused on phonology and morphology, he used a generalized organic model to explain language history, and argued that languages follow a universal pattern according to which "a prehistoric period of language development is followed by a historical period of language decay."[30] In sum, the methodology being developed in the historical comparative study of language made precise observations regarding language form, but did not necessarily look to these formal descriptions as causal factors when explaining language change over time.

For Veselovsky as well, the historical development of a poetic tradition is not determined by earlier states of that same tradition (understood as a reservoir of formal devices). He explained literary evolution with Hegelian "universal history." Maslov and Kliger describe Veselovsky's "historico-philosophical" framework as "a post-Hegelian or Spencerian assertion of the general movement towards human emancipation and individuation." His assumption is that "societies" universally "pass through a number of stages in the process of development from primitive communality to individualistic modernity." This "post-Hegelian idealist vision . . . that literary forms evolve in a way that is more or less uniform across cultures" was what "ma[de] possible systematic comparative inquiry into literature."[31] While Veselovsky's primary focus was the comparative study of poetic form, for him the study of verbal art is ultimately the study of the stadial history of social thought. In an 1894 publication, he explained this by beginning with the question: "What is the history of literature?" He answers: "Literary history is the history of social thought in its imagistic-poetic survival [*perezhivanie*] and in the forms that express this sedimentation. History of thought is a broader notion; literature is its partial manifestation."[32] The patterns derived from the inductive, comparative study of literary form were thought to result from the laws of history—not from the nature of literary forms themselves.

Inductive comparison was the mandatory method for scholarly work in the philological paradigm. However, it did not provide a complete framework for thinking about language as an object of study. A particularly interesting moment in the history of the philological paradigm occurred when Russian scholars sought to combine the comparative method with a Romantic philosophy of language. This line of thinking understands language, often in psychological terms, as inextricable from thought, and can be traced to the influence of eighteenth- and early nineteenth-century thinkers such as Johann Gottfried von Herder and Wilhelm von Humboldt. Robins articulates Herder's impact as follows: "The close connection between thought and language had been a commonplace of philosophy since antiquity," but while earlier writers had assumed a hierarchic dependence of language on prior thought, Herder's articulation of "the common origin and parallel development of both together through successive stages of growth and maturity was rather new."[33] This linkage between language and thought was extended to an identification between language and cultural identity, and, in the context of nineteenth-century nationalist "awakenings," an identification between language and national identity. The Slovak linguist and revolutionary Ľudovít Štúr, who is credited with codifying literary Slovak in the 1840s, exemplifies the link between a Herderian philosophy of language and a concept of national sovereignty:

> Every nation is most ardently coupled with its language. The nation is reflected in it as the first product of its theoretical spirit; language is, then, the surest sign of the essence and individuality of every nation. Just like an individual human being, the nation reveals its deepest inner self through language; it, so to speak, embodies its spirit in language.[34]

Similar statements can be found in the writings of patriotic philologists in Russia, as well as in Germany and among the foreign-ruled peoples of central Europe, such as the Slovaks. A widely embraced and fundamental truism of this philosophy was that language is inseparable from the historical and social reality of its speakers.

Humboldt and his student Heymann (Chajim) Steinthal developed this understanding of language in more precise detail. Like Herder, Humboldt believed that "language is the formative organ of thought" (*Sprache is das bildende Organ des Gedanken*) and shapes a speaker's "worldview" (*Weltansicht*). Ana Deumert explains Humboldt's philosophy as asserting that "human cognition and perception are historically and culturally embedded in the inner structures of specific languages, leading to a multiplicity of ways of seeing, conceptualizing, and assimilating the world around us."[35] As Humboldt wrote in 1812, "all languages taken together resemble a prism where each side shows the universe in differently tinted color."[36] Humboldt's articulation of the nature of the relationship between language, thought, and the speaker's social world would fundamentally shape Russian philologists' understanding of the nature of language.

The Russian tradition stressed two Humboldtian ideas in particular. The first was that language is to be understood as a creative act, which always entails a negotiation between the individual and the collective, between the speaker's creative impulse and the rules and norms within which any speaker/perceiver operates. As Humboldt wrote:

> Language, considered in its true nature, is something which is constantly and in every moment in transition . . . Language is not a product [*Ergon*] but an activity [*Energeia*]. . . . Language belongs to me because I produce it in my very own way; and since the basis of this lies in the speaking and having-spoken of all previous generations . . . it is the language as such which limits me . . . The study of language must recognize and honor the phenomenon of freedom, but at the same time trace carefully its limits.[37]

Deumert interprets Humboldt's understanding of linguistic limitations vs. freedom by stressing the latter: "speakers . . . are not at the mercy of their languages: they are subjects and as such capable of agency and creativity. Individual speech acts simultaneously reproduce and transcend the system in which they operate."[38] The second feature of Humboldt's philosophy crucial for Russian philology was his privileging of oral speech, and particularly speech in dialogue as the essence of language (*Energeia*). In Russia at the turn of the century, this concept was articulated as a focus on the "living word" (*zhivoe slovo*).

The meeting between the Humboldtian philosophy of language and the comparative method was a particularly important moment in the history that I am tracing. This is because there was an incomplete fit between them, and because scholars consequently attempted to reconcile them in different ways. The comparative method worked well with the collective aspect of the philosophy of language, or what Humboldt called *Ergon*, but the individual, creative part (*Energeia*) was not easily amenable to the method. The partial solutions that the philologists offered to surmount the rift between the two domains would become building blocks for the Russian Formalists. These included a programmatic methodology (referred to as "poetics"), inherited assumptions regarding the object of study (defined as *slovesnost'*), and criteria for scholarliness in the field of literary studies.

The Russian Formalists inherited an existing field of study, called the "theory of verbal art" or "poetics" (*poetika*). In describing his work as "historical poetics," Veselovsky saw his efforts as an improvement on the tradition of poetics associated with Aristotle.[39] In his 1870 address Veselovsky explains how the comparative method can be applied to the study of literature. This requires that literary works should not be treated as the isolated products of extraordinary individual creativity, of some "great man," but should be situated within a broader domain of popular verbal tradition.[40] The individual work cannot be the basic unit of analysis in this approach.

Veselovsky explains his perspective with a rhetorical question: "Does not each new poetic epoch work upon images inherited from time immemorial, necessarily operating within their limits, allowing itself only new combinations of the old, and only filling them with that new understanding of life which in fact constitutes its progress over the past?" The history of language provides an affirmative answer:

> At least the history of language suggests to us an analogous phenomenon. We do not create a new language, we receive it at birth ready-made, not subject to alteration; the actual changes effected by history do not alter the elemental form of the word, or else alter it so gradually that it occurs undetected by two consecutive generations.[41]

Literary studies should likewise proceed by identifying, through comparison, the repeating elements in literary history. Veselovsky and others used the term "tradition" (*predanie*), from the verb "give over" (*peredat'*), to refer to these repeating elements. Veselovsky's examples of the content of *predanie* include forms such as fixed epithets ("white" swan), particular symbols (e.g., a bird, flower, or color), metaphors (comparing clouds with enemies, or a battle with threshing), triadic repetitions, rhetorical devices, and formulas (prophetic dreams, boasts, curses, or typical depictions of battle).[42]

Veselovsky's concept of *predanie* is informed by his study of oral, folkloric genres. Folklore was amenable to the comparative historical method because these corpora (genres of oral verbal art such as tales, songs, or incantations) cluster into types and variants. By the early twentieth century, the dissection of (transcribed) folklore texts into minimal units was an established practice: folktales were understood to be made up of smaller parts, referred to as episodes, motifs, or formulas, which reoccurred in different performances.[43] In his work on folkloric material, Veselovsky demonstrated that the comparative method could successfully establish the collective, the rule-bound, and the normative aspects of literary history: those elements which limit the freedom of the individual speaker, according to Humboldt's model. However, the place of the individual—the source of novelty and creativity—remained an open question for philologists.

Veselovsky would suggest that the individual, creative act remains outside the limits of historical poetics, a research program defined by the comparative method. In lecture notes from the late 1890s, he wrote: "The task of historical poetics, as it appears to me, is to determine the role and the boundaries of tradition [*predanie*] in the process of personal creation."[44] This articulation echoes Humboldt's assertion, cited above, that "the study of language must recognize and honor the phenomenon of freedom, but at the same time trace carefully its limits."[45] Veselovsky adds that works of art which contemporaries may find utterly exceptional, may, with time, be revealed to be made up of traditional elements. In a frequently cited passage from his "Poetics of Plots" ("Poetika siuzhetov"), he argues that the plot structures found in folktales are an element of tradition (*predanie*), and poses the question of whether the comparative study of narrative could produce results for contemporary literature as well:

> Contemporary narrative literature with its complex plot structures and photographic representation of reality would seem to nullify the very possibility of such a question; but when for future generations it appears in the same distant perspective, like antiquity for us, from the prehistoric to the middle ages, when the synthesis of time, that great simplifier, passes through the complexity of phenomena, reducing them to the size of points receding into the depths, its lines will converge with those which reveal themselves to us today when we look at the ancient poetic past, and indications of schematism and repetition will emerge along the entire length.[46]

This text, and the implications of this passage in particular, directly inspired the Formalists' generation. The seminal narratological contributions of Viktor Shklovsky and Vladimir Propp can be seen as a competition to develop Veselovsky's proposal. Propp, who was not a member of the Formalist societies, but whose work was likewise informed by the Russian philological paradigm, cited this passage as the last paragraph of his *Morphology of the Folktale* (*Morfologiia skazki*, 1928), indicating that he viewed his work as a contribution to Veselovsky's larger project.

Veselovsky's argument is not just that methods developed in the study of folklore can be also applied to the study of written literature. The implicit argument shared within the philological paradigm is that folklore and literature should be studied together as manifestations of the same underlying processes. This idea was motivated by Romantic ideology regarding the relationship between a national language, folklore, and written literature. In the Russian tradition, the alliance between these domains was facilitated by the availability of a concept, "verbal art" (*slovesnost'*), which refers collectively to both popular, oral genres and written literature.[47] As Andy Byford points out, *slovesnost'* as a category was evoked as a way of "legitimately including folklore in the realm of 'literature,' as in the phrase *narodnaia slovesnost'*."[48] At the turn of the twentieth century, *slovesnost'* was used to describe poetic language or discourse in general. Vladimir Dal's dictionary defines *slovesnost'* as "the commonality of verbal works of the people [*narod*], writing, literature."[49] As this definition suggests, it is a category informed by Romantic nationalist thought, in that it is the verbal art of the "nation" or "folk" (*narod*).

As the dictionary definition reveals, the notion of *slovesnost'* is predicated on a refusal to distinguish between oral and written discourse, so that the term can be interpreted either way. However, scholars of literature working in the philological paradigm tended to embrace an oral understanding of *slovesnost'*.[50] Other discursive categories available to Russian literary scholars at the turn of the century were *pis'mennost'*, *literatura*, and *poeziia*. The first denoted "writing in general, especially when 'literariness' was not an issue." The second, *literatura*, referred to "published discourse, especially fine, educated writings, though not just fiction and poetry," and the last term, *poeziia*, referred to "not just verse, but also prose fiction and aesthetic literature in general" (synonymous with *iziashchnaia literatura*, literally "fine literature," a calque from the French *belles-lettres*).[51] These last two categories (literature and poetry) are probably more familiar as objects of literary studies. Yet, in Russia in the late nineteenth century scholars consciously avoided these categories.

The reasons for this are outlined in Byford's *Literary Scholarship in Late Imperial Russia*. A nationalist orientation in literary scholarship was driven by scholars' desire to assert their independence from the state, to view their work as dedicated "to the good of the Russian people," and to differentiate it from "Western science."[52] They also defined scholarliness in opposition to journalistic literary criticism. Academics thus often avoided artistic "high" literature and questions of aesthetics, which were seen as the province of journalism, and instead pursued historical, linguistically grounded research. For Russian philologists, academic or scholarly research focused not on "high" literary texts (*belles-lettres*) but rather on a wider range of verbal art, in particular folk poetry, and medieval or early modern writings.[53] These could be described by the term *slovesnost'*, which had the connotation of being "homegrown," or of the people (*narod*), in contrast to Europeanized *literatura* associated with educated society.

The concept of *slovesnost'* allowed scholars to propose that linguistic and folkloristic research was also relevant for understanding literature, since all verbal art—from a proverb to a novel—could be understood to follow the model of oral speech. This idea is articulated in a 1911 article by Dmitry Ovsianiko-Kulikovsky, a student of Potebnia's and popularizer of his work. In assessing the merits of Veselovsky's and Potebnia's theoretical legacy, which Ovsianiko-Kulikovsky refers to as the "linguistic theory" of verbal art, he writes:

> Thanks to Wilhelm Humboldt we know that language is *activity, work*, and that there are many signs or elements of artistry in this work. If you use these elements for the expression of your thoughts, then the phrase you utter, along with many others, is a manifestation of language's poetic work. *The difference between this manifestation and the "genuine" poetic composition of a poet is,*

in the end, only quantitative. The poet uses more artistic elements than we do, and their very artistry is greater, more suggestive, brighter. It is not hard to see that these differences are not qualitative, and that we are right to classify the compositions of world poetry with the artistic facts of everyday language [*obydennaia rech'*] of millions of people who cannot be called poets.[54]

Potebnia and his followers saw speech as an essentially creative act; everyday speech is not qualitatively (but only quantitatively) different from the work of a poet. In sum, the concept of *slovesnost'* allowed philologists to move between language, folklore, and written literature, and to apply the comparative method to the entire domain. This method allowed them to identify patterns within verbal traditions, with the understanding that identifying these regular forms reveals the limits on individual creativity. The individual creative will, or moment of inspiration, was understood to be inaccessible to scholarly study.

This combination of method and object of study (*slovesnost'*) became the definitive criteria of scholarliness (*nauchnost'*) in Russian academic studies at the turn of the twentieth century. The term *nauka*, like the German *Wissenschaft*, is translated into English as "science" or "scholarship" and refers to all systematic intellectual work. In both Russian and German, one can only distinguish between the humanities and the natural sciences by means of the additional adjectives "gumanitarnye *nauki*" (Geistes*wissenschaften*) or "estestvennye *nauki*" (Natur*wissenschaften*). The concept of scholarliness (*nauchnost'*), as it was developed by nineteenth-century Russian philologists, was focused on the identification of rules rather than on the description of highly valued individual objects. These rules were not understood as exceptionless laws, but more precisely as historical tendencies.

This philological concept of a science of literature was described in Russia, from the 1860s, as the "theory of verbal art" (*teoriia slovesnosti*).[55] As this phrase suggests, to produce "theory" meant to work with the category of *slovesnost'*. This is reflected in the titles of textbooks on the theory of literature (*slovesnost'*), such as *Educational Theory of Verbal Art* (*Uchebnaia teoriia slovesnosti*, N. Minin, St. Petersburg, 1861), *Theory of Verbal Art* (*Teoriia slovesnosti*, E. Voskresensky, Moscow, 1888), and *Theory of Verbal Art [Teoriia slovesnosti] for Secondary School Institutions* (P. Smirnovsky, St. Petersburg, 1895). The best-known titles among such a list would be Alexander Potebnia's published lectures, which appeared with the titles *From Notes on the Theory of Verbal Art [teorii slovesnosti]: Poetry and Prose, Tropes and Figures, Poetic and Mythological Thought, Appendix* (1905) and *From Lectures on the Theory of Verbal Art [teorii slovesnosti]: Fables, Proverbs, Sayings* (1894).

The Russian Formalists sought to outdo the philologists in producing a "theory" of verbal art. In this context, "theory" can be understood as synonymous with "poetics."[56] The Formalists referred to their own work as "theory" but also often as "poetics" or "scientific poetics" (*nauchnaia poetika*), as exemplified in the title used for the publications of OPOIAZ: *Poetics: Collections on the Theory of Poetic Language* (*Poetika: Sborniki po teorii poeticheskogo iazyka*). Contemporary scholars have seen "theory" in the humanities as originating with Russian Formalism. David Rodowick, for example, comments that the "Russian formalists almost certainly . . . invented 'theory' in the modern sense for the humanities."[57] In some ways this is true, yet I will show that they didn't really invent the theory that they were working with. More precisely, we can say that they pushed beyond Veselovsky and Potebnia to explain modern literature, using the framework provided by the philological paradigm. Their work can be described as a series of efforts to negotiate between scholarly (comparative) poetics and the "individual" element of verbal production described by Humboldt as *Energeia*. OPOIAZ theory did this by focusing on the individual author's performance (chapter 2). Shklovsky delved deeper into the psychology of creativity through his creative/theoretical writings, such as *ZOO* (chapter 3), and Jakobson and the Moscow Linguistic Circle stressed the capacity of individuals to consciously innovate in their language usage (chapter 4). The imperative to understand this relationship between the general rules, or accumulated traditions, and the individual act of creativity was, moreover, increasingly charged with political meaning in the early twentieth century, as the concepts of "collective" and "individual" were scrutinized and reinterpreted in the revolutionary period.

RUSSIAN FORMALISM AND THE PHILOLOGICAL PARADIGM

One of the contentions of this book is that situating Russian Formalism with respect to the philological paradigm reveals logical, straightforward explanations for aspects of Russian Formalism that otherwise appear ironic or paradoxical. A central puzzle has to do with the Formalists' motivations: Why did this group of students feel so passionately about apparently arcane subjects at a time of revolution and civil war? In 1919, for instance, the Moscow Linguistic Circle met as often as once a week to discuss presentations with titles such as "Trochaic Tetrameter with Dactylic Endings," and these presentations were followed by fierce debates.[58] The relationship between Formalism and the era in which it emerged has often been described as unintuitive. Carol Any, who views Formalism as a movement dedicated to an "intrinsic poetics" that "shut literature off from the world of politics and everything nonliterary," suggests that it is "ironic that Russian Formalism coincided with the years leading up to and following the Bolshevik Revolution, years when political and social upheaval would seem to have made ludicrous such an uncompromising attempt to divorce literature from the outside world."[59]

Although the Formalists themselves sometimes alluded to the vital importance of their work, these statements alone do not fully explain their motivation. Writing in Petrograd in 1919, Boris Eikhenbaum, for example, struggled to articulate the meaningfulness of scholarly poetics in a time when everyday life was falling apart:

> Now we—those who are alive and *want* to live—are artists. Because life has become difficult, enigmatic, new, meaningful [*preponiatnyi*], and at the same time, law-abiding, slow—and insanely fast. Grotesque, slapstick, circus, tragedy—all combined into a single grandiose performance. "The labyrinth of linkages," within which only an artist can move and see something. And this is the point, that life has become artistic in its very insanity, behind which are hidden some sort of iron laws.[60]

Shklovsky, at around the same time, likewise described the appeal of literary theory in the midst of dire conditions. He described the OPOIAZ Formalists at work in Petrograd in the winter of 1919, when the population was stranded without fuel or food:

> At times it seemed that we could not hold out any longer. Everyone would freeze to death at night in the apartments . . . We gathered and we sat in our coats by the stove, where books were burning. There were wounds on our legs. From a lack of fat, blood vessels burst. And we talked about rhythm, about verbal form and, now and then, about spring, which we had little hope of seeing . . . It seemed that we worked not by the head but by the spinal cord.[61]

For Eikhenbaum, massive changes in everyday life reveal the laws that it nonetheless abides by. He suggests that somehow this situation also allows the division between life and art to collapse. For Shklovsky, wartime deprivations allowed the Formalists to see art as essential for survival, rather than a luxury. These statements are moving, but we need more context to understand the Formalists' motivations.

Tihanov has stressed the legacy of Romanticism in explaining the emergence of Russian Formalism. He sees the relationship between their theory and its cultural context as a "foundational paradox" which "can be formulated in one ramified sentence. It is possible to think about and theorize literature per se, beyond national constraints, yet the importance of literature per se as a subject of theory is validated by analyzing texts that had been—or are being—canonized as nationally significant."[62] That is, the very idea of a science of literature is only conceivable in a society where the importance of literature is considered somehow self-evident (for instance in eastern and central Europe, as a result of the legacy of Romantic nationalism).

While I agree with this assessment, I hasten to clarify a potential point of misunderstanding. It was not that students took for granted that Pushkin's or Lermontov's writings are essential to Russian culture, thus enabling them to study metrical patterns, for example, without asking: Why do this? Rather, as I will show, the Romantic rationale for studying verbal art was carried over into Formalism on the level of the linguistic philosophy and methodology characteristic of the philological paradigm. The Formalists assumed a Romantic philosophy of language which dictated that the precise details of language usage shape the way that people think—what philosophers and cognitive scientists today refer to as a person's "cognitive architecture."[63]

Svetlikova eloquently argues for the necessity of contextualizing the Formalist project: She asks, "why did the formalists study philology?"

> How might the study of philology have appeared in the eyes of the formalists themselves? They did not wear scholarship like a necktie, to use Shklovsky's expression, and they did not sit out the requisite hours in scholarly institutions. They did not see their occupation as protecting cultural heritage, they were not its modest guardians. Behind that energy which the formalists applied to philology, there had to be an ideological motive, which slips away from us due to its historical character: it no longer acts on us.[64]

She proposes that there "was some sort of cultural stream, within which it appeared that philology did not study the details of culture, its '101 examples,' but the elementary mechanisms of its emergence . . . Philology had to study something that was the 'most important.'"[65] The lost ideological and cultural motivation that Svetlikova refers to can be explained as the product of the interaction between the assumptions of the philological paradigm and the fervor of the revolutionary period. The Formalists inherited the Humboldtian philosophy of language, which posited an intimate connection between verbal form and cognitive architecture. At the same time they were inspired by the modernist artistic experiments of their friends and colleagues, and saw in philology the study of how verbal art transforms the way people think. The study of the "laws" of poetics, of "rhythm" and "verbal form" which Eikhenbaum and Shklovsky mention is also implicitly the study of the underpinnings of cognition.

Svetlikova's central contribution is to point out that Russian Formalist thought was deeply embedded in turn-of-the-century psychologism. In her account, although the Formalists sought to study literature as an "autonomous" object of study, not reducible to another domain, the tools they used to do this "extremely frequently in one way or another abutted on psychology."[66] This was the mode of thinking which they inherited from their teachers, and was moreover one in which the study of language was the "most important" thing. As she puts it,

> In the era of psychologism there was a widespread conviction, deriving from Humboldt, that language (and then literature, and art) is an object of study which allows for a closer understanding of thought, and within the frame of psychologism this was in fact considered the most important and gripping task.[67]

For the Formalists, what is important is that "their predecessors, from whose ideas they took their point of departure, in one way or another, derived their energy for research from this conviction."[68] I agree with Svetlikova that this "energy" was carried over into the Formalists' work. However, in order to understand the importance of Humboldtian ideas for Formalist theory, I believe we must situate this philosophy within a larger paradigm for scholarship, which also included a commitment to the comparative method (a point to which I will return).

As Svetlikova has convincingly demonstrated, in order to understand how the Formalists were thinking about language, we must turn to associationist psychology. This is a tradition of thought that can be traced to British empiricism, particularly to John Locke's *Essay Concerning Human Understanding* (1690) and David Hume's *Treatise of Human Nature* (1738), and is closely tied to empiricist theories of mental life, as Eric Mandelbaum explains:

> Associationism has been the engine behind empiricism for centuries, from the British Empiricists through the Behaviorists and modern day Connectionists. . . .
>
> Associationism is a theory that connects learning to thought based on principles of the organism's causal history. Since its early roots, associationists have sought to use the history of an organism's experience as the main sculptor of cognitive architecture. In its most basic form, associationism has claimed that pairs of thoughts become associated based on the organism's past experience.[69]

Associative connections between ideas are understood to be formed by a mental process, which associationists argue is the only innate mental process: the ability to associate ideas. This flexible process accounts for both learning and thinking, and has been described as consisting of basic "types" of associative relations, such as contiguity, resemblance, and cause and effect. The relationship between experience and "Ideas" was described by Hume as the result of the "Copy Principle," which "demanded that there were no Ideas in the mind that were not first given in experience."[70] At the turn of the twentieth century, the mechanistic psychology of Johann Friedrich Herbart (1776–1841) was also an important influence. Herbart provided turn-of-the-century philologists with an understanding of consciousness as a psychic activity activated in response to a continuous stream of "representations" created by sensory contact with realia. The psyche is postulated to be "originally an utter *tabula rasa*."[71] Herbart described this activity in terms which are generally compatible with associationism. In the most general terms, associationism posits a psychological entity such as the Humean "Idea" or the Herbartian "representation" (*Vorstellung*), which is generated by an individual's experience of the external world. These entities enter into relationships with each other, which can be described in terms of "associations" (e.g., by similarity/contrast or continuity). Associationism was the overwhelmingly dominant theory in psychology in the last third of the nineteenth century, and it was against, and partially within, this framework that Sigmund Freud and William James developed their psychological theories.

How did associationism inform thinking about language? To explain, I will provide examples from the work of Nikolai Krushevsky (Mikołaj Kruszewski) (1851–1887) and Heymann Steinthal (1823–1899). Both used associationist psychology to develop a linguistic theory of formal structure and historical change. Krushevsky was a student of Baudouin de Courtenay at the University of Kazan. Like that of his teacher, his linguistic theory was psychologistic. Krushevsky sought to apply John Stuart Mill's laws of association to the study of language. Krushevsky, for example, claimed that "the two laws of association play the same role in linguistics as they do in psychology. The correspondence between the world of words and the world of ideas is the basic law of the development of language."[72] These laws are responsible for the way in which words are held together in the human mind: "the assimilation and use of language would be impossible if language presented a mass of uncoordinated words. Words are connected with one another directly (1) by similarity association and (2) by contiguity association."[73] As a result of these processes, an individual's mental lexicon is organized into "chains" or "series" (*riady*)—in the associationist terminology of the time—created by similarity and contiguity associations.

Krushevsky's idea of similarity and contiguity associations anticipates Ferdinand de Saussure's reference to "associative" relationships in his *Course in General Linguistics*.[74] However, Saussure's theory of language consciously moved away from psychology. In the structuralist reception of Saussure, it was of critical importance that linguistic structure is not derived from the mental processes of individuals, but rather from an abstract and collectively known system of knowledge. For structuralism, it is important that this collectively maintained structure precedes the individual's experience-based learning process.

These differences matter because the associationist, empiricist approach to language, which is psychologically and experientially grounded (e.g., Krushevsky), allows for a bidirectional causal relationship between social history and language change. To see how this was understood it is useful to consider Steinthal's philosophy of language, which has been described as an "improbable" and "original synthesis" of ideas derived from the work of Humboldt, Hegel, and Herbart. Following Humboldt's definition of language as a form of mental activity, Steinthal and his followers assumed that psychology is the discipline in which to study it; this meant, following Herbart, that "the units of language (words or sentences) must be taken in conjunction with mental representations (*Vorstellungen*) which have their origin in sensation."[75] Rooting his philosophy of language in psychological associationism allowed Steinthal to propose a way of describing language change as a process driven by social history. As Anna Morpurgo Davies explains, changes in language

> are caused by the way in which the mental representations enter in various associations with each other due to "objective" reasons (e.g., all members of a class such as that of colour words) or to the mediation of various factors ("white" is associated with "snow" which is associated with "cold") or through purely subjective individual connections (a famous event such as the battle of Leipzig is linked to the year 1813). Steinthal here adopts Herbart's views about the association of representations . . . In Steinthal's view this explains a large part of grammatical and syntactical change as well as part of sound change.[76]

In sum, this theory of language describes it as a structure held in the mind that is produced by the most general (non-language-specific) mental processes. It also holds that this structure, for each individual, is a product of that person's experience. These experiences are, in turn, shaped by the individual's place in society and by the cultural history that informs that social order. For the Formalists, the most important component of this philosophy of language is that the structure and content of an individual's linguistic knowledge can change; in other words, a change can occur in the way the mind works. They were particularly interested in how these changes were communicated between individual speakers. If one person, for example, a poet, begins using language in a new way, this can prompt a change in the mental structure of a reader. This assumption was essential to the Formalists' motivation for studying poetics.

24

Now that we have sketched out the psychological philosophy of language that informed Russian Formalism, we can return to the question of how their work emerged from the philological paradigm. One of the central arguments of this book is that this paradigm was "bifurcated" into two domains. One of these is the existing historical corpus of texts; in Humboldtian terms these are the "dead" utterances of the past, described as *Ergon*. This is contrasted to *Energeia*, which is the activity of producing and comprehending speech in the moment. In literary terms, this is the activity of composing a new work of art or of reading a text. Like their predecessors, the Formalists used the comparative method to study the first domain—the corpus of existing texts. This work allowed the theorist to postulate "laws" or regular tendencies which can be observed on the basis of this comparative work. The Russian Formalists departed from their philological predecessors, however, in their heightened interest in artistic production and perception. They were interested in contemporary art and literature—the sphere where innovation was taking place, and where new ways of thinking were being formed. They prized innovation and used the terms "defamiliarization" (*ostranenie*) and "orientation" (*ustanovka*) to refer to the mental processes that attend the creative use of language.

In the philological paradigm, as it was inherited by the Formalists, there was a gap between the two domains (i.e., the history of verbal art and the perception of verbal art); they were not assumed to be interconnected in a necessary, causal way. This meant that the historical patterns observed in the study of the corpus *do not* restrict individual, psychological processes of verbal production/perception in a predictable way. The history of literature belongs to a different domain from the production/perception of literature, yet these two domains are not entirely unrelated, because the psychological processes underlying creativity were assumed to be universal. A metaphor found in an ancient text and a metaphor constructed in 1920 were seen as similarly structured: both associate two ideas according to perceived similarities. Although a comparative history of metaphor will reveal patterns of development, these patterns do not allow the theorist working in 1920 to predict the metaphors a poet might produce in 1921, nor whether a reader in 1921 will find one of these contemporary metaphors to be novel or poetically effective. For the philological paradigm there is a gap between these two domains, resulting in a bifurcated theory.

Situating Russian Formalist theory within the philological paradigm allows us to see this theory as comprised of multiple "paths," each of which proposes a different way of understanding the relationship between the domains studied by poetics and psychology. A particularly well-known response is Yuri Tynianov's theory of literary evolution. In his writings from the mid-1920s, particularly the essays "Literary Fact" (1924) and "On Literary Evolution" (1927), he proposed that the entire corpus of "literature" can be described as a "system," whose evolution is dictated by the relationship between the elements of the system; for example, works of literature. This system is always in a state of "dynamic" change—which is driven by the requirement that any given element, to be perceptible (as "literary" or "poetic"), needs to stand out against other elements. Tynianov's proposal closes the gap between the comparative study of a historical corpus of texts and the psychological category of poetic perception. The way that he does this is informed by the philological paradigm—he relies on the philological, comparative method, and on the concept of poeticity as a mode of perception (explained by reference to associationist psychology). At the same time, his thinking is quite close to that of interwar structuralism—a movement which moves away from fundamental assumptions of the philological paradigm by adopting a systemic concept of language. Tynianov's ideas found support in Jakobson's structuralist historical phonology in the late 1920s, and their ideas—particularly their coauthored "Problems in the Study of Literature and Language" (1928)—have been seen as both the culmination of Formalism and the stepping-stone between Formalism and structuralism (see chapter 5).[77]

The existing scholarship on Russian Formalism has paid ample attention to Tynianov's contributions.[78] Without intending to discount the importance of his ideas, this book treats them as only one of a variety of possible paths taken by Formalist theory. The novel contribution of this book is to demonstrate that other Formalist theories did not close the gap between poetics and psychology in the way that Tynianov did. Chapters 2, 3, and 4 explicate Formalist theories which operated with the (philological) assumption that there is no necessary relationship between the history of verbal art and the perception of a text/utterance as artistic.

One of the advantages of reconstructing the philological paradigm as the intellectual context for Russian Formalism is that it allows non-structuralist theoretical proposals to be revealed as coherent, and thus potentially a resource for twenty-first-century literary studies. Much of Formalist theory makes better, logical sense when we acknowledge that the history of verbal art and the poeticity of a text/utterance constitute two disconnected domains. Failure to acknowledge this makes this theory seem paradoxical or contradictory. For example, Shklovsky is famous for his articulation of art's purpose as "defamiliarization" (*ostranenie*). In his formulation, the point of art is to make the thing described appear as if it is being seen *for the first time*: "The goal of art is to create the sensation of seeing, and not merely recognizing, things." He asks his reader to "remember the feeling you had when holding a quill in your hand for the first time . . . and compare it to the feeling you have when doing it for the ten thousandth time." This is the difference between art and non-art. Tolstoy, Shklovsky points out, tries to evoke this mode of perception by "not calling a thing or event by its name but describing it as if seen for the first time, as if happening for the first time."[79] Shklovsky thus equates the quality of artfulness or poeticity with a perception of novelty. At the same time, he is also known for asserting that there is no novelty in the history of art, which he describes as a cyclical movement of artistic tropes, genres, and "devices" in and out of a "canonical" position.[80] Steiner summarizes Shklovsky's theory of literary evolution as the "eternal return" of the same.[81] We thus arrive at the following paradox: Shklovsky privileges novelty as definitive of art, yet denies that there is any novelty in this history of art. The paradox disappears, however, if we admit that these contradictory positions indicate that the study of the historical corpus is separate from statements made about an individual's perception of or production of a work of art.

I will pause here to address the discourse of novelty in Russian Formalism. An important source for this was the rhetoric of the Russian modernist movements, especially Symbolism and Futurism. These artists often described the creative act as one of radical individualism, an "autonomous" utterance. The Futurists often used the adjective *samotsennyi* ("valuable in itself") to describe this creative use of language. This concept was a radical assertion of individualistic, unique expression, and was often expressed in opposition to an understanding of language as a collectively maintained set of rules. This was how the Futurist poet Aleksei Kruchenykh understood the idea of the autonomous, "transrational" poetic word in 1913:

> The artist is free to express himself not only in the common language (concepts), but also in a personal one (the creator is an individual), as well as in a language which does not have any definite meaning (not frozen), a transrational language . . . The artist has seen the world in a new way and, like Adam, proceeds to give things his own names. The lily is beautiful, but the word "lily" has been soiled and "raped." Therefore, I call the lily, "euy"—the original purity is reestablished.[82]

Kruchenykh argues that linguistic creativity consists of absolute freedom from normative constraints. This freedom is envisioned as an utterly novel, *re*-naming process: his creative act is an attempt to evoke the perception of a lily for the first time. This statement builds on the ideas of the French Symbolists: there are striking points of correspondence between the poetic theory of Stéphane Mallarmé, found in his *Crisis of Verse* (*Crise de vers*, 1896), and the ideas articulated by the Russian avant-garde.[83] Mallarmé, for example, writes that "an undeniable desire of my time is to distinguish two kinds of language according to their different attributes." The first is the speech of the "crowd": an "elementary use of discourse serving the universal *reporting*."[84] The second is the speech of "the Poet":

> Verse, which, out of several vocables, makes a total word, entirely new, foreign to the language, and almost incantatory, achieves that isolation of speech; negating, with a sovereign blow, despite their repeated reformulations between sound and sense, the arbitrariness that remains in the terms, and gives you the surprise of never having heard that fragment of ordinary eloquence before, while the object named is bathed in a brand new atmosphere.[85]

Mallarmé thus describes a widely held view at the turn of the century—that poetry can be understood in opposition to everyday communicative speech. What makes poetry different is the capacity of a poet to "isolate" the poetic word, to make it appear as something never before seen or heard. Thus poetry is the creation of a novel perception: a sense of "surprise" and a "brand new atmosphere."

The Russian Formalists, particularly Jakobson, Shklovsky, and Osip Brik, were close to the Futurists and collaborated with them on artistic and scholarly projects. At the same time, the Formalists positioned themselves as the successors of the scholarly poetics epitomized by Veselovsky and Potebnia. The Formalists wanted to produce an objective literary "science," and expressed their contempt for journalistic, subjective criticism or the speculative, mystical approaches to poetry associated with the Symbolist movement. How could they produce scholarship, a concept associated with poetics, which could also account for the most contemporary poetry—including the extreme subjectivity of an experimenter like Kruchenykh? This question is related to the apparent contradiction in Shklovsky's work—how to reconcile the fact that he defined "art" in terms of novelty, articulated in avant-garde terms, yet also argued that there is no novelty in the *history* of art.

The reception of Jakobson's long essay "The Newest Russian Poetry" (written 1919; published 1921), his first major work of literary theory, is instructive for answering this question. It is primarily a description of the language of Velimir Khlebnikov's verse, describing Khlebnikov's syntax, epithets, neologisms, sound repetitions, synonyms, and rhymes. Taking a broadly comparative approach, Jakobson compares Khlebnikov's language to a wide array of literary figures (e.g., Mayakovsky, Pushkin, Dostoevsky, Derzhavin), and more often with folklore. Jakobson refers to humorous tales (*pribakulochki*), limericks (*chastushki*), wedding songs, oral epics (*byliny*), oral narrative (*skaz*), riddles (*zagadki*), children's folklore, children's songs, proverbs (*poslovitsy*), and nursery rhymes (*pribautki*), as well as examples classed simply as "*fol'klor*." Jakobson's approach prompted questions from his audience about the place of individual creativity in his analysis. In the

Moscow Linguistic Circle's discussion of his essay, held in May 1919, Brik commented: "It appears that based on the presentation we have to accept the assertion that the entirety of Khlebnikov's poetics is merely the baring of preexisting devices. Where in this case is Khlebnikov's creativity? Where are the new devices he has created?"[86] Indeed, throughout his study Jakobson stresses that the novelty of Khlebnikov's poetry lies in the poet's making "age-old" devices newly visible. For example, in the published essay we find claims such as: "the device [i.e., the threading of motifs] has an ancient sanction, but in Khlebnikov's case it is 'laid bare,'" and "the play with suffixes has long been known to poetry, but only in new poetry, especially in Khlebnikov, does this become a conscious [osoznannyi], legitimate device."[87]

The study of poetics, as Brik confirms, reveals only what is general, what is collective—the traditional devices as studied by Veselovsky as pre-danie. To access the creativity that is responsible for "art" or "poetry," the Formalists assumed, in a move consistent with the philological paradigm, that one had to look to individual language use/perception. Recall Humboldt's argument that linguistic creativity is an individual activity, rather than the "dead" product of recorded past utterances: "Language is not a product [Ergon] but an activity [Energeia]. . . . Language belongs to me because I produce it in my very own way."[88] As Steinthal and others in this period assumed, to study language as Energeia meant to approach language using the tools of psychology. For Shklovsky and Jakobson, the distinction between Ergon and Energeia is reproduced as a split into two disciplinary fields: philology and psychology. This division is also between the collective and the individual, and between comparative poetics and the study of (psychological) poetic perception/production.

How did the Formalists use psychology? Svetlikova convincingly shows that the Formalists' references to the perception of verbal form relied on associative psychology. The Formalists' concept of "baring" (obnazhenie) a word or a device is traced to a passage in William James's Principles of Psychology, published in Russian translation in 1911. James describes how a word, if repeated over and over, becomes unfamiliar, or strange. As Jakobson puts it, we become "conscious" of the word or the device, which allows the word to be disassociated from its habitual associative ties. Disassociation, as Svetlikova explains, permitted established associative connections to be broken or disturbed, a process essential to creativity and to artistic imagination.[89] Jakobson refers to "disassociation" in his study of Khlebnikov, in passages where he attempts to define art:

The orientation towards an expression [ustanovka na vyrazhenie], on the verbal mass, which I have called the only essential characteristic of poetry, is directed not only to the form of the phrase, but also to the form of the word itself. The more habitual a mechanical association by contiguity [*mekhaniche-skaia assotsiatsiia po smezhnosti*] between sound and meaning is, the more quickly it is made. For this reason, everyday practical language is extremely conservative: the form of a word rapidly ceases to be felt. In poetry the role of mechanical association is reduced to a minimum, while the dissociation [*dis-sotsiatsiia*] of verbal elements acquires great importance. Dissociated fragments [*drobi dissotsiatsii*] are readily combined into new formations. Dead affixes come to life.[90]

Khlebnikov's poetry makes the perceiver conscious of an affix, and disassociates it from habitual associations, by combining it with a root in a new way. This reordering of associative chains is what Shklovsky refers to as defamiliarization. In his writings from the 1910s and 1920s, Shklovsky frequently refers to the discourse of association psychology, arguing, for example: "In order to make an object a fact of art, it is necessary . . . to remove [*vyrvat'*] the thing from the series of customary associations [*riad privychnykh assotsiatsii*] in which it is located."[91] Svetlikova concludes:

> Thus, *"ostranenie"* (the meaning of which can be described as a change in associations) . . . had a close synonym—"dissociation," the splitting of associations, which principally underlies all creativity. *"Ostranenie"* is not an isolated concept, it belongs to a rich tradition, the successors of which were not only the formalists.[92]

Jakobson's study of Khlebnikov moves between conclusions drawn from his comparative poetics, which reveals "ancient," well-known, widely used devices, such as the "play with suffixes" and references to contemporary psychology which describe the mental state of the perceiver of poetry—the way in which a perceptually novel use of an affix or suffix, for example, can precipitate a rearrangement of the associative chains stored in the perceiver's mind. It is in reference to the second, psychological domain of perception, not to that of formal devices, that Jakobson speaks about defining the "poetic."

How are we to understand the relationship between these two fields for Shklovsky and Jakobson? Their work in comparative poetics resulted in the collection of reoccurring "devices" or poetic tropes identified within the bounds of *slovesnost'*. They also referred to psychological concepts of the day to describe, in terms of perception, what is happening at an individual level. For Jakobson and Shklovsky, writing in the late 1910s, there was no deterministic connection between the two domains: neither individual poetic production nor perception was seen to be determined by relationships, patterns, or laws derived from the comparative study of the corpus. Shklovsky makes this remarkably clear in "Art as Device":

We know that expressions not created for artistic contemplation are often nevertheless experienced as poetic; [an] example would be Annensky's belief in the poetic qualities of Slavonic . . . Therefore, a thing can be (1) created as prosaic and experienced as poetic; (2) created as poetic and experienced as prosaic. This suggests that a *given work depends in its artistry—in whether or not it is poetry—on our perception.*[93]

It might seem counterintuitive to think that the Formalists' work in poetics (the identification of devices) is not more closely and necessarily bound to their statements on the definition of poetry. Yet a loose relationship between these two domains was productive and important for the Formalists' understanding of their work, particularly for its social and political relevance.

The individual, either the poet or the perceiver, situated in a particular historical context, is assumed to have agency to create his or her own unique artistic statement or interpretation. These processes are not understood through the matrix of a language system or grammar, but in psychological and empiricist-historical terms. The expectation that the goal of a linguistic study of a corpus is to arrive at laws that constrain production and perception is misleading when trying to understand Russian Formalism. As I have argued above, the philological paradigm did not look to the history of linguistic form for rules which would explain subsequent developments. The theoretical gap between comparative poetics and individual production/perception meant that the individual artist could consciously innovate; she could choose which aspect of a past tradition to draw on, and could seek to make new connections which would impact the thinking of her audience. The nonbinding connection between poetics and perception, between collective and individual, allowed the Formalists to approach their work as an applied discipline. In the context of the revolutionary period, application was a politicized activity.

The foundational concepts of Formalist theory were developed in the contexts of World War I, the February and October Revolutions of 1917, and the Civil War of 1918–22. The core Formalists—Osip Brik, Boris Eikhenbaum, Roman Jakobson, Viktor Shklovsky, and Yuri Tynianov—were all relatively young, between the ages of 20 and 30 in 1917. (Eikhenbaum was the oldest, ten years older than Jakobson, who was the youngest.) They were from Moscow (Jakobson, Brik), Petersburg (Shklovsky), Voronezh (Eikhenbaum), Rezhitsa (now Rēzekne) (Tynianov), and were educated at Moscow University (Jakobson, Brik) and St. Petersburg University (Shklovsky, Eikhenbaum, Tynianov). The particular political affiliations of the Formalists varied. Shklovsky sided with the Socialist Revolutionary Party, and in 1919 participated in efforts to overthrow the Bolshevik leadership and restore the Constituent Assembly. In his *Knight's Move* (1923), Shklovsky suggests that his activities in the 1910s were motivated by the promise of an international revolution: "I wanted happiness for the whole world—wouldn't settle for less."[94] As a result of his political activities, Shklovsky fled Bolshevik Russia in 1922, but returned in the fall of 1923 (having received political amnesty with the help of Maxim Gorky and Vladimir Mayakovsky). Brik embraced Bolshevik politics, and notoriously began working for the secret police (Cheka) in 1920.[95] Jakobson's political position is difficult to uncover, although there is some evidence that as a student he was a member of the Constitutional Democratic (Kadet) Party. In his correspondence from the time, and in reminiscences about the revolutionary period, Jakobson describes himself as adept at playing both sides of a political landscape—a natural "diplomat."[96] Jakobson would become a Soviet diplomat in the 1920s, in Czechoslovakia, where he lived until 1939.[97] Eikhenbaum's biographer, Carol Any, describes him as "profoundly apolitical" and skeptical of all Russian revolutionary politics, a position which he adopted after he moved to St. Petersburg for his university studies months after the suppression of the 1905 Revolution. Eikhenbaum's position, was, as Any points out, impacted by the political career of his older brother, Vsevolod, a leading Russian anarchist under the name of Volin, who joined the Makhno movement and was expelled from the Soviet Union in the early 1920s.[98] Yuri Tynianov's political sympathies in the revolutionary period are unknown to me.

Ascertaining the particular political leanings of the individual Formalists is not, however, necessary for arguing that their literary theory was viewed as a committed engagement with ongoing social processes. This is recognized, for example, by Kliger and Maslov, who write that "Formalism offers an activist (rather than autonomous or reflective) vision of the literary process, one that is not so much an effect of historical change as a full-fledged participant in it."[99] This is because, I would argue, all of the core Formalists (Brik, Eikhenbaum, Jakobson, Shklovsky, Tynianov) belong to the philological paradigm and assume the Humboldtian philosophy of language. They view the study of verbal form as important because it reveals how people think. Moreover, the gap between comparative poetics and artistic perception/production, which was inherent in the intellectual framework inherited by Formalism, encouraged them to insert their own theoretical and creative writings into literary and cultural history. Mapping the intellectual contours of the philological paradigm allows for a better understanding of why the Formalists approached creating literary theory in the way they did: there is no concept of a law-driven literary evolution that would not allow for individuals to consciously intervene and attempt to direct it toward their own ends. I hope to have shown in this section that the broader intellectual framework within which Formalism emerged allowed scholars to assume that the study of poetic form was immediately relevant to understanding, and shaping, social thought.

THE RECEPTION OF RUSSIAN FORMALISM AND CZECH STRUCTURALISM

One of the ideas I want to recontextualize is the view that Russian Formalism sought to establish the "autonomy of literature." Entries on Russian Formalism in encyclopedias and introductions to literary theory invariably introduce the movement by stressing the concept of "autonomy." For example, we can read that "the Formalists' ambition was to establish an autonomous science of literature," and that they "insisted on the autonomy of literature and, by implication, of literary study."[100] I believe we should distinguish between at least three distinct discursive sources for claims about "autonomy" which were available to the Russian Formalists. One source is the *modernist* artistic discourse of aesthetic "autonomy" as the unique, creative potential of an individual, as exemplified by the writings of Kruchenykh and Mallarmé. A second source is the concept of *disciplinary* autonomy. This autonomy rests on the identification of methodological procedures and an object of study that defines a disciplinary field. As Byford has argued, Veselovsky's historical poetics can be seen as a "key pre-Formalist project negotiating the autonomy of literary scholarship at the turn of the twentieth century."[101] At the turn of the twentieth century, the premises of the philological paradigm were understood as sufficient for asserting the "autonomy" of literary studies. It was thus not considered necessary to ground claims for the field's autonomy in a conception of linguistic form that is fully autonomous from cultural history. An example of such a fully autonomous concept of form can be found, for example, in the immanent linguistic theory embraced by French structuralism. This can be considered a third, and distinct, concept of autonomy. It rests on the concept of a "system" as a whole created by the relationships between its parts. The whole can be said to be autonomous in that its properties are, first and foremost, created by its internal components, rather than by factors external to it. In the mid- to late 1920s, Tynianov and Jakobson promoted a conjunction between the concept of a linguistic system and the notion of disciplinary autonomy. However, this conjunction was one development of Formalism, not a necessary starting point for literary theory.[102]

The Formalists are perhaps best known for their strident promotion of disciplinary autonomy for literary theory. They often used modernist rhetoric in order to make their argument more emphatic. For example, one of the most often-cited lines from Russian Formalist theory comes from Jakobson's study of Khlebnikov, where he argues for the disciplinary autonomy of literary studies using the avant-garde discourse of autonomy:

The plastic arts involve the shaping of self-sufficient visual impressions, music the shaping of self-sufficient sound material, dance the organization of the self-sufficient gesture; and poetry is the formulation of the self-sufficient, "selfsome," word [*samovitoe slovo*], as Khlebnikov puts it.

Poetry is language in its aesthetic function.

Thus the subject of literary scholarship is not literature but literariness [*literaturnost'*], that is, that which makes of a given work a work of literature.[103]

Despite Jakobson's use of modernist rhetoric, it does not inherently follow that he viewed his object of study as strictly autonomous from society, in the sense of Kruchenykh's pronouncement of the autonomy of his creative ego, or in the sense of the Saussurean system. The Formalists' motivation for studying poetics is only comprehensible once we see that they assumed the opposite: that (poetic) language is not distinct from (social) thought. Kliger and Maslov present this fact as a general truth, which holds not only for Veselovsky, but for Russian literary theory more broadly. Citing the work of Mikhail Bakhtin, Yuri Tynianov, Viktor Shklovsky, Lydia Ginzburg, and Yuri Lotman, they write that, in Russia:

Literature was predominantly understood as something of "a textbook of life" or "a theory of life," and the process of autonomization of the literary-aesthetic field from those of politics, society, and the broader culture that was in evidence in Western Europe throughout the nineteenth century seems to have never—neither in the nineteenth nor in the twentieth century—quite gotten off the ground in Russia. As a result, whereas the evolution of form-oriented approaches to art and literature find parallels in the West, the specific conditions of Russian historical development stimulated an understanding of literature as both specialized and intricately woven into the fabric of socio-political life.[104]

By placing Formalism within the philological paradigm I supply further context for this claim.

To demonstrate the outcome of collapsing these three discourses of autonomy, I will conclude with an episode from the reception history of Russian Formalism: the debate in the 1970s over the relationship between linguistics and literary studies, centering on "poetic language." One outcome of this debate was the solidification of a narrative about Russian Formalism which has remained largely unchallenged to this day. This is a narrative that synthesized Russian Formalism with post–World War II structuralism and New Criticism on the grounds that all three movements could be seen as "intrinsic" approaches in opposition to "extrinsic" scholarship.[105] The English-language reception of Russian Formalism was fundamentally shaped by a broader shift in American literary studies away from "intrinsic" New Criticism towards a Marxist-informed cultural studies. The discussion about poetic language was conducted, in part, in the pages of *New Literary History*, which devoted special issues to the "distinctiveness of literary language" (1972) and to the question: "What is literature?" (1973). In these and other contributions, the opposition between the intrinsic and extrinsic camps was articulated as positions in favor of, and opposed to, an empirical distinction between "poetic" and "ordinary" language. The legacy of Russian Formalism came to stand for a defense of this binary opposition, while the anti-Formalist camp sought to dissolve it. This is evident from the titles of articles alone: for example, Stanley Fish's "How Ordinary Is Ordinary Language?" (1973) and Manuel Duran's "Inside the Glass Cage: Poetry and 'Normal' Language" (1972). One of the most extended and explicit statements of the anti-Formalist position can be found in Mary Louise Pratt's *Towards a Speech Act Theory of Literary Discourse* (1977), which begins with a chapter devoted to a strident critique of Russian Formalism and Czech structuralism titled "The 'Poetic Language' Fallacy." For Pratt, this fallacy is equivalent to the "belief that literature is linguistically autonomous, that is, possessed of intrinsic linguistic properties which distinguish it from all other kinds of discourse." Pratt views this fallacy as the central legacy of Russian Formalism and Czech structuralism, movements which she treats as a single entity. Pratt's critique of this poetic language "doctrine" or "fallacy" is both ethical and empirical. She argues that the division of poetic from ordinary language is based on elitist prejudices inherited from Symbolist poets—she cites Rilke, Mallarmé, and Valéry—and she seeks to show that the devices found by Russian Formalists in "poetic" language are also found in "ordinary" language, such as in oral narrative. As evidence, she refers to William Labov's *Language in the Inner City* (1972), as well as Labov's and Joshua Waletzky's analyses of oral narratives of personal experience.[106]

The English-language reception of Russian Formalism has been decisively shaped by these debates on the possibility or desirability of drawing a line between poetry and non-poetry. After the 1970s, particularly in the Anglo-American tradition of literary studies, both Russian Formalism and Czech structuralism have come to be understood through this opposition between poetic and ordinary language, as evidenced by the summaries of these movements in textbooks and in introductions to literary theory for students. Terry Eagleton's popular *Literary Theory: An Introduction* (1983, 1996), for example, begins with Russian Formalism, defined here as a movement exemplifying the belief that literary texts have their "own specific laws, structures, and devices which were to be studied in themselves."[107] The Formalists, in sum,

> saw literary language as a set of deviations from a norm . . . : literature is a "special" kind of language, in contrast to the "ordinary" language we com-

monly use. But to spot a deviation implies being able to identify the norm from which it swerves . . . The idea that there is a single "normal" language, a common currency shared by all members of society, is an illusion.[108]

Both Eagleton and Pratt critique Russian Formalism by arguing that "poetic" devices can be found in "ordinary" language.

This introduction has argued that the Formalists described *poeticity* using concepts from the field of psychology. The comparative study of verbal art can reveal tendencies in literary history, but it cannot determine the poeticity of an utterance. Pratt and others cannot, however, be faulted for seeking to summarize Formalism in the way that they did. OPOIAZ theory did at one point explore the possibility of demonstrating the autonomy of poetic language on empirical (formal) grounds. This effort was led by Lev Jakubinsky, who published an important article in this vein in 1916. Yet the position that scholars such as Pratt and Eagleton take to be definitive of Russian Formalism as a whole was in fact disputed and rejected by other Formalists at the time. Jakobson, for example, argued in his 1923 book *On Czech Verse* that Jakubinsky's effort to define poetic language in formal, empirical terms is a "mistake."[109] Renunciations of the early OPOIAZ assertions regarding the specificity of poetic language were also made by Brik in 1923 and Eikhenbaum in 1924.[110] As I will demonstrate in my chapter on the Moscow Linguistic Circle, that society consistently sought to dissolve the study of "poetry" into the more general study of language (dialectology) in terms that recall Pratt's claim that poetic devices can be found in "ordinary language." For now, I conclude on this point of misunderstanding because it suggests how the reception of Formalism has obscured paths of development which do not easily fit into the intellectual framework of "intrinsic versus extrinsic," or the lens of a structuralist understanding of language, which have so powerfully shaped thinking about literary theory in the twentieth century. In order to reinvigorate our field, and to escape limiting frameworks of thought, we need to return to the historical context of the early twentieth century, and to do so in real detail. There is much to be gained from returning Russian Formalism to the philological paradigm. Doing so allows the Formalists to be seen not as policemen guarding the boundaries of literature against sociopolitical concerns, but rather as advocates for the study of form as a socially engaged, politically relevant activity.

Comparative Philology

THE RUSSIAN FORMALISTS are widely seen as the founders of modern, twentieth-century literary theory.[1] This status is in part a product of their own rhetoric. In their early, programmatic writings the Formalists often polemicized with their predecessors, attacking perceived weak points in their writings. Both Viktor Shklovsky and Roman Jakobson vociferously critiqued the ideas of competing authorities, especially the two preeminent philologists of their grandparents' generation—Alexander Potebnia and Alexander Veselovsky—as well as their older contemporaries, the Russian Symbolists. Shklovsky's debut as a literary scholar was as a sharp critic of Potebnia and Veselovsky.[2] For those familiar with Russian Formalism only in translation, the name "Potebnia" is obscure yet strangely prominent. Shklovsky, assuming that his readers know Potebnia's name and ideas, launches the first sentence of his "Art as Device" as a polemical response leveled against Potebnia's authority. Shklovsky's tone is dismissive—these days any "schoolboy" can be found parroting Potebnia, he claims. Jakobson also did not mince words when taking on opponents—for instance, he titled his talk on the Symbolist Valery Briusov's work on verse "A Specimen of Scholarly Charlatanism" ("Obrazchik nauchnogo sharlatanstva").[3] This combative stance was in keeping with the ethos of the avant-garde, with which both men had close ties.

The Formalists' attacks on authorities can be misleading. Although their ideas departed from the work of their predecessors in important ways, this book argues that Russian Formalism inherited an intellectual paradigm for literary and linguistic study that was formed in the mid-nineteenth century. The evidence that Potebnia's and Veselovsky's ideas were important for the Formalists is overwhelming; in fact, their influence has been acknowledged in the scholarship on Russian Formalism, and by the Formalists themselves.[4] In his well-known article "The Theory of the Formal Method," Boris Eikhenbaum explains that the Formalists don't seek to overthrow the legacy of Veselovsky and Potebnia, but rather to rescue it:

At about the time the Formalists emerged, academic scholarship—with its utter disregard of theoretical problems and its nonchalant making-do with obsolete aesthetic, psychological, and historical "axioms"—had lost the sense of its own proper object of study to such a degree that its very existence became illusory. Academic scholarship hardly needed attack. There was no call to force open the door, because, as it turned out, there was none. We discovered, instead of a fortress, a through alley. The theoretical legacy of Potebnja and Veselovskij, once handed down to their students, was left to stagnate as so much dead capital—a fortune which they were afraid to tap and so caused it to depreciate.[5]

Eikhenbaum clarifies here that the real targets of the Formalists' critique were not Veselovsky and Potebnia, but their numerous followers. Eikhenbaum describes the Formalists as revolutionary figures, storming the "fortress" of existing authority, yet this was no radical overthrow of an entire tradition: the Formalists saw themselves as the true inheritors of a wasted "fortune."

This chapter seeks to clarify which aspects of the preceding philological tradition were emulated by the Formalists, and which were discarded. The previous chapter introduced my understanding of the relevant tradition, which I am calling the "philological paradigm." In Thomas Kuhn's frequently cited *The Structure of Scientific Revolutions* (1962), he writes that an intellectual paradigm identifies not only the object of observation, but also the types of questions asked about it, and the structure of these questions.[6] The central questions that motivated the work of nineteenth-century Russian philologists reappear as the goals of the Formalists' research. The most important of these questions was: What is poetry? This was also formulated as: What is poetic language? A related question, oriented towards narrative, was: How is it that the same "plots" are found in tales from around the globe? These questions, and the method adopted by the philologists to answer them, also shaped the parameters of the Russian Formalists' research.

This chapter will show that there was no fundamental conceptual break between the philological paradigm and Russian Formalism. Demonstrating this is complicated by the fact that there are different types of literary and linguistic study which fall under the rubric of "philology." Admittedly, in the nineteenth century, philology was an extremely broad field of study. As James Turner has recently argued, philology can be seen as an undifferentiated amalgam of textual studies that predated the modern humanities and encompassed subsequent disciplinary fields such as anthropology, classics, comparative religion, literary scholarship, and branches of legal study and political science.[7] This sense of all-encompassing breadth is misleading, however, since it is possible to identify distinct lines of development within nineteenth-century philology. This chapter will winnow this broad category down to a specific branch of philological study which led up to and prepared the ground for the emergence of Russian Formalism.

The genealogy I will trace begins with Jacob Grimm's (1785–1863) comparative analyses of German grammar and mythology published in the 1820s and 1830s. Grimm's historical comparative method for the study of language and folklore was further developed by the founder of Russian academic literary studies, Fedor Buslaev (1818–1898), in his work on Russian mythology and folklore. The subsequent generation of Russian scholars, first and foremost Alexander Veselovsky (1838–1906) and Alexander Potebnia (1835–1891), extended the work of Buslaev and others to the study of written literature (*belles-lettres*) as well as folklore. In the 1910s and 1920s, the Russian Formalists assumed the central premises of this conceptual framework, including received notions regarding the nature of the literary domain, as well as the methods and goals of literary scholarship.

GERMAN PHILOLOGY

The far-reaching innovations of German scholars in the field of philology influenced work on both language and literature throughout Europe and in America. This impact was particularly strong in central and eastern Europe, where the linguistic philosophy of Johann Gottfried von Herder (1744–1803), which posited the indivisibility of language and cultural identity, was widely embraced by elites engaged in nation-building. The comparative study of the Indo-European languages pioneered by German philologists provided the Germanic and Slavic language groups with a continuous line of cultural development—stretching back to Gothic and Proto-Slavic, respectively—that was previously unknown. (For the Romance languages, by contrast, the reconstruction of a genealogy leading back to Latin only reiterated a well-established narrative.) Russian scholars frequently studied abroad in Germany, and thus swiftly adopted developments in language study they discovered there. German philology thus provides a necessary point of departure for understanding Russian thought on language and verbal culture. Just as importantly, this tradition furnishes a background against which the unique departures made by Russian scholars stand out.

There were two competing branches of philology in German-speaking lands in the early nineteenth century: classical philology and comparative philology.[8] These fields emerged in the 1790s and 1810s respectively, and were initially rivals, holding widely divergent conceptions of the origins and history of European languages. By the 1840s, however, the discoveries and methods of comparative linguistic study were increasingly integrated into scholarship on classical subjects. The initial rift between these two branches of philological study is, however, instructive for understanding the rise of the philological paradigm for literary study in Russia. To generalize, in Germany and western Europe, the method established by classical philology—known as textual criticism—came to dominate the philological study of literary texts. Comparative philology, on the other hand, developed into linguistics and also provided the conceptual basis for the comparative study of myth and folklore. Classical philology, then, was a mode of analysis which focused on static *written texts* and which often sought to establish an authorial version among variants of a manuscript. Comparative philology, by contrast, made *spoken language* its primary object of study and was oriented toward the comparative study of language and dialects or folk genres understood to be "authorless." It was the latter branch of philology—the comparative study of oral genres—which developed into the philological paradigm for literary study in Russia, including the Formalist study of literature in the early twentieth century. A brief review of the institutional history of academic literary studies in Germany and Russia helps understand why this was.

The historian of science R. Steven Turner tells us that classical philology was the first discipline to undergo professionalization within the German academy—having established itself as a specialized and self-sufficient field of study by 1835.[9] This gave it institutional primacy, and classical studies dominated the curriculum in both universities and in secondary schools.[10] Classical philologists produced detailed textual criticism, edited Greek and Latin texts, and sought to create broad historical reconstructions of the life of classical antiquity. Although this work continued, in part, the legacy of ancient Greek scholarship in the Alexandrian period, classical philology entered a new era in Germany in the 1770s and ended up becoming extremely influential, shaping generations of literary scholars in Germany and beyond in their approach to textual analysis.

The origins of the modern study of classical philology in Germany are typically traced to Friedrich August Wolf's (1759–1824) insistence on entering his name in the matriculation book at the University of Göttingen in 1777 as *Studiosus Philologiae*—the first student there to claim this as a primary field of study. From the University of Halle, where he taught for twenty-three years, Wolf is credited with initiating a renewal of interest in ancient literature in universities all over Germany.[11] Wolf's scholarship focused on the life of the ancient Greeks and Romans, which he called *Alterthums-Wissenschaft* (science of antiquity). He stressed the necessity of mastering Greek and Latin; grammar and language studies were for him "the first pillar of philology."[12] However, as his primary goal was reconstructing the world of ancients, he saw language as a tool rather than as an object of study in itself.[13] Classical philology was further exemplified by Karl Lachmann (1793–1851),

who is best known for having fine-tuned Wolf's method, and thus developing a systematic approach to the restoration of ancient texts called "textual
criticism." A scholar of Latin, Lachmann studied at Halle and taught at the
University of Berlin from 1825 to 1851.[14] Lachmann's name has become associated with the genealogical or "stemmatic" approach to the process of
reconstructing an original text. Using shared variants (often errors and omissions) as a basis for determining the relationship between texts, the scholar
then organizes these copies into a family tree. The goal of this procedure
is the reconstruction of an "archetype"—the original (lost) version of the
text—from the agreements between the different copies. Lachmann's most
famous work was his edition of the writings of the Roman poet and philosopher Lucretius, published in 1850. According to John Sandys, Lachmann's
efforts to establish the original form of the work went hand in hand with a
broader investigation of the author's personality. Next to the work of organizing the various textual witnesses, Lachmann sought to "form a judgment as
to what the writer was in a position to write . . . to examine his personality,
the time when he lived, the circumstances in which, and the means whereby,
he produced his work."[15] It is logical that this knowledge would be considered relevant for studies whose goal was to determine what an author actually wrote, as opposed to those textual elements which were added later.

The methodology of textual criticism, which was developed through the
study of ancient Greek and Roman texts as well as the New Testament, was
thus oriented toward the task of reconstructing an original source text which
was understood as an authorized version. This work was seen as the preliminary step to "higher criticism"—which focused on the origins of the text.
Before this could begin, however, scholars needed a stable, reliable version of
a text that was as close as possible to the original author's intent. Subsequent,
variant copies were relevant only for reconstructing or interpreting the
original. The way in which variations emerged and how they altered the text
were not of interest. This is an essentially textual understanding of language.
In his *In Praise of the Variant*, Bernard Cerquiglini argues that the emergence of these more exact methods for philological study in the early nineteenth century reflected the rise of modern thinking about texts.[16] Cerquiglini
links this mode of thought to the maturation of the printing industry and the
passage of laws granting authors the right to sell, distribute, or surrender
ownership of their works. Lachmann's method can be seen as a response to
the emergence of the modern, legal conception of the author and the availability of stable, reliable reproductions of texts. Textual critics sought to create
authoritative printed volumes for classical authors, whose works had hitherto
existed in scattered, redundant, and unwieldy manuscript collections.

Another important facet of German classical philology was hermeneutics. The career of August Boeckh (1785–1867) is instructive. He was

41

a student of Wolf's at Halle, and his studies focused on Plato, and Greek tragedy and poetry (especially Pindar). Boeckh also worked extensively on the economics of the Athenian constitution, and contributed to establishing the authenticity of Attic inscriptions.[17] He articulated his understanding of philology in his influential *Encyclopedia and Methodology of the Philological Sciences*, which he developed and taught between 1809 and 1866. For Boeckh, "hermeneutics is the basis for all philological studies, and philology is the universal discipline concerned with all aspects of human culture in its historical manifestations."[18] For example, his *Encyclopedia* states that

> since the great mass of verbal tradition is fixed through written record, the business of the philologist is with the text, in which he must gain understanding of three things: 1. The writing, the symbol of the thing signifying. 2. Language, the thing signifying. 3. The thing signified, the knowledge contained in the language. The paleographer stops with the proof of the symbol. The mere grammarian confines himself to the symbol of the thing signified, language. Only when one presses on to the thing signified, the thought, does genuine knowledge arise . . . [W]e treat not the audible aspect of language but only the concepts bound up with the words as objects for interpretation.[19]

Boeckh thus represents a tradition in which philology is understood as the study of the original meaning of (classical) texts, a project which entailed a broad understanding of the social, political, philosophical, and economic world to which the text belongs. Classical philologists studied the history of language, but their goal was to establish and, often and most importantly, interpret an authorized text.

This scholarly tradition can be contrasted with comparative philology, which emerged as a new field in the 1810s in response to Western scholars' discovery of Sanskrit in the 1780s. The first works in this new field were comparative studies of the grammars of Sanskrit, Greek, and Latin, which placed the origins of European language and culture in a more ancient East—in a direct challenge to the neo-humanist genealogies of the classical scholars. These included suppositions that Latin was a direct descendent from Greek, and that all languages are derived from Hebrew.[20] Foundational works by the German and Danish scholars Franz Bopp, Rasmus Rask, and Jacob Grimm, published in the 1810s and 1820s, put linguistic studies on a new, more rigorous footing. These scholars established methods for the systematic, comparative historical study of the grammatical structure and lexica of languages. Jacob Grimm built on the observations of Rasmus Rask, described in this book's introduction, in writing his seminal *Germanic Grammar* (*Deutsche Grammatik*, 1819, revised in 1822). Focusing on the grammar of Germanic languages (Old English, Old Norse, Old Saxon, Old High

German, and Gothic) in comparison with Greek, Grimm described regular patterns of consonant changes—"tendencies" he suggested, not exception-less "laws."

What makes Jacob Grimm important for this story is that he proposed an analogy between his linguistic theory and the study of oral traditions. In this, his work can be seen as a crucial point of origin for the philological paradigm for literary studies. This move is the central premise of his four-volume *Teutonic Mythology* (*Deutsche Mythologie*, 1835), in which he sought to establish a new, comparative historical method for the study of mythology based on an analogy with comparative grammar. For instance, in the preface to the second edition of *Teutonic Mythology*, Grimm writes that "as all the sounds of language are reducible to a few, from whose simplicity the rest can be derived"—and here he provides the example of the sound shift from "Th" to "D" to "T"—"so in Mythology I reduce the long array of divine personages to their unity, and let their multiplicity spring out of this unity; and we can hardly go wrong in assuming for deities and heroes a similar coincidence, combination, and gradation, according to their characters and particular functions."[21] Grimm thus proposes a detailed analogy between grammar and mythology based on his own comparative linguistic method. In other words, he suggests that the history of popular genres like myths and folktales will, like sound changes, show regular patterns over the course of their evolution. Using the terminology of the philosopher of science Ernest Nagel, Grimm's move could be called a "substantive analogy"—that is, an analogy "in which a theory is constructed on the model of another system which contains known laws."[22] This can be contrasted with the tendency among classical philologists to use historical linguistic knowledge as a preliminary tool for chronologically ordering different copies of a text. Grimm's substantive analogy paved the way for philological studies and then literary theory which studied verbal art (folklore and literature) as a domain which itself evolves in a way analogous to spoken language. This development can be seen as an origin point for the "linguistic turn" commonly located in the early twentieth century.

Due to differences between the political situations in the German lands and in tsarist Russia, Grimm's legacy in the fields of mythology and folklore studies had a greater impact in Russia than in Germany.[23] Before the unification of Germany in 1871, the development of German language scholarship had been stymied by an oppositional relationship between Germanists and local princes, which significantly slowed the creation of university chairs in the field. Until the 1860s, German lessons at secondary schools were often taught by masters of Greek and Latin. Only in 1866 did secondary school reforms raise demand for academic training in German as opposed to classical philology. Germanics, as a result, could not compete with classical

43

studies as a core discipline until the 1890s.[24] While philologists in classical studies, such as Wolf, Boeckh, Hermann, Lobeck, Lachmann, Ritschl, and Müller, held important positions at universities, Jacob Grimm spent the first twenty years of his career as a librarian.[25] This was typical of Germanists in the first half of the nineteenth century, who were more commonly engaged in the private collection of medieval manuscripts than in teaching.[26] As a result, classical philology and the methods of textual criticism and hermeneutics were the foundation and leading methodology for literary study in Germany. This tradition, moreover, formed the basis for literary studies in western Europe and the United States in the nineteenth and early twentieth centuries. Gerald Graff's *Professing Literature* describes how, beginning in the 1870s, literary studies in the United States were professionalized according to the German model—to the extent that Graff speaks of a "superstitious emulation of German methods."[27] In American institutions of higher education in the late nineteenth and early twentieth centuries, this meant studying the history of English by parsing old texts. Scholars sought to establish disciplinary legitimacy for the field by making the study of modern languages "as difficult as the classics."[28]

RUSSIAN ACADEMIC LITERARY STUDIES

In Russia, the political climate worked to a different end—the study of Russian literature was established as an academic field at the height of Romanticism, in the 1830s and 1840s, by a regime that sought to promote a Russian national identity. This allowed the nationally oriented, comparative mythological work pioneered by Grimm, which was quickly absorbed by Russian scholars, to become a cornerstone of the fledgling field of Russian literary study.[29] A pivotal moment in the history of the Russian university system was the university charter of 1835, which marked the culmination of important reforms undertaken by Nicholas I and the Minister of Education, Sergei Uvarov. The charter was part of a larger reorganization of higher education that was intended to professionalize Russian universities and remake them into centers capable of producing native-born scholars and a civil service elite who possessed patriotic values.[30] In the 1830s and 1840s the university system expanded and took root in Russian society. This development coincided with the principle of "official nationality" promoted by Nicholas's regime, which identified the state with the dominant "great Russian" ethnic group and the Russian language.[31] This Russian nationalist program was reflected in the creation of two new chairs in literature—in "Russian Verbal Art and the History of Russian Literature" (*Rossiiskaia slovesnost' i istoriia rossiiskoi literatury*) and in the "History of Slavic Literatures and Dialects" (*Istoriia i literatura slavianskikh narechii*)—as part of the 1835 charter. This is generally considered the institutional foundation of academic literary study in Russia.[32] These political-historical circumstances allowed the branch of German philology associated with Herder and Grimm—the comparative study of language and myth—to dominate Russian academic literary studies.[33]

Soviet scholarship on Russian literary studies in the nineteenth century breaks this history into several stages: the first, from the 1840s to the 1860s, was dominated by the "mythological school" of scholarship. Its leading representative was Fyodor Buslaev.[34] Buslaev studied at Moscow University in the 1830s, where he specialized in historical linguistics. As a tutor to the children of Count S. G. Stroganov, Buslaev spent the years 1839–41 in Italy and Germany, where he probably first encountered Jacob Grimm's new mythological and linguistic theories. Buslaev subsequently taught as a professor at Moscow University from 1847 until 1881, when he was named a member of the Russian Academy of Sciences. As Andy Byford has shown, Buslaev—like other scholars of his generation—understood his own work as "contributing to the forging of a national self consciousness."[35] The study of folklore as a repository of national identity, and a means of connecting scholarship with the life of the nation, was important for the legitimacy of academic literary study in Russia.

Buslaev dedicated the bulk of his studies to the history of language and what he referred to as the "epos" or "epic poetry," by which he meant all the verbal creativity of "the people" (*narod*).[36] He argued that language and myth are the two most fundamental forms of national consciousness, and determine the emergence and development of all national culture.[37] His most immediate followers were Alexander Afanas'ev and Orest Miller, known as the "younger mythologists." Afanas'ev, who was the closest to Grimm in his scholarship, is best known as the compiler of *Russian Fairy Tales* (*Narodnye russkie skazki*, 1855–63), inspired by Jacob and Wilhelm Grimm's *Children's and Household Tales* (*Kinder- und Hausmärchen*, 1812–15). Building on Buslaev's comparative studies of Slavic folklore and Jacob Grimm's *German Mythology*, Afanas'ev and Miller sought to recover the mythic underpinnings of more recent folkloric genres such as the folktale (*skazka*) and the oral epic (*bylina*).

Buslaev's most lasting impact was in the methodological precedent he set for subsequent literary scholarship.[38] Grimm's influence looms large in commentaries on Buslaev's work, although Franz Bopp, Rasmus Rask, and Wilhelm von Humboldt were also important sources of inspiration. In the words of Andrei Toporkov, Buslaev "attributed universal relevance to the comparative-historical method, extending it not only to the sphere of language, but also to the spheres of folk poetry, mythology, and ritual culture."[39] The lasting legacy of Buslaev and the mythological school was thus the importation and adaptation of Grimm's substantive analogy between comparative grammar and verbal art, and the establishment of this methodological basis as *the* foundation for Russian academic literary study. In *Teaching the Russian Language* (*Prepodavanie otechestvennogo iazyka*, 1844), Buslaev argues that "only philology and linguistics provide an indisputable basis for a theory of verbal art [*teoriia slovesnosti*] and protect it from the vulgar chatter of fiction writers [*belletristy*]."[40] Buslaev thus oriented the *scholarly* study of literature toward folklore as a privileged object of study and toward a methodology based on comparative historical linguistics.

Buslaev and his followers continued to flesh out the analogy between folklore and spoken language proposed by Grimm in his *Teutonic Mythology*. Buslaev argued that folk poetry and language were not only genetically related by an imagined common point of origin, but they shared a series of fundamental properties:

> Just as original, native epic poetry is the product of the entire mass of the people [*narod*], with an unknown moment of origin, having been formed and modified over the course of many centuries, and transmitted from generation to generation through tradition [*po predaniiu*], so language is the common property of the entire people, containing within itself the activity of many generations. Like the folktale [*skazka*], like oral tradition [*predanie*], language belongs to each and everyone; but no one can say when and by whom language was created.[41]

This observation allowed for the development of folklore studies based on the substantive analogy with linguistics; following Buslaev, Russian scholars would repeatedly argue that folklore and spoken language evolve in the same way. In the 1920s and 1930s this Romantic idea would be championed by Maxim Gorky, who cited Buslaev in his promotion of folklore as a model for socialist literature. Buslaev's ideas were also "partially rehabilitated" by Bogatyrev and Jakobson in their pioneering work in cultural semiotics.[42] In the context of the nineteenth century, what is important is that Buslaev firmly linked the concept of "scholarliness" with the comparative historical method.

While Buslaev looked to Grimm for methodology, his philosophy of language was largely inspired by Wilhelm von Humboldt (1767–1835). Humboldt's influence allows us to differentiate the strand of Russian comparative philology that led to Formalism from mainstream German comparative philology. As James Turner points out, Humboldt's theory of language was more influential outside of Germany than within it: in Germany his ahistorical approach to language jarred with the prevailing historicist tendency in comparative linguistics.[43] In Russia, however, Humboldt's influence was widespread; soon after the publication of his collected works (1836–39), his ideas were taken up by philologists such as K. P. Zelensky, I. I. Davydov, and M. A. Tulov, as well as by Buslaev and Alexander Potebnia, whose responses I will discuss in more detail in the next section of this chapter.[44]

As mentioned in the introduction, the Humboldtian conception of language focused on speech as a creative, yet rule-bound *activity*. This tendency to think of language as a constantly renewed creative (speech) act can be contrasted with the view underlying textual criticism, which focused on reconstructing an original, authorial text (a product, rather than an activity). These two diverging conceptions of language privledge either oral speech or written texts respectively. Humboldt believed that language really only existed in oral speech.[45] His focus was on the act of communication in spoken dialogue. In *On the Diversity of Human Language Construction and Its Influence on the Mental Development of the Human Species* (1836), Humboldt wrote:

> *Language*, regarded in its real nature, is an enduring thing, and at every moment a transitory one. Even its maintenance by writing is always just an incomplete, mummy-like preservation, only needed again in attempting thereby to picture a living utterance. In itself it is no product (*Ergon*), but an activity (*Energeia*). Its true definition can therefore only be a genetic one. For it is the ever-repeated mental *labor* of making the *articulated* sound capable of expressing *thought*.[46]

In this view, language is constantly re-created by the individual in dialogue with others. Together, interlocutors are involved in a creative activity, which is enabled and constrained by both parties. The (limited) freedom individuals have in this process allows for the historical development of a language and for the broader diversity of languages.

This view of language can be contrasted with the textual criticism developed by classical philologists. For textual critics, linguistic variation, as observed between the copies of a text, for example, was understood as *deterioration* rather than as a sign of the vitality of language. The Humboldtian view of language did not inform Grimm's work. German comparative-historical linguists described language change not as the result of creative use, but as a process of decay or decomposition. Of German comparative philology (e.g., the work of Grimm, Bopp, and Rask), Robins writes that "both the use of comparison as the clue to an earlier history and the conception of change as a degeneration from primitive integrity were common properties of the scientific thought of the time."[47]

The exemplar of this trend was August Schleicher (1821–1868), who developed an influential system of language classification resembling a genealogical tree, called *Stammbaumtheorie*. Schleicher assumed that linguistic evolution could be broken into a prehistoric period of growth and a historic period of decline, which could be traced like a branching tree. It is widely supposed that Schleicher's *Stammbaumtheorie* was partially inspired by the classical philologist Friedrich Ritschl's (1806–1876) method for *textual* reconstruction. Ritschl taught his students, including Schleicher, to reconstruct a lost original text by organizing extant and reconstructed manuscripts according to a "pedigree."[48] This suggests that, broadly speaking, in Germany (with the important exception of Humboldt), a *textual* approach to language was extended to thinking about *spoken* language.

This trend can also be found in German folkloristics, where a textual, reconstructive approach was often applied to oral folklore. Emblematic of this was the concept of *zersingen* (to alter by singing) in German folk song theory, which construes the act of singing a folk song as a potentially destructive act endangering the continued stability of the song. Much like scribal errors introduced into a copied manuscript, *zersingen* refers to "alterations of a destructive nature" which occur as songs are sung.[49] The folklorist Alan Dundes has referred to this widespread view as the "devolutionary premise" in folklore studies. Citing German, Finnish, Hungarian, and American folklorists, among others, Dundes shows that well into the twentieth century, the devolutionary premise remained unquestioned and widespread. Russian philologists, by contrast, often regarded folklore as an exemplary form of verbal creativity (following Humboldt) rather than as the destruction of a more authentic, primary source. Whereas in nineteenth-century Germany we find a textual approach applied to spoken language, in Russia the opposite occurred. Humboldt's generative philosophy of language, inspired by the act of oral communication, was applied to the study of *texts*.

POTEBNIA AND VESELOVSKY

The scholarship of Alexander Veselovsky (1838–1906) and Alexander Potebnia (1835–1891) had a far-reaching impact on Russian literary studies. As Boris Maslov has put it, this is an "open secret"; "for some, it's too obvious to comment on, whereas to most, it represents a long-forgotten chapter in the history of criticism."[50] More recently, scholars have returned to Veselovsky's legacy in particular, emphasizing his influence on the literary theories of Viktor Shklovsky, Vladimir Propp, Yuri Tynianov, and Mikhail Bakhtin, among others. Potebnia's and Veselovsky's importance for this younger generation has largely been considered separately from one another. This is in part because the two philologists' work gravitated in different directions; Potebnia is best known for his writings on the structure of the linguistic sign, while Veselovsky tracked the migration of plot motifs as they passed between Byzantium, the eastern Slavic lands, and western Europe.

Despite their different intellectual inclinations, both philologists considered their research to be part of the same general field, and they paid close attention to each other's work. Over the course of their long careers, Toporkov tells us, the two scholars "read each other's work with great interest, engaged in polemics, and each adjusted his point of view under the influence of the other's critique."[51] This was possible because they both worked within the common framework of the philological paradigm, using the methods of comparative philology and in accordance with a Humboldtian philosophy of language. As a student of both scholars, A. G. Gornfel'd, put it:

> Veselovsky talked about that which Potebnia did not touch upon—but in their conclusions they agreed. The questions of the *relationship between individual and collective elements of literary creativity*, which Potebnia decided on the basis of the phenomena of language and elementary poetic forms, were illuminated by Veselovsky through the study of more complex forms— plots, poetic genres, etc.[52]

That is, they shared an essential interest in exploring the nature of literary creativity. They both approached this topic using the tools of comparative poetics, focusing on repeating "forms" such as a "plot" or a "genre." At the same time, following Humboldt and Steinthal, they assumed that verbal creativity is to be understood psychologically, as a mental capacity.

Their shared intellectual framework can be traced to their training and sources of inspiration. Both were influenced by Buslaev; Veselovsky, who graduated from Moscow University in 1858, studied with him there.[53] Potebnia's debt to Buslaev, while indirect (he studied and taught at Kharkov University), is in many ways more obvious and is clearly manifested in his writings on the origins of language. A second common influence was the linguistic theory of Heymann Steinthal. Both Veselovsky and Potebnia were sent by the Russian Ministry of Education to study abroad, and both went first to Berlin, where they attended Steinthal's lectures in 1882–83.

Veselovsky's and Potebnia's shared interests can be situated in relation to Steinthal's and Moritz Lazarus's (1824–1903) project of *Völkerpsychologie*. This was a term used for a disciplinary field they proposed in the 1850s. It can be translated as "ethno-psychology" or "cultural psychology." In Russian the term was generally translated as the "psychology of peoples" (*psikhologiia narodov*). The movement had a journal, the *Journal for Völkerpsychologie and Linguistics* (*Zeitschrift für Völkerpsychologie und Sprachwissenschaft*), in which both Veselovsky and Potebnia published.[54] This field was particularly important for Potebnia, who "closely emulated" Steinthal's psycholinguistic model.[55] Potebnia's ideas are primarily known from a book of essays he published relatively early in his career, *Thought and Language* (*Mysl i iazyk*, 1862), and from two collections of his lectures published after

49

his death in 1891, by his wife and students (1894, 1904). As described in the introduction, Steinthal's language philosophy builds on Humboldt, using Herbartian psychology. Herbart's psychology has been characterized as a "mechanics of the mind" which describes the interaction of mental representations. Herbart postulated that the psyche is initially a tabula rasa, so that the source of any psychic differentiation must be sought outside of it, among the objects that affect it through the senses.[56] The result of this synthesis of Humboldt and Herbart has been described as a "relativized Kantian" view which locates the structure of thought in the psyche of the individual, but sees psychological processes as also shaped by history and culture.[57] As Steinthal and Moritz Lazarus wrote in an article on *Völkerpsychologie* in 1865:

> When Locke and Kant, when Spinoza and Fichte represent the activity and the development of human understanding, we find that they refer all of its moments directly to the individual. Allusions to historical conditions appear at best as fleeting exceptions. But in fact, in conditions of a developed culture [*Kultur*], even the seemingly simplest perception of nature takes place as a psychological process whose most important elements consist of thought forms and methods that are the result of the protracted accumulation and modification of given cognitive contents [*Gedankengehalte*]. It is true that everywhere and during every period the development of the human spirit [*Geist*] follows general psychological laws. Yet one is mistaken about the meaning of this very true proposition if one overlooks the fact that the conditions of law-governed events and their elements and presuppositions are fully different for different peoples and times; in such a manner that gradually new kinds of psychic events arise, and it is only with the appearance of these that the appropriate laws [relating to the objective *Geist*] appear.[58]

Veselovsky and Potebnia adhered to the concept of language articulated by *Völkerpsychologie*. In the quote above, this is articulated as the negotiation between "general psychological laws" and the fact that these laws are in turn conditioned by "specific peoples and times"—a premise that allowed Steinthal and Lazarus to explain historical changes in people's thinking. The Russian philologists used comparative poetics to study how individual thought and creativity are informed by, and limited by, culture-specific, collectively shared language.

It should be noted that within the Russian tradition, the comparative philological approach that Potebnia and Veselovsky developed was not universally adopted. Their generation of scholars, who began teaching at Russian universities after the reforms of Alexander II in the 1860s, was characterized by a turn to contemporary written literature (rather than mythology) and the embrace of historical positivism.[59] This gave rise to a "cultural-historical school" of literary studies and scholarship described as the "history of literature" (*istoriia literatury*) or simply "philology" by contemporaries. This philological work was closer to textual criticism, as described earlier in conjunction with Karl Lachmann. Russian historians and philologists of literature such as Aleksandr Pypin, Nikolai Tikhonravov, Iakov Grot, and Semen Vengerov sought to connect texts to their cultural and historical contexts. Like German classical philologists, these scholars sought to produce authoritative, scholarly editions of texts of national importance. Although literary historians stressed the need for breadth of study, they left their mark by publishing comprehensive collected volumes, with biographical studies, of Russia's great authors—such as Pavel Annenkov's edition of Pushkin, Grot's Derzhavin, or Leonid Maikov's Batiushkov.[60] This is the branch of philology that Russian Formalism emphatically rejected; particularly in their initial theoretical statements, the Formalists adamantly distanced their work from biographical author studies and historical contextualization.

The Russian Formalists did, however, retain the research questions which I see as definitive of the philological paradigm. These were: What is poetry? and Where do repeating plot structures come from? The first question is more central, since the question of narrative structure was answered by extending ideas developed in the study of poetry. In the introduction I argued that Formalist theory can be seen as bifurcated into two distinct objects of study: (1) the study of linguistic products, of the corpus, which is undertaken using the comparative method, and (2) the study of linguistic production and perception (mental processes), which is approached using concepts from associationist psychology. We can see this compartmentalization in Veselovsky's and Potebnia's writings when they seek to answer the paradigmatic question: What is poetry? Or, what is poetic language? They approach the question from two directions. Focusing on the individual psyche, they seek to describe the mental processes that allow for creative thought. Turning to the collective tradition, they describe the available formal devices that both enable and limit the creative use of language, in a culturally specific way.

In order to understand what Veselovsky or Potebnia meant by "poetic language," we must first set aside certain expectations that might attend the term "language," such as the notion that "language" refers to an abstract system of interrelated units (signs). Rather, "language" was understood in the terms described by Steinthal and Lazarus: as a "'linguistic continuum' unfolding in time and space through the linguistic activity of the totality of individuals that make up society."[61] So, what *did* Veselovsky and Potebnia mean when they asked: What is poetic language? To begin with, "poetry" was often contrasted with "prose," wherein poetry could refer to both lyric genres and narrative ones (fairy tales, novels, myths). "Prose" in this dichotomy refers thus not to narrative but to "science," in opposition to poetry, which is understood broadly as "the creative arts."[62] (This use of the terms "poetry" and "prose" to mean something like the "arts" versus "science" is also found in the Formalists' writings.)[63] Most importantly, when Veselovsky and Potebnia opposed poetry to prose, they made it clear that they were talking about two *modes of cognition*.[64] For the philological paradigm, claims about poetic language are claims about a mental capacity, not claims about a corpus of existing texts or recorded utterances. This psychological orientation was made explicit by Veselovsky and Potebnia. Potebnia, for example, begins a lecture titled "Poetry and Prose: Their Differentiation" with the introductory statement: "If we look at poetry first and foremost as a known mode of thought and knowledge [*myshlenie i poznanie*], then it is necessary to also look at prose in the same way."[65] Veselovsky likewise describes the "task" of poetics as follows: "Its task will be: the genetic explanation of poetry as a psychic act [*psikhicheskii akt*], determined by known forms of creativity."[66] What then are poetic thinking and prosaic thinking?

Potebnia argued that poetic thinking is defined by the capacity of a word (or longer utterance or text) to evoke more than one meaning. In this same lecture, he contrasts poetic and prosaic thinking as follows:

> The common formula of poetry (respective art) is A (image) < X (significance); that is, between image and signification there always exists an inequality such that A is less than X. The establishment of equality between A and X would destroy the poeticalness, would convert the image into a prosaic designation of a particular case, deprive it of the relationship with something else, or would even convert it into a scientific fact and its signification into a rule. X in relation to A is *always* something *different*, often even heterogeneous. Poetic thinking is an explanation of a particular by another heterogeneous particular. Thus if poetry is parable [*inoskazanie*], allegory in a broad sense of the word, then prose, as an expression of elementary observation, and science both tend in some sense to become tautology.[67]

As John Fizer explains Potebnia's thinking, he points out that poetry and prose (as modes of cognition) are not unrelated. Both are explained as efforts to go from "reality" towards a mental abstraction. As Potebnia wrote in *Thought and Language*, "Reality and idea are common constituents of poetry and prose; in both of them [our] thought strives to introduce connection and completion into the diversity of sensory data; but the different means and results peculiar to them demand that these two quests of [our] thought support and complement each other so long as mankind is 'striving.'"[68]

Veselovsky, when he addresses the same question, refers, like Potebnia, to the domain of psychology. He makes it clear that the difference between poetry and prose is not strictly formal:

The rudiments of poetic language are the same as that of the language of prose: the same constructions, the same rhetorical figures synecdoche, metonymy, etc.; the same words, images, metaphors, epithets. In essence, every word was at one point a metaphor, unilaterally-imagistically expressing one side or one property of an object, that which seemed the most characteristic, representative of its vitality.[69]

The difference between poetic and prosaic language has to do with the way that the mind operates with associations. Poetic thought works with associations between "images." These can be understood as personal memories of particular sensory experiences. The image is contrasted with the abstract "concept," understood as an idea which is not tied to particular memories of sensory experience. Veselovsky elaborates on his understanding of this process:

When we say a word, "house" [*dom*], "hut" [*khata*], and so forth, we unite with it some kind of general complex of features (construction, intended for living in, an enclosed space, and so on) which every person fills in in accord with his personal experience; but if we talk not about a house we know, whose image for some reason has been stamped in our memories, dear to us, and instead talk about a house in general, about house rental, and so forth, the contours [*ochertaniia*] of what this word connotes for us are not present, they do not appear to us. The word has become a bearer of a concept [*poniatie*], it evokes only associations with other concepts, not with images—which could then in turn evoke new juxtapositions with other images and new perspectives for generalization. The result is a unification of real-pictorial associations and psychological associations. The language of poetry, by renewing [*podnovit'*] the visual [*graficheskii*] element of the word, returns it, within certain limits, to that work which language at one time performed, imagistically [*obrazno*] acquiring phenomena of the external world and proceeding towards generalization through real [*real'nyi*] juxtapositions. We all, us non-poets, are capable, in moments of affect, sad or happy, of imbuing forms of reality— either seen or evoked by fantasy—with our memories, and from these images of reality moving on to new visions and generalizations. But this is a sporadic phenomenon; in poetry it is an organic property of style.[70]

In sum, these philologists drew on the psychology of their day and assumed that there are different modes of thinking, defined in terms of associative processes. It was understood that the question "what is poetry?" was ultimately a question about cognition.

I will now turn to the other aspect of the paradigm, comparative poetics. Comparative analyses, it must be stressed, are not on their own capable of producing an answer to the question "What is poetry?" or even "What is poetic language?" Instead, comparative poetics was understood to answer the question: What are the *limits* on individual creativity? (Or in Veselovsky's words, the "boundaries of tradition [*predanie*] in the process of personal creation.")[71] In "The Definition of Poetry" he acknowledges that his program of study has two sides, psychological and formal: poetics is the study of poetry "as a mental act," but also as an act "defined by known forms of creativity, which have consistently accumulated and sedimented [*otlagaiushchiisiia*] in the course of history." Here, I want to further explain Veselovsky's understanding of the formal side of poetics. He describes this as a process which is shaped by particular social environments and their histories. "Poetry, understood as a living process [*zhivoi protsess*], occurs in a constant exchange of offer and demand, personal creation and the perception of the masses; in this exchange its lawfulness is worked out." Poetry is an evolving tradition, a "living process," not a chronology of texts.

In his 1870 address Veselovsky explains that once one adopts the comparative method, literature is reconceptualized as a cultural process. He provides an overview of the way that "general literature" courses are currently taught in Germany, France, Italy, and England. His assessment (somewhat simplified) is that universities are teaching "theories of heroes." This is the practice of generalizing about literary history by focusing on the works of certain "great men":

> Usually chosen as the subject for research is some epoch remarkable from a cultural point of view: for example, the Italian Renaissance of the sixteenth century, Elizabethan drama, and the like. But more often some great man is made to answer for the unity of the viewpoint, for the integrity of the generalization: Petrarch, Cervantes, Dante and his time, Shakespeare and his contemporaries.

Veselovsky contrasts this approach with what he calls "modern scholarship"— by which he means German comparative philology—which he describes as having

> taken the liberty of looking into those masses who up to this time have stood mute behind these heroes; it has detected life and movement which were indiscernible to the naked eye, like everything that takes place in overly great dimensions of space and time. It was necessary to seek out the hidden springs of the historical process here, and, along with a lowering of historical research to more ordinary materials, the center of gravity was transferred to the life of the people.[72]

Comparative poetics, as Veselovsky argues, can make the study of literature a more rigorous, scholarly discipline by depersonalizing the study of texts—and approaching them instead from the perspective of comparative genre studies. He cites approvingly the work of Friedrich August Wolf, which cast doubt on the "individuality of Homer." Veselovsky argues that this kind of scholarship needs to go further, and compare the Homeric epics not just with other Greek material, but with other "impersonal" epics such as the *Kalevala* or with the French chansons de geste. Likewise, Veselovsky points to the possibility of enriching our understanding of "lyric poetry" by comparing the "art lyric" with the "folk song," and our understanding of "drama" by looking at "medieval mysteries and folk games." For Veselovsky, the goal of this comparative work is to elucidate the relationship between artistic forms and "world viewpoint." He is interested in "collective thought," not in the biographies of extraordinary individuals, and in questions of genre, not in interpretations of particular texts.[73] His early articulation of questions of literary theory was thus intertwined with what is cast as a democratizing motive; rejecting a focus on exemplary individuals in favor of studying the contributions of "the people."

Veselovsky's definition of scholarly poetics as a discipline which eschews the "great man" approach is central to Russian Formalism. Tynianov rephrased Veselovsky when arguing against the trend among literary historians to study "major (but also isolated) phenomena" and to turn "literary history into a 'history of generals.'"[74] What is less evident, yet an important component of this disciplinary methodology, is that the move to depersonalize the study of literature was largely accomplished by turning to folkloric genres; that is, popular, oral ones. In other words, the comparative poetic approach to literary history, as undertaken by Veselovsky and the Formalists, was not limited to bodies of written, "literary" texts. Instead, work in comparative poetics often approached questions about literary texts by situating them within a corpus that included oral and popular genres. This move is a hallmark of the philological paradigm.

Folklore studies were a central feature of the intellectual biographies of both Potebnia and Veselovsky. Potebnia, who was born in a village in northeastern Ukraine, began collecting folklore as a teenager in the early 1850s, when folklore collection in Ukraine was popular. His first informant was an aunt, who is reported to have been a talented folk singer and taleteller. Potebnia collected folktales, riddles, proverbs, legends, and incantations, but paid particular attention to folk song—collecting at least 350 distinct songs. In 1862, he convinced several friends to plan a trip around Ukraine with the goal of studying the people's lore and way of life. His letters reveal that he considered going on foot, dressed in traditional folk costume.

Potebnia's journey was cut short, however, because he was called to Moscow to prepare for his trip to Berlin.[75] In a letter written to a Czech Slavist in 1886, he recounted that

> due to the circumstances of my life it came to pass that, in my scholarly pursuits, the starting point—sometimes evident to others, sometimes not—was the Ukrainian language and Ukrainian folklore [*narodnaia slovesnost'*]. If this starting point and the feelings associated with it hadn't been there and if I had grown up without a connection to tradition [*predanie*], then, it seems to me, I would not have become a scholar.[76]

About half of Potebnia's scholarship was devoted to folkloristic subjects. He wrote on the symbolism of folk poetry and the mythological foundations of rituals and beliefs, and he also wrote numerous works on folk song.

Potebnia's view of folklore as a kind of creative font, from which his scholarly career grew, was consistent with his belief that oral tradition has a creative, generative function in literary and cultural history. As he told his students in a lecture titled "Civilization and Folklore" ("Tsivilizatsiia i narodnaia slovesnost'"): "Writing [*pis'mennost'*] is dead . . . it has never been and can never be a full reflection of life, and . . . therefore it can be useful only inasmuch as it is supplemented by oral tradition [*ustnoe predanie*]."[77] He reiterates here Humboldt's opposition between oral speech as the "living utterance" and writing as its "incomplete, mummy-like preservation." Potebnia also subscribes to the Romantic understanding of folklore (and the folk) as the source of a creative, vital energy which sustained literary, and even scholarly, development. He was sensitive to the differences between written texts and oral traditions, but he also rejected the idea that the two could be considered separately.

Veselovsky likewise dedicated much of his theoretical output to folklore. However, unlike Potebnia, he did not conduct fieldwork, and his interest in oral traditions was rooted in a broadly comparative approach. Veselovsky was particularly interested in how artistic forms travel, and his scholarship built on that of the influential German philologist and Sanskrit scholar Theodore Benfey, who sought to trace a common stock of tales found in Europe to their origins in India, developing what became known as the "theory of borrowing" in folklore studies. In an autobiographical sketch, Veselovsky stressed his parents' efforts to ensure his fluency in German, French, English, Italian, and Spanish at an early age. He mentions folklore, but seeks to distance himself from Romantic clichés, writing that "I, too, like everyone else, was told fairy tales [*skazki*], but I don't attribute my passion for folklore [*fol'klor*] to this."[78] In his *History of Modern Criticism*, René Wellek writes that "Veselovsky must be classed among the greatest literary scholars of the [nineteenth] century in breadth of knowledge and scope of competence."[79] He specialized in Italian Renaissance culture, worked on the ancient Greek novel, and wrote monographs on Boccaccio, Petrarch, and V. A. Zhukovsky.

While his interests were broader than Potebnia's, Veselovsky also dedicated at least half of his scholarship to folklore study. After Veselovsky's death in 1906, a commission was formed with the purpose of publishing his collected works. Although this plan never came to fruition, the commission produced a publication plan for 24 volumes. Of these, 12 were to cover folkloric subjects per se—legends, folklore, mythology, studies of the oral epic (*bylina*), and spiritual verses (*dukhovnye stikhi*).[80] This does not include Veselovsky's work in historical poetics (two volumes), which was also heavily skewed toward folkloristic material, in that one of his main concerns was explaining the origins of poetic language and narrative plots. The centrality of folkloristic material in the project is reflected in Boris Kazansky's assessment of Veselovsky's legacy in 1926: "It might seem that the title [i.e., historical poetics] should be retained only for research on that material which Veselovsky mainly studied, in general, as well as in his 'Historical Poetics,' that is, *primitive folklore* [*primitivnaia narodnaia slovesnost'*]."[81]

In sum, Veselovsky and Potebnia established a paradigm of study for which the central research question was: "What is poetry?" (or "What is poetic language?"). The answer, it was assumed, would have both a psychological and a formal component. The first of these—as was made explicit—was based on the premise that there is a particular mode of cognition which is responsible for artistic production and perception. The formal component was studied using the comparative method, particularly by locating repeating elements of verbal traditions, as viewed across literary and folkloric genres. This allowed them to replace the "great man" approach to literary history with the formal description of a reservoir of traditional devices. Russian Formalism inherited a paradigm that was bifurcated into an opposition between the collective and the individual. This splits the study of literature into two objects of study: the creative act (Humboldt's *Energeia*) and the inert product (*Ergon*). The first is the domain of the individual, and is described using concepts drawn from psychology. The second is the domain of the collective, and is studied using the method of comparative philology.

RUSSIAN FORMALISM

The three scholars who did the most to develop Formalism's core theoretical arguments, which were then taken up and modified or applied by others, were Osip Brik, Viktor Shklovsky, and Roman Jakobson. Brik was the first to develop key Formalist tenets, but then did the least to work these ideas out himself, in writing. He moved away from Formalism by the mid-1920s, and published relatively little. His most important publication for Formalist theory is "Sound Repetitions" (1917), while his only other major theoretical publication, "Rhythm and Syntax," appeared ten years later, in 1927. In a note accompanying the republication of these two studies in 1964, Jakobson describes Brik as a brilliant outsider in the world of academic literary studies:

> When in 1919 the erudite medievalist of Moscow University, B. I. Iarkho, was invited by MLC and delivered there his paper "On the so-called trochaic tetrameters in the Carolingian rhythms," he called me the next day to say how amazed he was by the unusual standard of the discussion, and especially by Brik's astute observations: "How could it happen that I have never met him before in our faculty; does he teach there or is he a research fellow?" Professor Iarkho did not want to believe that Brik, who actually was a graduate of the Law School, and had never studied in the faculty of arts and letters, nonetheless swiftly grasped and had keen observations to make both on the Medieval Latin versification and, to the great surprise of the classical philologist Rumer, even on the tangled problems of Ancient Greek prosody.[82]

Jakobson goes on to acknowledge that Brik's ideas influenced his own work, and also names studies by Boris Tomashevsky, Viktor Zhirmunsky, and Eikhenbaum which acknowledge Brik's important contributions. Brik "liked to cope with an intricate problem, then to recount his results, and felt quite happy if his listeners were ready to develop and utilize them, while he himself could go over to a new, unexplored domain." Jakobson refers to "a large number of painstaking studies loaded with new ideas and penetrating observations that remained uncompleted and unpublished"—a fact that he attributes to Brik's "total lack of personal ambition."[83] It is difficult to assess the reliability of Jakobson's account at this distance—although his picture of Brik as an incisive and eager interlocutor is confirmed by the minutes of the discussions held in the Moscow Linguistic Circle. Brik's contributions stand out for his capacity to identify the crux of a problem or a source of confusion. He also appears to have held the floor more than any other member, with the possible exception of Jakobson. Yet Brik has largely been overlooked in scholarship on Russian Formalism, because his contribution is difficult to assess. Svetlikova's book is an exception, and, like Jakobson, she stresses the importance of Brik's ideas for others, and attempts to account for Brik's decision not to write and publish more himself.[84]

Jakobson and Shklovsky are more easily recognizable as early leaders of the movement. Institutionally, they were founders and presidents: Shklovsky as the leader of OPOIAZ, and Jakobson as the student president of the Moscow Linguistic Circle. They both had long and prolific careers as literary scholars, and had a far-reaching influence on their peers and on subsequent literary theory. Shklovsky's articulation of the need to study the "device" (*priem*), and his idea that the function of art is defamiliarization (*ostranenie*) inform his colleagues' writings throughout. Jakobson was an incredibly effective institution builder, and is considered a founder of linguistic and literary structuralism. For these reasons, their responses to the philological paradigm—its concept of language and its framework for scholarship—are particularly important.

Shklovsky's and Jakobson's writings from the 1910s and early 1920s make the connection between Formalism and the philological paradigm particularly clear. They explicitly take up paradigmatic research questions, and the philological concept of the boundaries of the object of study (*slovesnost'*). During the winter of 1918 and spring of 1919 Shklovsky and Jakobson each produced long studies in which they laid out the ideas that would shape their careers as literary theorists. For Shklovsky this was "The Relationship between Devices of Plot Construction and General Devices of Style"; for Jakobson it was "The Newest Russian Poetry." At the time, the two men were apparently close friends; Shklovsky recalls that Jakobson hid him in his apartment in 1918, when Shklovsky was active in an underground organization (the Socialist Revolutionary Party) fighting against the Bolsheviks. In a letter to Jakobson, which Shklovsky published in 1926, he writes that "you and I were like two pistons in the same cylinder."[85] I would like to apply this metaphor to their two seminal studies produced at this time: they are clearly working together within the same conceptual "engine"—that of the philological paradigm.

Each of the studies takes up the questions that motivated the research of Veselovsky and Potebnia: "What is poetic language?" and "Why are the same narrative plots found all over the world?" Importantly, the Formalists approach these questions as if continuing an ongoing discussion. Jakobson begins by stating that a theory of poetic language exists, but can only be *advanced* by adopting a more sophisticated methodology (that of dialectology): "The advancement [*razvitie*] of a theory of poetic language will be possible only . . . when a kind of poetic dialectology will be founded."[86] For Jakobson, it is obvious that the pursuit of such a theory is worthwhile, and that its goal is to contribute a better answer to the question: "What is poetic language?" Shklovsky likewise assumes the paradigmatic question: "Why are the same plots found all over the world?" He begins not by justifying the question but by refuting others' answers to it, supplying his own (improved) approach. Shklovsky starts his discussion by citing Veselovsky's contributions; his own voice first appears with a "But . . ." refuting Veselovsky's position: "But a coincidence in plots is found even in cases where it is impossible to imagine borrowing."[87] The fact that both Jakobson and Shklovsky introduce their theoretical innovations as better responses to the existing, paradigm-defining questions alerts us to their adherence to the (philological) paradigm.

In addition to asking the same questions, the Formalists—with Shklovsky, Jakobson, and Brik in the forefront—also followed the philological paradigm in breaking the research problem (poetic language/narrative) into two domains: the psychological and the formal (comparative). The psychological half of their theory follows the paradigm in looking to association-ist psychology for concepts of how the mind acquires and stores information, and for the processes involved in creative thought. I have already noted that Shklovsky began his famous "Art as Device" (1917) by referring to Potebnia. His article begins: "'Art is thinking in images.' You can hear this phrase from a schoolboy, and it is also the starting point for a philologist beginning to construct a literary theory."[88] Brik's "Sound Repetitions" begins with a very similar formulation. Following Svetlikova, I would like to stress that, in critiquing the idea that "art is thinking in images," the Formalists are really rejecting only the ending of this statement, "in images." They retain the "art is thinking in . . ." part. As for Veselovsky and Potebnia, the Formalists' references to poetic or prosaic "language" were interchangeable with statements about poetic or prosaic "thinking." Jakubinsky makes this clear in his use of a parenthetical at the beginning of his influential 1916 essay: "Thus we are dealing with the system of *practical language* (linguistic thinking) [*iazykovoi myshlenie*])."[89]

In the opening paragraphs of Brik's study he suggests that the "images" part of this formulation can be replaced with an idea derived from the work of Veselovsky—in particular his 1898 study "Psychological Parallelism." This move is foundational for much of subsequent Formalist theory. It can be said that the Formalists replace the idea that "art is thinking in images" with the idea that "art is thinking in parallelisms." Brik puts the Formalists on this track with his detailed study of sound repetition in poetry. He argues that poetic language works as much with formal repetitions of sounds as it does with the semantic "referent" of individual words (i.e., the "image"). In Brik's usage, "image" means "referent" or semantic content. He writes: "I think that the elements of imagistic and sonic creativity exist at the same time; and every individual work is the resultant of these two heterogeneous aspirations."[90] Some of the simplest examples of a sound repetition for Brik are the following: (r-f, r-f) "i vnemlet a**rf**e se**raf**ima [and hearing the seraphim's harp]" or (l-zh-n, l-zh-n) "chto ia **lezhu na** v**lazhn**om dne [that I lie on the damp floor]."[91] The notion that poetic language is formally defined by "repetition" derives from the premise that poetic (artistic) thinking is, at its core, defined by the process of associations by similarity.

In their long studies from 1918–19, Shklovsky and Jakobson describe poetry/art as a mental activity in which relations of similarity can disrupt or "disassociate" connections established on the basis of habitual contiguity or causality associations. Recall that Jakobson argued that during "everyday linguistic thinking [*normal'noe prakticheskoe iazykovoe myshlenie*]" "associations by contiguity [*assotsiatsii po smezhnosti*]" dominate. However, when processing poetic language, these mechanical associations "retreat into the background."[92] In "The Relationship between Devices of Plot Construction and General Devices of Style," Shklovsky also contrasts "art" with "practical *thinking*":

> Practical thinking [*prakticheskoe myshlenie*] tends toward generalization, toward the creation of wide, all-encompassing formulas. In contrast, art "with its thirst for concreteness" (Carlyle) is based on stepped gradation [*stupenchatost'*] and the disintegration of even those things which are presented as abstract and indivisible. Stepped construction [*stupen'chatoe postroenie*] includes: repetition—with its particular case, rhyme, tautology, tautological parallelism, psychological parallelism, deceleration, epic repetitions, the triadic repetition of folktales, peripeteia, and many other devices of plot construction [*siuzhetnost'*].[93]

Shklovsky concludes: "We see that that which in prose can be designated as 'a,' in art is expressed by 'A1 A' (for example, psychological parallelism). This is the soul of all devices."[94] Here Shklovsky reiterates Potebnia's opposition between scientific and poetic thinking, arguing that the latter is metaphoric. Recall that Potebnia argued that "poetic thinking is an explanation of a particular by another heterogeneous particular." Moreover, Shklovsky's categories of "poetry" and "prose" are similar to Potebnia's in that concreteness is opposed to abstraction.

However, Shklovsky also uses Veselovsky's argument (and Brik's interpretation of it) that poetry is a product of similarity associations in order to further specify how poetic (i.e., metaphoric) thinking is manifest in language. Shklovsky, Brik, and Jakobson argue that the formal and semantic manifestation of poetic thinking is the production of sequences of sounds according to associations by similarity. For an author, poetic thinking results in an utterance whose sub-parts are related to each other by formal and semantic repetition; for the perceiver, poetic thinking is prompted by the perception of a succession of formal and semantic repetitions. An example from verse is Brik's sound repetitions. From narrative, it is Shklovsky's "stepped construction" (*stupen'chatoe postroenie*); his examples include first and foremost the repetition of tasks in folktales, but also general thematic "steps" as exemplified by Tolstoy's story "Three Deaths," which describes the death of a noblewoman, a peasant, and a tree.[95] The Formalists developed this line of thinking to account for the individual, creative side of their literary theory.

Moving to the collective or normative side of their theory, this is the domain defined by the comparative method. A wide range of literary scholars used some version of the comparative method to describe common features found within textual corpora. This kind of scholarship was, following Veselovsky, referred to as "poetics" (*poetika*). In a popular textbook, *Poetics* (1925), Boris Tomashevsky defines poetics as the identification of the "constituent parts" of a literary composition:

> In a theoretical approach literary phenomena are subjected to *generalization*, and thus are considered not in their individuality, but as the results of the application of general laws for the construction of literary compositions. Every work is consciously broken down into its constituent parts [*sostavnye chasti*]. In the construction of a composition, *devices* for similar constructions are distinguished, i.e., means of combining verbal material into an artistic whole. These devices are the primary object of poetics.[96]

While much was debated about many of the terms that Tomashevsky uses—"theory," "literary form," "the work," "general laws"—what *was* generally agreed on is the basic idea that poetics is comparative. Poetics is not the study of individual works, not interpretation, but is concerned with identifying the constituent elements that can be found in many different examples. Although comparison was mandatory for poetics, the scholar is, in principle, free to select any corpus for comparison. It was at this point that the different Formalists started to diverge in their responses to the philological paradigm. Some of them, primarily Shklovsky and Jakobson, continued to focus on a corpus which aligns with the contours of *slovesnost'* (i.e., a wide range of folkloric and literary examples). Others, namely Eikhenbaum and Tynianov, focused more narrowly on written, literary texts by known authors. Although, for example, Eikhenbaum and Shklovsky referred to shared theoretical concepts, such as "motivation" or "deceleration," the corpora they referred to differed. Eikhenbaum's "How Gogol's 'Overcoat' Is Made" (1919) can be compared in this regard to Shklovsky's "How *Don Quixote* Is Made" (1921). Eikhenbaum limits his analysis to a single text, while Shklovsky compares Cervantes's technique with that of Gogol, Tolstoy, Bely, Dickens, Sterne, Ovid, Shakespeare, Rabelais, Ostrovsky, Schnitzler, Conan Doyle, and Lesage, among others. The differences in corpora indicate different ambitions for their studies: Shklovsky is using comparison to extract reoccurring, potentially universal forms or devices, while Eikhenbaum is interested in how these devices work in specific instances. As Any puts it, "If Shklovsky leaned towards the general and the universal, Eikhenbaum addressed the individual and particular manifestations of that universal."[97]

Eikhenbaum and Tynianov were trained as literary scholars at St. Petersburg University, and both began their careers with training in a historical, and primarily biographical, approach to literary study. Eikhenbaum enrolled in the Slavic Division of the Philological Faculty at St. Petersburg University in 1907, but then switched into the Romance and German Division, where he studied under the Germanist F. A. Braun. Carol Any describes Eikhenbaum's early work as dedicated to using personal documents to uncover an individual writer's particular worldview—in other words, the "kind of articles that OPOIAZ was trying to sweep away." She identifies the year from summer 1917 through summer 1918 as a "turning point" for Eikhenbaum, which began when he became a regular visitor at the Briks' home. Scholars agree that he did not generally develop new theoretical ideas as much as test proposals through concrete applications. Any describes Eikhenbaum's writings during his Formalist period as "applied criticism."[98] Svetlikova describes his work as the "brilliant development of others' ideas"—in particular the ideas of Osip Brik. By Eikhenbaum's own account, Brik provided the core concepts for Eikhenbaum's three most important theoretical works in the late 1910s and early 1920s: "How Gogol's 'Overcoat' Is Made," *Young Tolstoy,* and *Melody of Verse.*[99]

Tynianov was also educated in the Philological Faculty of St. Petersburg University. Scholars of his intellectual biography stress the importance of Semen Vengerov's (1855–1920) Pushkin seminar for Tynianov, to which he belonged from 1913 to 1918. This was where he and Eikhenbaum reportedly met.[100] Catherine Depretto has argued that many of Tynianov's central subjects stemmed from this formative experience: his work on the archaists and Pushkin, on Tiutchev and Heine, on Kiukhelbeker and Pushkin.[101] It is unclear exactly when Tynianov joined OPOIAZ. Jakobson remembers that Tynianov did not join before he left for Czechoslovakia in the summer of 1920, which is consistent with published membership lists from the time.[102] Tynianov was particularly interested in literary history, a subject addressed in his first published article, "Dostoevsky and Gogol: Towards a Theory of Parody" (1921). As the subtitle indicates, Tynianov sought to understand history by studying the way in which individual words or phrases can be semantically or, as he puts it in this early study, "emotionally" recolored when they are transferred from one context to another.[103] His major theoretical treatment of this question was his 1924 *The Problem of Verse Language,* which I describe (in chapter 3) as an extension of the Formalist identification of parallelism as the core poetic device. Unlike Brik, Shklovsky, or Jakobson, Eikhenbaum and Tynianov frequently operate with a concept of a textual whole as a unit of analysis. For Eikhenbaum, this can be an individual text, such as Gogol's "Overcoat," or, more often, an individual author's oeuvre, as in his *Young Tolstoy* (1922), *Anna Akhmatova: An Attempt at Analysis* (1923), and *Lermontov: Effort at a Historical-Literary Evaluation* (1924). For Eikhenbaum, the unity provided by the author's oeuvre is described as a "system": for instance, he writes that the principal aim of his 1922 book is "to establish Tolstoy's system of artistic devices in its gradual development."[104] Even though Tynianov did not limit his studies to single authors or individual texts as often, his thinking also privileges the concept of a textual boundary—a semantic limit within which words take on secondary meaning or "recoloring." Both Eikhenbaum and Tynianov studied the way in which preexisting verbal forms (e.g., Tolstoy's use of a syntactic "turn of speech" typical of eighteenth-century philosophical constructions) are employed to a particular end, and given specific meaning, within the system of a text or corpus.[105]

The Formalists' studies of canonical literary texts often focused on the poets of the Romantic period (e.g., Pushkin, Lermontov, Fet, Zhukovsky) and on the poetry of the Russian avant-garde. Tihanov has argued that this indicates the importance of a Romantic nationalist valuation of literature, as an underlying motivation for the emergence of Russian Formalism.[106] Building on this claim, I will show that the broader social ambitions of Formalism can be accessed by situating their scholarship within a theoretical program which sought to make claims not only on the basis of individual (Romantic) texts, studied as semantic wholes, but on the basis of comparative claims about verbal art *in general*—literary texts as subjected to generalizing analysis (*obobshchenie*). As we have seen, general claims were necessary for "poetics" to be seen as a "science" (*nauka*). To produce these, a scholar needed to use the comparative method to study how poetic devices work across many instances. This kind of scholarship was understood to legitimize individual author studies such as Eikhenbaum's. The latter makes this clear in the introduction to his *Young Tolstoy*:

> The basic theme of this book . . . will be Tolstoy's poetics [*poetika*]. The central questions will concern his artistic traditions and the system of his stylistic and compositional devices. We are accustomed to call such a method of investigation "formal," although I would prefer to call it "morphological." . . . In the fields of folklore study and the study of plots [*obshchaia siuzhetologiia*], the morphological method is already firmly established. The next step is the question of applying this method to concrete historical and literary phenomena—individual creativity or the work of a certain literary era.[107]

Eikhenbaum's willingness to extend the comparative method to literary studies built on the pioneering work of Shklovsky and Jakobson.

Comparative philological analyses were seen as having produced general or scientific knowledge about verbal art. However, in actuality, as we have seen, "verbal art" (*slovesnost'*) was not, in practice, a universal category, but often a national one. Recall that in Dal's dictionary, *slovesnost'* is defined as "the commonality of verbal works of the people [*narod*], writing, literature."[108] As a result, conclusions derived from the *teoriia slovesnosti* are tacitly claims about the art of "the people." This was not irrelevant for the Formalists: they sought to contribute to a broader intellectual debate in the 1910s and 1920s regarding not just the concept of "art" in general, but the definition of national, popular, or proletarian "art." The inclusion of folkloric examples in Shklovsky's and Jakobson's writings (as well as, to a lesser degree, those of Brik and Eikhenbaum) is an important indicator that their theories were conceived within the framework of the philological paradigm. Jakobson and Shklovsky, in particular, seek to answer the question "What is poetry?" using a folkloristic corpus. In fact, their pioneering works in literary theory often modified existing approaches to the study of folklore.

Jakobson's intellectual biography makes it clear that his first "passion" was for folklore.[109] In a retrospective essay published in 1966, he begins with the proverb as a kind of seed for his own intellectual biography:

> A passion for gathering proverbs possessed me as soon as I learned to scrawl letters. Proverbial sayings were zealously seized upon to cover empty calendar sheets. Discussions with specialists in childhood psychology, Charlotte Bühler and Rosa Katz, have reinforced my conviction that such infantile predilections are neither fortuitous in their choice nor without consequence for the later lines of mental development. The proverb pertains simultaneously to daily speech and to verbal art . . . The proverb is the largest coded unit occurring in our speech and at the same time the shortest poetic composition.[110]

Here, folklore—the proverb—is the place where poetry and language meet. The intersection between poetic creativity and general linguistics is a major theme of Jakobson's intellectual biography. This interest can be seen as a product of the preoccupation of the philological paradigm: its pursuit of the elusive relationship between individual verbal creativity and collective norms. Jakobson recounts how he graduated from this childhood obsession with proverbs to the language of incantations, prompted by the Symbolists' interest in this genre. Later, Jakobson would describe himself in the 1910s as "a folklorist at heart," recalling that he would automatically attempt to transcribe an impressive folkloric performance wherever he was.[111]

Jakobson's university education included an important emphasis on fieldwork—he participated in expeditions to collect folkloric, dialectological, and ethnographic material. At Moscow University he enrolled in the

Historical Philological Department, where he majored in linguistics; as he put it later, this was "linguistics as it is connected with folklore and litera-ture . . . both general linguistics and Slavic philology."[112] During this period, 1914–18, Jakobson's thinking was shaped by his membership in several scholarly societies: the Commission for Folklore Study (Komissiia po na-rodnoi slovesnosti) within the Society of Devotees of Natural Science, An-thropology, and Ethnography, and the Moscow Dialectological Commission. Jakobson regularly attended the meetings of the Commission for Folklore Study between 1914 and 1917, and it was here, in 1915, that he presented his first scholarly work, an essay on "The Influence of Folk Literature on Trediakovsky," which sought to establish the impact of oral traditions on the Russian literary poetic tradition. The Commission funded his student field-work, which he conducted in the summers of 1915 and 1916 with his friend and frequent coauthor, the folklorist Petr Bogatyrev. As I argue in chapter 4, Jakobson combined his work on folklore with his training in dialectology to develop a particular method for Moscow Formalism—"poetic dialectology." These ideas were developed in meetings of the Moscow Linguistic Circle, a society which was originally founded, in 1915, as a student subsection of the Moscow Dialectological Commission. Jakobson's contributions to the field of folkloristics are too extensive to summarize here. What is important for the history of *literary* theory is that his folkloristic and linguistic training, which he approached in a synthetic manner, deeply informed his thinking about poetic language.

Shklovsky, according to his own accounts, managed to largely avoid gaining a systematic education in any field of study. When describing his education in *Third Factory* (*Tret'ia fabrika*, 1926), Shklovsky writes simply that "I was a bad student and I attended bad schools."[113] He mentions that he was already working on "prose theory" while a gymnasium student and at St. Petersburg University, although his efforts were, he stresses, unrelated to his official studies.[114] Shklovsky studied in the Philological Faculty at Petersburg University from 1913 to 1914 or 1916 (accounts vary).[115] This is not to say, however, that existing philological scholarship had no impact on him. In fact, scholars of Formalism view Shklovsky as the figure most closely bound to the legacy of Potebnia and Veselovsky.[116] Shklovsky later recalled that Vese-lovsky's ideas were alive and well at the university after his death in 1906.[117] In 1913 the first collected volumes of Veselovsky's works began to appear, including a volume dedicated to his works on poetics, and one containing his unfinished work on the "poetics of plots."[118]

Veselovsky's writings may have encouraged Shklovsky's interest in folk-lore. Some of Shklovsky's own folklore-heavy writings are those that most extensively engage with Veselovsky's ideas. Central among these is his long essay "The Relationship between Devices of Plot Construction and General Devices of Style" (hereafter "Plot Construction"). In his memoir, *Sentimental Journey* (1922), Shklovsky describes working on this essay during the course of his peripatetic underground efforts on the part of the Socialist Revolutionary Party in 1918.[119] He notes that he took several books with him, which he had "unbound . . . and divided into small parcels."[120] Maslov speculates that among these materials were sections of Veselovsky's collected writings. The essay is in large part a commentary on, and reinterpretation of, several ideas central to Veselovsky's work. The material analyzed by Shklovsky is largely folkloristic: his theoretical arguments hinge on observations made about the poetics of the oral epic and folktales. The essays in Shklovsky's *Theory of Prose* (*O teorii prozy*, 1925) reveal an obsessive interest in amassing folkloristic evidence for his claims. In an appendix to "Plot Construction," he lists fifty-eight different examples of a type of additive narrative structure found in folktales.[121] Shklovsky also reveals extensive research on riddles and folkloric plots; his early work on narrative was so tilted toward folklore that when Jakobson referred to these writings in a 1935 lecture on Formalism, he described them as Shklovsky's "folkloristic explorations [*folkloristické úvahy*]."[122] Yet Shklovsky's work has not generally been considered in the context of Russian folkloristics.[123]

The attention of folklorists, however, can be revealing. Andrei Toporkov has recently written on Shklovsky's use of Mikhail Speransky's (1863–1938) folklore textbook, *Russian Oral Verbal Art* (*Russkaia ustnaia slovesnost'*, 1917).[124] As Toporkov notes, Jakobson and Bogatyrev dedicated their *Slavic Philology* to Speransky, and they wrote that "the best textbook, which summarizes all that has been done in the study of Russian folklore, is academic M. N. Speransky's book *Russian Oral Verbal Art*."[125] Toporkov points out that Shklovsky's "Plot Construction" essay reproduces substantial portions of Speransky's book, without adequately citing him. Shklovsky's sections on "deceleration" and "repetition" closely follow identically titled sections in Speransky's textbook.[126] Shklovsky also reiterates key formulations made by Speransky regarding the goal of deceleration, the nature of poetic language, and the puzzle of reoccurring plot structures. Toporkov also points out that Speransky's terminology is "strangely" close to Shklovsky's—using the terms "structure," "poetics," "*fabula*," "*siuzhet*," "material," and "form" to describe the formal poetics of folklore genres.

The overlap between Speransky and Shklovsky can be explained in part as Veselovsky's general influence, since Speransky also relied heavily on Veselovsky's work. Toporkov's conclusion is that folklorists were already doing formal poetics before the Formalists, so it makes sense that the latter would find folkloristics helpful in formulating their approach:

If, for formal analysis, the literary scholar needs to "eliminate" the author with his psychology and ideology, then folklorists dealt with texts without an author, and existing in many variants, which required first and foremost some sort of systematization. Folklorists in the 1910s–1920s were well aware of the need to work with various variants of a text with one and the same plot [*siuzhet*], as well as the search for some sort of narrative [*siuzhetnyi*] invariants.[127]

Shklovsky was able to assume the position as the leading theorist of OPOIAZ—making him in hindsight a founding figure of modern literary theory—in part because he was willing to boldly transfer a method and its terms from the sphere of folkloristics to the analysis of literature. Yet Shklovsky's engagement with folklore is not merely a case of cross-disciplinary borrowing. His writings reveal a nuanced understanding of the nature of folkloric traditions and the specifics of oral composition. Although he did not, like Jakobson, go on officially sponsored fieldwork expeditions, he did record folklore, and made use of these examples in his papers on narrative theory.

Jakobson's and Shklovsky's interest in folklore is part of their positioning as the original theoretical leaders of the Formalist movement. The study of folklore, as Toporkov and others have pointed out, was already oriented toward comparative poetics. And comparative poetics, as I have shown, was considered by Russian philologists to be synonymous with "theory" (*teoriia*). The theorists most comfortable with analyzing verbal art for its component parts were best positioned to lead the development of literary theory in Russia in the early twentieth century. However, this is not the only reason why this folkloristic orientation was important. The decision to include (or even prioritize) folklore was intertwined with the social and cultural motivations of Formalist scholarship.

In the framework for humanities studies provided by *Völkerpsychologie* (ethno-psychology), the study of poetic form is understood as the means of understanding the way that a people think. Recall Steinthal's and Lazarus's relativized Kantian position, which acknowledged the role of "general psychological laws," but saw these as conditioned by particular cultural environments.[128] According to this rationale, the scholar's corpus for analysis is implicitly the reservoir of cultural forms which are shared by a given "people." For the Russian academic tradition, the operative concept of the "people" was largely equivalent to the Russian peasantry. The yoking of scholarly poetics with *slovesnost'* in nineteenth-century Russian philology meant that the oral culture of the Russian peasantry occupied a central position in this field. The politics behind these philological studies continued to play a role in the late 1910s and 1920s, in the form of an ongoing debate regarding the nature and contours of Russian popular identity and the legitimacy of different competing groups, each of whom aspired to position themselves as the "true inheritor" of this identity.

The Formalists, particularly Shklovsky and Jakobson, formulated their theoretical conclusions on the basis of comparisons between avant-garde poetry (e.g., that of Velimir Khlebnikov or Vladimir Mayakovsky) and examples from oral traditions. This can be seen as a way of legitimizing these authors as consistent with a broader, popular tradition. The Formalists were not alone in their interest in folklore. For example, during the Civil War, the cultural division of the Soviet government, Narkompros, collaborated with Petrograd intellectuals to organize a variety of entertainments approximating the traditional folk festival (*narodnoe gulianie*)—including puppet plays, *chastushki*, and dramatic improvisations for the 1919 May Day celebrations.[129] Also in this spirit, Aleksei Remizov wrote a version of the popular folk play *Tsar Maksimilian* that was staged in Petrograd in 1920–21. Shklovsky faulted Remizov for his superficial understanding of folk theater, contrasting Remizov's effort with Mayakovsky's *Mystery-Bouffe* (1918/1921):

> In its basis Mayakovsky's work is 10,000 times more popular [*narodnyi*] than all of Remizov's "Tsar Maksimilian." . . . Vladimir Mayakovsky took—intuitively, of course—the very device of folk [*narodnyi*] theater. Folk theater is entirely based on the word as its material, on the play with words, on word play. On the brilliant pages of "Mystery" . . . the popular device is canonized.[130]

Verbal creativity, "word play," as we have seen, is what comparative philology attempts to study. In publications from this period, Shklovsky repeatedly asserts that both the Formalists and the Futurists were allied with popular traditions due to their shared interest in verbal creativity, particularly puns, riddles, and metaphor.

This chapter has shown that the legacy of Romantic nationalism was deeply intertwined with the very concepts of scholarship (*nauchnost'*), method, and object of study (*slovesnost'*) for comparative philology. The Formalists were clear that their aim was to produce a more rigorous scholarly poetics, and in doing so they took over many of the assumptions of their predecessors. One outcome of this, as I demonstrate in subsequent chapters, was that they continued to produce engaged, activist scholarship. A second conclusion is that, due to the legacy of Romantic philology, the Formalists were committed to the study of non-elite forms of verbal creativity. Like Veselovsky and Potebnia, their interest was not in the individual "generals" of the artistic elite, but in verbal art as an aspect of everyday life.

The Author as Performer

THE PHILOLOGICAL PARADIGM provided a framework for thinking about verbal art as continual negotiation between a historical tradition, known and maintained by a collective, and the individual, creative act of speech. Nineteenth-century Romantic thought looked to peasant culture (i.e., folkloric verbal genres) for the sources of "collective" tradition and to the written literature of the intellectual classes to explore individual creativity. These assumptions were challenged on multiple fronts during the revolutionary period, from the mid-1910s through the mid-1920s. This chapter argues that Russian Formalist theory emerged as part of an effort to dismantle the class-based ideology that had defined artistic, written "literature" (i.e., *belles-lettres*) as a discursive category in the nineteenth century. This ideology relied on the opposition between the peasantry and the intelligentsia as the basis for contrasting oral and written verbal art, and folklore and literature. To reframe "literature," the Formalists continued the work of their philological predecessors by collapsing these oppositions, and applying concepts and methods primarily associated with the study of oral speech or folkloristic genres to the study of written literature. In the context of the revolutionary period, this move had political significance. The Formalists were developing a literary theory which would no longer assume that "art" or "literature" were categories that described the creative products of an elite class. One outcome was that the Formalists theorized literary "authorship" in performative terms: authors are not to be understood as owners of particular socially valued texts, but as creative performers who make use of a shared stock of rhetorical and poetic devices. This chapter recovers a lost branch of Formalist theory, according to which authorship is theorized as a dialogic performance that is both enabled and limited by a tradition.

The Russian Formalists made provocative and extreme statements rejecting the importance of the individual author. Some of their more frequently cited statements include brash rejections of authorial agency, such as Osip Brik's claim that "even if Pushkin hadn't existed, *Eugene Onegin* would have been written anyway."[1] Or Roman Jakobson's assertion: "To incriminate

70

the poet with ideas and emotions is as absurd as the behavior of the medieval audiences that beat the actor who played Judas."[2] Daniel Rancour-Laferriere has argued that the "Russian Formalists neglected the notion of a literary person"; they ignored "the writer, the reader, the narrator, the protagonist, the characters, etc.—any literary entity, in short, which might conceivably utter the pronoun 'I.'"[3] This suggests a total ban on the individual, a position that Rancour-Laferriere explains as a result of the *fallacy of misplaced personification*."[4] This is the tendency to treat the literary "device" as the real "hero" (i.e., agent), so that the device is in some way the real source of the text. Rancour-Laferriere sees this as a move that unites the literary scholarship of the Formalists with subsequent structuralist and post-structuralist theory.

The move to give the individual author's agency over to "language" is, generally speaking, close to the French structuralist position on authorship. This was the argument, made most famously by Roland Barthes and Michel Foucault in 1967 and 1969, that the author is "dead"—one manifestation of the broader French structuralist and post-structuralist "decentering of the subject."[5] For Barthes, the author's creative work is replaced by the self-contained workings of language or "writing" (*écriture*) as a system of signification: "writing is that neutral, composite, oblique space where our subject slips away, the negative where all identity is lost, starting with the very identity of the body writing. As soon as a fact is narrated . . . the voice loses its origin, the author enters into his own death, writing begins."[6] The French structuralist and post-structuralist articulation of the "death" of the author was intertwined with the movement's prioritization of writing (over speech) as the most self-sufficient manifestation of language. Writing was important because it showed how language is capable of generating a plentitude of meanings even in the absence of the author. For example, Derrida writes:

> For the written to be the written, it must continue to "act" and to be legible even if what is called the author of the writing no longer answers for what he has written . . . whether he is provisionally absent, or if he is dead, or if in general he does not support, with his absolutely current and present intention or attention, the plentitude of meaning.[7]

Russian Formalism likewise shunned the individual author's intentional meaning as an approach to texts. However, rather than replace the individual author with the text itself, or the system of language, the OPOIAZ Formalists replaced the author with the figure of the performer. The Formalists could not replace the biographical author with the system of language because the concept of language as a (structuralist) system was not available. Moreover, as we have seen, a sidelining of the biographical individual (or "great man") had been a cornerstone of the Russian philological paradigm for decades. In the philological paradigm, the function of the biographical author—the "individual" element of language (*Energeia*)—was located in the creative, dialogic performance of language.

"Performance" for the Formalists was understood in terms of the Humboldtian philosophy of language, and referred to the actual use of a speaker's linguistic knowledge in concrete situations. Humboldt argued that dialogue was the most central manifestation of language, and that language really only existed in the creative act of addressing another person:

> Particularly important for language is that duality plays a more crucial role in it than anywhere else. All speaking is based on dialogue . . . Humans speak, even in thoughts, only with the other, or with themselves as if they were the other . . . The potential for speaking presupposes address and reply . . . The word, born in solitude, too strongly resembles a mere imaginary object, language too cannot be realized by an individual, language can only be realized socially by connecting to a bold effort [of speaking] a new one.[8]

According to the Russian philologists' understanding of Humboldt, the novel use of language in dialogue with others is the closest that scholarship can come to pinpointing the creative aspect of language. They theorized literature using oral speech as a model, and posited that the creativity of speech in dialogue is the same creativity found in the use of verbal art forms—from the proverb to the novel.

In the revolutionary period, the primacy of oral, dialogical speech—language in performance—became a truism evoked by the reference to the "living word" (*zhivoe slovo*). Boris Eikhenbaum was one of the more eloquent in articulating the sense that this focus was an imperative. In a 1918 essay, "The Illusion of Skaz" ("Illiuziia skaza"), he wrote that "there are, of course, specifically written forms, but literature (or, more accurately, verbal art [*slovesnost'*]) is not accounted for by these, and, what's more, even in these forms you can find the traces of the living word [*sledy zhivogo slova*]." Identifying these "traces" allows the scholar to uncover the "organic forces" which give literature "life":

> For the artist of the word [*khudozhnik slova*], written language [*pis'mennost'*] is not always a good thing. The real artist of the word carries in himself the primitive but organic forces of living oral narration [*skazitel'stvo*]. That which is written [*napisannoe*] is a kind of museum. For our crazy, and at the same time creative times, what is characteristic is a return to the living word.[9]

Eikhenbaum here reiterates an idea articulated by Humboldt and Potebnia—that writing is a dead "mummy," a relic left behind by "living" oral speech.

He also writes that the revolutionary period calls, in a particularly insistent way, for an orientation toward oral speech.

Eikhenbaum is known today for his identification of the "skaz narrator," a narrative strategy that uses markers of oral speech. This was part of a broader interest in constructing a literary theory out of studies of oral speech. Eikhenbaum and the Formalists were not interested in orality, or the textual use of markers of orality, as a means to provide a more comprehensive description of literary devices. They were advancing a theory in which oral speech served as the base model for literary (oral and textual) authorship. Tamara Khmelnitskaia, a former student of Tynianov's, writes that he taught them that

> "living literature is a process and a direction, not clots [*sgustki*]." This living process was the object of our studies. In many of his articles and statements, Tynianov speaks about how the contemporary sees a living, flowing process of generation, forming, and growth, and, at the same time, the decline and disintegration of existing genres and styles. Only later do these living phenomena become embodied as clots [*sgustki*], as completed things.[10]

This description of literary history as a living process reflects the influence of a Humboldtian philosophy of language. In keeping with this framework, the Formalists approached literary authorship as a creative process embedded in a social context, in the way that oral dialogic speech more obviously is. This chapter explores in more detail two ways in which the Formalists developed a theory of authorship as performance. The first is OPOIAZ studies of poetic declamation and political rhetoric that focused on how particular devices evoke affective reactions in an audience. The second is Shklovsky's theory of authorship, in which the figure of the individual author is replaced by a "society of singer-writers [*obshchestvo pevtsov-pisatelei*]."[11] Their expertise and skill is a product of their dialogic relationship with a living tradition. The distinction between Formalist theory and (post)-structuralist theory can then be put as follows: for the Formalists, language (discourse) cannot write itself or operate autonomously without the author. Rather, the dialogic context, which is required for individual creativity, provides the contours which define authorship.

THE INDIVIDUAL AND THE COLLECTIVE IN FLUX

Before turning to the Formalist theory of authorship, this section provides the intellectual historical context for the particular understandings of hermeneutics and poetics in Russia at the turn of the twentieth century. At the time, these two approaches to literary analysis were conceived in opposition to each other. This was not unique to the Russian revolutionary period. This idea was also articulated by the structuralist Tzvetan Todorov:

> A study in poetics *is not in itself an interpretation of a particular work of art.* It is rather concerned with identifying the characteristic features present in a work of art—those which are purely verbal, those that are compositional, thematic, rhythmic, narrative, etc.—and with showing their resemblances to and differences from other similar structures, in other works of art.[12]

Poetics is described as a comparative approach, in contrast to hermeneutics, which focuses on a single work. Hermeneutics uses a given whole (a text) as the initial framework for ascribing meaning to the elements within it. As described by R. Lanier Anderson, the

> hermeneutic method approaches holistic cultural meanings by its famous circular procedure: first, the interpreter projects a hypothesis about the meaning of the whole, which she uses as background for understanding each part in turn; but the initial hypothesis is only tentative, and the interpreter allows her gradual discoveries about the meanings of the parts to influence her hypothesis about the whole, revisions of which, in turn, once again affect the way she sees the parts. Hermeneutic procedure consists in this repeated mutual adjustment, aiming at interpretive equilibrium.[13]

The methods of poetics and hermeneutics can be applied to both oral and written language. However, in the Russian philological tradition, the distinction between these methods was historically associated with a divide between the cultural products of different classes of society (the peasantry as opposed to the intelligentsia), and between different media (oral performance as opposed to writing).

The hermeneutic method of interpretation was associated with the written products of the educated elite, and these were valued as autonomous—as individual texts of an indecomposable, integral unity. The study of oral, more apparently formulaic genres was, however, more often conducted comparatively. Transcriptions of oral performances were not subjected to hermeneutic interpretation. Oral genres were approached as corpora, not as individual works with individual authors. This distinction in method was consequently understood as an implicit judgment on the author's social status. To choose an interpretative or a comparative poetic approach meant to take a stance on the status of the author as a subject: Is this person someone with an important, unique biography, or is he essentially interchangeable with anyone else (within the *narod*)? This opposition remains valid for Russian folkloristics. For example, the folklorist Sergei Nekliudov writes in his recent book that the study of "folklore typically does not entail 'hermeneutic' difficulties and does not require particular effort on the part of the interpreter for understanding its texts: the many variants of oral communication present, as a rule, one meaning."[14] At the turn of the twentieth century, the question of whether to apply the method of poetics or that of hermeneutics was drawn into the broader cultural debate regarding the relationship between the individual and the community.

Veselovsky and Potebnia subscribed to a stadial understanding of history, according to which society was progressing from a state of collectivism toward individualism. This meant that the category of *slovesnost'*, while it encompassed both oral and written genres, was not understood as a totally undifferentiated mass. Instead, the different genres of *slovesnost'*, ranging from a proverb to novel, could be ordered on a spectrum of relative collectivism to relative individualism. This opposition was also associated with medium. In an essay titled "Oral and Written Poetry" ("Poeziia ustnaia i pis'mennaia," 1905), Potebnia argues that writing allows for independent thought, while oral cultures allow collective opinion to retain greater authority:

> Only the sustained and successive use of writing and its continued development gives individual thought a degree of self-assurance which is particular to the way that we relate to the past these days . . . On the contrary, the closer one gets to the complete absence of writing and science . . . the more timidly individual thought clings to authority . . . "What everyone says, is true, what everyone does is right" . . . That which is individual is false and sinful—*vox populi—vox Dei.*[15]

In this essay, Potebnia concludes that oral poetry consists not of discrete works but of a multitude of variants, and individual performers of these variants don't think of them in terms of authorship or possession, as "my song" or "her song." In a world without writing, according to Potebnia, "the individual composition is so subordinated to tradition [*predanie*] in regard to meter, melody, means of expression—from constant epithets to complex descriptions—that it can be called impersonal. The poet himself doesn't see a reason to regard his composition as his own."[16] Potebnia thus describes the performer of oral traditions as limited by communal values, while the literate artist is a more rebellious individual who seeks to create something relatively new. These assumptions were increasing challenged in the early years of the twentieth century.

This critique did not emerge with the Revolutions of 1917. The idea of "collective creativity" had been under attack in Russian folkloristics since the 1860s. This was the idea, as articulated by Buslaev (and cited in chapter 1), that folklore ("native epic poetry") "is the product of the entire mass of the people [*narod*]" and, like language, it "belongs to each and everyone."[17] This kind of thinking was increasingly dismissed as unscholarly and incompatible with the ethos of positivism that dominated Russian philology in this period. Reform-minded, liberal folklorists in particular critiqued the Romantic view of folklore as collective creativity because it dismissed the contribution of individual performers. The result was a unique emphasis on the performer in Russian folkloristics, which included studies of an oral performer's repertoire and manner of performance, as well as the impact of his or her biography on the style and content of a narrative or a song.[18] The strength of Russian performer studies is reflected in the fact that outside of Russia it is referred to as the "Russian school" method.[19]

Performer studies was, on the one hand, an outgrowth of positivist philology. The practice of recording and publishing the name of the performer along with the items collected began with Pavel Rybnikov in the 1860s in order to provide evidence of the authenticity of his material.[20] This allowed Alexander Gil'ferding to "follow in his steps" in 1871, recording from many of the same people. Following Rybnikov's lead, Gil'ferding organized his recordings by village and by singer rather than by subject. He also included a biographical sketch of each performer, mentioning "artistic quality, manner of singing, feeling for rhythm, number of songs known, from whom the epics had been learned, and means of livelihood."[21] This became standard practice among Russian folklorists, and laid the groundwork for the early emergence of performer studies. In the early twentieth century this approach spread to tale studies, with Nikolai Onchukov, Dmitry Zelenin, and the brothers Boris and Yuri Sokolov promoting an approach that foregrounded the performer. This development was accompanied by increasingly rigorous (dialectological) documentation of the language of folklore, and its sociological and geographical context. Scholarship on the impact of the performer's personal experiences and his or her acquisition of material was part of this broader trend towards an expansive, exact collection of folkloristic data.

Politics also contributed to the strength of performer studies in Russia.[22] Folklorists like the Sokolov brothers were impacted by the surge in neopopulist sentiment among the intelligentsia following the failed 1905 Revolution and subsequent political reaction. This decade also saw a turn to the study of the tale (*skazka*)—a genre which was understood to be more variable than the *bylina* and more reflective of the personality of the tale-teller. In this context, there emerged a number of publications dedicated to the regional collection of folktales, impressive in their size and attention to detail—including analysis of the folklore performer.[23] The attention to individual performers was explicitly linked to egalitarian values. Nikolai Onchukov's study, published in 1908, articulated a new attitude towards the folktale:

The description of each of my narrators is given, as possible, before [present-ing] his tales, and those interested in types of narrators will find there, I hope, abundant material for themselves. Here I will only say that narrators in the north [of Russia] are very varied in terms of talent, brains, character, ability to narrate, and similar qualities. There are unsung jovial and gloomy people there, and people of serious and thoughtful mind . . . The singers of *byliny* and narrators [of tales] are undoubtedly exceptional people. This is the intel-ligentsia of the countryside, albeit illiterate, lacking diplomas as in the classes above the peasantry, but nonetheless genuine [intellectuals], outstanding for their intellectual quality by a natural path, or as the recipients of sometimes very great artistic gifts. This is the intellectual aristocracy of the countryside, and the person who is acquainted with it involuntarily acquires a deep respect for the intellectual strength of the countryside, hidden in its bosom, a poten-tial which only education can define and continue.[24]

As this quote indicates, scholarly interest in different performance styles was accompanied by an ethical stance which sought to see the peasantry as equal to their formally educated counterparts in the cities.

Performer studies developed along a few main lines in the 1910s and 1920s. Most important for my argument is the scholarship that sought to redraw the line between oral performance and literary texts, and between collective and individual authorship, by adopting a hermeneutic approach over a comparative mode of analysis. This trend began with efforts to iden-tify different "types" of narrators, as referred to in Onchukov's quote above.[25] However, the typological approach developed into more individualized stud-ies, which focused on a single artist. This can be seen in Mark Azadovsky's *A Siberian Tale Teller* (*Eine sibirische Märchenerzählerin*, 1926), an exemplary statement of the "Russian school" approach to performer studies.

Azadovsky's study focuses in large part on the creative personality of a single tale teller—Natalia Vinokurova. He stresses the literary qualities of her style, such as her gift for psychological realism and the absence of traditional formulas (e.g., "in some Tsar's kingdom . . .") and epic (ternary) repetitions. Azadovsky poses the question: "Can one decide . . . *what* must be placed on the one hand under personal elements, and on the other hand under general poetics of the folktale and local tradition?" He finds instances where personal biography and traditional poetics overlap (e.g., in the motif of poverty), forming an "inseparable union." Azadovsky concludes that "Vi-nokurova is always trying to break through the limitations of traditional po-etics. . . . One can follow her attempts to expand the traditional framework, to destroy the obligatory norms, and to find words and colors in order to portray her feelings for nature directly." These findings are consistent with the programmatic opening chapter of his study, in which he argues that the task of the folk narrator and that of the creative writer are fundamentally the same. Methodologically, this meant studying the folkloric performance as a work of literature: any tale is to be considered a "self-sufficient, artistic organism," and the researcher "must accept as his goal, the *ascertaining of meaning* for each and every form element in *the artistic whole* of the tale." This kind of research, for Azadovsky, is "inseparably bound up with the study of the creative individuality of the narrator."[26]

By arguing for a hermeneutic, biographical approach to folklore, Azadovsky makes not only a methodological claim, but also an ethical and political one—about the status of the peasant as an individual artist and the value of his or her creative products. The Sokolovs were also consistent proponents of performer studies. In 1915, they argued that "individual creativity" is too little valued in folklore studies while this same factor, of "self-conscious personality," is highly valued in other fields of study.[27] Almost a decade later, at a national conference on regional studies (*kraevedenii*) in 1924, Boris Sokolov stressed in similar terms the need to pay special attention to the study of the "creative individuality of the bearers of oral creativity."[28] This movement succeeded in promoting a reevaluation of popular art. For example, the classical philologist Boris Kazansky argued in 1926:

> One genre of "folk verbal art" [*narodnaia slovesnost'*] after another is losing its mystical aura of "the creativity of the very soul of the people": . . . the ballad and the epic song, the song and the fairy tale are being recognized, finally, as artistic forms developed by professional masters of the word in a particular poetic culture, at a definite time and in a definite place. *This is absolutely the same kind of poetry as the poetry of Lermontov or Blok.*[29]

As Kazansky's statement suggests, the reevaluation of folklore genres as "art" was framed as a rejection of the Romantic conception of collective creativity and a celebration of the equality between oral, folkloric art forms and written literary traditions. By the end of the 1910s, this ethical imperative made it taboo for folklorists to describe folklore as collective creativity. This was the cause of a quarrel between Jakobson and Petr Bogatyrev. In an obituary article written for Bogatyrev, Jakobson described them working together on a book on folk theater, working "in the winter months of 1919 at a temperature of 24°F in our room on Lubjanskij Alley with ice in our inkwell instead of ink, to the accompaniment of the sound of gun-fire from the neighboring street."[30] There was not just discord on the streets. According to Jakobson in his dialogues with Pomorska, he wanted to write in 1919 that folk theater was a form of "collective creation," but Bogatyrev refused to publish this argument because it was so different from reigning opinion. In response,

Jakobson had his name removed from the book.[31] The fact that they could not agree on this point is indicative of the intensity and instability of opinion on the questions of authorship and method in this period. Bogatyrev and Jakobson shared an interest in folklore, and went on collecting expeditions together (see chapter 4). They belonged to the same scholarly societies, and had the same teachers. Both were interested in the intersection between folklore, language, and art—and both were obsessed with the apparent similarities between folklore and avant-garde art. Their dispute reflects a real lack of consensus at the time regarding the fundamental concepts of collectivity and individuality.

An important factor in this instability was the effort among university-educated intellectuals to find common ground with less educated classes, both the proletariat and the peasantry, by theorizing written literature as collective creativity. For example, during the same summer of 1919, while Jakobson and Bogatyrev were collecting material for their book on folk theater, Vladimir Mayakovsky was in Pushkino working on his "*bylina*" *150,000,000* (the number is a reference to the population of the Soviet Union in 1919). This long poem generally receives cursory treatment in overviews of the poet's works, where it is described as a miscalculation.[32] Mayakovsky himself describes the work in these terms: "I published it without my name. I wanted anyone to add to it and improve it . . . but no one did add to it, and anyway everyone knew who wrote it. What's the difference. Publish it now under my name."[33] The poem uses elements of the *bylina* genre (such as a giant hero [*bogatyr*] with supernatural powers, and evil enemies hailing from a faraway land) to comment on the current political situation. The poem begins with a stanza on authorship:

> 150,000,000 is the name of the craftsman of this poem. / The bullet is its rhythm. / Its rhyme, a fire spreading from building to building. / 150,000,000 now speak through my lips. / This edition is printed / by rotary footsteps / on the cobblestone paper of squares. / Who would ask the moon, / who could compel the sun to answer: / why do you cause all these / nights and days? / Who can name the ingenious author of the earth? / So / of this / my / poem / no one is the creator.[34]

> 150 000 000 мастера этой поэмы имя. / Пуля—ритм. / Рифма—огонь из здания в здание. / 150 000 000 говорят губами моими. / Ротационкой шагов / в булыжном верже площадей / напечатано это издание. / Кто спросит луну? / Кто солнце к ответу притянет—/ чего / ночи и дни чините!? / Кто назовет земли гениального автора? / Так / и этой / моей / поэмы / никто не сочинитель.[35]

This opening suggests three different concepts of creativity: there is a unified, mass collective creativity, in which the entire population speaks through a single pair of lips; there is the ex nihilo creativity of the author of genius (*genial'nyi avtor*) akin to God; and then there is finally a kind of anonymous creation. The possible types of authorship are thus the collective, the great individual, and the anonymous negative (the "no one" [*nikto*] who created the poem). This opening should be read in the context of the political theme of the work: *150,000,000* was one of Mayakovsky's earliest efforts to write an extended, overtly engaged work of poetry. His choice of form—a folk epic (*bylina*)—is consistent with debates during this period regarding the creativity required by revolutionary art. His poem can be understood as an effort to speak from this third (anonymous negative) authorial position that is neither the mass voice nor that of the individual genius. It is also a poetic articulation of the desire to renegotiate the boundary between "folklore" and "literature" in the 1910s and 1920s.

In this period, a major influence pushing for a collective understanding of creativity was Proletkult (an acronym for "Proletarian cultural-educational organizations")—a loose coalition of clubs, factory committees, workers' theaters, and educational societies. Lynn Mally describes Proletkult's evolution from its origins in Petrograd in 1917 into a national movement which peaked in 1920 with "over four hundred thousand members organized in three hundred branches distributed all over Soviet territory." The membership, as Mally documents, was diverse, but proletkultists were generally ambitious in their understanding of their mission: they wanted to create a unique proletarian culture, from new art forms to ethics, that would inform and inspire the new society.[36]

Proletkult emerged in the flourishing of alternative cultural programs under the Provisional Government; among these, Mally writes, it was the Petrograd factory committees that succeeded in founding a unified network, in large part because they had the support of the Vpered (Forward) circle.[37] The ideological foundations of Proletkult were particularly influenced by Alexander Bogdanov, who was the central theoretician of the Left Bolsheviks between 1905 and 1917. Bogdanov argued that a socialist revolution would be fomented by a distinct proletarian culture. This was understood as a total ideological framework based on collectivism, which encompassed art as well as science and philosophy. This was articulated, for example, in the foreword to *Essays on the Philosophy of Collectivism* (*Ocherki filosofii kollektivizma*, 1909) authored by Bogdanov, Gorky, Lunacharsky, and others:

Our basic idea, our point of departure, is that the worldview of the proletarian class—the embryo for the universal ideology of the future society—is in its essence *collectivism* [*kollektivizm*]; a complete, resolute collectivism of practice and cognition. Indeed, as the proletarian progresses in his class development he increasingly lives in the collective and with the collective, fusing his aspirations with its interests, his activities with its creative work, his feelings with its experience. In this way the proletarian frees himself from countless individualistic illusions . . . Humanity appears before him as a giant system of collaboration of people in space and time, like a higher life form [*vysshaia zhiznennaia forma*], developing towards a harmonious, active unity [*edinstvo*].[38]

In his writings and speeches after 1917, Bogdanov continued to argue that a new, conscious collectivism was the foundation of proletarian culture. In a speech at the 1920 Proletkult Congress, he argued:

Conscious collectivism transforms the entire meaning of an artist's work, giving it new incentives. Previously, the artist saw in his work the revelation of his individuality; the new artist understands and feels that in him and through him a grand unity creates—the collective. For the old artist originality is the expression of his "I," a means for his exultation; for the new artist originality is the deep and wide reach of collective experience and is the expression of his share in the active participation in the creation and development of the life of the collective . . . Conscious collectivism, by deepening people's mutual understanding and their emotional bonds, allows for . . . an immediate collectivism in creative work [*tvorchestvo*], i.e., the direct collaboration of many people, up to and including the mass [*massovyi*] collaboration.[39]

In theory then, proletarian art was to be "collective," to express the shared interests and experiences of the proletarian class as a whole. It was to be based on a new, deeper, mutual comprehension between people, and even to allow for a new kind of *direct, mass cooperation.*

These ideas inspired a wide range of efforts to produce proletarian, collective art. In order to replace the lyrical "I" with the first-person plural "we," authors published their work anonymously or stressed heroic, cosmic, or planetary themes. All of these features appear in the opening stanza of Mayakovsky's *150,000,000.* Mayakovsky's desire to have others modify his epic, and his use of a traditional folk genre, further speak to an interest in articulating the collective ethos of the revolution. Mally mentions examples such as a music studio in Penza which put on a "leaderless concert" without a conductor in 1920; and a collective poem, "In Memory of the Fallen," produced by a Moscow studio in 1919. In theater, "collective creation" was explored through improvisational evenings or choral declamation.[40]

An argument that emerged within Proletkult over amateurism versus professionalism in the new proletarian art is particularly revealing. Mally shows that in 1919 and 1920, as Proletkult "gained a mass base, it had little internal unity," partly because many of its members were not proletarians. She describes an "internal duel of utopias" between "those who argued for an egalitarian, mass-based organization and an inclusive approach to cultural activities" and an "elitist" group which "addressed Proletkult work to an exclusive, restricted, and gifted working-class constituency."[41] The collision between these two positions came to a head in debates at a Moscow Proletkult conference in 1919 on the issue of whether the organization should create special studios where full-time professional proletarian artists would be supported with scholarships and freed from their jobs. Those in favor of professionalization cited the low quality of amateur proletarian art and argued for creating an accomplished vanguard, a "workers' intelligentsia" that would free proletarians from their dependence on bourgeois intellectuals.[42] This position ultimately won—and was expressed in the leadership's renunciation of the goal of being a mass organization.

This position was not, however, unanimous. The opponents of professionalization articulated alternative understandings of art and creativity. Platon Kerzhentsev, for example, argued that "a proletarian artist would be something entirely new, someone who did not specialize in art alone." Others, Mally reports, "denounced the notion of artistic genius as a degenerate remnant of capitalism. The purpose of the revolution was to bring out the creative potential in everyone." Organizers of the Kostroma Proletkult argued that "proletarian culture will not be made by loners [*odinochki*], but rather by the entire class. Individual 'gifted' workers who stand higher on the cultural ladder will only create new cultural values if they are not alienated from the working masses."[43] Arguments advancing a concept of the artist as ideally an "amateur" (*liubitel'*) can be seen as a shift toward the Romantic concept of collective creation that folklorists such as the Sokolovs and Azadovsky had rejected.

In sum, folkloristics and literary criticism were moving towards and often past each other in this period. Folklorists such as Azadovsky regarded the folktale as a product of individual creativity, while Proletkutists theorized artistry as collective creation. Two publications exemplify this contrast: Onchukov's *Northern Tales* (*Severnye skazki*, 1908) and the collection *Essays on the Philosophy of Collectivism* (1909). The first was seen as a seminal rejection of the mythological school in folkloristics, and an attempt to replace its concept of "mass creation" with "the personality of the creator."[44] This can be contrasted with Maxim Gorky's contribution to the *Essays*, "The Destruction of Personality" ("Razrushenie lichnosti"), which begins by explicitly evoking the mythological school and its emphasis on collective creativity. Anticipating his speech at the First Congress of Soviet Writers in 1934, Gorky's article holds up folkloric creation as a positive model for literary authors who have lost the ability to speak for the collective. In order to describe the old, collective creativity that produced "epic personality," Gorky cites Fyodor Buslaev:

> In myth and the epic, as in language, the primary mover of an era, the collective creativity of the entire people [*kollektivnoe tvorchestvo vsego naroda*] is clearly articulated, not the personal thought of a single person. "Language," as F. Buslaev says, "was an integral part of that indivisible activity in which every person actively participates without standing out from the united mass [*splochennaia massa*] of the entire people [*narod*]." That the constitution and formation of a language is a collective process is irrefutably established both by linguistics and by the history of culture. The unsurpassable and remarkable-to-this-day beauty of the myth and epic is explainable only by the gigantic power of the collective.[45]

Thus, just when folklorists were distancing themselves from the Romantic concept of collective creativity, Gorky was evoking it in a programmatic study on the place of the collective in literature.

Juxtaposing Russian folktale studies and Proletkult theory in this period reveals the extent to which the understanding of artistic authorship was in flux. A widespread interest in rethinking the categories of collective versus individual entailed the revision of the domains of "folklore" and "literature" in the process. In the academy, the instability of these concepts fostered productive interdisciplinary work under the capacious heading of philology. In the next sections I will show how the Formalists, particularly Viktor Shklovsky, took advantage of this situation to propose a new understanding of the literary author—one which would replace the Romantic dichotomy of collective creation versus individual genius. The ideas outlined above reveal a tendency to adopt one of these two established positions: innovative thinking often entailed switching from one to the other, rather than attempting to formulate a third option. The Formalist theory of authorship is thus particularly interesting for attempting (like Mayakovsky) to articulate a new, middle position. This was done in two ways. The first was by effacing the dividing lines created by medium: OPOIAZ Formalists set aside the textuality of literature to focus on the oral performance of poetry or narrative. The second way was by effacing the distinctions drawn between popular and elite creativity. Shklovsky in particular sought to show that there is no difference between the creativity involved in folkloric production and that in literary production. The Formalists did not want to commit to the established hermeneutic method for the study of literature, since this was associated with liberal ("bourgeois") individualism. At the same time, the Romantic concept of collectivity was suspect because it was imprecise, and also (for some) because it unethically negated particular, historical individuals and traditions.

OPOIAZ POETICS AND ORAL PERFORMANCE

Scholarship in the philological paradigm grouped oral folklore and written literature together within the broader concept of verbal art (*slovesnost'*). It was not, however, a given that this conceptual framework would continue into twentieth-century Russian thought. Cultural factors specific to the revolutionary period encouraged the Formalists to retain an oral, Humboldtian model for thinking about literature. To begin with the most general factors, European modernism privileged the spoken word; poetry and theater were particularly popular across Europe in this era. As a pan-European movement in the arts and culture, modernism has been described as a crisis of faith in the communicative transparency of language. As Bradbury and Mc-Farlane put it, modernism "is the art consequent on the dis-establishing of communal reality and conventional notions of causality . . . on the linguistic chaos that ensues when public notions of language have been discredited and when all realities have become subjective fictions."[46] This uncertainty regarding language's referential capacity coincided with a heightened interest in its performance; no longer a transparent tool of communication, language entered center stage as the performance of sound. The Futurists' "evenings" (*vechera*) in which they performed their trans-sense (*zaum*) poetry, sometimes while dressed in scandal-provoking costumes, are a prime example. The phonic aspect of poetry and its mode of delivery were foregrounded; this hallmark of poetic modernism has been seen as akin to the focus on the texture of paint in the visual arts.

In the postrevolutionary period, additional historical factors heightened the interest in the oral dimension of literature. One of these was the collapse of the print industry during the Civil War. The historian Jeffrey Brooks describes a "precipitous decline" in publishing: "only a quarter of the number of copies and titles produced in 1917 was issued in 1920 and 1921."[47] These trends took time to reverse; Brooks argues that it was at least a decade before a new Soviet publishing industry was really established, and concludes that "the scarcity of printed material resulted in increased reliance on oral communication and oral traditions." Although, as Brooks asserts, "the reduction of the role of the written word in people's lives was greatest in the countryside," the intelligentsia (including the Formalists) in Petrograd and Moscow argued that even urban culture was returning to a state of orality.[48] Writing in Petrograd in 1919, Eikhenbaum exclaimed:

O, how far we are from "aestheticism"! And, really, how close we have come to art! To its core [*do zhuti*]. And this is why we now don't need the book, nor the monk's cell, nor the poet, but something else. It's true, we are returning to some kind of fabled time when poetry was the voice, and not the printed letter, and when theater was the town square, and not rows of seats.[49]

As this quote suggests, the breakdown of established institutions and conventions encouraged modernist tendencies to dispute a perceived divide between "art" and "life"—as literature was freed from the page by the more primal, affective medium of the "voice."

Martha Hickey argues for the importance of voice and performance for writers in Petrograd:

> Displaced from the pages of books and the press, the writer's word was being heard, after 1918, from the stages of Petrograd's newly organized literary, professional, cultural, and political organizations. . . . In a city where presses had been widely silenced, the voice was for a time the writer's primary, though not perhaps natural, instrument. Writers of narrative prose, in particular, found themselves in an arena that both promoted a consciousness of the audible word and suggested a performance model for their activity as authors.[50]

According to contemporary reports, readings arranged in the House of Writers, the House of Arts, and in Proletkult groups met with "extraordinary success," and these institutions sought to embrace the oral medium in forms such as the "living almanac" and the "oral periodical."[51] In an article dating to 1926, the linguist Sergei Bernshtein suggested that an obsession with poetry and oral performance began with the Futurists' "oral propaganda of their poetry and theories" in 1913–14, noting that the practice of poets performing their own poetry had been relatively rare, but became more frequent after this time.[52] He notes that 1922 saw a sharp decline in interest in "sounding verse" and poetry more generally, and traces this to the beginning of the New Economic Policy.[53]

At the same time, new sound-recording technologies increasingly became available to intelligentsia in the cities.[54] The intersections between oral performance, recording technology, and politics was explored in the Institute of the Living Word (Institut zhivogo slova), founded in fall 1918 by the actor and theater scholar Vsevolod Vsevolodsky-Gerngross (1882–1962) as a section of Narkompros. The core membership of OPOIAZ was affiliated with this institute: Lev Jakubinsky was its secretary, while Eikhenbaum, Tynianov, and Shklovsky all lectured there. Sergei Bernshtein was also an active member of both societies. The institute combined pedagogical and practically oriented work, such as teaching rhetoric, pronunciation, and declamation, with scholarly laboratory work on the auditory aspects of poetry. According to Rafaella Vassena, the institute was unique in its scholarly ambitions, which included a widely interdisciplinary approach to the study of "the living word," to be studied from the perspectives of philology, declamation, linguistics, music, physiology, psychology, and sociology.[55]

The study of the art of speech was implicitly if not always explicitly connected to the political importance of oratory at this time. To mention only the most obvious example, Vladimir Lenin succeeded in consolidating his power after the February Revolution in large part due to his effective oratorical skills. The historian Stephen Kotkin suggests that there was a Dada-esque quality to the Bolsheviks' seizure of power. Without real control over the situation, Lenin asserted new realities and claimed broad authority through performative gestures. In the context of a chaotic power vacuum accompanied by a widespread desire for revolutionary reform, a convincing rhetorical performance could immediately bring new social realities into being.[56] The power of rhetoric as a weapon in the Civil War was clear to the political leadership, and Anatoly Lunacharsky (Commissar of Enlightenment) appears to have supported the foundation of the Institute of the Living Word for its potential to connect advances in linguistics and technology with the Bolshevik political cause. At the first meeting of the institute, Lunacharsky stressed the need to study the "psychology of the crowd and of listeners" and to include the study of mimicry (*mimiki*) and gestures as part of expressive speech.[57]

The revolutionary moment encouraged bold and sometimes utopian thinking, which Vassena concludes was a central attribute of the institute—accounting both for its rise and collapse (in 1924):

> In addition to financial disorder, there was also the methodological problem which was constantly present in the agendas of the meetings of the scholarly committee and which was connected with the difficulties of realizing a utopian "theory of intonation" *super partes*. Vsevolodsky-Gerngross's memoirs reveal that his enthusiasm and that of colleagues soon ran up against the impossibility of determining the objective criteria which govern the language of the masses and which are independent of particular, individual vocal characteristics.[58]

These utopian aspirations were inspired in part by the promise of new technologies—in particular the use of the phonograph to record and study spoken language. Sergei Bernshtein, a leader in this field, used the Phonetic Laboratory at the Institute of the Living Word and the Laboratory of Experimental Phonetics at St. Petersburg University to produce a detailed study of "Blok's Voice."[59] Bernshtein and other scholars and artists associated with the

Institute of the Living Word were inspired by work being done in Germany, such as that of Edward Sievers, whose seminal *Rhythmisch–melodische Studien* (1912) initiated an acoustically oriented method for the study of poetry often called *Ohrenphilologie*.

Boris Eikhenbaum's *Melody of Russian Lyric Verse* (*Melodika russkogo liricheskogo stikha*, 1922) introduces this field in terms reminiscent of Humboldtian language philosophy. Citing a German follower of Sievers, Eikhenbaum affirms that "the printed poem is only an indication for pronunciation [*Sprechanweisung*]; the artistic work lives only when and as long as it is perceived."[60] In keeping with the Humboldtian view that the true manifestation of language is in dialogic production, these scholars believed that poetry must be studied in its performance. The Phonetic Laboratory in the Institute of the Living Word primarily studied poetic declamation, which was the subject of a special Commission for the Theory of Declamation, founded in the spring of 1921 and headed by Eikhenbaum. Its members included Bernshtein, Vsevolodsky-Gerngross, Boris Tomashevsky, and Tynianov. Tynianov taught a course on "The History of the Russian Ode," and his article "The Ode as an Oratorical Genre" (written 1922; published 1927) reflects the interest in what he and others called "sounding verse" (*zvuchashchii stikh*).[61] By the end of 1921, the institute had recorded more than 6,000 poems read by 30 individuals, including Blok, Nikolai Gumilev, Andrei Bely, Vladimir Piast, Vsevolod Rozhdestvensky, Fedor Sologub, and Vladislav Khodasevich.[62] The institute also dedicated significant resources to research on folkloristic subjects. This included the collection of bibliographic materials on Russian folklore, folk theater, folk beliefs (*verovanie*), and "superstitions, customs, revelry [*igrishcha*], and festivals." Members were sent on expeditions to collect folktales (*skazki*), and Vsevolodsky-Gerngross taught a course on the vocal intonation and study of "Russian folk art of the word" (*russkoe narodnoe iskusstvo slova*). In the institute, *byliny* by famous performers were transcribed and recorded using a phonograph.

According to Vassena's assessment, the theoretical and utopian ambitions of the Institute of the Living Word ultimately ended in failure; she highlights a discrepancy between the institute's focus on the performances of recognized masters (of folkloric and literary genres) and the desire to uncover general principles governing the "language of the masses." We can, however, glean what kind of theory these scholars *wanted* to develop by looking at their writings on gesture and communication. A central concept that emerged from the Formalist study of poetic performance was that of the "sound gesture" (*zvukovoi zhest*), a concept employed by members of OPOIAZ, including Shklovsky, Tynianov, Eikhenbaum, and Evgeny Polivanov, as well as the Symbolist poet Andrei Bely.[63] The idea came from Wilhelm Wundt's *Völkerpsychologie: Eine Untersuchung der Entwicklungsgesetze von*

Sprache, Mythus und Sitte—a project which would become a ten-volume, cross-cultural study of myth, religion, and language. Wundt's project has been described as the "successor" to Steinthal and Lazarus's *Völkerpsychologie*. And while scholars stress important differences between Wundt's thinking and that of his predecessors, what is important for our purposes is that Wundt, like Steinthal and Lazarus, was pursuing a theory of language that would explain its development by reference to the history of culture.

In the first volume of Wundt's *Völkerpsychologie*, titled *Die Sprache* (1900), Wundt dwelt at length on both imitative sounds (e.g., onomatopoeia) and imitative gestures (*nachbildende Geberde*). He argued that the source of the apparent similarity between German words such as *bummeln* (to stroll), *torkeln* (to lurch), *kribbeln* (to tickle), and the actions they denote is not their sounds, but the movements made by the tongue and lips in their articulation.[64] The tongue mimics in its movements the swaying motion of strolling, incidentally producing the sounds of *bummeln*. There is thus a mimetic relationship between the verb and its referent, yet this has nothing to do with sound, but with physiological processes that "take place beneath the level of free ideas."[65] In "On Poetry and Zaum Language" ("O poezii i zaumnom iazyke," 1916), Shklovsky goes beyond Wundt's observations about imitative gestures by combining the latter's mimetic and articulatory explanation of sound and gesture with William James's conception of the physiological origins of emotions. Shklovsky's understanding of James is that "every emotion is a result of some physiological state (a pounding heartbeat—the source of fear, tears—the source of sadness)." In synthesizing Wundt and James, Shklovsky proposes an understanding of communication that obviates the referential dimension of speech. Shklovsky suggests that the conventional meanings associated with speech sounds are not of primary importance for the communication of emotion. Instead, he reinterprets Wundt to suggest that the act of *comprehension* has to first pass through an articulatory moment: "In the perception of another's speech . . . we silently reproduce with our own organs of speech the movements which are necessary for producing the given sound." Emotions, such as fear or sadness, may also be communicated in speech in this way: "It is possible to say that the impression made on us by the timbre of someone's speech can be explained by the fact that we reproduce the facial expressions [*mimiki*] of the speaker and therefore experience his emotions." Shklovsky thus uses Wundt's gestural mimicry and James's physiological theory of emotion to describe communication as a mimetic "dance of the organs of speech" between speaker and listener.[66] Shklovsky concludes that there is a yet-to-be-discovered relationship between emotion and the articulatory movements of the vocal tract, and that the apparently meaningless sounds (of Futurist poetry or infants' babble) may actually communicate emotion in a precisely definable way. One important feature of this proposal is that it obviates the crisis in referential meaning that troubled and inspired modernists. The communication of emotions is mimetic even without reference to shared knowledge, and moreover, it is speculated that the quality of this communication is subject to quantification: speech sounds and physiological reflexes (i.e., Shklovsky's "dance" of vocal organs in speaker and listener) can be measured.

Shklovsky's article on *zaum* represents a convergence of Futurist, Formalist, and also Symbolist theories of language. Andrei Bely also relied on Wundt's concept of the sound gesture in his *Glossolaliia* (1922), a work which begins with drawings illustrating the similarities between bodily gestures and the movement of the tongue.

The Symbolist interest in incantations and the phenomenon of speaking in tongues (glossolalia) is a point of overlap between Symbolism and early Russian Formalism.[67] An interest in these phenomena was widespread in the 1910s. D. G. Konovalov's widely read *Religious Rapture in Russian Mystical Sectarianism* (*Religioznyi ekstaz v russkom misticheskom sektanstve*, 1908), for example, provided literary scholars and artists with abundant examples of glossolalia and incantations—which he explained in physiological terms. The broader interest in nonsense speech was driven by the desire to understand how non-referential speech sounds can impact a listener physiologically and emotionally.

In the postrevolutionary period the Formalists moved away from Symbolist ideas, which they cast as mystical and vague in contrast to their own efforts to produce objective, fact-based scholarship. However, the desire for a non-referential, physiological theory of communication remained. For example, Sergei Eisenstein's effort to develop a theory of movement for the theater in the early 1920s has fundamental points of similarity with the ideas Shklovsky articulated in his 1916 essay. Eisenstein argued that "attractions" or shocks to the spectator were the key to ideological art. In a manuscript coauthored with Sergei Tretiakov in 1923, Eisenstein argued that "expressive

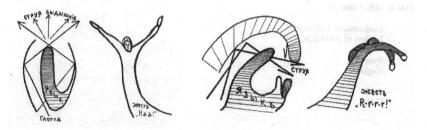

Drawings from Andrei Bely, *Glossolaliia: Poem über den Laut* (*Glossolalia: A Poem about Sound*), originally published in 1922.

actions"—such as "the arching of an eyebrow, the unfolding of a fist, the kissing of a foot, the chattering of teeth"—could be used to deliver "mathematically calculated" shocks.[68] Referring, like Shklovsky, to William James's physiological theory of emotion, Eisenstein and Tretiakov discuss the possibility of evoking emotions in the audience through a kind of physiological mimicry. They write that

> expressive movement assures the arousal of the intended emotions in the spectator. It is precisely expressive movement, built on an organically correct foundation, that is solely capable of evoking this emotion in the *spectator, who in turn reflexively repeats in weakened form the entire system of the actor's movements*: as a result of the produced movements, the spectator's incipient muscular tensions are released in the desired emotion.[69]

Like Shklovsky, Eisenstein and Tretiakov focus on the mimicry that takes place between performer and audience: their "aim [is] not for the 'sincerity' of the actor's movement, but for its imitative, mimical infectiousness."[70]

This interest in the emotional impact of artistic performance informed OPOIAZ scholarship on sound in verse and narrative. For example, Eikhenbaum's well-known essay "How Gogol's 'Overcoat' Is Made" treats Gogol's story as an oral performance. Eikhenbaum is interested in the same questions that motivated his colleagues at the Institute of the Living Word—such as how to account for the effect of Alexander Blok's declamation.[71] Eikhenbaum begins by reconstructing Gogol's performance style, using attestations from people who had heard him recite his stories. The reception of Eikhenbaum's essay has focused on his departure from the tradition of Russian social criticism.[72] Less acknowledged is Eikhenbaum's effort to understand Gogol's story in terms of a different mimetic relationship: in place of the relationship between the historical, social world and the text, Eikhenbaum points to a mimetic relationship between the author and the audience.

The first step is to discover the relationship between an author's performance style and his or her text. Eikhenbaum argues that "the structure of a short story depends in large part on the kind of role which the author's *personal tone [lichnyi ton]* plays in its composition."[73] Likewise, in his 1923 study of "Chamber Declamation," Eikhenbaum stresses the need to listen to poets performing their own works in order to perceive their essential rhythmic and melodic structure.[74] Eikhenbaum argues that "his [Gogol's] text is made up of [*slagaetsia iz*] live spoken performances and the emotions of speech."[75] In Gogol's text, he argues,

> words and sentences are selected and ordered not according to the principle of mere logical speech, but more according to the principle of expres-

sive speech, in which a special role is played by articulation, mimicry, sound gestures, etc. Whence the appearance in his language of the semantics of sound: the sound "envelope" of a word, its acoustic characteristic becomes meaningful in Gogol's speech independently of its logical meaning or material referent.[76]

Gogol's text is organized by the techniques of expressive oratory. These "infect," to use Eisenstein and Tretiakov's term, an audience with a desired emotion, using a physiological rather than a semantic channel of communication. In "The Overcoat," Eikhenbaum argues that Gogol's performance (and the text of the story that results) is constructed by alternating "the mimicry of laughter with the mimicry of sorrow . . . accompanied by a controlled alternation of gestures and intonations."[77] This alternation is what creates the particular effect of Gogol's story—that of the "grotesque."

It is worth reiterating the differences between the OPOIAZ study of sound as performance and the French structuralist and post-structuralist analysis of texts because there are apparent similarities between the two.[78] Eikhenbaum sidelines Gogol's own interpretation of his stories: "In the work of art not a single sentence can be in itself a simple 'reflection' of the personal feelings of the author."[79] Barthes, like Eikhenbaum, argues that the personal intent of the author is irrelevant; both of these thinkers seek to separate the text from the real-world referents of that text. However, the major difference between Eikhenbaum's approach and a French structuralist reading is the approach to the meaning of the text. A French structuralist would interpret the text in light of the multiplicity of meanings encoded in the language of the story. The OPOIAZ approach instead focuses on the (ostensibly mimetic) communication of affect via rhetorical devices and their physiological impact on the audience. For example, Eikhenbaum focuses on Gogol's manipulation of kinds of intonation. Gogol, he argues, uses "an enormous sentence, building up the intonation to enormous tension toward the end," which causes the audience/reader to experience a mounting sense of expectation. But the sentence is "resolved with unexpected simplicity," which results in "the impression of a comic disparity" in the reader/audience.[80] This kind of analysis is not about the meaning(s) or codes in a text, but about how the author-performer uses language to produce a particular emotional impact on the reader.

This approach is close to that of classical rhetorical analysis, which was a staple of secondary schooling in Russia in the nineteenth and early twentieth centuries. Looking back on his career, Jakobson told Krystyna Pomorska that Formalism was essentially a resurrection of the "sound principles of classical rhetoric," and mentioned Quintilian as an example. He recalled reading through "textbooks on literary theory" as a high school student to get some grasp of the elementary concepts, . . . routine definitions . . . tropes and figures of speech. . . . I quickly saw that the habitual formulae were quite sterile, and that it would be necessary to revise this entire outdated arsenal in order to transform it into a genuine scientific tool.[81]

Tynianov's 1922 essay "The Ode as an Oratorical Genre" begins by arguing that the second edition of Lomonosov's *Rhetoric* (1748) privileged an understanding of rhetoric oriented to the study of what is "emotionally affecting," as opposed to the study of "logically persuasive" oratorical language. That is, he finds in Lomonosov an understanding of rhetoric which is consistent with that of the Formalists themselves. Tynianov also approvingly quotes Longinus: "Grandeur does not persuade the listener, but, rather, astonishes him. That which genuinely astounds always takes the upper hand over the persuasive and the agreeable."[82]

Rhetoric, from its roots in classical Greece, has been understood as both a discursive skill used to produce a desired effect on an audience, and the study of the techniques a person should employ to produce such an effect. The two (of five) traditional "canons" of rhetorical study that are closest to Formalism are the study of "style" and "delivery": Michael Burke writes that historically these typically included "the use of style figures (*tropes* and *schemes*) to produce differing linguistic and cognitive levels of parallelism and deviation in order to draw in, delight, and ultimately persuade listeners and hearers." He further notes that the study of performance typically "put much focus on intonation, prosody, voice, rhythm, and gesture."[83]

The link, implicit in rhetoric, between the study of linguistic form and the impact of form on the audience is useful for understanding the Formalists' goals. The Formalists used comparison to identify techniques commonly utilized by authors. They referred to these, as a category, by using a very broad term: *priem*. The term *priem* is usually translated into English as "device," but it can also be translated as a "move," in the sense of a wrestling or fencing move. This meaning of the word is helpful to keep in mind because, as they identified verbal *priemy*, the Formalists were focused on the *tactics* employed to bring about a desired effect.

The compatibility between Formalist poetics and rhetorical analysis was demonstrated in a 1924 collection of articles published by Shklovsky, Eikhenbaum, Tynianov, and Jakubinsky that was devoted to the analysis of "Lenin's language."[84] Tellingly, in their analyses of Lenin's language, the Formalists emphasized the same poetic devices they had identified in literary works. Eikhenbaum, as in his study of Gogol's "The Overcoat," focused on the contrasting registers in Lenin's speeches, and stressed that Lenin used features of everyday, conversational speech in written expression.[85] Carol Any sees this as "one of Eikhenbaum's most successful Formalist articles" and points out that it replicated the analytical framework he used for a 1921 study of Pushkin's prose—dividing it into units which function as stanzas.[86] Tynianov, who was invested in the study of parody and its role in literary history, wrote about Lenin's ironic use of the language of his opponents. Shklovsky described Lenin's style in terms almost identical to those he used to describe Tolstoy: "Lenin is against naming things [*protiv nazvan'ia*], he continually establishes a new relationship between a word and its referent, not naming things and not fixing a new name." Shklovsky had argued that *ostranenie* is a product of this very tactic—writing that Tolstoy "does not call [*ne nazyvaet*] a thing by its name." He concludes that Lenin defamiliarizes language "in order to get rid of a false tone, to shake it up [*rasshevelit' ego*]," again using terms he used to define defamiliarization as a poetic device.[87] The Formalists' 1924 articles on Lenin suggest that whether they are analyzing a story, poem, or political speech, the "devices" they identify are the same—shifts in register, parody, metaphor—and in both literature and in political speech these serve to capture an audience's attention. This overlap between OPOIAZ poetics and the classical study of rhetoric reveals that, in the revolutionary period, OPOIAZ scholarship was invested in explaining how oral performances can wield power—by transmitting emotion, exciting expectations, arresting attention, and "astonishing" the listener.

Eikhenbaum's study of Lenin's language questions the opposition between poetic and nonpoetic language:

> In our works on the study of poetic language we generally assumed it to be opposed to "practical" language. This was important and fruitful during the first stage of determining the distinctive features of poetic speech. But it has since been shown on more than one occasion (L. Jakubinsky), the area of so-called "practical" language is extremely wide and diversified. There is probably no type of speech in which our relationship to the word is thoroughly mechanized, in which the word is completely "known"; as for forms such as oratory, despite their "practical" nature, they are in many respects very close to poetic speech. The only characteristic of poetic language is the highlighting of particular elements of speech and their specific implementation (especially in verse language).[88]

Any notes that at this juncture, in 1924, Eikhenbaum "put forward as his positive criterion of 'poeticity' the construction of a hierarchical system. This was the best he could do in answer to the charge that the Formalists were unable to establish a positive definition of poetic language."[89] Any's assessment is echoed by other scholars on Russian Formalism, who describe OPOIAZ theory as gradually moving away from a hard-line stance—that poetic language is empirically differentiated from nonpoetic—toward a more nuanced view of poetry as a hierarchical system. This approach relied on the aesthetic concept of the *dominanta*, which Eikhenbaum borrowed from Broder Christiansen's *Philosophy of Art* (1912). For Christiansen, the dominant is that factor of an "aesthetic object" which "comes to the fore and assumes a leading role . . . The dominant is the same as the structure of bones in an organic body: it contains the theme of the whole, supports this whole, enters into relation with it."[90] For Eikhenbaum, the dominant element was that aspect of a work, or an artist's oeuvre, which gives it its unique character and unitary quality. Any writes that "in Akhmatova's poetry he [Eikhenbaum] considered the deforming *dominanta* to be the articulation of selected vowels and consonants through the repeated, strenuous movements of the lips, tongue, and jaw."[91] Tynianov took up the concept of the *dominanta* as a way of describing the factor that recolored the semantics of words when used in a line of verse.

Any argues that Eikhenbaum and Tynianov adopted the concept of a hierarchical system, organized by a dominant element, to assert that even if there is no empirical difference between the language or devices used by Pushkin and Lenin (i.e., between poetic and nonpoetic language), poetic works can still be considered as autonomous, or quasi-autonomous, wholes by virtue of the fact that they are internally organized. In the mid-1920s, Tynianov extended the concept of a hierarchical system to the study of literary history. The standard view of OPOIAZ theory casts the movement as moving away from empiricism, a definition of form derived from the measurable sonic properties of language, and thus away from stringent claims for the autonomy of poetry. These ideas were replaced by a semantic or "dynamic" definition of form, and a systemic model that allows for a work of art to be only *relatively* autonomous.[92] Without disputing this narrative, the recovery of an early OPOIAZ theory of poetic performance allows for a recontextualization of this theoretical trajectory.

The theoretical legacy described in this section shows that early OPOIAZ theory was not always primarily motivated by a desire to demonstrate that poetry is distinct from everyday language. Rather, their work sought to understand how a poetic work is (emotionally) impactful. We have seen that OPOIAZ theory was not invested in sidelining the author in favor of a self-sufficient, meaning-generating system. Rather, it sought to understand authorship in terms of an interaction between performer and audience. It was presumed that, for an author, the rationale for using a device (e.g., for shifting registers) was not to differentiate a message from nonpoetic messages, but rather to engage an audience. The distinction between these two rationales (poetic differentiation versus impact) can be collapsed, but OPOIAZ theory recognized that they are not necessarily the same thing. In Tynianov's "The Ode" essay, he argues that

literary systems are interrelated with the extra-literary series closest at hand—speech; this includes both the material from neighboring forms of verbal art and everyday speech. . . . This is where the term *orientation* [*ustanovka*] comes into play. Orientation refers . . . also to the function of a work (or genre) vis-à-vis the closest extra-literary series. This is why the speech orientation is so tremendously important in literature.[93]

Tynianov's stress on the "speech orientation" of literature reflects the Humboldtian philosophy of language, which prioritized oral speech in dialogue. His essay suggests that the history of literature is driven by an author's need to be "effective," to capture an audience's attention. To do so an author relies on shared knowledge of everyday speech, as well as the works of other authors.[94] The categorization of one speech act as literary and another as nonliterary is the concern of the scholar, not that of the author; it is a retrospective assessment, not the immediate force driving literary history.

OPOIAZ work on poetry as performance allows us to see these theorists as themselves in dialogue with the political and cultural interests of the revolutionary period. They approached authors as skilled manipulators of rhetorical devices, motivated by a desire to impact their audiences. The theory they produced largely focused on the exceptional individual (e.g., Blok, Akhmatova, Gogol, Lenin). Shklovsky's work on narrative theory would attempt a more egalitarian approach to this topic.

SHKLOVSKY'S THEORY OF AUTHORSHIP

This chapter argues that OPOIAZ theorized authorship as performance by collapsing categorical oppositions: between oral and written discourse, and between collective and individual creativity. In this section, I highlight efforts to collapse a perceived opposition between folkloric creativity and literary creativity. My focus will be on Shklovsky's work on narrative, written during the Civil War period (1918–22), which exemplifies the intersection between Formalist theory and contemporary political thought. It is a more radical theory of authorship than the OPOIAZ poetics of performance described above. Shklovsky's departure from his peers coincided with his shift from the study of poetry to prose narrative. His writings on Futurist poetry, the earliest of which date from 1914 and 1916, are separated from his work on prose, which he began in the summer of 1918, by only a few years.[95] This was, however, a period of intense activity. Between the summer of 1917 and January 1919, Shklovsky was engaged in active combat—in Galicia and Persia in the Russian army under the Provisional Government, and then as a conspirator in an underground movement affiliated with the Socialist Revolutionary Party to restore the Constituent Assembly (which the Bolsheviks dissolved in January 1918). His participation in this movement would later force Shklovsky into exile in Berlin from spring 1922 to fall 1923. During these years he also wrote dozens of articles, at least six long studies, and three books, which combine memoiristic accounts with literary theory.[96] It was at this time that Shklovsky developed his original theory of narrative, based on an original theory of authorship.

Between 1919 and 1922 Shklovsky published much of his writing in the theatrical daily *Life of Art* (*Zhizn' iskusstva*), for which he was on the editorial board. He republished most of these articles in a book titled *Knight's Move* (*Khod konia*, Berlin, 1923). The articles in this book are generally short, and most respond to contemporary developments in the cultural sphere. Shklovsky begins *Knight's Move* with a preface that establishes a major theme in his essays:

> The book is called *Knight's Move* [*Khod konia*]. The knight moves edgewise . . . there are many reasons for the oddity of the knight's move, and the most important of them is the conventionality [*uslovnost'*] of art . . . I write about the conventionality of art. The second reason is that the knight is not free—he moves edgewise because the straight path is forbidden to him. The articles and feuilletons in this book were all printed in Russia between 1919 and 1921. They were printed in a tiny theatrical journal, *The Life of Art*, and this very journal was a knight's move.[97]

Here, Shklovsky overtly likens the indirectness and conventionality of artistic rules to the rules of chess. I will argue that when Shklovsky claims that art is "conventional" or "not free," he is theorizing literature as a product of a creative process modeled on oral performance. I will focus on several, interrelated results of this approach. First, if literary creativity is fundamentally like oral performance, then the literary text is not seen as an inviolable whole, but as a variant. A second outcome is that authorship is understood as an engagement with a shared tradition. Third, as a performer, the author is not seen as a unique, inspired "genius" but as a "craftsman."

The grounds for Shklovsky's theorizing were prepared by the conditions outlined above: the tendency to think of literature in oral terms, the trend to treat folklore in individualistic terms, and efforts to rethink literary authorship as collective creativity. Shklovsky's understanding of literature borrows explicitly from folkloristics—not the performer studies of Onchukov or the Sokolovs, but that of an earlier generation (of the 1860s–1890s). The folkloristics that was productive for Shklovsky is conceptually situated in between the collectivism of the mythological school and the individualism of performer studies: he most often cites Alexander Veselovsky, Pavel Rybnikov, and Mikhail Speransky. Shklovsky's thinking was also impacted by the modernist orientation toward performance, and theater in particular. He served in the Theatrical Section of Narkompros in 1919 as part of the repertory commission. This entailed reading through hundreds of plays produced by Proletkult studios.[98] In 1921 Shklovsky even wrote sixteen plays himself, reportedly to supplement the living rations he was receiving from the Writers' Union.[99]

Finally, it is significant that Shklovsky's innovative theory of authorship emerged when he turned his focus away from poetry and toward prose narrative, often prose in translation. His seminal articles on narrative theory, which were published as *Theory of Prose* (*O teorii prozy*) in 1925, contain extended analyses of novels by Cervantes, Dickens, and Sterne, as well as abundant references to texts originally written in Arabic, Georgian, German, Greek, French, Finnish, Latin, Sanskrit, and other languages.[100] His approach is broadly comparative; he is not interested in the linguistic specificity of these texts. Emily Finer, in her study of Shklovsky's work on Sterne, notes that "Shklovsky ignores the fact that he is reading texts at several removes from their original language versions, both when he cites directly from translated works and from translations borrowed from secondary sources. Furthermore, he is unaware, or uninterested, in the accuracy of translated material." She explains this as partly a result of the fact that Shklovsky did not know any foreign languages.[101] I would also stress that Shklovsky's willingness to work with translated material is consistent with his dismissal of the specifics of textual form as unimportant. He is more interested in how each textual performance is derived from a poetic tradition.

Shklovsky theorizes narrative as something essentially open-ended and malleable, like the script of a play or the schematic plot frame of a folktale. He dismisses the idea that a text is a stable whole with inviolable integrity. For example, he does not distinguish between intertextual borrowings which precede the composition of a text (e.g., Goethe's knowledge of Shakespeare's writings) and subsequent authors' rearrangements of a text (e.g., an adaptation of Shakespeare's *Hamlet*). Shklovsky articulates these ideas in a review praising Yuri Annenkov's irreverent rearrangement of Leo Tolstoy's anti-liquor play "The First Distiller" ("Pervyi vinokur"):

Of course, the text of a work is not something inviolable [*neprikosnovennyi*], as people thought at the end of the 19th and beginning of the 20th centuries. In any event, we do not have the right to say that playing freely with another's text is a sign of "bad taste." After all, Goethe remade Shakespeare, and even Shakespeare's text is made up of a layering [*naplastovanie*] of many people's, maybe even actors' remakes [*peredelki*]. What is more, every reproduction of a work entails its reconstitution [*peresozdanie*], its rearrangement [*perekomponovka*]. This is very clear from studying copies made from one and the same work over a period of, say, twenty years.[102]

Shklovsky moves here between a number of kinds of collaboration or co-authorship: one author borrowing from another, the layering of many persons' contributions within a text, and the reproduction of a text over time—through performance or even "copying." The repercussions of this stance can be seen in his treatment of the text as a unit.

In a chapter in *The Hamburg Score* (*Gamburgskii schet*, 1928), Shklovsky describes one of the most important aspects of his thinking: "What is important is a feeling of the disconnectedness of forms [*razobshchennost' form*] and the free treatment of these forms. The sense of the unity [*slitnost'*] of a literary work is, for me, replaced by a feeling of the value of the individual piece. Rather than unifying the pieces, I am more interested in their contradictions."[103] When describing his own writing process, Shklovsky repeatedly speaks of the process of composition as an arrangement of pieces, one not driven by any overarching, all-encompassing concept, but rather a processual, ad hoc procedure:

> I am of the opinion that a work, especially a long one, is created not by realizing the work's objective [*zadanie*]. Yes, an objective exists, but the technique of the work re-creates [*peredelyvaet*] it entirely. The unity of a literary work, it seems, is a myth; at least it seems that way to me, someone who has written semi-belletristic things and who has observed many others write them.[104]

Shklovsky describes the composition of his epistolary novel *ZOO* in these very terms: "When I put the pieces of the finished product on the floor and sat down on the parquet to stick the book together, another book resulted—not the one which I had been making."[105] Shklovsky also took this approach toward others' texts. In an essay published in 1927, he describes taking apart Konstantin Fedin's *Cities and Years* (*Goroda i gody*) in these terms:

> Fedin is angry at me and says that I didn't read the novel. No, I divided it (the novel) into lessons [*uroki*] and read those. I cut the novel up into pieces and am assembling new novels from them, in the manner of Walter Scott, Dickens, and Ehrenburg. I can, by casting the witticisms and play under Sterne, turn the lyrical spots into Turgenev.[106]

Shklovsky is not just non-reverential toward texts: he refuses to see the text as a whole as a meaningful unit. Fedin critiques Shklovsky's focus on technique and tradition. As Fedin writes, "I am speaking on behalf of the naive reader: I believe in inspiration, I believe in the soul." For Fedin, this means believing in the writer as an extraordinary individual, as someone "inspired." He connects this with the reader's undisturbed engagement with the writer's artistic illusion. For this reason he objects to Shklovsky's mixture of theory

and artistry, which "bares" (*obnazhat'*) the device, as a disruption of the illusion which makes him lose faith in the theorist-author.[107]

Shklovsky, on the other hand, was sharp in his rejection of "inspiration"
in an article titled "Compromisers" ("Soglashateli") published in *Life of Art*
in 1920:

> You can't cast a cannon out of inspiration [*po vdokhnoveniiu*], you can't act a
> play out of intuition [*nutrom*], from your guts. A play can only be made. Revo-
> lutionary theater wanted to be a theater of spontaneous impulse [*poryv*], of
> inspiration, but it couldn't escape technique [*tekhnika*]. It refused to look
> for it—and as a result we got strange, old, garbage technique [*otbrosovaia
> tekhnika*].[108]

In rejecting "inspiration," Shklovsky goes against Fedin's belief in the
autonomy of the individual and of the text as whole. These values informed
the arguments presented above regarding the method of literary interpretation (hermeneutics). To return to Azadovsky's folkloristics, as an example,
we have seen that to treat a *skazka* narrated by Natalia Vinokurova as an
inviolable "work," worthy of interpretation as a meaningful whole, is to acknowledge her as an autonomous subject. The concept of self that is Natalia
Vinokurova is more than the sum of its parts; her identity cannot be broken down into component pieces. The same principle applies to her stories. Shklovsky's theory disregards this logic, relentlessly dismantling literary
texts—those authored by others, as well as his own.

Commenting on Shklovsky's propensity to fragment texts, Ilya Kalinin
describes his method as "decomposition." He writes that "on the one hand,
the decomposition method exposes the structure of the text and reflects the
fragmentary structure of a human experience immersed in history . . . On the
other hand, however, text gives the body the unity it has lost, but this time
it does not have organic status—rather it is the status of a certain historical
structure."[109] I would add that we can understand Shklovsky's theory not only
in terms of "text" and "body," but also in terms of a performance which em-
ploys collectively owned devices. Shklovsky repeatedly describes the "self"
as a place of intersection. As he writes in "I and My Coat": "Like air with
raindrops, life is permeated with other lives, other worlds. One wheel is
turning and intersecting with another wheel. The machine is working in another machine . . . Perhaps our life itself is like rain piercing another life."[110]
Shklovsky's concept of self is nonautonomous; and he similarly views authorship as reliant on a historical tradition of devices and techniques known and
developed by others. This is a modified, post-Romantic collectivism.

Shklovsky consistently stressed technique (*tekhnika*) in opposition to
"inspiration" as a way of understanding literary creativity. As we saw above,

he stresses that technique has to be "sought"; if this process is superficial, "garbage technique" (*otbrosovaia tekhnika*) can ruin the effort to create new art. Shklovsky is not just criticizing his contemporaries; he also has a positive argument in his writings as to what the successful search for technique might look like. To understand this positive argument, we can start with the "pieces" into which Shklovsky fragments literary works. This is neither an act of total destruction nor an idiosyncratic act of individual caprice: the elemental units in Shklovsky's theoretical arguments are not the "pieces" of Fedin's novel or the letters that make up his novel *ZOO*. The recycling process that is literary history is not to be imagined as an individual cutting up a manuscript with scissors, but rather as a process akin to the oral performance of a skilled storyteller. Shklovsky makes this explicit in his writings. He makes considerable theoretical use of a letter written in the 1860s by the folklorist Pavel Rybnikov, which Shklovsky repeatedly refers to in his own essays.

This letter describes the process of oral performance in terms that Shklovsky would borrow to describe literary (artistic) creativity more generally. Rybnikov tries to convince Vsevolod Miller that the *skazka* is composed with more freedom than the *bylina*. Rybnikov describes the variation in tale-tellers' performances, suggesting that each performer composes in performance by stringing words together, like "beads" on a string. Importantly, each time this is done, the result is different:

> Let's listen to the storyteller. If he is a good one, his words will weave themselves into place like beads on a string. You can hear the rhythm itself. Whole lines of verse. . . . Force him to repeat and he will express much of it differently. Ask him if anyone else knows the story, and he'll point to a *fellow villager*, a certain So-and-So, and he'll tell you that this So-and-So heard the story along with him from a certain old man or minstrel. Then go ask this So-and-So to tell this same story, and you will hear the story told not only in a different language and with different figures of speech, but often in a different key. One storyteller introduces (or preserves) the piteous details, another contributes (or perpetuates) the satirical point of view in certain episodes, while a third storyteller adapts a denouement from another tale (or from the *general fund* [*obshchii sklad*] that is available to all storytellers, of which later). In addition, new characters and new adventures appear on the scene . . . The well-known, communally shared conceptions put on a certain costume and were expressed with a certain turn of speech. "Story = Shaping [*skazka—skladka*]."[111]

Rybnikov's letter describes the creative process that allows for considerable flexibility in the composition of a folktale, but he does not go so far as to treat the resulting tale as a work of "literature." That is, he does not isolate the individual narrator and his performance from tradition (the stable elements and their mode of transmission). Rybnikov notes that a traditional "fund" of shared elements is maintained by tale-tellers listening to others perform (the full text of the letter goes into more detail on this). This fund is made up not of whole stories but of smaller elements; thus, an ending from one tale can be separated and combined with other material. This traditional "fund" is what Shklovsky found most suggestive in Rybnikov's description.

This letter anticipates oral formulaic theory. In *The Ethnography of Rhythm,* Haun Saussy describes the genealogy of this idea, which is largely associated today with Albert Lord's *The Singer of Tales* (1960). Saussy reveals that the French writer and critic Jean Paulhan had articulated the outlines of oral theory in his 1913 book on the poetics of *hain-teny*, a genre of oral performative poetry in Madagascar. Paulhan's book included the following suggestive description of this tradition:

> One might imagine a language consisting of two or three hundred rhythmic phrases and four or five hundred verse-types, fixed once and for all and passed on without modification by oral tradition. Poetic invention would then consist of taking these verses as models and fashioning new verses in their image, verses having the same form, rhythm, structure, and, so far as possible, the same meaning. Such a language would quite closely resemble the language of Malagasy poetry.[112]

Saussy describes the evolution of this idea, as it was revised by Marcel Jousse in a 1925 book, and then by Antoine Meillet, who was Milman Parry's teacher in Paris in the 1920s. Parry is known for pursuing this idea in detail, using phonograph recordings made in the 1930s of the performances of epic songs in the territories of what are today Serbia and Bosnia and Herzegovina. Lord, who assisted Parry in his fieldwork, carried on this work after Parry's death in 1935. While there are basic commonalities between the oral formulaic theory of Parry-Lord and the ideas of Rybnikov, they differ on an important point. The theory developed by French and American scholars was understood as a means of describing a particular, non-written tradition. Lord is explicit that the capacity for this kind of creativity is contingent on illiteracy.[113] The French Paulhan, writing about the people of Madagascar, and the Americans Parry and Lord about the South Slavic singers, stress how different this mode of verbal production is from literate, modern, individualistic art. Within the Russian philological paradigm, by contrast, scholars more frequently sought to theorize oral and written art within a single synthetic model. In keeping with this trend, Shklovsky used the concept of oral performance to describe both oral and written verbal creativity.

In his article "Collective Creativity," first published in *Life of Art* in

September 1919, Shklovsky uses the folkloristic understanding of composition in performance to respond to the debates on the subject of "collective creativity" fueled by Proletkultists and others in the Civil War period. Shklovsky's key point is that *all* literature is "collectively" created. He further specifies what he means: "By collective here I mean not the entire masses, the whole population, but a society of singer-writers [*obshchestvo pevtsov-pisatelei*], regardless of whether we are talking about so-called folk [*narodnyi*] or so-called artistic creativity."[114] He thus denies any difference between traditional oral folkloric performance and the work of the literary writer. As we have seen, this view became increasingly accepted in the 1910s. However, unlike the Sokolovs or Azadovsky, Shklovsky does not take this to mean that folklore is to be studied like literature, using the hermeneutic method, but rather that literature is to be understood like folklore, and thus studied using the method of comparative poetics.

Shklovsky elaborates on this argument by discussing the origins of the components of narrative structure, and the process by which a narrative is composed. He breaks narrative into a plot schema ("frame") and the "material" that is used to fill out the frame. For Shklovsky, both of these are "traditional"—that is, they come from a "fund" of shared knowledge. Shklovsky explains this by using commedia dell'arte as an example:

> One takes a script [*stsenarii*], at the basis of the script is some kind of plot [*siuzhet*]; plots themselves, as you know, are not a product of individual [*lichnyi*] creativity, they move from one chronological stratum of creators of art to another, changing under the influence of the ever-present desire for material to be palpably experienced. Into this basis [*osnova*] the performers of roles insert their jokes, enlivening and decorating the traditional speeches. But, as anyone who has heard or told a joke knows, these jokes are themselves a kind of fund of spare parts [*sklad zapasnykh chastei*]. In this manner, the artist-improviser [*artist-improvizator*] inserts into the traditional (in the broad sense of the word) frame, a traditional filling.
>
> This is how the creativity of the epic singer is accomplished.
>
> This is how Rybnikov described the creativity of telling folk tales. He talked about a fund that is common to all tale-tellers. It seems to us that so-called individual creativity is not accomplished this way, but this is just a result of the impossibility or, more accurately, the difficulty of seeing the present day in general terms.[115]

The ending of this quote reiterates Veselovsky's assertion in the "Poetics of Plots" (cited in the introduction) that subsequent generations will see modern literature to be schematically conventional in the way that moderns now see older, formulaic genres. Aligning himself with the philological paradigm, Shklovsky uses post-Romantic folkloristic research of the 1880s to argue for an understanding of creativity that is neither individualistic, nor the "mass" creation described by Bogdanov and Gorky. In the terms of the ongoing debate on creativity, it allowed him to argue against a "bourgeois" understanding of creativity, but to retain a view of art as something created by specialists or professionals.

This brings us back to the question of technique, and Shklovsky's stress on the importance of an informed search for the right technique. Folk art serves Shklovsky as a privileged model for thinking about traditions of techniques. What seems to appeal to him is how oral traditions reveal the importance of a dialogic connection between the artist and the audience. Shklovsky's theoretical project was accompanied by his own creative writing and mentoring of young writers, and constituted his effort to contribute to the search for a new, revolutionary literature. This was articulated by Konstantin Fedin, who described Shklovsky as "preoccupied with his quest for the most 'sound' tradition from which to begin without fail the dance of the new literature."[116] "Dance" (*tanets*) is a metaphor for writing that Shklovsky often used in his writings. Recall, for example, his description of the relationship between author and audience as the "dance of the organs of speech."[117] For Shklovsky this is always a partner dance; a dance between writer and reader. To perform effectively, the writer must be attuned to the current moment and his audience. Brik articulated this in his 1923 article "The So-Called Formal Method." He, like Shklovsky, seeks to reframe literary creativity as a craft. He also emphasizes that this craft is inseparable from what he calls the "social demand":

> The poet is the master of his own trade, and that is all. In order to be a good craftsman [*master*] one needs to know the needs of those for whom you are working, you must live one life with them. Otherwise the work won't come off and will be useless. . . . The poet is a craftsman of the word, a word-creator, serving his own class, his own social group. The consumer [*potrebitel'*] tells him what to write about.[118]

Brik argues that the work of OPOIAZ is central to the efforts of "proletarian cultural construction." Formalist poetics shows proletarian poets that "everything great has been created in answer to the questions of the day, that the 'eternal' today was then a topic of the time, and that the great poet does not reveal himself, but simply carries out the social command [*sotsial'nyi zakaz*]."[119] Brik, like Shklovsky, stresses that rather than study individual authors, the "*mass study of the devices of the poetic craft is necessary*"—and the outcome of this work (comparative poetics) was understood to provide knowledge that would allow contemporary writers to do a better job of responding to the needs of the current moment.

Shklovsky likewise understood poetic, technical know-how in terms of a social contract, but he also suggested that the craftsman's success hinges on the selection of a relevant historical tradition. Commenting on Annenkov's successful adaptation of Tolstoy, Shklovsky writes: "It is interesting to note that, like any innovator, Annenkov turns out to be the true inheritor of a tradition [*traditsiia*]."[120] The idea that successful innovation requires a deep knowledge of the past was a basic tenet of OPOIAZ Formalism. This was succinctly articulated in Shklovsky's proposed title for Tynianov's collected essays: "Archaists—Innovators" ("Arkhaisty—novatory").[121] The turn to the "archaic" as the source of the new informs Shklovsky's turn to folkloristics for developing a new theory of literature. The apparently marginal traditions of the past are the most likely candidates for innovation in the current moment. This idea was, again, aphoristically articulated by Shklovsky as the principle that the history of literary schools is not "linear" but rather is filled with "discontinuities," because "inheritance with the change of literary schools does not go from father to son, but from uncle to nephew."[122] Shklovsky also described this as the L-shaped move of the knight in chess. The Formalists, when looking to the past for inspiration, knew that they needed to look outside the line of "canonized saints" of Russian literature. Tynianov memorably described this as a personal preference for historical "failures": "I respect the rough, unfinished losers, mumblers, whose speech you need to finish for them. I love the provincials, in whom history is clumsily layered, and who are therefore rough around the edges. There are quiet uprisings, which have been hidden in a box for 100 and 200 years."[123] This conviction that forgotten or peripheral traditions are more interesting, more useful for the present than the canon of "great men" can be seen in Tynianov's work on the Russian poet Vilgelm Kiukhelbeker, known primarily as a lesser poet and friend of Pushkin. Tynianov produced several studies of Kiukhelbeker's poetry, and wrote a historical novel based on his life. For Shklovsky, the appeal of marginal or non-canonical art manifested itself in his interest in folklore (folktales, riddles, puns, anecdotes).

In addition, the class origins of folklore could also have been important to Shklovsky for political reasons. Shklovsky's celebration of folklore as a model for literary theory can be understood as part of his active resistance to Bolshevik political theory and cultural policy. He criticizes Bolshevik vanguardist cultural policy from the perspective of an advocate for a populist, socialist revolution. It is remarkable that Shklovsky's seminal statement on narrative theory, "The Relationship between Devices of Plot Construction and General Devices of Style," was begun while he was in hiding in 1918 as part of an anti-Bolshevik action.[124] It is widely assumed that Shklovsky's actions were part of the SR resistance, and it can be surmised that his political views were close to those of the Socialist Revolutionary (SR) Party. The Socialist Revolutionaries cast themselves as the representatives of the peasantry, and as the immediate successors to the populists of the 1870s and 1880s.[125] One of the basic demands of the SR program was the "socialization of land," based on the premise that the peasantry was essentially communalist in its thinking. This idea was accompanied by the assumption that a socialist revolution required a massive popular uprising among the peasantry. In the revolutionary period the SR platform had considerable popular support—in the universal suffrage elections held in November 1917, the SRs received four-fifths of the vote among the population that lived in the countryside.[126]

A pro-peasant, populist ethos was also common among the so-called fellow travelers—intellectuals who were sympathetic to the revolution but who did not side with the Bolsheviks. Trotsky sought to explain and dismiss this "neo-populism" as superficial and idealistic:

All these groups [fellow travelers] reflected, in an extremely uneven form, the state of mind of the village at the time of forced requisition [of foodstuffs]. It was then that the intelligentsia sought refuge from hunger in the villages and there accumulated its impressions. . . . The non-communist intelligentsia which has not thrown in its lot unreservedly with the proletariat, and this comprises the overwhelming majority of the intelligentsia, seeks support in the peasantry . . . [and] this process . . . expresses itself (with hindsight) in the idealization of the peasant elements of the Revolution. This peculiar neo-populism [*novonarodnichestvo*] is characteristic of all the fellow-travelers.[127]

Bolshevism cast itself as the representative specifically of the working class (over the peasantry) and took a vanguardist (as opposed to populist) approach to cultural revolution. In the cultural sphere, vanguardism is described by Sheila Fitzpatrick as a relationship of "tutelage" between intellectuals and workers.[128] For the Bolshevik leadership, such as Lunacharsky or Lenin, the cultural education of the workers was a problematic topic: neither the existing cultural heritage of the vanguard (i.e., the aristocratic-bourgeois culture of the society in which Marxist intellectuals were educated) nor the popular culture of the working class or peasantry was thought to be acceptable as a candidate for proletarian culture. As Fitzpatrick puts it,

All Marxist intellectuals were agreed, without even thinking about it, that proletarian culture had little or nothing to do with observable popular lower-class habits and cultural tastes. "Vulgar," "tasteless," or "trivial" culture was obviously not proletarian; and if workers liked it that only showed that they had been infected with petit bourgeois attitudes.[129]

The Bolshevik leadership thus leaned toward an educational policy which thought of socialist culture in terms of education or enlightenment—bringing "culture" to workers who were otherwise uncultured. A different line of thinking, discussed earlier in this chapter, was represented by Proletkult, which sought to nurture a spontaneously emerging proletarian culture. The intellectual leaders of that organization, such as Bogdanov, theorized proletarian culture in relatively utopian, or at least highly abstract, terms as a kind of mass-collective creativity.

Shklovsky's writings propose a Socialist Revolutionary alternative to both these options. His articles from the Civil War period repeatedly engage with "popular" art, and theorize authorship as socially engaged creativity. His thinking is closer to a Marxist position than might be expected. In his article "Collective Creativity" Shklovsky critiques a bourgeois, individualist understanding of creativity, using arguments from contemporary Marxist discourse:

> When issuing patents for inventions [*izobreteniia*] they note not only the day, but the hour and even the minute an application is submitted; practice has shown that it is very possible that another inventor will appear with the very same invention. It happened with the application for a patent on the telephone! In general, establishing priority for an invention or a discovery is very difficult; the era prepared the preconditions for a construction, and several people not connected to each other feel that they are authors [*tvortsy*]. In this case a human and the human mind are nothing other than a geometric point of intersection for lines of collective creation.[130]

This same argument appears in the entry on "Invention" ("Izobretenie," published in 1933) in the *Great Soviet Encyclopedia*. The entry points out that "the multitude of examples of simultaneously emerging inventions in different places, often isolated from each other, is a clear indication of the social-economic conditionality of invention."[131] Shklovsky uses these examples of "simultaneous" scientific invention as evidence for the collective nature of artistic creativity.

However, Shklovsky's argument regarding the social nature of creativity differs from the Marxist understanding of art or science. For Shklovsky, simultaneous artistic invention occurs not because of similar socioeconomic conditions, but because two creators are both working from the same "fund of spare parts." They are part of the same "society of singer-writers" (*ob-*

shchestvo pevtsov-pisatelei).[132] Shklovsky's recourse to folkloristic research is continually presented as a counter-argument to the presumption that the lower classes lack culture, or that an emerging socialist culture needs to be organized or instilled from above, by a leading vanguard class. In *Knight's Move* he is explicit on this point, writing that "the greatest misfortune of our time is that the government is regulating art without knowing what it is. The greatest misfortune of Russian art is that we discard it like a husk of rice." One of the most frequently cited lines from Shklovsky's writings is his provocative claim that "art has always been free of life. Its flag has never reflected the color of the flag that flies over the city fortress."[133] This statement is often cited as evidence of the Formalists' hard-line stance regarding the "autonomy" of art from everyday life, and particularly from politics. I would argue that it is more accurate to read this aphoristic claim as rejecting top-down regulation or tutelage in the artistic sphere. Shklovsky does not totally isolate art from social reality, but rather promotes his own (socialist) model for thinking about art as something collectively created by a collective of specialists. His privileging of peasant specialists is consistent with the SRs' anticapitalist, neopopulist vision for a socialist revolution.

This was not a fleeting provocation. Shklovsky uses the rhetoric of a precapitalist or anticapitalist mode of production—that of the handicraftsman—throughout his writings. As he put it in *Sentimental Journey*: "At its basis the formal method is simple. A return to craftsmanship [*masterstvo*]."[134] Shklovsky consistently refers to writers as "masters" (*mastera*), art as "mastery" or "craftsmanship" (*masterstvo*), writing as a "craft" (*remeslo*), to "technique" (*technika*), and to "devices" (*priemy*). This is a concept of creativity as an artisanal craft: work done by the individual, by hand, according to a learned tradition. Shklovsky also opposes artistic craftsmanship to the products of mechanized processes or automatization. In his early essay "Resurrection of the Word" he contrasts real, "living" art with dead "marketplace art," or "bazaar monstrosities" (*rynochnoe iskusstvo, bazarnye merzosti*) which are "dead."[135] The opening of his "Plot Construction" essay makes this contrast more explicit. In a work of art,

> the word approaches another word, the word feels the other word, like a cheek feels a cheek. The word is dismantled, and rather than a single complex—an automatically [*avtomaticheski*] articulated word, thrown out like a chocolate bar from a vending machine [*avtomat*]—a word-sound is born, a word-articulatory [*slovoartikuliatsionyi*] movement.[136]

Shklovsky is playing on an association between the psychologically "automatic" (*avtomaticheski*) and the product of a machine (*avtomat*). Automatization is a product of habitual associations, and is also the routinization of creative processes due to industrialization. This critique can be compared to Walter Benjamin's Romantic anticapitalism.[137] Shklovsky's thinking is particularly close, for example, to Benjamin's 1936 essay on Nikolai Leskov, "The Storyteller," in which he celebrates storytelling as "an artisan form of communication" in which "traces of the storyteller cling to the story in the way the handprints of the potter cling to the clay vessel."[138]

Kalinin has argued that Shklovsky's interest in combating the automatization of perception is analogous to Marx's critique of the emotionless, abstract perception of objects as "commodity-forms." He writes that, in search of an "alternative political-economic model that frees a person from automatization and alienation," the Formalists looked to "the handicraft work of the solitary craftsman [*kustar'-odinochka*], who turns out to be the prototypical figure of the artist as such."[139] Kalinin's arguments corroborate my own, although I would stress that the Formalists' prototypical craftsman is not necessarily a "loner." For Shklovsky it is important that the craftsman's specialized knowledge is maintained by a group. Recall that for Shklovsky, the self can be described as intersecting with other selves, like one "machine . . . working in another machine." Despite his proclivity for mechanistic metaphors, Shklovsky argues that the work of art has to be constructed by hand, each time anew, so that its parts ("words" in Shklovsky's quote above) are perceived as individual units, contrasting with and dismantling each other. To do this the artist has to be in dialogue with his audience, and must have studied the social craft of writing.

One of the claims of this book is that placing Russian Formalism in the context of the philological paradigm unravels apparent paradoxes in the Formalists' thinking. One such paradox is that Russian Formalism began as an apparently vehemently anti-biographical movement, but then its leaders—Shklovsky, Eikhenbaum, Tynianov, and Jakobson—all turned to biographical studies, or even to inserting their own biographies into their scholarship in the mid- to late 1920s. Jan Levchenko, who has studied what he calls the Formalists' "search for biography," writes:

> Early revolutionary formalism, with its fear of psychological determinism, led to the phantasmal assertion of the latter. Shklovsky, who advanced the concept of mechanical turnover of impersonal forms, Tynianov, who thought of history . . . as an anonymous process of struggle and turnover, Eikhenbaum, planning an all-encompassing biography of Tolstoy by starting with the morphology and genesis of his literary devices—each sublimated a sharply personal attitude to history, a desire to enter in its ranks.[140]

Levchenko describes "early" Formalism as an "ascetic" movement which "fed on a need for isolation." However, as he puts it, this "strict rule inevitably anticipates its violation."[141] Any likewise describes Eikhenbaum's Formalist career as marked by an early period of severe personal negation, followed by a moment of "crisis," which was then remedied by adopting a more moderate position.

While I don't want to deny that Russian Formalism evolved in its thinking, what I hope to have shown in this chapter is that early Formalism did not negate the subject of the author to the extent that critics have assumed. The Formalists' study of authorship as performance can be seen as an effort to more fundamentally embed the author in a social context, using the oral-dialogic model of art as performance. The Formalists' turn to biography doesn't have to be understood as the resurgence of a repressed individualism, as a reversal, but can be seen as a development of their early interest in the performer's impact on his audience. This is articulated in a diary entry that Eikhenbaum wrote in 1925:

> Somehow I keep coming back to the idea of biographies. Of writing a book, not on one writer, but on many . . . Interweaving the question of how to build one's life (art as an act) with the epoch, with history . . . I feel that a book like this, oriented toward *people*, is necessary historically as well as for me personally—at the same time that it is work, it is also an act.[142]

Eikhenbaum articulates a commitment: to "build one's life . . . with history," to perform "acts" which are "oriented towards *people*." This stance is not in conflict with the OPOIAZ poetics of performance which I have described in this chapter. Levchenko's final assessment of Formalism affirms this: "The radicalism of Petersburg Formalism results from the fact that literature was understood not as an object of study, but as a specific means of existence [*sposob sobstvennogo sushchestvovaniia*] which was, in addition, an object of study."[143] To see the author as a performer is to see authorship as only conceivable in the context of a real, socially specific audience. Shklovsky goes further to stress that the performer needs not only an audience, but also a society of fellow creator-performers from whom she can learn the craft. This position was, in turn, a product of the Formalists' belonging to the ethos of their own milieu. Their study of the rhetorical impact of poetic devices, and their promotion of a theory of authorship as collective creativity, were part of the dialogue which accompanied the Russian revolutions and the Civil War.

The Psychology of Poetic Form

FOR ALEXANDER VESELOVSKY individual crea-
tivity was a mystery, a subject which was ultimately inaccessible to scholarship. In the conclusion of an 1886 essay he writes:

> The process of individual creation is "covered by a veil, whom no one has
> ever raised or will raise" (Spielhagen); but we can define more accurately its
> *boundaries*, by following the centuries-long history of literary developments
> and by trying to clarify its internal lawfulness [*zakonnost'*] which limits indi-
> vidual achievement, even that of a genius.[1]

Veselovsky relied on a Hegelian philosophy of history as the ultimate source
of these "laws." For instance, when discussing the conditions necessary for
the emergence of *national* epics in medieval Europe, he stresses the stage of
self-consciousness that a society has reached. Even if a people (such as the
Russians) had an epic poetic tradition available, without a consciousness of
a national-political unity, there could be no national epic such as the French
chansons de geste.[2] Thus Veselovsky's "laws" that limit individual achievement are not derived from the reservoir of verbal devices (*predanie*) alone.
The Formalists developed their literary theory in a period when there was
no single, clear orthodoxy regarding a philosophy of history. They emerged
committed to continuing the scholarly work of comparative poetics, but they
did not inherit a philosophy for explaining apparent patterns in literary history. In the late 1920s, Tynianov and Jakobson famously argued that the lawfulness of literary history is a product of the systemic nature of language and
literature. However, this was not the only explanation that Formalism proposed. In this chapter and the next (chapter 4), I describe efforts to account
for regularities in the history of literature by referring to extraliterary forces.
This chapter focuses on the Formalists' recourse to psychology—their efforts
to lift the "veil" covering individual creativity.

A commonplace in the reception of Russian Formalism is that it was an
"anti-psychological" movement.[3] However, this is an overgeneralization. At

the turn of the century, psychology was the master discipline against which the emerging disciplines of linguistics, sociology, and literary studies fought to disentangle themselves. One tactic employed in this struggle was to define psychology in narrow terms. When the Russian Formalists rejected "psychological" approaches to literature, they did so by identifying psychology with the study of a biography. For example, Shklovsky wrote in 1924:

> There is no point in getting carried away with the biography of the artist. He writes first and looks for motivations later. And least of all should one get carried away with psychoanalysis. Psychoanalysis studies the psychological traumas of one person, while in truth, an author never writes alone. A school of writers writes through him. A whole age.[4]

Yet a year earlier, in his *Sentimental Journey* (*Sentimental'noe puteshestvie*, 1923), Shklovsky also wrote: "I'm not a socialist, I'm a Freudian [*freidovets*]!"[5] Shklovsky thus sees himself as a "Freudian" in some sense but rejects "psychoanalysis" as the study of the personal or biographical. So, what kind of psychology did he consider relevant for understanding literature?

In *The Sources of Russian Formalism: The Tradition of Psychologism and the Formal School*, Ilona Svetlikova reveals the importance of nineteenth-century psychology for the Formalists' thinking and describes how Brik, Tynianov, Shklovsky, and Jakobson relied on ideas from British associationist psychology. This field provided a theory of mental structure which underpinned some of the most significant Formalist contributions, such as Shklovsky's concept of *ostranenie*, Jakobson's articulations of the "metaphoric" and "metonymic" modes of thought, and Tynianov's first "law of verse": "the unity and compactness of the verse series" (*edinstvo i tesnota stikhovogo riada*).[6]

Associationism was linked to empiricism, and sought to explain the mind as a product of an individual's lived, sensory experiences. Associationists argue that there is only one innate mental process: the ability to associate "ideas." Following David Hume, associationism has focused on three basic principles of association: resemblance, contiguity in time and place, and causation.[7] Associationism was the dominant theory in psychology in the last third of the nineteenth century. The view that ideas are ordered in the mind according to laws of association found expression, for example, in James Frazier's opposition between sympathetic and contagious magic in *The Golden Bough* (1890), and in Sigmund Freud's principles of displacement and identification articulated in his *Interpretation of Dreams* (1899).[8] The principal difference between Freud's psychology and associationism is that the latter, following John Locke, posits that the individual mind is initially a tabula rasa, while Freud developed a complex theory of innate mental structure.[9]

VESELOVSKY AND PSYCHOLOGICAL PARALLELISM

Veselovsky's writings provide great insight into how Russian philologists understood the relationship between language and the mind at the turn of the twentieth century. In "The Definition of Poetry" he described his work on the history of poetic language in psychological terms: "In the sphere of poetry I am interested in the association [*assotsiatsiia*] of images with images, the reasons for their attraction [*pritiazhenie*] to each other and the laws governing the latter." He views the evolution of social thought as an increasingly complex accumulation of "ready-made associations" (*gotovye assotsiatsii*). Veselovsky describes this process: "Associations of sounds, colors, and images . . . are primary [*pervichnyi*]; precisely this simplest association of images among themselves is the source of symbol and metaphor, just as allegory—the conscious extension of a comparison to a series of facts—reveals the workings of reason or intelligence." As an illustration, Veselovsky cites an example from Potebnia's research on Ukrainian folk songs: "The horns will play, like thunder from the sky, / The swords will flash, like lighting in the sky, / The arrows will shoot, like light rain" ("Zaigraiut trubi, iak grim na nebi, / Blisnut mechemi, iak mol'nia v nebi, / Puste strilochki, iak droben doshchik").[10] Veselovsky then explains how the primary "convergence" (*sblizhenie*) between the noise of thunder and the noise of battle becomes the basis for an expanding, collectively shared network of associations:

> The understanding of battle is transferred to summer thunderstorms, the rumble of thunder to the rumble of battle or a feast; from here new convergences: battle with a feast, with the brewing of beer. . . . In each case the starting point is the association of two images, but each image carries along, by contiguity, other images; what results is two parallel series of facts [*parallel'nye riady faktov*], which in turn interpenetrate and create the possibility for new associations.[11]

This outline for the evolution of poetic imagery reveals how Russian scholars at the turn of the twentieth century understood the articulation of social thought in language: it was assumed to be based on the continual, gradual evolution of ideas, developing in complexity and abstraction through a cumulative process of associative connections. Tracing this process allowed Veselovsky to "follow the personal moment in the creation of ready-made, elemental materials for convergence [*materialy sblizheniia*], for the artist associates not just his own impressions, but also ready-made associations. At this point the freedom of imagination borders on its history, on what we call poetic tradition."[12]

Veselovsky, along with Potebnia, sought to uncover the mechanisms of this process by studying the poetic tradition (*predanie*); this was understood as the communal repository of formally recognizable symbols and images, which accrue in an expanding and changing network of meanings over generations. In "The Language of Poetry and Language of Prose" ("Iazyk poezii i iazyk prozy"), Veselovsky described how the history of poetic language can provide a key to uncovering the evolving associative chains that comprise social thought:

> The fact is that poetic language is made up of formulas, which over a certain period of time evoked certain groups of imagistic associations, either positive ones or associations by contrast . . . This is the work of centuries-old tradition [*predanie*], unconsciously established conventions, and, in relation to a particular individual, of training and habits. Outside of established linguistic forms one cannot express thought, thus rare innovations in the sphere of poetic phraseology are composed within its existing frames.[13]

When described in broad strokes, this associationist view of the history of language and thought can seem hopelessly vast and complex. This complexity is evoked by Shklovsky: "The word in poetry is not just a word. It draws in its wake dozens and thousands of associations. It is permeated with them just as the Petersburg air during a blizzard is permeated with snow."[14] Yet, despite the apparent immensity of this "blizzard" of associations, Veselovsky and the Formalists turned to the laws of association to study the fundamental properties of poetic language. They did this by focusing more narrowly on a basic manifestation of the "law of similarity": parallelism. The laws of association (i.e., similarity, contiguity) are mental processes. Parallelism is the formal manifestation of mental similarity associations in language.

Veselovsky made the connection between psychology and verbal form explicit in his term for the phenomenon: "psychological parallelism." Each of the original leaders of Russian Formalism—Brik, Shklovsky, and Jakobson—staked out his understanding of verbal art in dialogue with Veselovsky on this very point.[15] Veselovsky's central study on this subject was "Psychological Parallelism and Its Forms in the Reflection of Poetic Style" ("Psikhologicheskii parallelizm i ego formy v otrazheniiakh poeticheskogo stilia," 1898).[16] A basic definition of poetic parallelism is: the expression of the same idea in different verbal forms in two contiguous lines of verse.[17] For example, a parallelism from a Serbian oral epic: "Without the fated hour there is no dying, / From the fated hour there is no flying" ("Bez eđelja nema umiranja, Od eđelja nema zaviranja").[18] Parallelism is a formal device found in various genres and traditions, most notably in ancient Hebrew poetry and Chinese verse, as well as Finnish, Turkic, and Slavic folk poetry.[19] In his study of specifically *psychological* parallelism, Veselovsky focused on parallels that juxtapose man and nature. Typical examples for him include: "green little birch, why are you white, not green? / Pretty little girl, why are you sad, not gay?" ("zelenaia berezon'ka, chemu bela, ne zelena? / krasna dzevochka, chemu smutna ne vesela?") or "Oh maple green, don't you rustle at me, / O my dear, dark-browed one, don't get angry at me" ("Oi iavore zelenen'kii, ne shumi zh na mene / a ti milii, chernobrivii, ne svaris' na mene").[20]

Veselovsky privileges these human-nature parallels because he believes they reflect the *origins* of poetic language. He relies here on the work of the English anthropologist Edward Burnett Tylor, who proposed that "animism" is the universal starting point for all human religions. Veselovsky uses this idea to explain the "source" of what he calls "poetic" or "lyrical" language:

> This source is the animism, or anthropomorphism, anthropopathism—call it what you will—of the ancient worldview. That is, man transposes his "I" onto nature, especially onto those objects which match his form of life; all of nature seems to be somehow alive. Anthropomorphism indicates the equivalence between natural and human life; it would appear that man does not set boundaries, does not distinguish himself from nature. This is the beginning of the entire development [of poetic language].[21]

This "psychological" fact underlies the parallels cited above (e.g., *zelenaia berezon'ka*). Veselovsky explains: "At hand is not the *identification* of human life with nature and not *comparison*, presuming a consciousness of the separateness of the compared objects, but their juxtaposition [*sopostavlenie*] according to a characteristic action or movement: the tree sways [*khilitsia*], the girl bows—as in the Belorussian song."[22] At the basis of parallelism is a similarity association based on similarities of "action."

Matching the universalism of Tylor's animism, Veselovsky finds psychological parallels in a wide variety of folkloric traditions. In "Psychological Parallelism" he provides not only East, South, and West Slavic examples, but also evidence from Lithuanian, Latvian, Italian, French, Spanish, German, Georgian, Tartar, Bashkirian, Chuvash, Turkish, Arabic, Prakrit, Chinese, and Polynesian folklore. He concludes: "I have selected these examples from everywhere, perhaps in a manner that is not sufficiently broad or uniform, but I think that in my selection they give a sense of the commonality [*obshchnost'*] of the device [*priem*]."[23] He convinced the Formalists at least, whose writings assume that psychological parallelism is a universal phenomenon. For Veselovsky, its universality derives from the premise that *animism* is a universal, early stage of human social thought. The Formalists disputed the connection with animism, instead replacing Veselovsky's anthropological psychology with a psychological foundation that is not tied to an argument about the origins of poetry in the distant past.

The most critical aspect of Veselovsky's study for subsequent Formalist theory was his emphasis on psychological over formal parallelism. His statement on this became *the* point of departure for Russian Formalist theory:

I will start with the simplest form of folk-poetic parallelism, with (1) *two-part parallelism*. Its general type is the following: a picture of nature, and next to it a similar picture of human life; they repeat each other despite the difference in objective content. Between them there is consonance, explaining what they have in common. This sharply distinguishes [*rezko otdeliaet*] a psychological parallel from repetitions that can be explained by the mechanism of their performance in song (choral or amoebaean). Psychological parallels are also different from tautological formulas in which one line of verse repeats in other words the content of the preceding line or lines: rhythmic parallelism, known in Jewish or Chinese poetry, as well as in the folk epics of the Finns, Native Americans, and others. For example, from the "Edda":

> The sun did not know, where was its peace,
> [*Sòl þat ne vissi hvar hon sali átti*]
> The moon did not know, where was its power,
> [*Máni þat ne vissi hvat hon megins átti*]

Or the schema of four-line stanzas typical in the poetry of the skalds:
> (Such-and-such) a king unfurled his banner,
> He bloodied his sword (in such-and-such a place),
> He sent his foes fleeing,
> They (such-and-such foes) ran before him.
> . . . .

This kind of tautology made the image seem clearer; it is distributed over rhymed lines of the same meter, and has a musical effect. *Also, formulas of psychological parallelism, at a certain stage of degeneration* [razlozhenie], *can descend* [spustit'siia] *into a strictly musical, rhythmic effect.*[24]

In this passage, Veselovsky initially suggests a "sharp division" between psychological parallelism and formal parallelism. The former is based on mental "content"—the association of images. The latter is defined by the reoccurrence of formal (musical, rhythmic) markers. And yet, at the same time, Veselovsky opens the door for a connection between the two categories (content and form) by suggesting that psychological parallelisms can "degrade" or "descend" into formal ones. He also describes this evolution as "distortion" (*iskazhenie*).[25] This statement is a seminal moment in the history of literary theory. Veselovsky appears to have shown that a parallelism is universal and primary—rooted in psychological (and anthropological) constants. Furthermore, he suggests a connection between conceptual and formal parallelism. For him, the latter is a secondary manifestation of the first: a conceptual parallel can only degrade into a formal one.

This is the point at which the Russian Formalists intervened. They argued against Veselovsky's separation of the psychological from the formal, while retaining much of his groundwork. What they sought to overturn was the relative importance of the two categories: while Veselovsky saw conceptual associations as primary, degrading into formal repetition, the Formalists would argue that conceptual and formal repetitions operate at the same time. The fact that Russian Formalism got its start in the midst of an argument over the relationship of form and content in psychological parallelism is significant: it meant that assumptions regarding the universalism of parallelism and its source in psychological laws were carried over into the foundations of their theory.

RUSSIAN FORMALISM AND
PSYCHOLOGICAL PARALLELISM

The first of the Formalists to respond to Veselovsky's argument was Osip Brik. Brik's seminal study "Sound Repetitions (Analysis of the Sound Structure of Verse)" ("Zvukovye povtory [Analiz zvukovoi struktury stikha]"), written in 1916 and published in the second OPOIAZ "collection," or *Sbornik* (1917), was a critical first step for much of subsequent Formalist theory. Brik begins in a typical, polemical Formalist fashion by attacking the idea that sound plays a "subsidiary" (*sluzhebnyi*) role in poetry and is merely a decorative, external addition to the content. His ammunition *against* this view is Veselovsky's "Psychological Parallelism." On the first page of his article, Brik cites the passage from Veselovsky's study discussed above. He highlights Veselovsky's idea that conceptual parallelism can become formal parallelism, citing Veselovsky's statement: "Conceptual [*soderzhatel'nyi*] parallelism turns into [*perekhodit v*] rhythmic parallelism; the musical moment predominates when the distinct relationships between the details of the parallel weaken." Brik responds to this claim with a bold revision: "If we take the term 'turns into' [*perekhodit v*] . . . *not as a chronological, but as a logical category*, we can conclude from the words of Prof. Veselovsky that in folk poetry one encounters, along with images, examples of musical creativity which are exclusively rhythmic-acoustic in nature."[26] Brik here lays the groundwork for Formalist work on poetic language by removing the hierarchical primacy which Veselovsky accorded to conceptual parallelism.

Brik makes his next move by analyzing a folk riddle:

> I think that the elements of imagistic [*obraznyi*] [i.e., conceptual] and acoustic creativity exist at the same time; and each individual work entails the equal action [*ravnodeistviia*] of these two different poetic aspirations.
>
> A curious example of this kind of "equal-action" can be found in the Russian folk riddle: "a black horse jumps into the fire" [*chernyi kon' prygaet v*

ogon'] (answer: poker [*kocherga*]). If one breaks the acoustic complex of "ko-cherga" into pieces: "ko," "cher," "ga," then it becomes clear that all of these pieces are found in the expression: *chernyi kon' prygaet v ogon'*, which becomes as a result not just an imagistic description of the object, but also a full paraphrase of the sounds of its appellation.[27]

The folk riddle is "curious" in that it appears to be describing the "poker" (*kocherga*) in terms of the conceptual similarities—something black in a fire—but the description also hints at the sonic side of the concept. What Brik is getting at is the idea that the mental structure of the word "poker" (*kocherga*) is a product not just of conceptual associations—connected to "fire" or "stove" by contiguity, or to "black" or "iron" by similarity—but also of associative chains based on the sonic properties of the word. From this "equal-action" of sound and meaning, Brik moves on to examples in which a sonic association will override conceptual ones. This is the domain of the pun. Brik cites (from Veselovsky) the French physiologist and psychologist Charles Richet: "The mind works in puns, and . . . memory is the art of creating puns, which lead eventually to sought-for ideas."[28] Memory is structured according to sonic associations as much as conceptual ones. The mental work that puns require can seem trivial. Let's take, for example, a riddle such as "What turns but does not move?" (milk).[29] To solve the riddle requires disassociating the ideas which cluster around "to turn" 1 (meaning "to change direction") in order to adopt the different series of ideas associated with "turn" 2 ("to go bad.") Shifting from one meaning of "turn" to the other may not seem profound, but the Russian Formalists and the Russian avant-garde viewed puns as a prime example of how art can rearrange a perceiver's mental architecture.

As Svetlikova tells us, thinkers such as Alfred Bain, William James, and Théodule Ribot viewed conceptual associations based on similarity as more creative, and those based on contiguity as more conservative. The law of contiguity, it was thought, was responsible for a wider range of mental associations; these required less mental effort and led to the formation of habits. In the domain of language, the law of contiguity results in associations between sound and meaning, as well as clichés and commonplaces. The law of similarity, on the other hand, allows for inventive mental activity based on comparison, including scientific classification and generalization.[30] This fed interest in studying how art (poetry) can create new conceptual associations. Broadly speaking, this was not a new idea, particularly if we look at the history of associationist psychology. As early as the 1770s, for instance, the English chemist Joseph Priestley argued that "the best works [of art] are those which most disturb our normal trains of association and force the mind into the active construction of new associative connections."[31] However, the

Formalists' achievement lies in their more precise and thorough investigation of this idea.

Their ambition to do this was fueled by the psychologically grounded linguistics of the late nineteenth century, exemplified by Nikolai Krushevsky. As discussed in the introduction, Krushevsky believed that all linguistic structure could be derived from the observation that "words are connected with one another directly (1) by similarity association and (2) by contiguity association." To explain how these laws work, Krushevsky described the process of language acquisition. He argued that in order to learn the Russian verb form _vedët_ ([she/he] is leading), the speaker relies on the perception of a similarity between the first part of the word (_ved-_) and other words, such as _vedësh'_ ([you] are leading) or _vedenie_ (conduct; authority). The acquisition of the second part of the word (_vedët_) is likewise enabled by knowledge of words like _idët_ ([she/he] is walking) or _nesët_ ([she/he] is carrying). These are associations of similarity based on sonic properties. The law of contiguity association results in habitual associations between items in a lexicon. These are conceptual, rather than sonic. For example, for Krushevsky, "the word _iznosit'_ [to wear out] calls forth the words _plat'e_ [dress], _obuv'_ [footwear]; the word _vnesti_ [to invest] calls forth the word _den'gi_ [money]."[32] To return to my sample pun riddle, "What turns but does not move?" the answer "milk" prompts the audience to move from a series of contiguous conceptual associations in which "turn" 1 is located, which includes "movement" or "change of direction," to a series which includes "sour smells" or "fermentation." The connection made between these two different conceptual series is created by a sonic similarity association; "turn" 1 and "turn" 2 are homonyms.

This kind of mental reordering becomes less trivial once we recall the empiricist conception of language to which associationism belonged. As Krushevsky put it: "The correspondence between the world of words and the world of ideas is the basic law of the development of language."[33] To reorder the associative relations among words is to reorder the way people think. This idea was infused with revolutionary and utopian ambitions in Russia in the 1910s and 1920s. A classic example is the montage theory of Sergei Eisenstein. Eisenstein is famous for the use of metaphoric sequences in his films, such as the shots of workers being killed juxtaposed in a "cross-montage" with the butchering of a bull in an abattoir in _Strike_ (1925). His assumption that this kind of filmmaking could change the way people think was based on an associationist language philosophy. "Though the subjects are different," Eisenstein wrote, "'butchering' is the associative link." For instance, in a 1929 essay he asked: "Now why should the cinema follow the forms of theater and painting rather than the methodology of language, which allows wholly new concepts of ideas to arise from the combination of two concrete denotations of two concrete objects?"[34] This kind of thinking about language also informed the poetic experimentation of the Russian Futurists. It arguably stands behind the Futurist slogan (also cited by the Formalists) that "once there is a new form it follows that there is a new content."[35] As Aleksei Kruchenykh argued in a 1913 manifesto, "Our new devices teach a new understanding of the world . . . the irregular structuring of a sentence (in terms of logic and word formation) generates movement and a new perception of the world."[36] Formalist work on sound structure, understood in the context of associationism, was guided by the idea that novel associations based on sound could change thought itself.

Shklovsky's description of defamiliarization relies on the idea of associative chains stored in memory; like Veselovsky and others, he calls them "series" (*riady*).[37] For example, he writes:

> In order to make an item a fact of art, it is necessary to remove it from the list of facts of life. For this it is necessary, first of all, to "shake up the thing," like Ivan the Terrible "sorted out" his minions. *It is necessary to tear the thing out of the series* [riad] *of habitual associations it belongs to*. It is necessary to turn the thing over, like a log in the fire . . . In this way the poet creates a semantic shift, he *snatches a concept from the semantic series in which it belongs and transfers it, with the help of a word (trope), to another semantic series.* This allows us to feel the novelty of the location of the item in the new series. The new word sits on the item like new clothing.[38]

Shklovsky's description of the mechanics of defamiliarization here shuttles between metaphors (referring to Ivan the Terrible, a burning log, and clothing) and the (italicized) discourse of associationist psychology. His use of metaphor appears to be an effort to demonstrate his argument through example. The idea that the work of the poet is similar to the violence of Ivan the Terrible (selection of word = selection of a minion to be purged) is an effort to describe poetic defamiliarization in a way that in itself is defamiliarizing. Jakobson also subscribed to the idea that disassociation was the aim of poetry, and that it had far-reaching, revolutionary potential. For example, in "The Newest Russian Poetry" he contrasts "everyday linguistic cerebration [*normal'noe prakticheskoe iazykovoe myshlenie*]" with both emotive and poetic language. The latter are "more revolutionary, insofar as habitual associations by contiguity [*smezhnost'*] retreat into the background."[39] In sum, what Brik accomplished with his reinterpretation of Veselovsky's psychological parallelism was to posit psychological grounds for the idea that art (e.g., poetry or film), due to the way it is produced and perceived, is inherently "revolutionary." This was a powerful idea which set the course for much of the

Formalist theory that followed: in order to understand art, one must examine both the formal manifestation of similarity associations (parallelisms) within the artwork, and the way the perceiver processes those parallelisms.

The major works of Formalist theory that appeared in the early and mid-1920s explored these processes, taking two distinct approaches: the analysis of how psychological parallelism impacts the semantics of discrete texts (i.e., the verse theory of Tynianov and Eikhenbaum); and the analysis of devices reoccurring across different works as manifestations of psychological parallelism (i.e., Shklovsky's narrative theory). The first approach focuses on the surface structure of a text and the interaction between formal features and semantics. The second uses psychology to explain the production and processing of narrative on an ostensibly pre-semantic level. Shklovsky's theory can be seen as an effort to explain narrative devices as a product of psychological-biological "drives" or "instincts."

Tynianov's development of psychological parallelism can be contrasted with those of Shklovsky and Jakobson. All three men depart from the premise that verbal art is fundamentally a product of similarity associations, manifested formally as parallelism (which Brik also called "repetition" [*povtor*]). The divide between semantic and non-semantic (psychological) theories is not clear-cut. Rather, all three theorists make arguments that appeal to psychological laws as well as to semantic meaning. However, the relative importance of these domains differs for each of them. Tynianov's contribution most relevant to this discussion is his *The Problem of Verse Language* (*Problema stikhotvornogo iazyka*, 1924). As Svetlikova has shown, Tynianov's theory of verse is deeply indebted to Herbartian psychology. However, despite his reliance on a psychological model, Tynianov's theory is overwhelmingly oriented towards the study of textual meaning within segments of discourse, defined as "unities" (*edinstva*). Tynianov initially titled his book *The Problem of Verse Semantics* (*Problema stikhovoi semantiki*), but this title was rejected by the publisher, which replaced it with *The Problem of Verse Language*.[40] Svetlikova concisely summarizes Tynianov's argument: "Verse semantics cannot be considered outside of a description of its connection with verse construction. The meaning of a word included in a line of verse [*stikh*] does not coincide with the meaning of that word outside of that line, but is changed in accordance with the principles of its construction."[41]

Tynianov's book hinges on his central claim that "*it is precisely the unity and compactness of the series which is the objective sign of rhythm.*" Rhythm for Tynianov is a property of language that emerges when it is very densely patterned; that is, when there are many repetitions of sound or stress in close succession. This creates a "boundary" around this series, which "transforms" and "isolates" it.[42] Within this boundary, associations based on sonic similarity override existing contiguity relations. Within the boundary, a word's "prosaic" meaning is weakened, and it takes on new secondary mean-ings as a result of its association by similarity with other words in the series. This process is called "lexical coloring" (*leksicheskaia okraska*). For example, Tynianov cites a stanza from Pushkin's "To F. N. Glinka":

Когда средь оргий жизни шумной	When amidst the noisy orgies of life
Меня постигнул <u>остракизм</u>,	<u>Ostracism</u> had befallen me,
Увидел я толпы безумной	I saw the reckless crowd's
Презренный, робкий <u>эгозим</u>.	Contemptible, timid <u>egotism</u>.[43]

Tynianov argues that "egoism," in Pushkin's time, would typically be perceived as a "barbarism" or "prosaicism." However, in this verse series, "egoism" is "recolored" due to its proximity and formal similarity to "ostracism," which is not a "prosaicism" but a "Greekism." As Tynianov puts it: "The 'Greek' suf-fix of the word '*ostrakism*' [ostracism] calls forth the same lexical coloring in the suffix of the word '*egoizm*' [egotism]. The entire word is thereby colored anew. From a 'prosaicism' '*egoizm*' is recolored a 'Greekism.'"[44] Tynianov's book can seen as an effort to extend Brik's observation that poetry works on the basis of the "equal-action" of sonic and conceptual similarity associations. Tynianov does this by describing verse as a succession of quasi-isolated se-mantic systems ("series"). Similarity associations within these units override habitual, conceptual associations of the individual words.

In contrast to Tynianov's theory, which relies on a semantic boundary that isolates textual segments (series), Shklovsky makes it clear that he does not want to work with the concept of the textual "whole." However, parallel-ism is still at the heart of Shklovsky's theory of verbal art. In "Plot Construc-tion" he summarizes this idea: "We see that what in prose can be designated as 'a' in art is expressed by 'A1 A' (for example, psychological parallelism). *This is the soul of all devices.*" The underlying principle for all poetic devices is thus psychological parallelism, or similarity associations. Because I will be discussing Shklovsky's work at length in the last sections of this chapter, I will limit myself here to pointing out that he used the term "device" (*priem*) to refer alternatively to psychological and to textual structure. For example, he repeatedly refers to universal principles of art using the term "device." He writes about the "device of defamiliarization" (*priem ostranenii*) or the "device of deceleration" (*priem zaderzhaniia*). The latter refers to ways that a narrative can be conceptually "slowed down"—for example, by a narrative digression from a primary plot line. In the same studies, however, Shklovsky also uses the term "device" to refer to specific motifs, such as the "device of three arrivals" (*priem trekh prikhodov*) or the "device of abduction" (*priem pokhishcheniia*).[45] Rather than assume that Shklovsky uses the term "device" indiscriminately, I would suggest that he is talking about two different orders of phenomena: the "device of three arrivals" is a means of effecting the broader psychological "device of deceleration." It might have been preferable if Shklovsky had used different terms: one for the psychological effect, and another for the formal cue. I stress that, according to Shklovsky's theory, the perceptual mode of defamiliarization *may* be cued by a formal device (e.g., the "device of three arrivals"), but there is no guarantee that this will happen. Perceptual defamiliarization, that is, the perception of a semantic shift, is a universal capacity, but it is contingent on the knowledge and expectations of the individual. Because the individual perception of novelty is not subject to generalization, Shklovsky turned to the relationship between psychological "drives" and general devices of repetition to get at the laws of verbal creativity (a point I return to).

In *Dialogues* Jakobson states: "There has been no other subject during my entire scholarly life that has captured me as persistently as have the questions of parallelism."[46] If we can say that Shklovsky gravitated to the psychological side of parallelism in his narrative theory, and Tynianov to the textual and semantic side, Jakobson's thinking is not so easily summarized. In 1919, Jakobson articulated his understanding of poetic language in terms quite close to Shklovsky's pronouncement that psychological parallelism is the "soul of all devices":

> Poetic language possesses a certain rather elementary device: the device of rapprochement [*sblizheniia*] of two units of speech. In the area of semantics, varieties of this device are: parallelism; simile—a particular case of parallelism; metamorphosis, that is, a parallelism developed in time; and metaphor, that is, a parallelism reduced to a single point. In the area of euphony, modifications of the device include: rhyme, assonance, and alliteration (or, more broadly speaking, sound repetition).[47]

Here Jakobson appears to summarize Veselovsky's contribution as modified by Brik. Poetic language is a product of the equal action of semantic (i.e., conceptual, *obraznyi*) and formal (sonic) parallelism. Jakobson lists an array of devices which he sees as "modifications" of this basic principle.

In *Dialogues*, Jakobson reports that the topic of parallelism in epic poetry was one of his earliest scholarly interests (in the 1910s), but that he was only able to fully address the topic in publication in the 1960s. He recalls that a central concern of the Moscow Linguistic Circle was the language of the Russian *bylina*, and he dwells on the impact of hearing, in 1915, Maria Krivopolenova's performance of epic verse in Moscow.[48] In 1917 he began working on a seventeenth-century narrative song, "Sorrow-Misfortune" ("Gore-zlochast'e"):

I promised to contribute an article on the subject to the forthcoming issue of the *Sbornik po teorii poeticheskogo jazyka* (*Collection on the Theory of Poetic Language*), which the OPOIAZ was preparing at the time. The issue appeared in 1919, but without my article, which I rightly considered as an immature sketch that needed extension and revision . . . I allowed this analysis of these twenty-one lines of the "Misfortune" poem to ripen for half a century before using it in my monograph on grammatical parallelism and its Russian facet, published in 1966 in the American periodical *Language*.[49]

In his 1966 publication, Jakobson returns to the passage from Veselovsky cited above. In the 1960s, he argues against Veselovsky's division of parallelism into conceptual and musical (formal) categories, by moving the discussion of parallelism into the domain of grammar.

Jakobson's concept of "grammatical parallelism" can be seen as an answer to the challenge posed by Veselovsky's "psychological parallelism": how to understand the relationship between cognitive structure (the psychological) and formal, textual structure (the parallelism). At the end of his career, Jakobson described parallelism as "a system of steady correspondences in composition and order of elements on many different levels; syntactic constructions, grammatical forms and grammatical categories, lexical synonyms and total lexical identities, and finally combinations of sounds and prosodic schemes."[50] In the oral epic tradition, for example in "Sorrow-Misfortune," the importance of parallelism is obvious. For example, the song includes the following sequence:

1. A i gore gore-gorevan'ice! . . .	1. And grief, grief—little grieving . . .
6. Ne byvat' pleshatomu kudria-vomu,	6. No way for a bald one to be curly,
7. Ne byvat' guliashchemu boga-tomu.	7. No way for an idle one to be rich.
8. Ne otrostit' dereva sukhoverk-hogo,	8. No way to grow a dead-topped tree,
9. Ne otkormit' konia sukhoparogo	9. No way to fatten a withered horse
10. Ne uteshiti ditia bez materi,	10. No way to console a child without a mother,
11. Ne skroit' atlasu bez mastera.	11. No way to cut satin without a master.
12. A gore, gore gorevan'ice,	12. And grief, grief—little grieving,[51]

We see here the repetition of entire lines of verse ("total lexical identities"), such as in a musical or poetic refrain, in lines 1 and 12, and the repetition of grammatical syntactic constructions (*ne* + infinitive *bez* + genitive noun) in lines 10 and 11. However, by delving into deeper "levels" of the text—into grammatical categories—Jakobson finds parallelisms even in texts which are not obviously structured on this principle. The best-known application was Jakobson's analysis, coauthored with Claude Lévi-Strauss, of Baudelaire's "Les Chats" (1962)—which they treat as a work profoundly structured by the principle of grammatical parallelism. In his influential critique of their approach, Michael Riffaterre argued that the perception of repetition on the order of words or phrases is categorically different from the repetition of grammatical categories; the latter can be identified by a linguist, but are not perceptible to an ordinary reader: "Constituents that cannot possibly be perceived by the reader . . . must therefore remain alien to the poetic structure."[52] For example, in Jakobson's analysis of lines 8–9 and 10–11 of the epic song cited above, he points out that "both lines of the distichs 8–9 and 10–11 exhibit an identical syntactic combination of the same morpho-logic categories. Genders are the only admitted variables, and this variation is constantly utilized."[53] For example, gender alternates in lines 8–11: "tree" in Russian is neuter, "horse" is masculine, "child" is neuter, "satin" is mascu-line. Riffaterre's point is that while any listener can perceive the repetition of the dative forms and constructions, it is less likely that a non-linguist will perceive a "constant utilization" of gender variation.

However, if we keep in mind that Jakobson is developing a theory that is not only about textual structure and semantics, but also about cognitive universals (poetic thinking), then the extension of parallelism into grammatical categories makes sense. Jakobson's grammatical parallelism can be used to support Tynianov's argument about the semantics of verse; the density of the structure can create associations within the bounds of the series (within the poem and the poem as a whole) which could be said to create seman-tic "coloring." Yet Jakobson is not only interested in the semantics of verse language. From the 1910s into his later writings, he makes it clear that he is interested in poeticity as a cognitive "function," a mode of thinking which, as he puts it, operates independently of the material to which it is applied. For example, at a meeting of the Moscow Linguistic Circle in December 1919, Jakobson spoke about the poetic and communicative functions of language. The poetic function is thought in which similarity associations predominate. It is formally repetitive and semantically redundant. The communicative function, in contrast, strives for maximum efficiency in communication.

Jakobson makes this point in the context of a utopian-sounding discus-sion of language politics and the possibility of a "universal" language which will be more efficient than existing language habits:

For us it should be clear that linguistic habits [*iazykovye navyki*] are a negative element of language in its communicative function. The life of the future language should be based on a refined linguistic pedagogy, which will fight against synonymy, equivocations, the paralyzing negative side of expression. Here we run into aesthetic arguments . . . Certainly the creation of a universal language will be possible only on the basis of a rupture with the poetic tradition. But this does not mean the end of poetry. Poetry is not at all tied to the national language, and is possible on any foundation [*na vsiakoi osnove*].[54]

For Jakobson, poetic language is not in its essence a special dialect or "language," but is the *result* of a cognitive tendency which can be applied to "any foundation."

The poetic function is a more sophisticated way of describing what Potebnia called "poetic thought." It is based on a universal mode of thinking according to similarity associations. Jakobson explored the cognitive and even neurological basis for this mode of thinking in his publications on aphasia, which he worked on from the 1940s through the 1960s.[55] His central argument was that two major types of aphasia (which affect different areas of the brain, and are referred to as Broca's aphasia and Wernicke's aphasia after the two areas of the brain impacted) correlate with the ability to make associative connections according to similarity and contiguity. The implication is that these two modes of thought (one of which is definitive of poetic thinking) are localizable in two particular areas of the brain. The psycholinguist Hugh Buckingham, in a review of Jakobson's impact on the study of aphasia, concludes that an "essentially Aristotelian theory [was] taken by the structuralist Roman Jakobson and scaffolded across the cerebral cortex. . . . In a sense, it was a major attempt to bridge the mind (functional associationism) with the lobes of the human brain."[56] Jakobson's effort to show the operation of parallelism on so many levels—from the semantic (tautology) to the cognitive (grammar), and even potentially on a neurological level—is consistent with Veselovsky's and Potebnia's assumption that "poetry" is a universal mode of thinking.

SHKLOVSKY'S NARRATIVE THEORY

While there has been an abundance of excellent recent scholarship on Shklovsky, which provides insightful historical contextualizations and interpretations of his ideas, mainly *ostranenie*, much less attention has been paid to the central focus of his intellectual output: his narrative theory.[57] It appears to be largely taken for granted that Shklovsky's primary contribution to narrative theory is the distinction between *fabula* (discourse or story) and *siuzhet* (plot). I believe that this is a misunderstanding of Shklovsky's work, which may derive from the tendency to interpret Russian Formalism through the lens of subsequent theory. The distinction between *fabula* and *siuzhet* is indeed seminal, and its importance cannot be overstated for the field of structuralist (or "classical") narratology. In this field, the commonly accepted use of these terms follows Boris Tomashevsky. According to Tomashevsky, "the artistically arranged distribution of events in a work is called the *plot* [*siuzhet*] of the work," while "the totality of these events in their internal [i.e., causal] relationship we call the *story* [*fabula*]."[58] The distinction can be paraphrased as that between the order of the events as presented in a narrative text (*siuzhet*) and their chronological order as constructed in the mind of a reader (*fabula*). Shklovsky's narrative theory does not dwell on this distinction; he only mentions the terms in passing, in his essay on Sterne.[59] Moreover, the logic behind this contrast between *fabula* and *siuzhet* places much significance on the particular textual detail of a narrative; it is the specific order in which events appear on the page that is definitive for the structuralist understanding of *siuzhet*. I have argued (in chapter 2) that Shklovsky treats narrative texts as essentially open-ended and malleable, and that he explicitly dismisses the view of texts as stable, inviolable wholes. This disregard for the specificity of textual detail, for narrative surface structure, is incompatible with the structuralist definition of *siuzhet*.

By contrast, Shklovsky constantly uses the terms "deceleration," "stepped construction," and "parallelism." In "The Relationship between Devices of Plot Construction and General Devices of Style," he devotes several pages to Veselovsky's differentiation between psychological and formal parallelism. Shklovsky engages with Veselovsky in a subsection of this essay titled "Stepped Construction and Deceleration" ("Stupen'chatoe stroenie i zaderzhanie"). Shklovsky proceeds by providing examples of different kinds of repetition (*povtor, povtorenie*), including the use of paired synonyms in folkloric discourse, for example, *vishenka-chereshenka* (cherry-sweet cherry), *velela-kazala* (she ordered-she commanded), and *gorit-kuritsia* (it burns-it smokes); the repetition of entire episodes in folktales; and Gogol's and Pushkin's use of synonyms. He concludes that all of these examples should be considered together as evidence of a single underlying rule: "Form creates its own content."[60] To elaborate, Shklovsky summarizes Veselovsky's "Psychological Parallelism," and concludes with Veselovsky's suggestion that psychological parallels can over time become formal ones. This is the same point to which both Brik (in 1917) and Jakobson (in 1966) responded. Here is Shklovsky:

> Thus even Veselovsky admits, if not a relationship between, then a gravitation of these two kinds of construction towards each other [i.e., between psycho-

logical and formal parallelism]. They contain the total unique gait [*postup'*] of poetry. In both cases, what is expressed is the need to slow down the imagistic mass, to create from it a series of original steps [*stupeni*]. In one case, for the creation of steps, what is used is the non-equivalence [*nesovpadenie*] of images, and in the other case a linguistic-formal [*slovesno-formal'noe*] non-equivalence.[61]

As for Veselovsky and Brik, the terms "image" or "imagistic" (*obraz, obraznyi*) can be understood to refer to the conceptual or semantic content of language, and these are opposed to "formal" or "musical" (sonic) repetitions. Shklovsky wants to discuss both semantic and formal repetition together, as manifestations of a single underlying principle: the need to "slow down" the exposition. In order to see that the "content" (meaning) of poetic and narrative works is determined by formal principles (i.e., "form creates . . . content"), Shklovsky argues that both aspects of language are determined by the same underlying rule. This is the mode of cognition that Potebnia calls "poetic thinking" and which Jakobson describes as the "poetic function." It is based on the assumption that the process of associating mental content according to principles of similarity can be described as a mode of thinking. In his writings from the early 1920s, Shklovsky sought to further explore the psychology that might support this idea.

I will start with the formal side of his narrative theory. The challenge for Shklovsky is to get from the concept of metaphor, the juxtaposition of two isolated units, to a theory which describes an extended discourse. Shklovsky's approach appears to have been inspired by Veselovsky's suggestive, unfinished fragment "Poetics of Plots" ("Poetika siuzhetov," 1913). In a discussion of plot (*siuzhet*) which would be taken up by both Shklovsky and Vladimir Propp, Veselovsky proposed that plots are made up of motifs:

> The simplest type of motif can be expressed through the formula a + b: an evil old woman dislikes a beautiful girl and assigns her a dangerous task. Every part of the formula is capable of modification: b in particular is subject to augmentation; there may be two, three (a favorite folk number) tasks or more; the epic hero meets someone on his path, but he may meet several people. *Thus the motif grows into a plot* [siuzhet] *in the way that a formula of lyric style, based on a parallelism, can expand, developing one or another of its parts.*[62]

In "Psychological Parallelism," Veselovsky had described how parallelism can extend over successive lines of verse at length, and he provided numerous examples of songs in which one or both of the halves of an initial parallel are "spun out" (*razvertyvaetsia*) over the course of the song. For example, he provides the following song, recorded in the Kursk province. The song is spun out of a base parallel, which Veselovsky defines as "The falcon chooses for himself a jackdaw / Ivanushka [chooses for himself]—Avdot'iushka."[63] The song is comprised of two parts, each of about fifteen lines: the first part is about a falcon and a jackdaw: the second is about Ivanushka and Avdot'iushka. I am quoting the opening six lines, followed by the corresponding lines from the beginning of the second part of the song.

a.) Па пад небисью исмен сокол лятая,

a.) And from the sky the bright falcon flew

Сы палёту чёрных галок выбирая,

On its flight he was choosing a jackdaw,

Он выбрал сабе галушку сизуя,
Он сизуя, сизуя, маладуя.
Сизая галушка у сокола прашалась:
«Атпусти мене, исмен сокол, на волю . . . »

He chose for himself a grey jackdaw,
He a grey, grey young-one.
The grey jackdaw asked the falcon:
"Let me go free, bright falcon . . ."

b.) Па улицы, улицы шырокай,
Па улицы Иванушка праезжая,
С карагоду красных девок выбирая,

b.) And on the road, the wide road,
On the road Ivanushka was passing,
From the dance he was choosing a beautiful woman,

Он выбрал себе девушку любуя,
Ох любуя, любуя, Авдотьюшку маладуя.
Авдотьюшка у Иванушки прашалась:
«Атпусти мине, Иванушка, у гости . . . »

He chose for himself a lovely woman,
Oh lovely, lovely, Avdot'iushka, young-one.
Avdot'iushka asked Ivanushka:

"Let me go to my family, Ivanushka . . ."

To return to Veselovsky's point in "Poetics of Plots," he is saying that the way this song is created from a core parallel can serve as a model for narrative structure.

This articulation is suggestive, but it certainly leaves room for development—and this is where Shklovsky takes over. He takes up Veselovsky's suggestion that the smallest element of plot structure can be thought of as a parallelism, which can be expanded to create a longer, plotted narrative. This is the first step to elaborating a theory of narrative from the concept of metaphor. Veselovsky's associationist approach, which starts with the juxtaposition of two images according to the law of similarity (falcon and jackdaw = man and woman), extends this principle to explain the structure of a longer work. Shklovsky also tried to build a theory of narrative out of constructions that result from similarity associations between units. As he put it in the quote cited above, narrative, like poetry, is constructed out of "steps" which are related to each other according to the perception that they "repeat" each other (*povtorenie*) and are also "non-equivalent" (*nesovpadenie*). By contrast, Propp departs from Veselovsky's work by focusing on the sequence of motifs that make up a fairy tale's plot. Propp focuses on the action of a motif as its central feature, and his theory famously proposes a rule describing the order in which these actions occur in the genre of the wonder tale. The assignment of tasks, which Veselovsky refers to, for Propp becomes function 12, "the hero is tested," and what is important to him is that this function comes after the "hero leaves home" (function 11), and before "the hero acquires the use of a magical agent" (function 14).[64] Tomashevsky likewise approaches the concept of *siuzhet* from a thematic, holistic perspective. The starting point for him is the assumption that any narrative has "an idea that summarizes and unifies the verbal material in the work." From here, he distinguishes between elements of the story (motifs) which are either essential or inessential ("bound" [*sviazannyi*] versus "free" [*svobodnyi*]), based on what is needed for an acceptable paraphrase of the narrative.[65] Bound motifs include essential events, such as a kidnapping, which change the situation; free motifs include descriptions of nature, furniture, and local color, which do not.

Shklovsky's approach is more abstract, and treats narrative structure as an open-ended process.[66] Inspired by Veselovsky, he focuses on two principal ways in which parallelism is used to create a narrative plot, or what Shklovsky calls *siuzhet*. These two forms of plot construction are epitomized by folkloric genres, but are also found in complex works of written narrative. The first is what Shklovsky calls "circular construction" (*kol'tsevoe postroenie*); it is exemplified by jokes, particularly riddles and puns. The second is "stepped construction" (*stupenchatoe postroenie*); it is exemplified by epic verse, and triadic repetition in folktales. Both of these principles are based on parallelism, and on the perception of both "repetition" and "non-equivalence" between two elements in parallel. I will start with circular construction, then move on to discuss stepped construction, and conclude by showing how these inform Shklovsky's *Theory of Prose* (1925, 1929).

One of the clearest expositions of Shklovsky's narrative theory can be found in "Plot in Dostoevsky" ("Siuzet u Dostoevskogo," 1921).[67] In this essay, he describes circular plot construction using two variants of a narrative joke (one which he heard in Nikolaev, the other in Petersburg). The joke refers to the emergence of new slang terms for money and to extreme inflation:

First tale [*rasskaz*]

A customer asks the vendor at the market how much a thing costs. He replies *dve kosykh* [lit. "two slanted"]. The customer tears a thousand note slantwise and pays. There's a fight. The court decides in favor of the customer.

Second tale [*rasskaz*]

A sailor asks a vendor at the market how much a thing costs. He answers *piat' kuskov* [lit. "five pieces"]. The sailor tears a thousand note into five pieces and gives them to the vendor. A fight. The court decides in favor of the sailor.

What kind of organization of the material are we dealing with here?
1. The old name for an object.
2. The new name for an object.
3. Resolution.[68]

Shklovsky presents a narrative built on a pun; "*kosoi*" and "*kusok*" each have two meanings, a "new" meaning, which refers to a unit of currency, and an "old" meaning: "slanted" and "piece." The circular plots juxtapose the new and old meanings, creating a conflict. Shklovsky's approach contrasts with narrative theories which stipulate that narratives are about characters in conflict with each other. While the joke does refer to a fight and a trial, Shklovsky is interested in the conflict between two meanings.

The joke epitomizes "circular construction." As Shklovsky explains, "At the basis of 'circular construction' there is usually a 'task/problem' [*zadacha*], 'question,' 'choice.'" Shklovsky is particularly interested in the moment of realization experienced by the reader/audience when the question is solved. He described this as "the unexpected . . . 'equivalence' of two unequal quantities."[69] To take our example of the riddle "What turns but does not move? (milk)," the circular aspect that interests Shklovsky is the perceptual connection created by the sonic similarity between "turn" 1 and "turn" 2. He seems to envision a perceptual closing of a loop, which creates an "equivalence" between two disparate series of associations: for example, directional movement and fermentation.

Stepped construction is Shklovsky's other principle of narrative construction: "Stepped construction is based on incomplete repetition." Unlike the circular riddle, a parallel which needs only two phrases to work, stepped structure allows for the limitless expansion of a narrative. His examples are from what Veselovsky called tautological or rhythmic parallelism in epic verse, such as the *bylina* about Ilya Muromets. In figure 3.1, I have arranged eight lines of the epic in a step-like fashion to illustrate Shklovsky's point:[70]

Выезжая Илья на высок бугор,
    на высок бугор на раскатистый,
            расставлял шатер-полы белые,
            расставя шатер, стал огонь сечи,
                    высеча огонь, стал раскладывать,
                    разложа огонь, стал кашу варить,
                            сваря кашу, расхлебывать
                                    расхлебал кашу...

Ilya rode onto a high hill,
    onto a high hill rolling,
            he set up the white tents,
        after he set up the tents, he began cutting firewood,
            after he cut up the firewood, he built a fire,
                after he built the fire, he started to cook kasha,
                    after he cooked up the kasha, he started to eat it,
                        after he ate up the kasha...

Stepped construction in epic verse.

Each new line, or piece, of narrative partially repeats the previous one, while adding something new. Shklovsky describes parallelism as a means of making an object "perceptible." To demonstrate, Shklovsky refers to the lyrics of a popular song of the Civil War period:

> A thing doubles and trebles through its reflections and oppositions.
>   Oh, little apple where are you rolling?
>   Oh, mama I want to get married—sings a Rostov tramp . . . Here are given two concepts, completely non-equivalent, but dislocating each other from a series of habitual associations.[71]

Shklovsky here reiterates his cardinal principle of art: the "a" in prose becomes "A1, A" in poetry. A single idea (a woman wants to marry) is doubled (apple rolling = woman leaving home). This allows Shklovsky's principle of defamiliarization to serve as the core process which produces narrative structure. He concludes his discussion of circular and stepped construction with the following summary:

> "Stepped construction" is based on incomplete repetition, "ring" construction on the unexpectedness of the "equivalence" of two unequal quantities. Ring construction in its pure form is found only in jokes [anekdoty]. Usually it is interlaced with stepped construction. In fairy tales the ring type is usual, but fairy tale repetition [obriadnost'] (for example, triadic repetition of episodes) is a phenomenon of stepped composition.[72]

In sum, then, parallels can be used to create beginnings and endings, and to fill out the narrative in steps between these end points.

These two principles are taken in their "pure form" from oral, folkloric genres such as the riddle, the epic song, and the folktale. However, Shklovsky aimed to show that the principles also underlie the structure of a much wider range of narrative. The essays in his *Theory of Prose* follow a progressive order, moving from shorter, oral genres to longer, written ones. He starts with defamiliarization, which is paradigmatically represented by the genre of the riddle (his chapter 1). He then moves to discuss (chapter 2) the elementary mechanism of plot construction: parallelism as a means of "deceleration," demonstrated largely on the basis of folktales and medieval or oral epic narratives. The third chapter concludes that individual novellas can be "strung together" to create longer works, while chapter 4 argues that the novel *Don Quixote* exemplifies this stringing technique. Chapters 5 and 6 return to circular (joke- or riddle-based) construction, as seen in the mystery novella and Dickens's mystery novels. Shklovsky extends his theory to seemingly unorthodox narrative compositions in chapters 7 (*Tristram Shandy*) and 8 (Rozanov's "plotless" fiction). He argues that even these works operate with the same basic principles of circular and stepped construction.[73]

Extending principles from folkloric genres to written literature is often accomplished by making a more abstract or general argument. Shklovsky analyzes Tolstoy's early story "Three Deaths," which describes the deaths of a noblewoman, a peasant, and a tree, as a straightforward example of the use of stepped construction. A more abstract example of stepped construction is Tolstoy's development of characters as parallels, such as: Napoleon = Kutuzov, or Anna/Vronsky = Levin/Kitty. Shklovsky also suggests that in *War and Peace* the three Rostov siblings can be seen as the "spinning-out [*razvertyvanie*] of a single type." Shklovsky stresses that stepped construction can be applied indefinitely, as he writes: "I have noted the stepped type of accumulation of motifs [*motivy*]. These accumulations are in essence endless, just as the adventure novels constructed on them are endless. This is the source of all the countless tomes of Rocambole, as well as the 'Ten Years Later' and 'Twenty Years Later' of Alexander Dumas."[74]

To get at circular construction, Shklovsky asks: "What is necessary for a novella so that it is perceived [*osoznat'sia*] as something finished?" He answers, "This finished-ness comes from the fact that we have at first a false recognition [*uznavanie*], followed by a revelation of the real state of things."[75] Shklovsky here is referring to what is known from Aristotle's *Poetics* as tragic anagnorisis; the revelation that things are not what they seemed to be. This is also the structure of riddles, as Aristotle also recognized.[76] Building on this, Shklovsky uses Chekhov's stories as an example of this principle in literary fiction. Chekhov's stories often use, Shklovsky argues, the device of "error" (*oshibka*) followed by the "recognition" (*uznavanie*) of the original error. As an example, he refers to Chekhov's story "The Bathhouse" ("Bania"). The story is set in a bathhouse in prerevolutionary Russia during Lent. A barber, seeing a man with long hair whispering under his breath, assumes that he is a nihilist and insults him. It turns out that he is a priest. Shklovsky reduces the story to the following: "Given: both priests and socialists have long hair. It is necessary to confuse them. Motivation—a bathhouse."[77] The plot can also be cast as a riddle: Who has long hair and mutters but is not a nihilist? (A priest). This is what Shklovsky described as circular construction, a plot that is based on the "unexpectedness of the 'equivalence' of two unequal quantities."

In sum, Shklovsky established two basic principles of plot construction in his writings from the late 1910s and early 1920s. Both are based on parallelism, which Osip Brik and Roman Jakobson argued was the foundation for poetic language. Parallelisms are based on a similarity association between two units, but also allow for the perception of their non-equivalence. This relationship was described by Shklovsky as repetition (*povtorenie*) and non-equivalence (*nesovpadenie*). Defamiliarization is achieved by creating unexpected parallels; a narrative gains depth from developing an idea in "steps." This can defamiliarize the object described, as in Tolstoy's "Three Deaths," in which a similarity association is prompted between a woman's death and the death of a tree. Recognizing the similarity between two items which are unexpectedly shown to be in a parallel relationship allows for a satisfying sense of closure—termed "circular" construction.

SHKLOVSKY'S PSYCHOLOGY OF NARRATIVE

In his narrative theory, Shklovsky often refers to forward-directed pressure and counter-pressure; he uses the terms "pressure" (*davlenie*) and "deceleration" (*zaderzhanie*). He describes ring construction as a source of pressure, and stepped construction as a means of decelerating this pressure. In "Plot in Dostoevsky," Shklovsky uses the image of a car tire metaphorically to describe the pressure created by circular plot construction:

> Ring structure seeks closure; it has a tendency to quickness. The ring is elastic. The material that spins out the plot [*razvertyvaiushchii siuzhet*] (for example, descriptions of everyday life, psychological analyses) slows down the action. The naive reader feels this and often skips these parts. This material is under pressure from the plot [*pod davleniem siuzheta*] in the way that a wheel [*koleso*] feels the pressure of the steel after a tire, put on heated, cools down.[78]

Shklovsky elsewhere writes that the riddle, as a device used by Dickens, creates "pressure," "squeezing" the material interpolated into the plot: "The compositional role of these unfolding chapters [*razvertyvaiushchie glavy*] is deceleration. If we consider them to be central, then we must point out that, *having fallen into the grip of the riddle* [v tiski zagadki], *they feel the pressure of the plot* [davlenie siuzheta]."[79] How are we to understand this idea? It seems that Shklovsky views the riddle in particular as a plot device that creates "pressure." He describes this as a tendency for the plot to "seek closure," or as the reader's tendency to hasten to the end; the "naive," plot-oriented reader skips the parts that delay the desired ending, the closing of the circle.[80]

Shklovsky's references to the psychological "pressure" created by the riddle can be understood in the context of the popularity of Freudian ideas in Russia in the 1910s and 1920s. As Alexander Etkind and Martin Miller have documented, Freudian psychoanalytic theory was well known in Russia at the time when Shklovsky was working on his theory of prose.[81] The systematic translation of Freud's writings into Russian began in 1909, at which point his fame spread rapidly. There was a Russian journal dedicated to the subject, *Psychotherapy* (*Psikhoterapiia,* 1910–14), the only such journal outside of Freud's own *Jahrbuch für psychoanalytische und psychopathologische Forschungen* at the time. There was also a Russian Psychoanalytic Society (1922–27), independent psychiatric clinics, and even a state-run State Psychoanalytic Institute, which operated from 1923 to 1925.[82]

Given this Freudian context, it is possible that Shklovsky's "pressure" (*davlenie*) was inspired by Freud's theory of "instincts" (*Triebe*). Freud's account of instincts or drives explains how an infant develops into a conscious, socialized adult. The most primal instincts, self-preservative and sexual, Freud argued, are subject to "vicissitudes" which inhibit, deflect, or delay those instincts' aims, thus allowing the individual to break their compulsion and transform his own nature. Freud's essay "Instincts and Their Vicissitudes" ("Triebe und Triebschicksale," 1915) lists the following psychological means of transforming an instinct: "reversal into its opposite, turning round upon the subject, repression, sublimation."[83] Freud's earliest theories treated human psychology as a natural science, applying principles of thermodynamics to the study of the nervous system.[84] Although he moved away from this approach, he continued to be influenced by physics in that he retained a scientific worldview "of force and counterforce, of energies involved in violent power struggles."[85] Psychic "energy," for Freud, had its source in somatic, instinctual drives, and he defined these "in terms of a determining force which gives the life process a definite 'direction' [*Richtung*]."[86] This basic dynamic of Freud's psychology appears to be compatible with Shklovsky's approach to narrative.

However, any analogy between Shklovsky and Freud must be made cautiously. Shklovsky was writing in the early 1920s—and it is not clear how much of Freud's writings were known to him, or how they were understood. What is more, Shklovsky was not interested, as Freud was, in the *interpre-*

tation of (dream) narratives or their symbolic meaning, but rather in the generation of narrative. For this reason, there is surprisingly little overlap between Shklovsky's Freudian narrative theory and Peter Brooks's *Reading for the Plot* (1984). Brooks shares with Shklovsky an interest in describing the "reading of plot as a form of desire that carries us forward, onward, through the text."[87] However, Brooks often bases his arguments on interpretive analysis of the worlds depicted in fiction. Shklovsky is instead interested in an erotically grounded, theoretical poetics. If we recall Shklovsky's rejection of psychoanalysis as the useless study of "the psychological traumas of one person," we can conclude that he had little interest in the hermeneutic dimension of Freudian theory. So, while there are aspects of Freudian psychology that are critical to understanding Shklovsky's narrative theory, it would be a mistake to think of Shklovsky as a "Freudian" in the usual sense of the term.

The central point of overlap between Freud and Shklovsky can be seen in their use of the Oedipal myth. Ilya Kalinin has argued that Shklovsky's theory of literary evolution as passing from "uncles to nephews" reflects Freud's interpretation of Oedipal conflict in *Hamlet*—a special case discussed in *Interpretation of Dreams* (which was translated into Russian in 1913).[88] It is instructive to consider Shklovsky's theoretical use of Oedipal narratives and erotic riddles in his writings from the late 1910s and early 1920s. In "Plot Construction," for example, he lists eight instances of Oedipal plots found in different folklore collections:

> Interesting are the different expositions—constructions allowing for the possibility for patricide and incest. For example, Iulian Milostivyi kills his sleeping father and mother who have come to visit, confusing them for his wife and a lover. Compare the parallel in the folktale "About Hunger-Want" in the Belorussian folktale from the Viatka province, "Returning from an absence, a merchant saw two young men in his wife's bed and wanted to kill them. They were his sons" in Zelenin, No. 5. Compare to Afanas'ev, No. 92 or "A Good Word" in Onchukov, No. 12 and 82, or Erlenvein, no. 16; see also V. N. Perets' "The Source of Folktales"; and A. N. Maikov's collection dedicated to V. I. Lamanskii vol. 2, 1908, pgs. 827–829.[89]

Shklovsky provides further folkloric Oedipal examples in "The Mystery Novel." The abundance of examples and bibliographic exactitude stands in contrast to Shklovsky's treatment of contemporary literature.[90]

One reason why Shklovsky might have been drawn to these tales is that Freud had demonstrated that popular narratives, such as myths or folktales, can be seen as reflecting universal psychological drives. In his analysis of *Oedipus Rex*, Freud argued that the myth at the basis of the narrative is universal: it is the story of every human being. As Freud wrote about the

Oedipus myth: "The ancient world has provided us with a legend whose far-reaching and universal power can only be understood if we grant a similar universality to the assumption from child-psychology we have just been discussing [i.e., the child's desire for the death of a same-sex parent]."[91] That is, the myth is universal because the psychology that informs it is universal. In Freud's focus on the formative traumas of childhood—the Oedipal conflict—he argued for the importance of pre-individual, universal aspects of human psychology which repeat with every generation. As Herbert Marcuse summarizes: "To Freud, the universal fate is in the instinctual drives . . . At their beginning is the experience of domination, symbolized by the primal father—the extreme Oedipus situation. It is never entirely overcome: the mature ego of the civilized person still preserves the archaic heritage of man."[92] In Formalist terms, the Oedipal plot is a reoccurring "device." The reason why it continues to reappear, over and over again in literary history, is because the universal processes of human cognition continually reproduce it.

In my view, Shklovsky is not primarily interested in the specifics of Freud's account of childhood sexuality. It would run contrary to Shklovsky's theory to suggest that he would view an Oedipal story as a representation of actual sexual desires. For Shklovsky, the Oedipal examples are important in that they suggest a connection between circular construction and somatic, biologically generated "pressure" (energies, drives). The Oedipal tale is a classic example of the error-recognition plot. It is a circular construction, like a riddle. Recall that Chekhov's story based on this kind of construction could be reduced to the parallel priest = nihilist. In one of Shklovsky's Oedipal examples, Iulian Milostivyi kills his sleeping father and mother who have come to visit, confusing them for his wife and a lover. Here, the parallel can be stated as: mother and father = wife and wife's lover. This, again, can be formulated as a riddle: She arouses sexual jealousy, who is she? (two possible answers: wife, mother).

The reception of Shklovsky's concept of defamiliarization has largely focused on his examples from Tolstoy's writings. However, in addition to quotes from *War and Peace* and "Kholstomer," Shklovsky also cites an abundance of riddles and examples of erotic defamiliarization drawn from seven different sources, primarily from collections of folklore published between 1900 and 1913.[93] In *Theory of Prose* he refers to "Art as Device" as his "chapter about erotic defamiliarization," suggesting that he viewed this "erotic" section as the chapter's essential argument.[94] Shklovsky also dwells on the erotic riddle as a fundamental plot device in his analysis of Charles Dickens's *Little Dorrit*.[95] Shklovsky begins this chapter with an overview of different types of riddles and scholarship on the subject. His central claim is that Dickens's novel is built on the same structural and psychological principles that inform the erotic folk riddle. We have already seen Shklovsky argue that the riddle, as a circular plot, is a means of providing closure for a tale. He further argues that it also creates suspense; the reader is compelled to read/listen due to the "pressure" created by this plot device.

In his chapter on Dickens, Shklovsky develops his thinking about riddles in more detail. Again arguing with Veselovsky, he writes: "*A riddle is not just a parallelism with a missing second part, but a game with the possibility of creating several parallels.*"[96] He is apparently referring to Veselovsky's analysis of the riddle in "Psychological Parallelism," where he writes that the "riddle is constructed on omissions [*vykliuchenie*]," for example, "beautiful/red [*krasna*], but not a young woman, green, but not an oak grove (carrot)."[97] Shklovsky departs from Veselovsky at this point by prioritizing what are called "catch riddles." These are riddles which suggest an obscene answer, but which catch the audience by providing a non-obscene answer. For example, "What is it that sticks out of your pajamas in the morning, strong enough to hold up a hat?" (Answer: Your head).[98] Shklovsky argues that Dickens uses this kind of riddle to organize his novel. The mysteries in *Little Dorrit*, Shklovsky argues, hint at something "more awful than that which we find." The primary instance of this is the multiple allusions to an incestuous relationship between Dorrit and her father. "This device," he asserts, "is canonical for Russian folk riddles of the type 'It hangs, swings back and forth, everyone tries to grab it,' answer—'A towel.'" He reiterates his point with a second folk narrative in which a protagonist tells a suggestive riddle. The audience thinks of the worst case possible (*podumal na khudoe delo*), but they remain silent; no one can guess. The protagonist then solves the riddle herself with a non-taboo answer, along the lines of the "towel" answer above. Shklovsky concludes, and this is his crucial point: "and so we see that the false solution is a very common element of the mystery story or novel. The false solution is the true solution [*lozhnaia razgadka—istinnaia razgadka*] and provides the technique of organizing the mystery. The moment of transition from one solution to another is the moment of the denouement. The interrelationship of the parts is the same as that in plots founded on puns."[99] What Shklovsky adds here is that the "false" solution to the riddle, the answer no one can say out loud because it is taboo, is actually the "true" solution because it provides the "pressure" that compels the reader to read, or the listener to listen. Like Freud, Shklovsky stresses that strategies for sublimating taboo desires do so by replacing them with a socially acceptable replacement.

Shklovsky's "pressure" is thus structurally equivalent to Freud's repressed instincts. Shklovsky implies that circular constructions are universal because they engage somatic (sexual) energy in a way that allows for its partial release, while socializing it by diverting and forestalling it. Shklovsky is particularly interested in circular plot constructions that allow repressed desire to be *partially* fulfilled. The unspeakable suspicion on the reader's part that the answer to the riddle/mystery will fulfill a taboo desire is like the compromise between the repressed desires and consciousness that Freud sees in the act of dreaming. Shklovsky's understanding of circular construction can seem overly deterministic, arguing for the necessity of repression and the triumph of the status quo. Yet, this is balanced by Shklovsky's other central device of plot structure, stepped construction, which is more open-ended.

As we have seen, Shklovsky argued with Veselovsky's separation of "conceptual" (*soderzhatelnyi*) from "formal" parallelism. He did this by subsuming both kinds of parallelism to a single, more fundamental "device"— that of "deceleration" (*zaderzhanie*). Deceleration features everywhere in Shklovsky's narrative theory. It is the principle most commonly evoked to explain narrative structure. On a formal level, deceleration has been described as the "soul" of all devices: poetry turns "a" into "A1, A." A single concept is doubled, trebled, or, using "stepped construction," spun out in parallel steps indefinitely. Deceleration is also central to Shklovsky's "device of defamiliarization," which is a claim about perception. As Shklovsky put it in "Art as Device": "The device of art is the device of the defamiliarization of things and the device of made-difficult form, increasing the difficulty and length of perception."[100]

Stepped construction uses parallels to create forestalling complications that counter the pressure of the plot. Recall the stepped parallels in the *bylina* about Ilya Muromets. This kind of structure slows down perception, forcing the reader-listener to linger on the thing described. The psychological dimension of this structure can be compared to Freud's "vicissitudes": the mechanisms which inhibit, deflect, or delay "instinct" (i.e., repression, reversal, or sublimation). To use Freud's Oedipal conflict as an example, the child's instinctual violent feelings towards the father are sublimated into a socially acceptable outlet. These mechanisms allow children to develop from instinct-driven infants into socialized adults. Shklovsky's understanding of stepped construction also appears to view this opposition between raw instinct and narrative as a kind of socialization of instinct.

This is suggested in Shklovsky's memoiristic writings, which relate what happens when instinctual "pressure" becomes too intense—such as during his experiences of World War I and the Russian Civil War. In an article titled "Petersburg during the Blockade" ("Peterburg v blokade," 1922), Shklovsky describes the ways in which starving residents of the city adapted to a situation of extreme privation: people ate things formerly considered inedible, burned their possessions for warmth, and abandoned social norms of modesty or politeness. He describes this as a state of extreme "pressure": "When the pressure [*davlenie*] doesn't exceed a certain magnitude, then objects can change their form in a variety of ways, but when the pressure is enormous [*davlenie gromadno*], it obliterates the differences between a hardness of straw and a hardness of iron. It all takes a single form." In conjunction with this statement, Shklovsky tells the reader that sexual desire and fertility also disappeared under extreme pressure: "Men were almost completely impotent and women ceased to have their periods." All people, as he puts it, "had but one fate."[101] As we know, Shklovsky described psychological parallelism in the terms he used for defamiliarization. As he put it, "In a parallelism what is important is the lack of convergence despite similarity."[102] Both straw and iron can be described as "hard," but one is light and the other heavy. Here, Shklovsky suggests that this type of thought is impossible when there is too much "pressure"—people see only similarities. During the blockade of Petersburg, people burned anything that was flammable—books and furniture become indistinguishable from firewood. In a circumstance where survival instincts create too much pressure, he suggests, difference is obliterated and art is impossible. Shklovsky stresses the importance of stepped construction as a means of blocking or decelerating the pressure of raw instinct. It does this by revealing differences despite similarity. In the same way that Freudian theory posited that socialization is brought about by blocking and rerouting the energy of instincts, Shklovsky suggests that by forestalling instinctual pressure, artistic narrative is a product of psychological mechanisms which allow humans to create pleasure out of compulsion.[103] As he suggestively put it, the devices of narrative slow down time, creating the "torture of delayed pleasure" (*pytka zaderzhannogo naslazhdeniia*).[104]

Shklovsky's consistent sexualization of his narrative constructions may reflect the influence of Freud, who argued that all instincts can be derived from two core categories: the life instinct (Eros) and the death instinct (Thanatos). More importantly, it suggests an effort to explain these constructions by reference to drives which have a significant physiological component. Chapter 2 introduced Shklovsky's interest in the possibilities of a physiologically grounded theory of communication, which he described as a mimetic "dance of the organs of speech" between speaker and listener.[105] Shklovsky did not pursue this articulatory premise in further detail. His narrative theory did, however, attempt to describe its universal structures in terms of devices that engage and forestall psychic or somatic energies. Circular constructions (riddles) activate a flow of energy, which is experienced as "pressure." Stepped constructions decelerate this forward driving pressure; each step perpetuates while slightly diverting this force. In both cases, the pressure Shklovsky describes manifests in repetition—either as a return to the beginning of the story (making a circle), or as an immediate reiteration in the next line (as in the steps of an epic poem). The universality of the psychological premise (that any human can be described as an energy-system) is what causes the similarities observed when comparing different narratives over time and space. Shklovsky's *Theory of Prose* sets out to illuminate the "internal laws" (*vnutrennie zakony*) of literature.[106] In the final assessment, the source of these laws comes from human psychology, not from "language," i.e., formal structure or semantics, or from "literature" itself, i.e., a traditional corpus of texts or particular literary "devices" (such as the "device of abduction").

ZOO, OR LETTERS NOT ABOUT LOVE

Formalist theory emerged in a series of efforts to connect the study of poetics with the individual experience of the artistic, which is understood as a perception of novelty prompted by metaphoric thinking. Of all the Formalists, Shklovsky most insistently sought to go behind the "veil" that hides the process of individual creation and perception. He did this by turning his own experiences into literary narratives: *Sentimental Journey* (1923), *ZOO, or Letters Not about Love* (1923), *Knight's Move* (1923), *The Third Factory* (1926), and *The Hamburg Score* (1928). Jan Levchenko has argued that Shklovsky's "idée fixe" was to destroy the boundaries between criticism and literary discourse. He interprets Shklovsky's writings from the 1920s as fundamentally about a search for identity.[107] I agree with Levchenko's conclusions, but I would add that Shklovsky's collapse of theory and biography was also motivated by a desire to understand the psychological origins of literary devices. In the remainder of this chapter, I will look at his *ZOO, or Letters Not about Love*, highlighting moments where Shklovsky argues that the structuring principles of literature come from a place deeply buried in the mind of the writer (perhaps in the Freudian unconscious).

Shklovsky developed his ideas while working as a creative writing teacher in Maxim Gorky's Translators' Studio and at the Petrograd State Institute of Art History, where he taught a course called "Theory of Plot" ("Teoriia siuzheta").[108] He was also working as a creative writer himself. Shklovsky was thus in a position to enact his own literary theory. He often did this by explaining through examples—we have seen him explain defamiliarization by comparing a poet's selection of words to Ivan the Terrible's selection of minions for purging. Shklovsky's epistolary novel *ZOO, or Letters Not about Love* can be seen as an extended demonstration of how circular and stepped construction can be used to produce a work of literature. Moreover, the novel is presented as his introspective investigation of the correspondence between psychological universals and universals of narrative construction.

ZOO was written in the spring of 1923 while Shklovsky was living in Berlin. In early 1922 he had fled Russia for political reasons. In Berlin, he

watched as his SR allies were tried in Moscow in a show trial in the summer
of 1922 and initially condemned to death.[109] By 1923, when he was working
on *ZOO*, Shklovsky's cause had been defeated, but he nevertheless decided
that he would prefer to return to a Bolshevik Russia than remain abroad
as an émigré. The novel ends with a letter to the Communist Party of the
Soviet Union in which Shklovsky declares that "I want to go back to Russia . . . I raise my arm and surrender."[110] Yet the novel appears to be primarily about a romantic affair. It is made up of a fictionalized correspondence
between Shklovsky and Elsa Triolet. Elsa was the sister of Lilia Brik, the
wife of Formalist Osip Brik and Vladimir Mayakovsky's muse; Shklovsky's
literary wooing of Elsa thus can be seen as creating (a perhaps desirable)
parallel between Shklovsky and Mayakovsky. It is also perhaps significant
that Roman Jakobson was also pursuing a romantic relationship with Elsa
in the early 1920s.[111] The two Formalists' romantic competition has been
cited as one reason for their falling out around this time.[112] The premise of
ZOO is that Shklovsky is in love with Elsa, but she does not share his feelings and has forbidden him from writing her about his emotions. As a result,
Shklovsky's letters discuss primarily literary subjects, while constantly allud-
ing to the forbidden theme.

It is impossible to judge the sincerity of Shklovsky's first-person narrator in *ZOO*. Nevertheless, his literary material has been shown, in several
instances, to coincide with historical-biographical facts. Scholars have ascer-
tained that Triolet did actually write some of the letters attributed to her.
And Shklovsky's contemporaries in emigration recall that he behaved as if
he was in love with Triolet at the time—Valentina Khodasevich recalls that
Shklovsky would buy Elsa flowers, and played the part of the pining lover.[113]
The letter to the Communist Party which concludes the novel is a modified
version of one Shklovsky actually sent, a copy of which has been found in
Osip Brik's personal archive.[114] It is significant that Shklovsky used his own
real, personal experiences as the raw material with which to demonstrate
his narrative theory. This does not mean that the novel should be read as a
straightforward confession of his sincere feelings, or as a factually accurate
account of events. It does suggest, however, that Shklovsky used his own
biography as a testing ground for his psychological poetics.

Shklovsky uses circular and stepped construction to structure *ZOO*,
and notes how these constructions impact his own understanding of his experiences. The result is a narrative that is both personal and impersonal: it
details his own experiences and behavior, yet his choices are influenced by
universal laws. As we know, Shklovsky argued that a narrative plot can be
built in steps, each of which repeats part of the previous one while adding
something new. Veselovsky mentioned that rhythmic parallelism can be the
product of an "amoebaean" performance style, in which two singers alter-

nate lines or stanzas with each other. Parallelism in this case is manifest in the dialogic structure of call and response. Shklovsky utilizes this possibility by using the genre of the epistolary novel to construct a narrative which remains relatively close to the principle of stepped construction. Each letter responds to and repeats an element of the previous letter, while also introducing new material.

Structured as a dialogue between two people, the book can be described as a "game" with alternating moves. In Letter Eighteen Shklovsky writes to Triolet: "I pronounced the word 'love' and set the whole thing in motion. The game begins. And I no longer know where love ends and the book begins. The game is underway."[115] He brings his own personal experiences, and perhaps even his own feelings, to the game—but this does not make it entirely his own story. The metaphor of writing as a turn-based "game" played by two people recalls Shklovsky's description of writing as a partner "dance." As I argued in chapter 2, he understands writing as a dialogic process. This is a position, widely accepted at the time, that derives from a Humboldtian philosophy of language. Because the text is part of a dialogue, it is not the author's alone to control and direct.

ZOO is also based on Shklovsky's analysis of the riddle as the prototype for circular plot construction. The novel's preface suggests that erotic folklore provides a clue to understanding this work: "I built the book on a dispute between people of two cultures; the events mentioned in the text serve only as material for the metaphors. This is a common device in erotic things, where the series of the real is repudiated and the metaphoric series is affirmed. Cf. the *Forbidden Tales* [*Zavetnye skazki*]."[116] As we have seen, Shklovsky was particularly interested in catch riddles. In his chapter on Dickens, he uses the terms "true" (*istinnyi*) and "false" (*lozhnyi*) to refer to the two different answers for the riddle. In his preface he uses the terms "real" (*real'nyi*) and "metaphorical" (*metaforicheskii*). The genre of the catch riddle requires that the strongly suggested, "real" or "true" solution is explicitly denied by the riddler, who replaces it with a "false," "metaphoric" answer. The first solution evokes pleasurable suspense, allowing readers to entertain taboo desires. The second answer instead refers to something relatively boring. This convention helps us understand the ending of *ZOO*: the final letter, addressed to the Executive Committee of the Communist Party. This letter can be read as the riddler providing the non-erotic "answer." Shklovsky instructs his readers as to what it all means. The novel, he reports, is a plea for political mercy. He writes:

> Don't be surprised that this letter follows some letters written to a woman. I'm not getting a love affair involved in this matter. The woman I was writing to never existed. . . . Elsa is the realization of a metaphor. I invented a

woman and love in order to make a book about misunderstanding, about alien people, about an alien land. I want to go back to Russia . . . I raise my arm and surrender.[117]

At both the beginning and end of the novel, Shklovsky thus asserts that the narrative about his love for Elsa is a "metaphor," and not the "real" subject. If we read Shklovsky's frame as a circular construction, as the onset and answer to a riddle (which is spun out using stepped construction), then we can apply the rules of the catch riddle genre to interpret Shklovsky's meaning. The overt answer is that the book is about a politically expedient "surrender." Shklovsky's narrative theory suggests that this overt answer can be considered a "false" solution in the way that "towel" is not the only, or most important, answer to the pretend obscene riddle. The true answer is one that the riddle hints at but denies. Shklovsky also reiterates this denial of the erotic within the stepped construction of *ZOO*; his letters dwell on literary subjects because love is a "forbidden" topic. Reading *ZOO* in the context of these theoretical statements allows us to see that Shklovsky's narrative utilizes the "pressure" of erotic desire, decelerating it with steps (letters). It also allows for an interpretation of the novel's ending as something generically required, and not entirely "true."

Yet Shklovsky did return to Russia and "surrender" to the Bolshevik government. He suggests that this ending (literary and biographical) is to be understood as satisfying a genre requirement. This claim gains depth when we consider that Shklovsky has been arguing for the fundamental identity of narrative and psychological constraints. To return to Letter Eighteen, here is the full passage in which he describes writing as a "game":

> I am completely bewildered, Alya [Elsa]! This is the problem: I am writing letters to you, at the same time, I'm writing a book. And what's in the book and what's in life have gotten hopelessly jumbled. You recall that I wrote you about Andrei Bely and about method. Love has its own methods, its own logic—set moves established without consulting either me or us. I pronounced the word "love" and set the whole thing in motion. The game begins. And I no longer know where love ends and the book begins. The game is underway. After a hundred pages or so, I will be checkmated. The beginning is already played out. No one can change the denouement.[118]

The (purported) dialogic aspect of the novel is not the only factor which limits Shklovsky's control over the writing process. In *ZOO* he repeatedly alludes to psychological factors, which are described as a powerful determining force. Thus far, we have largely considered the concept of "pressure" in terms of the audience; the reader is compelled by a kind of "pressure" to keep reading. The majority of Shklovsky's examples suggest that he understands this pressure to be something like Freud's life instinct or Eros. He also gestures towards something like a death drive (*Todestrieb*) when he mentions being "checkmated." In an earlier letter in *ZOO* he articulates this idea using the metaphor of a car. "In art, too, method leads a life of its own. A man writing something big is like the driver whose 300-horsepower car dashes him against a wall—as if of its own volition. Drivers say that a car like that will 'do you in.'"[119] In the passage above, Shklovsky argues that the boundary between life and writing (the "book") has disappeared. His professed confusion here can be related to the fact that he traces the rules of narrative structure to the same psychological drives that govern his behavior in everyday life.[120]

Why might Shklovsky have used stepped construction (the epistolary form) and circular construction (the framing catch riddle) to narrate his decision to return to Russia? He stresses that both constructions limit his authorial agency. The novel is a reflection on the ideas about art that Shklovsky described in *Knight's Move* using the metaphor of the L-shaped move of the chess piece. That book began with the statement: "There are many reasons for the oddness of the knight's move, and the most important of these is the conventionality of art . . . The second reason is that the knight is not free [*ne svoboden*]—he moves sideways because he is not allowed to take the straight road."[121] The two main "reasons" (*prichiny*) for the knight's L-shaped movement are also the two main reasons why Shklovsky returns to Russia. There is the conventionality of art, and then there is outright constraint, "un-freedom." The source of this un-freedom is, Shklovsky seems to be arguing, not political, but psychological. His interest in constraint is referenced in the first half-book's title, *ZOO*, and is thematically explored in passages where Shklovsky describes the caged lifestyle of Russian émigrés in Berlin. They are not free in Russia, nor are they free in Germany. This conclusion is backed by Shklovsky's Freudian-inspired understanding of psychology, which is considerably more deterministic than associationism. Humans are driven by powerful instincts (i.e., Eros and Thanatos), which they attempt to steer like drivers of an out-of-control car. As a human being, Shklovsky is therefore ultimately un-free regardless of where he is, due to the nature of human psychology. His "surrender" to the Bolshevik government is thus portrayed as the outcome of forces beyond his control (both psychological and narrative). To narrate his experiences in this way may appear deterministic, but it also suggests that the forces that dictate his direction can be countered by the devices that allow humans to create art, and pleasure, out of constraint.

Russian Formalist theory was, at its core, based on the assertion that poetic language is produced by a mode of thinking in which similarity associations predominate. As Jakobson put it, the essence of poetry is "bringing two elements together." Shklovsky explored this mode of thinking in terms of pressure. He describes the production of verbal art as a compulsion to build in (partially repeating) steps. For the audience, this cues an expectation of repetition. Shklovsky describes this compulsion/expectation as pressure, and it appears to be a kind of "un-freedom." However, it is also a source of defamiliarization. Repetitions based on similarity create metaphors, and possibly novel associations. The need to repeat forces the writer to create tautologies which are not complete equivalences (steps), and to equate things that are not obviously the same (circular form). This allows for the realization that a thing or concept has a "novel" or unexpected dimension to it: despite their sameness, there is difference (stepped form), or, despite their difference, there is sameness (circular form). Shklovsky describes himself as compelled to return to Russia by psychological and poetic forces beyond his control, which are reduced to the same underlying concept: pressure. He stresses that desire and narrative are in some way fundamentally the same; and according to his theory of defamiliarization, this may allow us to understand both in a new light, removed from their habitual associations.

Inside the Moscow Linguistic Circle:
Poetic Dialectology

BEFORE ROMAN JAKOBSON moved to Czechoslova-
kia in the summer of 1920, he developed a method for the study of poetics
which, like other work in the philological paradigm, traced the sources of linguistic or poetic regularities *not* to the system of language or literature itself,
but to extralinguistic social history—in this case, primarily to the migration
of individuals and language contact (that is, the mutual influence of speakers
of different varieties on the speech habits of the other).[1] This chapter exca-
vates, largely from archival records, a lost branch of Russian Formalism—a
Moscow Formalism grounded in the study of dialectology. The focus is on
the Moscow Linguistic Circle (MLC), which was founded in 1915, with
Roman Jakobson as its president, as a student group within the Moscow Dialectological Commission (Moskovskaia dialektologicheskaia komissiia). In
the late 1910s the MLC developed into the second center for Russian Formalism, collaborating intensively with OPOIAZ. Within the MLC, dialectology was used to develop not "linguistic poetics"—the field that Jakobson
would champion in the 1950s—but a distinct, *socio*linguistic poetics.

The study of dialectology at the turn of the century conformed with
the neo-Humboldtian philosophy of language: language is acquired through
individual experiences and the associationist learning process. As a result,
an individual's stored language knowledge is shaped by his or her particular
social environment. Dialectology focused on the language of the individual
(now called an "idiolect") as the only real object of study. Each idiolect is
unique. For philologists in this paradigm, such as the teachers of the Formalists, to speak of the "language" of a society or a people is to speak only
of "a combination of languages of individuals who engage in certain relations thanks to the unity of their common origin."[2] This philosophy of language predated the Russian revolutions, but it was highly amenable to revolutionary aspirations. If the forces that ensure linguistic (cultural) continuity over time are exclusively *individual* (e.g., contact and mimicry between

individuals), then the conservative nature of linguistic change over time is only a result of the conservative nature of society. A major social disruption, it follows, will precipitate dramatic language change. The MLC adopted this notion and sought to exploit it. They believed that individuals exercise considerable agency within the process of language change, and argued that linguistic innovations could be consciously developed and "decreed" in an effort to change how people think.

THE MOSCOW LINGUISTIC CIRCLE AND OPOIAZ

In practice, Russian Formalism is considered to be synonymous with OPOIAZ, while the Moscow Linguistic Circle, by contrast, remains relatively obscure. One reason for this disparity is the publication history of the two societies. OPOIAZ was, even by its own members, defined by reference to its publications, the OPOIAZ "collections" (*Sborniki po teorii poeticheskogo iazyka*).[3] The first of these appeared in 1916, followed by volume 2 in 1917, and volume 3 in 1919. The subsequent three volumes were not collections but individual monographs, by Eikhenbaum (1922), Jakobson (1923), and Bogatyrev (1923).[4] Publication became increasingly difficult as a result of the collapse of institutions and infrastructure during the Civil War. During this period the publication of the OPOIAZ *sborniki* was funded by Osip Brik. Their back cover carried the stamp "OMB"—Brik's initials.[5] The Moscow Linguistic Circle, in contrast, did not succeed in publishing its work before the society disbanded in 1923.[6] This is cited by Maksim Shapir as a primary reason for the Circle's absence from mainstream histories of literary theory. Shapir notes that the MLC

> was perhaps the most significant association of Russian linguists and literary scholars . . . The contribution of the Circle in, not only domestic but international, linguistics and poetics in the twentieth century is not comparable with any other. But the lack of their own print organs and publishing facilities, the lack of avant-garde brilliance in the organization of [its] scholarly life, and also deep internal contradictions led to the fact that the symbol of Russian Formalism became the world-famous OPOIAZ, while the main work towards creating a new philology was conducted within the MLC.[7]

Shapir's knowledge of the MLC is based on access to the society's unpublished archive, which consists largely of minutes of its meetings. OPOIAZ originated in salon-like meetings in the Briks' St. Petersburg apartment in 1916–17. It was initially a less formal society, and did not keep official records. The MLC began as an organization of students of the Historical Philological

Department at Moscow University in 1915.[8] Records in the society's archive reveal that the practice of keeping minutes was, at least in part, motivated by a desire to counteract the dearth of publishing opportunities. At a meeting on December 9, 1919, it was noted that the minutes were to be typed up and disseminated as a recompense for the fact that members of the MLC were unable to publish their work.[9]

In chapter 2 I described the overlap between OPOIAZ and the Institute of the Living Word, and argued that considering these two societies together allows for a clearer understanding of the conceptual goals of Formalist work—such as Eikhenbaum's studies of authors' (e.g., Gogol's or Akhmatova's) performance styles. In this chapter I explain Moscow Formalism by connecting the work of the MLC with that of the Moscow Dialectological Commission (MDC) as well as the Commission for Folklore Study within the Society of Devotees of Natural Science, Anthropology, and Ethnography (Komissiia po narodnoi slovesnosti pri OLEAE).[10] The Moscow Dialectological Commission was formed within the Russian Academy of Sciences in 1904 and was charged with producing a dialect map of European Russia (a preliminary map was published in 1915). Fedor Korsh (1843–1915), who was the chairman of the MDC from 1909, was to be the official sponsor of the MLC, but he died just as permission to establish the group was granted (January 3, 1915).[11] The seven founding members of the Moscow Linguistic Circle were F. N. Afremov, P. G. Bogatyrev, A. A. Buslaev (the grandson of Fyodor Buslaev), R. O. Jakobson, S. I. Ragozin, P. P. Sveshnikov, and N. F. Jakovlev. All but one (Ragozin) were also members of the MDC.[12] Of the twenty-seven additional members who joined the MLC between January 1915 and January 1920, nine were also members of the MDC.[13] Many of these young scholars also belonged to the Commission for Folklore Study. This was a society founded in October 1911 and run by V. F. Miller (president until his death in 1913, when replaced by V. A. Gordlevsky), N. V. Vasil'ev (treasurer), and E. N. Eleonskaia (secretary).[14] The scholars who belonged to both the MLC and the Folklore Commission in the years between 1915 and 1920 included P. G. Bogatyrev, A. A. Buslaev, G. G. Dinges, Y. M. Sokolov, B. V. Shergin, R. O. Jakobson, N. F. Iakovlev, and B. I. Iarkho. In sum, the core group of Moscow Formalists were students trained as both dialectologists and folklorists.[15]

It was in the context of these societies that long-lasting intellectual relationships and collaborations were established. Jakobson met Nikolai Trubetskoi (1890–1938)—with whom he would develop the principles of structuralist phonology in the 1920s and 1930s—in the Commission for Folklore Study in 1915. Trubetskoi had begun his scholarly career as a teenager interested in ethnography, initially "Russian folk poetry," but soon thereafter Finno-Ugric languages and folklore, on which he published as early as

1905.[16] He was a member of the Commission for Folklore Study, but not of either the MLC or MDC. When the two men resumed contact in 1920, after both had left Russia, Trubetskoi's first questions to Jakobson concerned their mutual acquaintances in the Commission for Folklore Study.[17] Another important collaborative relationship was that between Jakobson and Petr Bogatyrev (1893–1971). Bogatyrev was one of the founding student members of the MLC; he moved to Czechoslovakia soon after Jakobson did, and also helped found the Prague Linguistic Circle. A specialist in folklore, Bogatyrev is considered a pioneer of semiotic ethnography, and is best known for his analyses of folk theater and folk costume written in the 1930s. Jakobson and Bogatyrev were frequent collaborators, and both attended virtually every meeting of the Commission for Folklore Study between 1915 and 1917.[18] In their separate reminiscences, Bogatyrev recalls that it was Jakobson who "constantly led me to the linguists," and Jakobson recalls that it was Bogatyrev who introduced him to both the Commission for Folklore Study and the MDC.[19]

Shapir mentions "deep internal contradictions" in addition to publishing difficulties as a reason for the relative obscurity of the MLC. He is referring to a split in the society after Jakobson left Russia in 1920, described by Glants and Pil'shchikov as a divide between the "empiricists-positivists" who gathered around Jakobson and the "phenomenologists" who were led by Gustav Shpet, who joined the Circle in 1919.[20] Boris Gornung, who belonged to the latter camp, described the antagonism in 1922 as one between scholars oriented towards recent, "strictly scholarly achievements in aesthetics" and the "so-called scholarly theories . . . created by folklorists and dialectological scholars."[21] The dissolution of the Circle in 1923 resulted in the transfer of its members to the State Academy for the Scientific Study of Art (Gosudarstvennaia Akademiia Khudozhestvennykh Nauk), of which Shpet was the vice-president.[22] My focus in this chapter will be on the folklorists and dialectologists, and the efforts at a synthesis between this group and OPOIAZ.

A period of significant collaboration between OPOIAZ and the MLC began in the spring of 1919, partly prompted by the fact that Osip and Lilia Brik and Vladimir Mayakovsky moved from Petrograd to Moscow in March 1919. Mayakovsky moved into 3 Lubiansky proezd—the building where Jakobson's parents had an apartment (abandoned after the revolutions), and where Jakobson also lived before he left the Soviet Union in 1920.[23] Osip Brik played a central role in discussions between April 1919 and 1922; his voice dominates the debates in the MLC almost as much as Jakobson's.[24] During a three-year period, from spring 1919 to spring 1922, OPOIAZ founders Osip Brik and Viktor Shklovsky regularly attended meetings of the MLC and presented their research there. Bernshtein, Zhirmunsky, and

Tynianov were also members of the MLC, although Tynianov, unlike the others, did not actively participate in the activities of the Circle.[25] The years 1919 and 1920 were the peak years of operation for the MLC, during which it met as often as four times a month. A summary account for Narkompros written up by the MLC in April 1920 described its transformation:

> Although the Circle has existed for already more than 5 years, its work began to develop only after the revolution and especially during 1919. The general turn [*povorot*] in Russian life also stimulated the Circle, turning it from a quasi-legal closed student corporation into an open society of young scholars. During 1919 the Circle held more than 30 meetings.[26]

During these years the Circle emerged as a society with a strong orientation toward poetics, with meetings focused on poetic language, plot structure, versification, and literary history. The leaders of the MLC and OPOIAZ even planned a joint publication divided into two sections, each representing the respective strengths of the two institutions, to be titled "Folklore, Ethnography, and Dialectology" and "Poetics."[27]

The philological paradigm entailed certain assumptions regarding the study of "poetic language," including the idea that there are "poetic" and "prosaic" modes of thinking, and that the former can be described as thinking in metaphors or similarity associations. In chapter 3 I described the different ways this idea was developed—in the study of verse semantics (Tynianov), in grammatical parallelism (Jakobson), and in a psychologically grounded narratology (Shklovsky). While the two societies agreed on the psychological impulse for poetic language ("poetic language" is characterized by the dominance of similarity associations in its production and perception), they disagreed when it came to the more fundamental concept of what a *language* is.

In *Slavic Philology during the Years of War and Revolution* (*Slavianskaia filologiia v Rossii za gody voiny i revoliutsii*), a booklet published in Berlin in 1923, Jakobson and Bogatyrev offer one of the few published accounts of the societies' disagreements and compare the MLC's strictly linguistic approach, which was historically and sociologically grounded, with OPOIAZ theory, which was more insistent on the total "autonomy" of artistic form:

> At the same time that the Moscow Linguistic Circle starts from the position that poetry is language in its aesthetic function, the Petrograd group [i.e., OPOIAZ] argues that a poetic motif is very often not a product of the development of linguistic material. Furthermore, at the same time that the first group proves the necessity of a sociologically grounded history of the

development of artistic forms, the other insists on the complete autonomy of these forms.[28]

This passage condenses a number of different ideas and disagreements. The first opposition in the passage refers, I believe, to a dispute between Shklovsky on one side and Jakobson and Grigory Vinokur on the other; in a talk on plot construction in film, Shklovsky had discussed "non-linguistic defamiliarization" (*neiazykovoe, bytovoe ostranenie*), a concept which the Muscovites vehemently rejected.[29] The second opposition contrasts OPOIAZ "autonomy" of form with a sociologically grounded history of form. I am particularly interested in the MLC's rejection of poetic autonomy, but before turning to this I will quickly review the significance of "autonomy" for OPOIAZ theorists in the late 1910s.

The first two OPOIAZ collections, published in 1916 and 1917, were largely devoted to phonic questions, and featured programmatic articles arguing that "poetic language" qualitatively differed from "practical language." Both volumes opened with a piece by Shklovsky, followed by a more technical study by the linguist Lev Jakubinsky. Both of Jakubinsky's articles, "On the Sounds of Verse Language" ("O zvukakh stikhotvornogo iazyka") and "The Accumulation of Similar Liquid Consonants in Practical and Poetic Languages" ("Skoplenie odinakovykh plavnykh v prakticheskom i poeticheskom iazykakh"), aimed to demonstrate empirical, formal differences between the use of language in verse and in everyday speech. The second article, for example, argued that the tendency toward the dissimilation of liquid sounds is not as strictly observed in poetic language. Jakubinsky's article included suggestive statements such as: "The fate of the dissimilation of liquids in practical and poetic language shows to what extent these two linguistic systems differ."[30] This claim suggests that "poetic language" could be thought of as a separate, or "autonomous," linguistic system.[31]

Perhaps with this idea in mind, Osip Brik butted heads with Jakobson over the concept of "poetic language" when he attended his first meeting of the MLC in April 1919. Brik gave a presentation on the poetic epithet, and was voted a member of the Circle at the conclusion of the meeting. The minutes record the ensuing exchange between Jakobson and Brik:

JAKOBSON: In general one cannot think about poetic and practical language as two sharply differentiated spheres [*razgranichennye rezko oblasti*]. One can speak only of two tendencies [*tendentsii*], whose limits are antipodes [*predely koikh—antipody*].

BRIK: R[oman] O[sipovich]'s point of view sends us back to the approach of Pot[ebnia] and Ves[elovsky]. If we take this point of view, we cannot speak about poetic language but only about heightened speech, only about poetic tropes [*poeticheskie oboroty*].[32]

Brik, it appears, had been speaking about "language" (poetic or otherwise) as a "sphere" (*oblast'*) which is "bounded" (*razgranichennyi*). Jakobson, in contrast, argues that there are no such spheres, but only observed "tendencies" (*tendentsii*) within linguistic production.[33] At this point, in 1919, Brik argues that without a concept of language as a bounded sphere, one cannot speak of "poetic language." (Brik would subsequently reject this division of poetic from nonpoetic language in the 1920s.)[34] It follows that the definable boundaries of poetic language as a sphere are what allow for its autonomy. As we have seen, Jakobson and Bogatyrev state that the autonomy of artistic forms was an important concept for OPOIAZ, but was rejected by the MLC. What alternative did Jakobson and the MLC propose?

The answer to this question lies in the dialectology in which Jakobson and the other members of the MLC were trained. The Moscow Formalists sought to apply this training to the development of a "scholarly poetics," as is clear from the opening of Jakobson's study "The Newest Russian Poetry," which he presented to the MLC in May 1919 (and also in Petrograd, in 1919).[35] This work was eventually published in Prague as *The Newest Russian Poetry: Approaches to Khlebnikov* (*Noveishaia russkaia poeziia: podstupy k Khlebnikovu*, 1921). However, it was initially titled "Approaches to Khlebnikov (an Experiment in Poetic Dialectology)" ("Podstupy k Khlebnikovu [opyt poeticheskoi dialektologiia]").[36] The change in title between 1919 and 1921 does not indicate that Jakobson gave up on the "dialectological" approach. The published version includes a footnote which reiterates his claims for the legitimacy of the dialectological "method."[37]

The first section of the study calls for a new poetic method, which Jakobson calls a "poetic dialectology": "The development of a theory of poetic language will be possible only when poetry is treated as a social fact, when a kind of poetic dialectology is created. From the point of view of this dialectology, Pushkin is the center of a poetic culture of a particular time, with a definite zone of influence."[38] I will start with the obvious questions that emerge: What is a "dialect" for Jakobson? How can Pushkin be described as a dialect? The answers will clarify the implicit assumptions underlying Jakobson's disagreement with Brik.

Bogatyrev posed this very question to Jakobson in the discussion of the latter's presentation on Khlebnikov in May 1919:

Bogatyrev objects to the use of the term "dialectology" for the study of the poetic language of only one poet. This is an individual language, [while] a dialect is the language of a given class of people. It would only be possible to describe a given school of poetics using the term "dialect."

Jakobson indicated that he does not determine the boundaries of the facts [*granitsy faktov*]. And the only source for scholarship is in fact individual language. Dialect is always more or less a fiction [*fiktsiia*].[39]

In his response, Jakobson echoes a tenet of the Neogrammarian linguistics of his teachers. For example, Aleksei Shakhmatov (1864–1920) uses strikingly similar terms: "Only the language of every individual [*individuum*] has a real existence [*real'noe byt'e*]; the language of the village, the city, the region, the nation is a known scholarly fiction [*nauchnyaia fiktsiia*], for it consists of linguistic facts belonging to groups—territorial or tribal—of individuals."[40] Jakobson's thinking at this point in his career overlaps greatly with Shakhmatov's work. Not only did Shakhmatov's ideas inform the work of the MDC, but Jakobson also appears to have cultivated a personal relationship with the esteemed scholar.[41] For Shakhmatov, like others of his generation impacted by Neogrammarian linguistics, the only real object of study was the immediately observable, positive, linguistic fact. Jakobson's statement is striking for those who are more familiar with Jakobson the structuralist. One might recall, for instance, a very different statement made by Jakobson in 1953:

> Everyone, when speaking to a new person, tries, deliberately or involuntarily, to hit upon a common vocabulary: either to please or simply to be understood or, finally, to bring him out, he uses the terms of his addressee. There is no such thing as private property in language: everything is socialized. Verbal exchange, like any form of intercourse, requires at least two communicators, and *idiolect proves to be a somewhat perverse fiction.*[42]

Jakobson retains the formula that "x . . . is a fiction," while reversing his position as to whether it is idiolect or dialect that is the fiction. This 1953 statement—particularly the line that "there is no such thing as private property in language"—was cited by Roland Barthes in *Semiology* (1964) to buttress his own understanding of writing as *écriture*.[43] In the 1910s and 1920s, the Formalists were developing their thinking in a landscape where the concepts of "collective" and "individual" were being reconsidered. By the 1950s and 1960s, following the rise of structuralism, the tension between the study of language in the individual (idiolect) and the abstract *langue* of the collective was decided in favor of the latter.

The contrast between Jakobson's statements in 1919 and 1953 underscores the fact that the Formalist theory which he promoted in the 1910s was, in its epistemological foundations, quite different from the structuralist poetics for which he is known. An introductory textbook, *Dialectology* (1998), remarks that at the turn of the twentieth century "the first reaction of the dialect geographers seems to have been a profound suspicion of linguistic theorizing under almost any guise. . . . The result was that dialectology and linguistics came to have little contact with one another."[44] "Poetic dialectology" indicates a genuinely different path. Jakobson's Neogrammarian response to Bogatyrev was not a flippant, one-off statement. This position provided the epistemological foundation for Moscow Formalism, and allowed scholars to pursue a revolutionary poetic theory. (Poetic) dialectology offered a theory of language history (diachrony) by focusing on change as it occurs in the collisions between individuals' speech habits in practice. It accorded significant agency to individuals, and broad importance to the impact of particular poetic innovations on an individual's mental architecture.

INTELLECTUAL-HISTORICAL CONTEXT: DIALECTOLOGY

When Brik rejected Jakobson's position, he said that Jakobson's "point of view sends us back to the approach of Pot[ebnia] and Ves[elovsky]. If we take this point of view we cannot speak about poetic language but only about heightened speech, only about poetic tropes [*poeticheskie oboroty*]."[45] He is referring to philological research on "poetic language" (*poeticheskii iazyk* or *iazyk poezii*) as a storehouse of elements, which lack a systematic relationship among themselves. As we have seen, the philologists tended to focus on oral traditions when analyzing "poetic language," attributing their continuity to the gradual nature of social change. Veselovsky described the evolution of a poetic/literary tradition as a process of selection: "We expect an exchange of songs similar in expression and in their everyday references. Among them a selection process [*podbor*] takes place with regard to substance and style; a brighter, more expressive formula will win out over others expressing the same relationships."[46] With the passage of time, Veselovsky supposes that

> from the diversity of regional images and figures of speech [*oboroty*] in song could have begun the development, in the sense of a poetic style, of what we call a *koiné* . . . In this way, from an *exchange of dialects* [*iz obshcheniia govorov*], was formed that middle, central language which was destined, in the right historical circumstances, to become known as the literary language.[47]

Here and elsewhere Veselovsky uses the terms "poetic style," "poetic language," and "literary language" interchangeably. Jakobson was aware of Veselovsky's concept of a poetic *koiné* (equivalent to what he elsewhere described as a *predanie*). When lecturing his students in Brno about Veselovsky's "theory of a poetic *koiné*," Jakobson defined it as "the vast reservoir of conventional formal resources, ready schemas, and diverse clichés which any poet draws on."[48]

We can find a similar articulation of "poetic language" in the writings of Fedor Korsh, the chairman of the MDC and a mentor for the students in the MLC.[49] In *On Russian Folk Versification* (*O russkom narodnom stikhoslozhenii*, 1901), Korsh, like Veselovsky, describes the emergence of a "conventional poetic language" as a process that emerges from contact and selective mimicry:

> In folk poetry . . . language always appears more or less colorful and, within certain limits, changeable, as a result of the mixture [*smes'*] of dialects from different regions and eras which is continually generated by the transmission of a song from one part of the country to another and from one generation to the next. This eventually results in a conventional poetic language [*uslovnyi poeticheskii iazyk*] which, of course, is not strictly maintained, but is still fixed enough that subsequent folk poets have it in mind as a model.[50]

Korsh contrasts this folk poetic language with both "literary" (*literaturnyi*) language and the "conversational" (*razgovornyi*) language of a milieu. Korsh's name comes up repeatedly in the archival materials of the Circle, and special meetings were held to mark the fifth and sixth anniversaries of his death, in February 1920 and in March 1921.[51] In April 1919, the Circle discussed a proposal that Brik publish some of Korsh's work on versification, which Jakobson and Bogatyrev would prepare for publication.[52] This publication did not come to light, however, perhaps in part because Brik did not share the Muscovites' veneration of their mentor. When Jakobson criticized Brik's presentation on syntax and rhythm in poetry in October 1919, and exhorted him to read Korsh, Brik retorted that "as for Korsh's research on folk verse, in the final analysis his method did not lead to anything."[53]

Jakobson aimed to convince Brik otherwise, since Jakobson was committed to Korsh's approach to language study. This did not mean, however, halting the study of poetic language with the observation that, over time, people reuse the same poetic devices. When arguing for a "poetic dialectology," Jakobson meant the application of principles observed in the study of language variation and change in order to better understand the mechanisms by which traditions emerge and change over time. He sought to bring more rigor to the observations of their teachers by using the cutting edge of theory in contemporary linguistics: dialectology. Jakobson extolled dialectology as the "avant-garde" of linguistics as late as 1929—a claim that Jindřich Toman has described as oddly "anachronistic," in that linguists had been advocating dialect study since the 1870s.[54] Yet this claim reflects the deeply formative impact of the MDC on Jakobson in his student years. This is evidenced in the opening to his study "The Newest Russian Poetry." Here is the continuation of the passage cited in part above:

> The development of a theory of poetic language will be possible only when poetry is treated as a social fact, when a kind of poetic dialectology is created. From the point of view of this dialectology, Pushkin is the center of a poetic culture of a particular time, with a definite zone of influence. From this point of view, the poetic dialects of one zone, when they gravitate toward the cultural center of another, can be subdivided, like dialects of practical language, into: transitional dialects which have adopted a set of canons from the center of gravity; semi-transitional dialects which adopt certain tendencies from the center of gravity; and mixed dialects which adopt occasional alien elements or devices.[55]

This passage has been overlooked as an apparently irrelevant and inscrutable proposal; its terminology is not familiar to scholars of literature or Russian Formalism.[56] Admittedly Jakobson is not easy on his readers, or, apparently, on his listeners in the MLC. He does not take pains to connect his methodological proposal with the analysis of Khlebnikov's poetry that follows. Hence Brik's exasperated reaction to Jakobson's presentation: "The lecture doesn't have a topic, doesn't have clearly set goals: What did the lecturer want to achieve?" Jakobson responded: "The lecture has a thoroughly defined topic and goal. Its goal is the task of poetic dialectology."[57] It is helpful to review the structure of Jakobson's study, which has nine subsections. The first contains his methodological proposal (poetic dialectology); parts 2 and 3 contrast Russian and Italian Futurism; but then settles into a description of Khlebnikov's "poetic dialect" in parts 4 through 9. These last parts most obviously cohere with Jakobson's proposed method. In them, he describes Khlebnikov's syntax (part 4), his use of epithets (5), neologisms (6), sound repetitions (7), synonyms (8), and rhymes (9). These, presumably, are the features of Khlebnikov's dialect that other speakers may adopt as they gravitate toward him as a "cultural center."

Jakobson insisted on this method outside of this conversation, and he referenced poetic dialectology in other works besides "The Newest Russian Poetry."[58] Strikingly, the minutes from subsequent meetings of the MLC show that Jakobson's proposal was gaining traction. Just a month after Jakobson's (May 11) presentation on Khlebnikov, Jakobson and Brik discussed the contemporary poetic landscape using dialectological terminology. Jakobson asserts that "in contemporary poetry schools play a huge role. The arbiters of one school or another play the role of cultural centers," to which Brik responded: "In this sense we have transitional dialects [*perekhodnye dialekty*]. Compare the Moscow branch of Proletkult with the Petrograd branch." Their conversation then moves on to discuss "cultural centers" established in the past, with Jakobson concluding with an analogy between "Pushkin" and "the Moscow dialect"—both being a "huge source" (*gromadnyi istok*) of influence.[59] Jakobson and Brik are using the terminology that Jakobson introduced in the opening of "The Newest Russian Poetry" which was also that of the Moscow Dialectological Commission.

In describing the basic contours of MDC dialectology I want to stress two points: a "dialect" is not an abstract system, and dialectal change is understood in social terms. Dialectology is a diachronic approach to language; the Moscow Dialectological Commission was interested in language *change* over time. In the introduction to his Khlebnikov study, Jakobson describes this as the "gravitation" of smaller dialects toward a dialect with a more weighty "zone of influence." Dialectology thus pertains to the history of language, and is fundamentally a theory of how social factors (the movement of people, and contacts between them) impact this history. This theory—which can be called the "cultural centers" model of language change—was developed by Aleksei Shakhmatov and Nikolai Durnovo and then adopted as the common platform of the MDC, as a correction to the "wave" theory (*Wellentheorie*) formulated by the German linguist Johannes Schmidt in 1872.[60] According to Schmidt's model, a linguistic innovation spreads outward, like ripples of water, from a central area into a surrounding transitional area where it will be found in varying degrees depending on the distance from the center.[61]

The Russian dialectologists in the MDC amended Schmidt's model by making it more sociological. Shakhmatov, who is considered the founder of modern Russian dialectology, defined dialectology as an "ethnographic discipline"; his lectures from the 1910s stress that dialectology "has as its object the study of *the population* according to characteristics presented in its language."[62] This definition underscores the fact that, at the turn of the twentieth century, dialectology was regarded as part of a more general complex of disciplines oriented to the historical description of Russian language and culture. In their modification of Schmidt's wave theory, the MDC and Shakhmatov introduced the idea of a "cultural center" towards which dialects gravitate. Nikolai Durnovo explained this concept by noting that the size of the "center" corresponds with the size of the dialect it creates: "Individual local dialects [*govory*] group around minor centers such as trade settlements, factories, monasteries, etc.; major regional centers sometimes facilitate the formation of a larger, regional dialect [*narechie*]; finally the grouping of certain regions into entire states facilitates the creation of a language [*iazyk*]."[63] The linguists Walt Wolfram and Natalie Schilling-Estes note that the transmission of linguistic innovations is impacted by the same factors that the communication scholar Everett Rogers outlined for the diffusion of customs, ideas, and practices: the nature of the phenomenon itself (e.g., a dialect's formal features), communication networks, distance, time, and social structure.[64] In the study of language change, the dialectologist weighs formal factors, such as phonology, against social ones, such as communication networks.

This approach in the MDC entailed careful formal (phonological, morphological) description of the dialects, but the factors understood to drive formal change over time were primarily social. This is where the concept of "gravitation" comes in. The MDC's dialectology shares some features with the "gravity" or "hierarchical" model in historical dialectology developed in the 1970s by Peter Trudgill. According to Trudgill's model,

> the diffusion of innovations is a function not only of the distance from one point to another, as with the wave model [i.e., Schmidt's *Wellentheorie*], but of the population density of areas which stand to be affected by a nearby change. Changes are most likely to begin in large, heavily populated cities which have historically been cultural centers. From there, they radiate outward, but not in a simple wave pattern. Rather, innovations first reach moderately sized cities, which fall under the area of influence of some large, focal city, leaving nearby sparsely populated areas unaffected.[65]

In 1911, Shakhmatov similarly describes language change through social networks:

> The diffusion of a *koiné* occurs through units which are similar to those in which it itself emerged . . . Local dialects of a rural population can retain their ancient form in close proximity to a city which has established a *koiné*, while the same *koiné* will penetrate distant cities and commercial centers, which are connected to each other by similar cultural or political interests.[66]

These models use patterns in people's geographical movement to explain patterns of change in the history of language.

Jakobson's rebellious stance towards intellectual authorities did not extend to the Dialectological Commission.[67] He wrote a favorable review of the commission's dialectological map in 1916 and he evidently formed a close relationship with Durnovo, the vice-chairman.[68] In *Slavic Philology*, Jakobson again praised the model since it allows for "intersecting dialectological influences, and places *linguistic influence in immediate dependence on the gravitation of speakers* of a given dialect to a specific cultural center."[69] This focus on individual speakers appears again in Jakobson's own dialectological study, "Phonetics of a North Russian Dialect." Based on his fieldwork, he concludes that one cannot describe the "dialect" in question as a single coherent dialect governed by internal "laws": "One cannot talk about the dialect of the village of Kostiunin, but only about a multiplicity of individual and short-term dialects: *it is virtually impossible to speak about phonetic laws, but only about phonetic inclinations and tendencies.*"[70] Here we find the same discourse that Jakobson used to counter the idea that a "poetic language" is a sharply differentiated sphere: as he said to Brik, "One can only speak of . . . tendencies."[71] Again, Jakobson's argumentation here stands in sharp contrast to his later structuralist work. Beginning in the late 1920s, in his work on historical phonology, Jakobson would argue that any phonetic change must be studied from the perspective of the existing "phonemic system" of a language, which limits the kinds of changes possible for the language.[72] For the structuralist, the intrinsic, abstract phonological system is a primary causal factor in change, while social factors (such as cultural centers and social networks) are of secondary importance.

Jakobson's arguments from the 1910s were consistent with the principles of dialectology at the turn of the twentieth century. Dialectology emerged in the late nineteenth century as a continuation of, and then a reaction against, the Neogrammarian (*Junggrammatiker*) school of linguistics. The Neogrammarian movement was initially developed at the University of Leipzig in the 1870s, when a group of scholars (including Karl Burgmann, Hermann Osthoff, Karl Verner, and Hermann Paul) challenged the field of historical comparative linguistics. They called for a focus on the present usage of language, rather than on reconstructing the ancient past (e.g., Indo-European), so as to make the study of sound change more rigorously scientific in a positivist sense. As we have seen, the Neogrammarians argued that the idiolect is the only legitimate object of linguistic investigation, since it is the only form of language which is directly, empirically observable. As a result, Neogrammarian linguistics encouraged the expansion of work on dialects. Their fine-grained investigations of language eventually came into conflict with the Neogrammarians' first (of two) "methodological principles" (*methodische Grundsätze*): "Sound change occurs according to mechanical laws which suffer no exceptions (the regularity principle)."[73] At the time of Jakobson's fieldwork in the 1910s, dialectologists in France, Germany, and Russia were arguing against the "regularity principle." As Robins explains:

The most important and radical arguments against the neogrammarian position . . . came from specialists in a branch of linguistics that they had been at pains to encourage, the study of living dialects. . . . The more narrowly a language was scrutinized, the more it was seen that geographical dialect divisions are in constant fluctuation and far from clear-cut, as more gross and superficial descriptions imply. The number of coincidental isoglosses [a line on a dialect map which marks the boundary between areas where language features, such as the pronunciation of a vowel, differ] required to delimit a dialect must be arbitrary, and if one presses differences in detail at all levels, including pronunciation, to their logical limits, then the dialect becomes the idiolect.[74]

In sum, fieldwork in dialectology was encouraging scholars to argue that sound change cannot be described by exceptionless laws, and, going even further, to argue that abstractions about the phonological structure of a language or even of a dialect are ultimately fictions. Yet dialectologists nonetheless sought explanations for general, observable patterns of change. The sources for these were sought in geography, but also, within a region, in social factors such as education, class, age, and gender.[75]

In their student work, Jakobson and Bogatyrev applied the MDC theory to the study of phonology, as well as to the analysis of folklore. This intersection was encouraged by the fact that folklore studies and dialectology were particularly close, in that both relied on the collection of speech data.[76] Jakobson and Bogatyrev went on their first joint expedition in the summer of 1915, during which they recorded, according to their own report, "200 folktales and narratives, many songs, several examples of religious verse [*dukhovnye stikhi*], incantations, and a series of accounts on folk medicine and beliefs. In addition, proverbs, riddles, jokes [*pobaski*], etc. and finally wedding and festive rituals were also described."[77] At the same time, Jakobson was making dialectological notes.[78] Afterwards, Bogatyrev and Jakobson jointly presented the results of their trip to both the Commission for Folklore Study and the MDC; both societies appear to have provided funding for the expedition.[79] Their report for the presentations, written in Bogatyrev's hand, begins by contesting the practice of looking for folklore in isolated communities, remote from urban centers and industry. Referencing Dmitri Zelenin's work on the tales of the Perm *gubernia* as representative of this approach, Bogatyrev and Jakobson stress that they found material which surpassed that of Zelenin's best tale-teller (*skazochnik*) "within three minutes' walk from the railroad."[80]

What is particularly interesting is that they used the MDC "cultural centers" model to interpret both folkloristic and dialectological data. Their interest was not in folklore as something pure and unchanging (and found in isolated regions), but in the way folkloric traditions absorb innovations. Both Jakobson and Bogatyrev focused on the *otkhodnik*, the village dweller who travels to a local cultural center, such as a larger city or a factory, for work.

This practice has been studied by historians as a measure of the modernization of European Russia in this period. As Sheila Fitzpatrick writes,

> In the years immediately before the First World War, about nine million peasants took out passports for seasonal work outside their native village each year, and almost half were working outside agriculture. With one in every two peasant households in European Russia including a family member who left the village for work . . . the impression that old Russia survived almost unchanged in the villages may well have been deceptive. Many peasants were in fact living with one foot in the traditional village world and the other in the quite different world of the modern industrial town.[81]

Jakobson and Bogatyrev were studying how these migrant workers were spreading cultural and linguistic innovations.

In one of Jakobson's first scholarly articles, written in 1916, he presented the results of his 1915 expedition with Bogatyrev, describing the impact of Muscovite pronunciation (i.e., of a cultural center) on local dialects.[82] In his essay he explains that male villagers in Kostiunin spent a significant amount of time in Moscow, which allowed the Muscovite dialect to influence the dialect of their native village; even those who had never been to Moscow adopted principles of the Moscow dialect from those who had, adapting them to their own way of speaking.[83] Likewise, the two students' presentation of their folkloristic fieldwork to the Commission for Folklore Study focused on how urban culture was absorbed into an existing folkloric repertoire.[84] In their report, Jakobson and Bogatyrev note that new information and verbal forms are incorporated into preexisting traditions, including stock narratives and melodies. They focus on the Tsindel textile factory in Naro-Fominsk (a town 70 km southwest of Moscow) as a cultural center that serves as a "breeding ground [*rassadnik*] for all kinds of tales, superstitions, and songs." As a place where peasants from different villages meet, the Tsindel factory transforms village "culture"—people's views, norms, and poetry—into urban (*gorodskoi*) culture.[85] This topic was of considerable political import in the revolutionary period. Jakobson and Bogatyrev, following Shakhmatov's lead in approaching dialectology as the study of "the population according to characteristics presented in its language," claimed that their research documented the modernization of Russian culture, one person at a time, through contacts between individuals.[86] The application of ideas from the study of dialect to the study of literature (poetics)—"poetic dialectology"—followed the example set by the intersection between dialect study and folkloristics. Poetic dialectology, as applied to the works of Khlebnikov, was a continuation and radicalization of Jakobson's student work focused on the language and culture of a group of individuals.

Chapter Four

AVANT-GARDE PHILOLOGY

From the outset, the Formalists were concerned with theorizing Russian Futurism. Shklovsky's public debut as a literary theorist was in a defense of Futurism at the Stray Dog (Brodiachaia sobaka) café in December 1913.[87] Jakobson collaborated with the Futurists in the group Hylaea in the 1910s and even coauthored a book of "transrational" poetry with them, published in 1915. One of the earliest monographs on Russian Formalism, Krystyna Pomorska's *Russian Formalist Theory and Its Poetic Ambiance* (1968), was dedicated to this specific connection. Pomorska began the book under Jakobson's supervision at MIT in 1960.[88] She argues that Russian Futurist manifestoes and verse, with their focus on the sounds of poetry, provided a starting point for Formalism. My point is related, but ultimately different: that the research program developed in the Moscow Linguistic Circle in the late 1910s and early 1920s was, at its core, motivated by an avant-garde ideology. This ideology can be described using Peter Bürger's terms. In his classic study *Theory of the Avant-Garde* (1974), he defines the avant-garde as a movement which rested on "two intertwined fundamental principles": "the attack on the institution of art and the revolutionizing of life as a whole."[89] The Futurists and the MLC adhered to these principles in their rejection of the autonomy of art; verbal art was not to be thought of as individual, stable works or texts with identifiable authors and interpretable, holistic meanings. Instead, they saw verbal creativity as inseparable from the broader "verbal mass" (*slovesnaia massa*)—the language they lived in, understood as the aggregate of idiolects, constantly in contact with each other. As Bürger points out, this position logically implies a loss of status: "By renouncing the idea of autonomy, the artist also gives up his special social position and thereby his claim to genius."[90] However, the trade-off is that the work of the artist or "speech-crafter" (*rechar*) (the Futurists coined new terms to describe new concepts) can immediately impact the lives of other people.[91]

It was this avant-garde concept of verbal creativity that Jakobson and others in the MLC sought to study with dialectological methodology. Khlebnikov or Pushkin in this framework is not an individual artist but rather a cultural center. This reformulation entails these same trade-offs. It is an inflation of the artist's status, ascribing a greater social impact to their work, but it is also a demotion. The *rechar* is not an extraordinary individual, whose irreducible works carry weighty authority or encode timeless meanings. His importance lies only in the fact that linguistic features found in his language (idiolect) have spread into the idiolects of others. Because this way of thinking depends on the premise that there is no dividing line between poetry and the broader "verbal mass," MLC theory did not make a distinction between

162

language contact between poets (e.g., Khlebnikov and Mayakovsky) and contact between Khlebnikov and the average speaker.

The reception of Velimir Khlebnikov by his contemporaries exemplifies this view. In 1977, Jakobson recalled being "stunned" as a student by Khebnikov's famous 1910 poem "Incantation by Laughter," prompting Jakobson to visit the poet, equipped with a collection of incantations:

> Xlebnikov rented an apartment somewhere at the end of the world, at a place called something like Kamenoostrovskie Peski. I recall that as I was looking for his apartment there was a raw chill in the air, penetrating even for a Moscovite, so that I had to hold my handkerchief to my nose the whole time. The author of "Laughter" had no telephone, and I had come unannounced. He wasn't at home, but I 'asked them to tell him that I would return the next morning. The next day, December 30, 1913, I turned up at his place, along with a special copy I had made for him of a collection of excerpts I had compiled at the Rumjancev Museum from various collections of incantations, some transrational, some half-transrational. A part of them had been taken from Saxarov's anthology: songs about demons, incantations, and children's counting-out rhymes and tales as well. Xlebnikov immediately began to look at them with undivided attention, and soon was to use them in his poem "A Night in Galicia," where the mermaids "are reading Saxarov."[92]

Even as it is retold more than sixty years later, Jakobson's account suggests that his meeting and poetic collaborations with Khlebnikov were significant to him. Jakobson also recalled that Khlebnikov dedicated "A Night in Galicia" to him in several memoiristic accounts.[93] It was evident to contemporaries that there was a particular affinity between some of the Formalists and the Futurists. Boris Gornung, as a member of the phenomenological camp within the MLC, provides an informative, if uncharitable, assessment of the allegiance between the dialectologists and the Futurists. In 1922, he critiqued Moscow Formalism as "so-called scholarly theories, which gave support to Russian futurism . . . which were created by folklorists and dialectological scholars sympathizing with the movement." He continues:

> These sympathies are clear. Futurism appeared in literature, according to its own pronouncement, "without family without tribe" [*bez rodu bez plemeni*], and genealogical researches for the forefathers of Khlebnikov led to Russian folklore and dialects. The folklorists were quite flattered that the object of their scholarly work went from the backyard into the literary salons, and they took up providing a scholarly foundation for the arts of these homegrown innovators.[94]

163

Gornung describes the allegiance between the dialectologists-folklorists and the Futurists as one of mutual social advancement. The scholars provide the upstart poets with status by providing them with genealogies, while the poets in turn allowed the humble researchers to share the Futurists' limelight. I would call attention to the acknowledgment that the bond between these two groups emerged from their position as "outsiders" in relation to the world of "high" art—they spent their time scrutinizing "backyards" (*zadvorki*), or they were "homegrown" (*domoroshchennyi*), and their creations lacked prestige and pedigrees. The Formalists and Futurists themselves embraced this outsider identity. Rather than see themselves as social climbers seeking to legitimize their work in the salons of high society, they aimed for something much more ambitious and radical: to annul the old, bourgeois concept of art.

The Formalist-Futurist project, as pursued within the MLC, was to utilize an ostensibly non-bourgeois model for verbal creativity (borrowed from folklore and dialect study) to attack the institution of art. At a meeting of the MLC in December 1919, Jakobson argued that all previous poetry is fundamentally alien to the "people" (the minutes register an uncertainty as to whether he said "the proletariat [proletariat]" or the "peasantry [*prostonarod'e*]") and that only avant-garde art operates with principles that prompt an aesthetic response among people other than the elites:

> Regarding the objections made to the presenter, first of all it is completely unclear what facts suggest a significant closeness of the poets of the preceding generations to the ~~proletariat~~ the folk [*prostonarod'e*]? Both new and old poets are equally foreign to him. There is a whole series of facts providing evidence for this. . . . The report of Shklovsky about the excursion to the Tret'iakov gallery, where Repin's "Barge Haulers," despite all the efforts of the guide, was in no way perceived by the visitors. Just the opposite, the people [*narod*], when perceiving literary phenomena, remake them into something avant-garde [*zaumnye*]. This is the character of folklore itself. Critics of futurism have always supported their hostility towards futurism by arguing that it is an uncultured phenomenon, and that similar facts can be found in the village: counting rhymes, petty-bourgeois songs, etc.[95]

Jakobson argues here that avant-garde poetry, like folklore, is distinct from the existing, social (bourgeois) concept of art. These claims can be compared with Shklovsky's efforts, described in chapters 2 and 3, to analyze narrative outside of existing social concepts such as that of the work, or the author. Jakobson's claim is also characteristically avant-garde in its rejection of the immediate past, particularly the cultural history of their parents' generation.

The radicalism of Jakobson's poetic dialectology is indicated by the difficulty with which his contemporaries received his work. Nikolai Trubetskoi was apparently confused and frustrated by Jakobson's "Newest Russian Poetry." In his letters to Jakobson from 1921, he strenuously objected to Jakobson's project:

> It seems to me that one must not lose sight of the fact that literature is a factor of social life. And as soon as you approach it from that perspective then your viewpoint immediately turns out to be insufficient, incomplete. In order for a given work to become a social fact [*fakt sotsial'nogo poriadka*], it is necessary that it pass victoriously through the "test of taste." Only then will it satisfy readers and evoke imitation, even if only potentially. And, strictly speaking, only under these conditions does it become a work of art and enter as a link into the history of literature. . . . Meanwhile, in your approach [*v Vashei nauke*], Pushkin, uncle Mitiai, and the schoolgirl trying to write verses, these are all completely similar and equal objects of study.[96]

For Trubetskoi, a scholarly poetics must acknowledge that its object of study—literature—is a socially defined category. This is also the essence of Pavel Medvedev's critique of Russian Formalism:

> The very concept of "poeticity" is concretely historical. "Poeticity" is not a property of language, like a linguistic concept, but is the artistic use of certain linguistic elements of a language in the creative practice of a given school or movement, according to their tastes. And since taste is a social category, and since succession of tastes and styles is the "aesthetic" result of the succession of social class . . . thus "poeticity" and "poetic language" are concrete sociological concepts, not abstract linguistic ones.[97]

These critiques implicitly reject the utopian project that inspired the MLC: Moscow Formalism sought to redefine its object of study—to see Khlebnikov's or Mayakovsky's poems not as literature or art but as language. Medvedev and Trubetskoi argue that one cannot study "poetry" if one does not take into account that the category is itself socially determined. However, poetic dialectology consciously rejected the category of "poetry" *because* it was socially defined—by bourgeois tastes. Trubetskoi was responding to this when he objected that *anyone's* effort at verbal creativity ("Pushkin, uncle Mitiai, and the schoolgirl trying to write verses") would be of equal value in Jakobson's approach. Poetic dialectology, by integrating the study of poetic creativity into the study of language, replaces "poetry" with an array of dialectal features (syntax, epithets, neologisms, etc.). Ultimately, what distinguishes

Khlebnikov as a cultural center is not the way that his usage of language differs from everyday speech, but rather the dialectological evidence that his usage was being adopted by other speakers.

In their explorations of a new, non-bourgeois conception of poetry, the Futurists turned to philology, or, more accurately, to the history of the Russian language. Khlebnikov was described by his peers not as a "poet" in the old sense, but as a kind of linguistic force. His work was seen as an intervention in the process of language change. Benedikt Livshits, a member of Hylaea, articulated this in his memoir, *One-and-a-Half-Eyed Archer* (*Polutoraglazyi strelets,* 1933). Describing the visit of the founder of Italian Futurism, Filippo Marinetti, to Russia in 1914, just before the outbreak of World War I, Livshits recalls that the Hylaea group received Marinetti with hostility. Livshits himself said to Marinetti:

> Unfortunately Khlebnikov for you is an empty sound: he is completely untranslatable in those of his works where his genius is most strongly apparent. Rimbaud's most courageous daring is child's prattle in comparison to what Khlebnikov does, blowing up thousand-year-old linguistic stratifications and fearlessly submerging himself in the articulatory chasms [*artikuliatsionnye bezdny*] of the primeval word. . . . We are more consistent than you are. Already five years ago we destroyed punctuation marks . . . by this we underscore the continuity of the verbal mass [*slovesnaia massa*], its elemental cosmic essence.[98]

Livshits thus emphasizes that Khlebnikov's poetry is revolutionary not in its referential meaning, but for its linguistic revelations. Khlebnikov uncovers new possibilities for the Russian language, combining verbal elements that belong to different centuries, and endowing morphological features such as prefixes or suffixes with new meanings. Livshits implies that Khlebnikov's innovations are not confined to discrete texts, but instead participate in the larger, communally shared reservoir of the lexicon and linguistic norms. Mayakovsky also stressed that Khlebnikov did not write in discrete units definable as poems:

> Khlebnikov has no poems. The finishedness [*zakonchennost'*] of his printed things is a fiction. Evidence of the finishedness is most frequently the work of his friends. We selected from the whirlwind of his discarded drafts those which seemed most valuable and sent them to be published. Often the tail of one sketch was pasted to a foreign head, prompting merry bewilderment from Khlebnikov. You couldn't allow him to edit—he would cross out everything and create a completely new text.[99]

Mayakovsky's and Livshits's descriptions of Khlebnikov should ultimately be situated within a larger discourse which in fact mythologized Khlebnikov as an extraordinary individual. However, in a contradictory way, the Futurists and the Moscow Formalists insisted that they valued Khlebnikov not as an author of poems, but for his potential influence on Russian dialects.

LANGUAGE POLITICS AND KHLEBNIKOV AS A CULTURAL CENTER

Moscow dialectology looked to population movement and contact between speakers as the engine of linguistic change: one person adopts a feature from another. Some of the linguists reacting to the Neogrammarian school at the turn of the century stressed the role of individual consciousness in this process. The German linguist Hugo Schuchardt (1842–1927) became well known for his critique of the Neogrammarian doctrine of the "absolute exceptionlessness of sound laws" from this perspective:

> I will therefore probably not be mistaken if I consider the exceptionlessness of sound laws to be irreconcilable with the influence consciousness has in my opinion on language change. What influence does the school not have even where public education plays only a marginal role? How widespread is the wish to sound educated among the uneducated, to sound metropolitan among those in the provinces?[100]

This kind of argumentation was gaining ground at the turn of the twentieth century, as evidence mounted against the Neogrammarian position that sound change follows natural laws. Jakobson likewise stressed that language change could be conscious, and saw this to be central to poetic dialectology and what the MLC referred to as "language politics."

The capacity of individuals to consciously change their own speech is central to verbal creativity. Thus far, we have seen the discourse of consciousness in the discussion of poeticity: to become conscious of language is for it to be "laid bare" or "defamiliarized." Jakobson and the MLC were interested in using this capacity to further a political cause. Cultural leaders, such as scholars or politicians, can consciously develop and promote linguistic innovations so that they are adopted by others. This was the subject of an extended exchange between Jakobson and Boris Kushner, following the latter's presentation "On the Languages of Small Peoples and Language Politics" ("O iazykakh malykh narodnostei i iazykovoi politike") in December 1919. Jakobson links the need for a "language politics" to the emergence of a new scholarly consensus that an individual can consciously direct linguistic evolution:

> In the science of the recent period, along with demands for the analysis and study of given facts, the problem of applying already accumulated scientific experience becomes ever more insistent. The question of language politics [*iazykovaia politika*] has to date never been raised. Meanwhile a solution to this question is necessary. Already a priori one can establish two points of view on this question. The first, which can be called romantic, looks at language as an elemental phenomenon, which is completely independent from human will . . . which absolutely does not allow individual interference in the process of the development of language. The second point of view allows within certain limits free creation [*proizvol'noe tvorchestvo*] in the process of the development of language. Even recently the second point of view would have been considered a heresy and would have been compared with old linguistic errors, but today this approach to language has fully matured [*nazrel vpolne*]. Having established the social character of linguistic facts . . . we can speak about conscious organizational acts [*soznatel'nye organizuiushchie akty*] in the development of language.[101]

Jakobson's thinking is arguably informed here by his dialectological fieldwork on the impact of migrant workers on village dialects. Any individual speaker has the capacity to consciously change his or her own speech, and potentially that of others. Jakobson's "language politics" suggests the possibility of consciously steering this change. When Jakobson refers above to recent thinking which allows for "free creation" in the study of language, he may be referring to the work of Schuchardt, or to that of Karl Vossler or his followers, who were known as the "idealist" or "aesthetic" school.[102] Vossler's approach to language change was, in its basic contours, similar to Jakobson's poetic dialectology. Vossler argued that

> all linguistic change begins with innovations in individual speech habits, and those that are going to give rise to some alteration in language do so by being imitated by others and thus diffusing themselves. . . . Certain individuals, through their social position or literary reputation, are better placed to initiate changes that others will take up and diffuse through a language.[103]

Vossler stressed that the individual behaviors of innovation and imitation were conscious choices. In the continuation of his discussion with Kushner, Jakobson uses this premise to argue for the extreme malleability of "language." Unlike French structuralists who later attributed to linguistic (social) norms an agentive force which is impossible for individuals to escape, Jakobson believes that sweeping changes are possible and can be consciously directed. In his presentation on the "Languages of Small Peoples," Kushner referred to tendencies that reveal a "will towards linguistic unity [*edinoiazykiia*]" or a "tendency towards a common language." At the conclusion of his monologue cited above, Jakobson refers to the idea of a "universal language":

> Finally, regarding the possibility of a universal language [*universal'nyi iazyk*], it will never come about through natural [*estestvennyi*] development. The only way for this to happen is through artificial propagation [*nasazhdenie*] and by decree [*dekretirovanie*] . . . Of course, here, a general unification [*obshchee ob"edinenie*] is necessary (meanwhile, not necessarily a socialist one).

Kushner responded to Jakobson by suggesting a more cautious approach:

> We do not have sufficient evidence to estimate the possibility of language change by decree [*dekretirovanie*]. Propagation of language change must correspond with the basic tendency in development. And this tendency can only be established in an absolute sense. Meanwhile, it is necessary to keep in mind that language change by decree cannot remove dialectical particularities, which will inescapably emerge in a universal language [*v mirovom iazyke*].

Jakobson, however, was undeterred, replying:

> Just the opposite, there is no evidence that would contradict this basic tendency. Conservatism is possible in all kinds of spheres, but not in the sphere of dialect. Here we can see a constant and unchanging gravitation towards the cultural center [*stremlenie k kul'turnomu tsentru*], towards simplification [*nivellirovka*]. *Linguistic conservatism is always connected with political separatism.* If we remove political considerations, then we cannot find a single fact contradicting the basic tendency of development. Thus it is possible to talk about change by decree, and about the possibility of artificial propagation.[104]

Jakobson here explains language evolution by reference to sociopolitical factors. Since "linguistic conservatism is always connected with political separatism," the obverse may also be true: political unification—or what Jakobson refers to as a "general unification" (*obshchee ob"edinenie*)—will allow for revolutionary changes in language.

The mechanisms by which such change could occur are "decree" or "propagation." This sounds antidemocratic, particularly in contrast to Kushner's appeal to popular usage and the ubiquity of diversity. Jakobson's language appears to be compatible with the discourse and politics of the Bolshevik Party, which had seized power in the name of a "dictatorship of the proletariat."

In April 1920, the Moscow Linguistic Circle applied to Narkompros for state funding. In a letter of application, the Circle described itself as a society dedicated to questions of "applied philology [*prikladnaia filologiia*]"—citing members' research on questions of "language culture [*iazykovaia kul'tura*]" and "language politics [*iazykovaia politika*]." The Circle promised to help the government reshape the population through language reform and literacy education.[105] The letter uses the uncompromising discourse seen in Jakobson's comments above: "Many of the measures taken by Narkompros in these spheres [i.e., language pedagogy] can be subjected to objective-scholarly criticism, much is guilty of eclecticism and 'conciliation' [*soglashatel'stvo*]."

Tellingly, the MLC seeks to establish common ground with the government on the basis of the kind of "language politics" that Jakobson articulated in his debate with Kushner. The letter specifically praises the government's effort to change language "by decree":

> The question of linguistic self-determination [*iazykovoe samoopredelenie*], which has been newly and soberly articulated by the Soviet government, is still met in the most varied circles with a mess of romantic hold-overs. The question of Soviet terminology, one of the first efforts at language change by decree [*dekretirovanie iazyka*] is extremely important both practically . . . as well as theoretically.[106]

In essence, the MLC here suggests that the top-down direction of language is possible and that they are eager to help the Soviet government with this project. One of the more obvious cases of language reform or language change at the time was the emergence of new words, and particularly new words created from abbreviations—such as Narkompros, a portmanteau word, created from the words *Na*rodnyi *kom*issariat *pros*vesheniia. This was a widespread and novel phenomenon, which was discussed following Kushner's presentation on "Contemporary Words Created from Abbreviations" (October 24, 1920) and A. A. Buslaev's "Several Observations on Syllabic Word Coinage" (December 21, 1920). As Jakobson noted, this practice emerged from the use of telegraph abbreviations before and during World War I, and became widespread in the military. In the period of the October Revolution, he recounts, these abbreviations flooded print language.[107]

To return to the relationship between the Futurists' avant-garde ideology and the language politics promoted by Jakobson and the MLC, Leon Trotsky's assessment of Futurism in *Literature and Revolution* (1924) reveals that he actually understood the movement in the same way that the Futurists themselves did. Echoing, to some extent, Gornung and Mayakovsky,

Trotsky argued that the linguistic innovations of the Futurists "are philology of a doubtful character, poetics in part, *but not poetry*."[108] However, while Gornung and Trotsky suggest that this is a failure, the Futurists might call it a success, since their goal was to create a new form of verbal creativity. Even more striking is Trotsky's admission that the Futurists' neologisms "may . . . facilitate the development of the living and even of the poetic language, *and forecast a time when the evolution of speech will be more consciously directed.* But this very work . . . is outside of poetry."[109] Trotsky thus sees the value of the movement in the way that the MLC did, not as poetry in terms of the old cultural institution, governed by implicit rules of taste, but as a conscious effort to direct the course of the "living" (spoken) language.

We can now return to Jakobson's "Newest Russian Poetry" as an "experiment in poetic dialectology" that is focused on Khlebnikov's idiolect (or "dialect" in Jakobson's terms). And we can now understand why he attempts to identify features of this individual language: so that the MLC can trace the way these are picked up by other people and incorporated into their own idiolects. Jakobson was not alone in this task. For example, Grigory Vinokur (1896–1947), who was a member and secretary of the MLC from 1919 and its chairman in 1922–23, also described the Futurists' poetry as a direct intervention in the history of the Russian language. In an article titled "Futurists—Builders of Language" ("Futuristy—stroiteli iazyka," 1923), he argued that the task of Futurism is to create a new "language of the street"; their poetry is not only to be understood against the background of other literary works, but against "language in general."[110] The Futurists, he writes, have drawn their "material" from the "spoken language of the masses" and have "overcome" it, in an effort to create a new language.[111] Vinokur, like Jakobson, likened the Futurists' influence on the Russian language to Pushkin's, with the difference that Pushkin created a new language for the noble classes while the Futurists were oriented toward the language of the people.[112] Vinokur in fact cites Jakobson's Khlebnikov study in the spirit in which it was intended: as an inventory of the lexical innovations that Futurist poetry was introducing into everyday spoken Russian.

Mayakovsky expressed, in his own words, a version of this argument in his obituary for Khlebnikov:

> The poetic fame of Khlebnikov is immeasurably lesser than his importance. Of the hundred who have read him, fifty called him simply an obscure scribbler [*grafoman*], forty read him for pleasure and were surprised to find nothing there, and only ten (poets-Futurists, philologists in OPOIAZ) knew and loved this Columbus of new poetic continents, now inhabited and cultivated by us. Khlebnikov is not a poet for consumers. You can not read him. Khlebnikov is a poet for producers.[113]

This is another way of describing Khlebnikov as a cultural center. In Maya-kovsky's geographic metaphor, Khlebnikov discovered new poetic lands, into which other poets then moved. In the dialectologists' geographical terms, these poets "gravitate" towards him, where they pick up features of his dia-lect. One difference between Mayakovsky's formulation and that of Vinokur or Jakobson is that Mayakovsky appears to restrict Khlebnikov's impact to the sphere of other creative writers—a group he calls "producers." This was not the case for poetic dialectology.

This is made clear in a talk Jakobson gave at the Manes Art Society in Prague in 1932, titled "What Is Poetry?" ("Co je poesie?"). In his conclusion, Jakobson vehemently rejects the accusation that Formalist and structural-ist theory divorces literature from society—that it amounts to "an 'art-for-art's sake' approach . . . following in the footsteps of Kantian aesthetics."[114] Jakobson clarifies his position by reference to the Czech avant-garde poet Vítězslav Nezval's profound, if unnoticed, impact on Czech culture: "I am convinced," he writes, "that the year 1932 will go down in the history of Czech culture as the year of Nezval's 'Havelock of Glass,' just as 1836 is for Czech culture the year of Mácha's 'May.'" This, Jakobson admits, may seem paradoxical because the social importance of poetry is not overtly obvious.

> It is poetry that protects our formulas [*formule*] of love and hate, revolt and reconciliation, faith and denial from automatization and corrosion. The per-centage of Czechoslovak citizens who have read Nezval's verse is perhaps not large. But as long as they have read and accepted it they will, unwittingly, joke with friends, swear at opponents, intone arousal, profess and experience love, and politicize somewhat differently. Even if they have read Nezval but reject him, they will not remain without changes in their speech and daily rituals . . . And from these admirers and deniers of Nezval's poetry its motifs and into-nation, words and connections [*vazby*] will spread wider and wider and will form the speech and whole habitus of even those who have only heard of Nezval in the daily news.[115]

This echoes Jakobson's 1916 statement that even "people who have never been in Moscow adopt from those who have, principles of Moscow vowel reduction [*akan'e*], remaking them [*perelitsovyvat'*] in their own way."[116] In the same way, Nezval's innovations can be adopted even by those who don't read him.

The core of Jakobson's 1932 argument about society and poetry relies on the concept of an abstract system. He argues that "art is an integral part of the social structure, a component that interacts with all the others and is itself mutable, since both the domain of art and its relationship to the other constituents of the social structure are in constant dialectical flux."[117]

172

It appears that, as Jakobson strove to *really* convince his audience of Nez-val's social relevance, he moved in his conclusion from a structuralist framework into a dialectological one. Similarly, at the beginning of Jakobson's famous "Linguistics and Poetics" paper, which he first gave at the 1958 Indiana Style Conference, he invokes a dialectological argument as his first positive argument for treating poetics as a subfield of linguistics: "There is a close correspondence, much closer than critics believe, between the question of linguistic phenomena expanding in space and time and the spatial and temporal spread of literary models."[118] This is clearly an echo of his original dialectological understanding of poetics. Yet, in his 1958 statement this claim is easily overlooked as a brief aside; it is unrelated to his central argument regarding the six functions of language.

The conceptual framework that informed Jakobson's thinking about language changed substantially between the 1910s and 1950s. His isolated references to a dialectological argument in the 1930s and 1950s are curious in that the structuralist theory which he began to develop in the late 1920s appeared to be incompatible with the core tenets of dialectological poetics. These tenets include the claim that the language of the individual is the only real object of study; the view that changes in language are primarily driven by extralinguistic factors such as migration, contact, and individual consciousness; the rejection of the idea of a language as a bounded sphere in favor of a multitude of idiolects; and the avant-garde rejection of the concept of the poem or work as the object of study for poetics. The central idea of poetic dialectology is to look not at poems, or even at idiolects, as wholes, but to focus on individual features (e.g., a word, a string of words, or the pronunciation of a sound) and their variation over space and time. The central premise of structuralism, by contrast, is to study linguistic features in their relationship to other features within a bounded system (e.g., the system of Russian phonology) or in a subsystem of a system (e.g., the system of sounds in a poem written in Russian).

The difference between dialectology and structuralism is also important when we consider their psychological dimension. The psychologistic linguistic theory of the late nineteenth century posited the human mind to be initially a blank slate, and each individual's mental architecture to be entirely a product of biographical experience (as organized by the laws of association). This experience is shaped by contact between individuals: individuals with a new way of speaking (such as Khlebnikov or Nezval) can thus change the idiolect (and mental architecture) of those who come into contact with them. Structuralist theory, by contrast, posited a socially maintained, homeostatic system of values—also described as a "collective consciousness"—which provides a priori an inescapable framework for individual thought. In this theoretical model, the "conservatism of language" is a result of the inherently systemic nature of language, not a result of the conservatism of society or "political separatism," as Jakobson argued in 1919. Any change in the way an individual speaks, for the structuralist, is contingent, first and foremost, on the allowances and restrictions of the collectively shared *langue*. Poetic dialectology is thus a very different literary theory than structuralist poetics. Jakobson does refer back to dialectology after he began developing his structuralist linguistics—but when he does this he is departing from structuralist theory.

MLC DIALECTOLOGY AND THE RUSSIAN CIVIL WAR

As a method for the study of language, dialectology had considerable appeal in a time of cultural upheaval. There are a number of affinities between dialectological poetics and the social situation in which it developed—the Russian Revolutions of 1917 and particularly the Civil War, which erupted in 1918. During the Civil War a second, rhetorical battle was being fought. The Formalists describe Lenin's language in these terms. For example, Shklovsky writes that "Lenin's arguments with his opponents, whether they are enemies or party comrades, usually start with an argument 'about words'—with an assertion that words have changed."[119] Eikhenbaum further argued that, for Lenin, "every political party for him is not just a certain worldview, but a certain system of speech style."[120] The OPOIAZ studies of rhetoric, discussed in chapter 2, including the articles on Lenin's language, focus on highly performative acts of oratory in speeches that sought to influence and inspire. However, the verbal civil war was also fought in a more diffuse way—in everyday communication, exemplified by the spread of rumors. For instance, Kotkin recounts that, to disguise the train in which Lenin traveled from Petrograd to Moscow in 1918, "Bonch-Bruevich sent two teams of agents unknown to each other . . . to eavesdrop on nearby 'tea' houses, and spread rumors of a train being prepared for doctors heading to the front."[121] In their student fieldwork, Jakobson and Bogatyrev focused on the village tea room (*chainaia*) as a kind of cultural center for oral narrative: "Here, people read the paper aloud and discuss the events of the war and voice considerations about future developments."[122] The tea room produces new "legends," or "formulas": as Bogatyrev wrote, "Often a kind of formula is made up which subsequently is repeated and disseminated."[123]

As students who largely came of age during the revolutionary period, the Formalists were, unsurprisingly, deeply impacted by this context. Particularly during the Civil War, Jakobson and his peers took a position in relation to these events which was not that of disengaged observers, but of combatants. This was often true in the literal sense—the minutes of Circle meetings refer to creating a commission for the distribution of Red Army rations, the "militarization" of student linguists, and students' military service obligations.[124] I am also using "battle" and "combatant" in a metaphoric sense, to describe the position of the dialectologists in relation to language change. The accepted view in historical linguistics is that change cannot be directly observed.[125] The historical linguist operating with a tree model of sound change identifies changes after the fact, once they have been adopted as a new standard. Historical linguistics also frequently studies the evolution of languages over centuries. Dialectology studies this process as if under a microscope, revealing "variation and coexistence between new and old forms in the process of change."[126] As Wolfram and Schilling-Estes write,

> Dialect variation brings together language synchrony and diachrony in a unique way. Language change is typically initiated by a group of speakers in a particular locale at a given point in time, spreading from that locus outward in successive stages that reflect an apparent time depth in the spatial dispersion of forms.[127]

Jakobson's background in dialectology may well have informed his conviction that the past and future of a language are visible at any given moment; he would repeatedly insist that "archaisms" must be considered a real feature of the contemporary linguistic-literary landscape.[128] In the context of the Civil War, the movement of people and the contacts between them become more intense—more rapid, forceful, and loaded with significance. The young Moscow dialectologists arguably saw themselves to be caught in a battle of dialects. There was no escape from the messy and violent process in which multiple cultural centers around them were generating innovations, which were being dispersed by colliding networks of speakers.

The MLC's members made pragmatic use of their own linguistic consciousness in the Civil War period in two ways. The first usage was relatively straightforward: the use of their technical knowledge as a unit of exchange in negotiations with political authorities. (The second, which I will come to, was the application of the cultural centers model to contemporary discourse.) The MLC letter to Narkompros cited above reported that the Circle had repeatedly provided the Bolshevik government with "valuable" information. It mentions that the Scholarly Division of Narkompros had requested information in connection with proposals for orthographic reform, and the negotiation of the Russo-Ukrainian border with Skoropadsky's government in 1920. Jakobson is cited as having provided "valuable materials" regarding the linguistic and ethnographic boundary between Russia and Ukraine.[129] Marina Sorokina has determined, on the basis of new archival research, that the Ukrainian negotiators were citing the 1915 dialect map published by the MDC, and as a result that Dmitry Ushakov was contacted by the Soviet Peoples' Commissariat of Foreign Affairs for his aid as a specialist. However, rather than Ushakov, Jakobson ended up representing the MDC on this question.[130] The MLC reminds Narkompros of this aid when asking that the Circle be incorporated into the network of state-funded scientific and artistic institutions, Glavnauka, a division of Narkompros. (This request was granted, and the MLC received subsidies from the government budget until January 1, 1923.)[131] The letter ends with a reference to an exchange of funds for services:

> The Circle also appeals to the Scientific Department [*Nauchnyi Otdel*] with a request to accept the circle as one of its institutions, and to not deny it the modest financial support requested by the Circle. For its part, the Circle pledges to submit reports on its studies to the Scientific Department and to perform any [*vsiakie*] special tasks that will be assigned to it by the Scientific Department.[132]

The MLC is asking to become a government institution, and promises to fulfill any assignment that the government asks of it. Dialectological knowledge can be exchanged not only for funding, but for power and protection. Sorokina notes that between 1918 and 1921, Ushakov and his colleagues, including Jakobson, repeatedly consulted with the Commissariat of Foreign Affairs, and prepared scholarly materials and special reports relating to border negotiations with Poland and Latvia.[133] Already before April 1920, some of the work presented at meetings of the MLC had been officially sponsored by the government. This included a presentation by M. Peterson on "The Question of the Introduction of the Latin Alphabet," solicited by the Academic Division of Narkompros, and Boris Kushner's presentation on "The Languages of Small Peoples and Language Politics," connected to the Division of the Education of National Minorities.[134]

At a meeting held on April 25, 1920, the MLC discussed the organization of an archive related to "contemporary living language [*sovremennyi zhivoi iazyk*] . . . language culture and politics" that would include materials on the language of small nationalities and language politics, on language pedagogy, new phenomena in the sphere of Russian language, and urban folklore. The initiators of this project were Jakobson and Maksim Kenigsberg. While I am not aware of the history of this archive itself, the existence and the concept of project are reflected in some of the publications of MLC members. For example, Vinokur's book *The Culture of Language* (*Kul'tura iazyka*, 1924) can be seen as an extension of this project. One source of information on the Circle's work on contemporary language change was Jakobson's article "The Influence of the Revolution on the Russian Language"

("Vliv revoluce na ruský jazyk," 1920), in which he notes that the MLC has been collecting materials on this question and on the language politics of the revolutionary governments.[135] His own study of this material is evidenced in the article, which discusses the formation and spread of neologisms, new abbreviations, and "ornamental" epithets and clichés. Jakobson classifies his material according to different social groups. He appears most familiar with what he calls "oppositional" language usage (the language of educated urbanites), although he also refers to the language of the press, speeches of political leaders such as Lenin and Trotsky, and the language of villagers.

In the article, the main source of linguistic innovation for Jakobson is oppositional language: "Humor, polemics, political animosity, and hatred produce many new sayings [úsloví], some of which die out, while others remain the property of groups' speech [mluva]."[136] For example, Jakobson reports that the originally oppositional phrase "to put to the wall" (postavit' k stenke), which means "to shoot," has "became very common and has entered quasi-official usage."[137] The political relevance of this research is clear. For instance, he comments on alternative forms and meanings of the word "comrade" (tovarisch) which had been competing with each other in Russia for the previous three years.[138] Jakobson's article teems with examples of ironic jokes and word play at the expense of the Bolshevik revolutionary project, although this does not necessarily indicate that the MLC was anti-Bolshevik in its politics. Shklovsky, who was present at a meeting where this material was discussed, stresses this point in his 1922 article "Towards a Theory of the Comic":

> I was present at a meeting of a linguistic society in Moscow which certainly did not have an oppositional attitude towards the Soviet government. Someone read a presentation on "Soviet words." The presenter was a philologist-communist. And the entire evening was spent in a merry demonstration of various linguistic curiosities.[139]

Shklovsky's point is that linguistic innovations are often perceived as comic—regardless of a person's political sympathies. Shklovsky's response to this material is characteristically psychological-physiological—he is interested in the impulse to laughter provoked by novelty. Jakobson is interested in how new words spread and in the struggle between different groups over their meaning; describing this competition is to describe the Russian Civil War in dialectological terms.

The second use of dialectological theory in the Civil War period was the use of the cultural centers model to understand the flow of information and the shaping of public opinion. The volatility and high stakes of this cultural battlefield meant that a theory of how innovations tend to disseminate was taken seriously. This is exemplified by the Circle's extended discussion of contemporary folklore. In May 1919 the Circle met twice to discuss legends and songs (*chastushki*) responding to prerevolutionary and current events, following a report given by Yuri Sokolov.[140] This was the only instance recorded where more than one meeting was dedicated to a single presentation. The material that Sokolov presented was overwhelmingly antirevolutionary (*oppozitsionnyi*) and also antisemitic. The central question debated was prompted by Brik's suggestion that the legends were "fabrications"; Brik asked: "Haven't these legends been specially prepared and planted among the people [*narod*]?" As we have seen (in the examples of Bolshevik rumor-planting), this was not an unreasonable suggestion. The Circle debated whether knowing the source of folklore was theoretically important, and whether folklore emerges in the "center" or in the villages. While the group came to a consensus that folklore always originates in a center rather than the periphery, in this case—"a specific, partially educated environment [*polu-obrazovannaia sreda*]"—the group was divided as to whether establishing the *source* of the legends ought to be the focus of their investigation.[141]

Brik and Jakobson dominated the discussion of how to determine the source of these legends, a question which they broached using formal analysis. As Jakobson put it, "to establish the source is very important, for different kinds of legends differ in their initial structure." Jakobson and Brik both sought to split the material into two groups; Brik used the political categories of "oppositional" as opposed to "official" (*oppozitsionnyi, offitsial'nyi*) verbal art, while Jakobson used an opposition between "artistic" legends and those that seek to explain events (*osmyslenie sobytii*). Both men sought to differentiate the materials on the basis of formal criteria; Brik was explicit on the need for a "formal analysis [*formal'nyi razbor*]," and compared the style, plots, and verse structure of the materials in an attempt to discern their sources.[142] Jakobson concluded that the more "artistic" legends tended to pile on details—motifs, characters—in an effort to create a "juicy [*pikant-nyi*]" story. Rationalizing folklore, he claimed, is formally simpler. While the two men's discussion ultimately resists synthesis, it reveals how the dialectological model (formal description and centers of gravity) was applied to questions of immediate political and personal significance. Jakobson noted that the "stock character [*okamenevshii personazh*]" of the "Commissar Jew" is a widespread feature of rationalizing legends—and is found in narratives among the intelligentsia (in Saratov) and in academic circles. The spread of demonizing rumors about the role of Jews in the revolution could affect many of the Formalists personally—Jakobson, Brik, and Filipp Vremel', among those present.[143] Understanding how popular opinion (including folklore like legends, rumors, or jokes) spread, and estimating its source, was politically and personally useful knowledge during the Civil War.

Jakobson's reference to the stock character of the "Commissar Jew," which was spreading through language contact, highlights the way in which dialectological theory allowed for a "sociologically grounded history of the development of artistic forms."[144] This stock character can be traced as a feature of idiolects which travel from one person to another. A particularly vivid example of this kind of travel appears in the report of the trip made by Jakobson, Bogatyrev, and Jakovlev in 1915. It describes how, while the students were in the village of Novinskoe, a woman initiated a rumor which cast the student-ethnographers as hostile foreign agents. Bogatyrev writes that her tale successfully integrated the students into the existing repertoire of "anecdotes and rumors" about German spies. Their movements, their bags, papers, and glasses were all incorporated into this existing narrative framework. When the students arrived in another town about eight miles away several days later, they discovered that these tales had preceded them. Decades later, Jakobson described this event ironically, writing that "the tricks of the three malefactors whose perfidy deceived people's vigilance remained a trite and commonplace topic of horror stories, told with an ever-growing set of new adornments not only in Novinskoe but also in surrounding villages."[145] The report from the time, however, makes the physical threat sound more serious; the villagers in Novinskoe had decided to "drive them out and do away with [*raspravit'sia*] them," but violence was fortuitously averted by a nearby army officer.[146]

This episode demonstrates the practical importance of studying poetic devices and understanding how they travel. These devices are not to be understood in the context of an abstract autonomous system, but rather as features of particular idiolects—that of a woman in Novinskoe, or an academic in Saratov. It is as features of idiolects that these devices were capable of transforming individuals, including the Formalists themselves, into characters, such as "German spies" or "Commissar Jews." Here, we may recall Shklovsky's interest in merging his literary theory with the narration of his own personal experiences in *ZOO*. In both cases, Formalist theory explores the way in which "poetic" devices give form to lived experiences. However, while Shklovsky looked to the subconscious as a source for the regular structure and psychological effectiveness of these devices, Moscow Formalism suggested that linguistic consciousness and the geographic tracking of poetic forms could allow the theorist to shape the course of cultural and political history.

Structuralisms

SCHOLARSHIP IN THE philological paradigm was based on the comparative method; it focused on identifying isolated, reoccurring forms, which were viewed as a loose collection of unrelated elements that can travel from speaker to speaker, over space and time. The individual histories of these forms were explained by reference to psychology, as well as to cultural history. Structuralism emerged as part of a sweeping rejection of this kind of positivist scholarship. The concept of a verbal "form," for structuralism, was now defined, first and foremost, by its place in a holistic system.

Peter Steiner has stressed that, in contrast to Russian Formalism, Czech structuralism was a highly coherent school, organized around an officially established method and epistemology. Jindřich Toman's research on the Prague Linguistic Circle (PLC; Pražský lingvistický kroužek) complements this argument, revealing that the PLC's scholarly culture demanded an "unreserved assertion of methodological conformity," with bylaws that reserved the right to expel members who opposed the Circle's official method and research goals.[1] Russian Formalism, which emerged in two different centers with diverse approaches, was not nearly as tightly organized as a movement. Jurij Striedter presents the evolution from Russian Formalism to Czech structuralism as a series of stages. I agree with these scholars that structuralism was more coherent than Formalism and that one can chart a general progression, or series of shifts, in the intellectual history of thinkers like Jakobson and Bogatyrev from the 1910s to 1940s. However, my analysis aims to highlight differences rather than search for continuities and coherence. Stressing these differences clarifies earlier ideas, allowing some of them to emerge as lost paths which were alien to mainstream postwar literary theory—that is, of Claude Lévi-Strauss and French structuralism— that became dominant in the 1960s.

FROM ATOMISM TO HOLISM

The epistemological shift that accompanied the emergence of structuralism has been understood as revolutionary. Fredric Jameson describes the "Saussurean revolution" as

> corresponding to a historic shift in the subject-matter of the sciences in general, where the visible, physical independence of a given object (the organism of animals, the characteristics of chemical elements) no longer seems a useful way of distinguishing the appropriate units of study; where the first task of a science henceforth seems the establishment of a method, or a model, such that the basic conceptual units are given from the outset and organize the data (the atom, the phoneme).[2]

Jakobson also stressed this notion of an epistemological revolution across the sciences. In his 1929 book on historical phonology, he concluded that the "notion of system" was currently transforming contemporaries' understanding of architecture, physics, artistic painting, psychology, biology, geography, and economic science, as well as linguistics, of course.[3] In February 1945, days before his sudden death, Ernst Cassirer gave a talk at the Linguistic Circle of New York, titled "Structuralism in Modern Linguistics," in which he summarized the sea change across the sciences as a turn towards "holism." In situating structuralist linguistics in relation to contemporary developments in biology, psychology, and philosophy, Cassirer focused on the use of the term "Gestalt." He credited Gestalt psychology, a movement that emerged largely in Prague and Berlin in the 1910s, with developing a "new concept and a new description of empirical knowledge."[4] I will follow Cassirer in focusing on Gestalt psychology: it clearly exemplifies the turn to holism in early twentieth-century scholarly thought, and it provided structuralist linguistics with an epistemological model for distinguishing their work from nineteenth-century philology. Gestaltism is also widely understood in opposition to associationism, which provided the underpinnings for the philological paradigm.

Gestalt psychology informed Jakobson's thinking about structuralist linguistics in the late 1920s and early 1930s. His 1931 "Principles of Historical Phonology" articulates the methodological difference between his structuralist approach and the historical phonology of the Neogrammarians by referring to Kurt Koffka's "Psychology" (1925). The new phonological method Jakobson advocates is, like Gestalt psychology, an "integrating method," according to which "every phonological fact is treated as part of the whole." This is contrasted to the Neogrammarians' "isolating method."[5] Jakobson's turn to psychology as an epistemological model echoed the intellectual environment of Prague in the 1920s. Gestalt psychology, which had intellectual roots in Charles University, insisted on its radical methodological and epistemological break with older psychological theories.

The history of Gestalt psychology is said to have begun with a founding statement, "On Gestalt Qualities" (1890), by the Prague-based Austrian nobleman Christian von Ehrenfels. Ehrenfels pointed out that we can recognize two melodies as identical even when no two notes in them are the same. A melody can be played using any set of pitches; as long as the relation between those pitches is held constant, it is considered to be the same melody. Ehrenfels concluded on this basis that the "form" of the melody must contain something different from the sum of its elements. He termed this perception of the whole its "Gestalt quality" (*Gestaltqualität*). Ehrenfels's proposal was followed by two decades of debate on the apparent divide between bottom-up, empirical (associative) theories of perception and top-down, rationalist, and holistic methods and models.[6] This debate culminated in the 1910s with the successful demonstration of Gestaltist claims using experimental research, which spurred the coalescence of the movement as a school. The critical experiment was devised by the Prague-born Max Wertheimer, who had studied with Ehrenfels at Charles University in the late 1890s. In 1912 Wertheimer demonstrated what was called the "phi phenomenon": the "motion" seen when two stationary light sources alternately flash at a given interval. Wertheimer's experiment was understood to reveal that this phenomenon is not deduced from the separate sensation of two optical stimuli (first light A flashes, then light B), which are then added together; instead movement is perceived directly, as a whole.[7] The psychologists John Anderson and Gordon Bower have described this as "a clear demonstration that the mind imposes organization on incoming sensory data, that the perception of the whole series takes on emergent properties above and beyond the properties of its parts."[8]

Wertheimer thus laid the ground for an epistemology "based on the claim that not sensations, but structured wholes, or *Gestalten*, are the primary units of mental life."[9] The best-known Gestalt rule is the overarching "law of *Prägnanz*": individuals tend to perceive any given visual array in a way that most simply organizes the different elements into a stable and coherent form. The more specific Gestalt laws of similarity, proximity, closure, and good continuation are special instances of this more general law. In the 1910s, this new psychology was part of a broader debate between the empiricist position that the mind is a "blank slate" and the opposing view that the mind operates with innate mental structures. Gestaltism was a challenge to associationist psychology, which was characterized as "atomizing" or "mechanistic" rather than holistic. Associationist theories, as we have seen, identified the basic components of the mind with sensory experience and proposed simple, additive rules to predict the properties of associative configurations from the underlying sense data. But as Wertheimer put it, "the whole cannot be deduced from the characteristics of the separate pieces, but conversely; what happens to a part of the whole is, in clear-cut cases, determined by the laws of the inner structure of its whole."[10] Anderson and Bower articulate the logical conclusions of the debate between the two positions:

> The Gestalt-associationist controversy was not over what the atomic elements might be in a psychological analysis, but over whether such elements existed at any level. The Gestalters insisted that psychology would only succeed if it considered the whole phenomenon "from the top down." The "whole" was alleged to have emergent properties that could not have easily been predicted by examining the parts. These wholistic properties determined how the parts would be perceived, and not vice versa.[11]

For the broader academic community, including Jakobson and the Prague Linguistic Circle, the success of Gestalt psychology was proof that science must proceed by the deductive study of holistic structures rather than the inductive identification of primary elements.[12]

This intellectual environment influenced the reception of Ferdinand de Saussure's *Course in General Linguistics* (1916) in Prague. Although Saussure does not reference Gestalt psychology, his ideas were understood as analogous to the Gestaltists' revolutionary claims. Saussure argued for an epistemological distinction between the study of language history (atomizing and inductive) and language structure (holistic and deductive). In his view, the discovery of the principles of operation for a language "system" as a whole must precede the analysis of its component parts. As he put it, apropos of the "sign":

> It is a great mistake . . . to isolate it [the sign] from the system to which it belongs. It would be to suppose that a start could be made with individual signs, and a system constructed by putting them together. On the contrary, the system as a united whole is the starting point, from which it becomes possible, by a process of analysis, to identify its constituent elements.[13]

Saussure's *Course* encouraged scholars like Jakobson and Trubetskoi to take up the study of the system of sounds in language, understood as a "united whole."

Trubetskoi's seminal *Principles of Phonology* (*Grundzüge der Phonologie,* 1939) characterizes the discipline of phonology as a methodological revolution by opposing holism to mechanism. Like Jakobson, Trubetskoi used terms from Gestalt psychology to explain phonology, arguing, for example, that each word is a "Gestalt" that "always contains something more than the sum of its parts (i.e., the phonemes)."[14] The linguist Zelig Harris laments this aspect of Prague school terminology as obfuscating: the "mystical use of philosophical terms" and "undefined psychological terms" does not bring clarity to the subject.[15] These terms came from the intellectual milieu of central Europe, in which arguments for the identity of a new discipline—such as Gestalt psychology or structuralist linguistics—sought support by referring to epistemological debates. Trubetskoi relies on these terms when distinguishing between phonetics and phonology. The former studies speech sounds in all of their acoustic and articulatory properties. The latter is not interested in *all* possible speech sounds; it approaches the study of sound deductively, from the top down: it "needs to consider only *that aspect of sound which fulfills a specific function in the system of language.*"[16] Like Gestalt psychology and Saussure's concept of language as a "system," Praguean structuralist phonology approached its object of study in holistic terms (of "structure" and "function") and opposes this work to an empiricist methodology.

This opposition was also used to distinguish structuralism from both Formalist theory and nineteenth-century philology. In the 1930s, Jakobson sharply discounted "early" Formalist theory, which he associated almost entirely with the work of Victor Shklovsky, whom he criticized in a 1935 lecture:

> In the earlier works of Shklovsky, a poetic work was defined as a mere sum of its artistic devices, while poetic evolution appeared as nothing more than a substitution of certain devices. With the further development of Formalism, there arose the *accurate [správný]* conception of a poetic work as a structured system, a regularly ordered hierarchical set of artistic devices.[17]

Jakobson also attacked Neogrammarian scholarship—even though, as we have seen, he himself adhered to some of its principles in 1919. In his speech "What Is Poetry?" (1934) he lambasts outdated cultural trends, including "positivism and naive realism in philosophy, liberalism in politics, the neogrammarian school in linguistics, scrupulous illusionism in literature and on the stage . . . atomizing methods in literary studies (and in the sciences in general)."[18] Toman has pointed out that Jakobson frequently used the terms "mechanical" and "atomism" to critique misguided methodology.[19]

The analogy between linguistics and Gestalt psychology did not mean, however, that Prague structuralism was a psychological understanding of language. In fact, both Prague structuralism and Saussure explicitly argued for a *social*, rather than a psychological, conception of language (see the appendix). Saussure viewed language (*la langue*) as a corpus or inventory of elements, which he described as a fund or "treasure" belonging to a collective:

It [*la langue*] is a fund [*trésor*] deposited by the members of a given community through their active use of speaking, a grammatical system that has a potential existence in each brain, or, more specifically, in the brains of a group of individuals. For the language is never complete in any single individual, but exists perfectly only in the collectivity.[20]

Saussurean linguistics studies the system of language derived from this inventory of elements—the shared "treasure" or "sum of words and phrases" available to any speaker.[21] The structuralist method takes this *socially shared knowledge* as the ultimate object of study, in contrast to the philological paradigm, which viewed language structure as the individually variable product of psychological laws of association. The structuralists' social definition of language can also be contrasted with Noam Chomsky's generative grammar, introduced in the late 1950s, which views grammatical rules as resulting from an innate mental capacity or "biological endowment."[22]

Following Saussure, structuralist theory argued that language can be understood as a system of "values," which is arbitrary in the sense of arbitrary *social convention*. The Prague school linguists adopted and extended this idea. Trubetskoi distinguishes phonetics from phonology by analogy with the social sciences:

> The basis for this distinction [between phonology and phonetics] is that the system of language *as a social institution* constitutes a world of relations, functions, and values . . . The same type of relation is found in all the social sciences insofar as they deal with the social evaluation of material things. In all such cases, the social institution per se must be strictly distinguished from the concrete acts in which it finds expression, so to speak, and which would not be possible without them.[23]

The historian of linguistics John Joseph has documented how Saussure replaced psychological with sociological explanations in the changes he made between his second (1908–09) and third (1910–11) course of lectures on general linguistics: although Saussure never ceased to view the language system as both a social and a psychological fact, he increasingly stressed its social nature. Joseph explains this as an act of "academic *Realpolitik*"—an effort to buttress the autonomy of the new linguistics against the "strong academic interests of psychology."[24] Those interests

> threatened to swallow up whole any emerging "general synchronic linguistic" enterprise—unless that enterprise began with a strong and reiterated claim that its object of study was actually language as a *social* fact—not a creation of the human mind or human minds, but a wholly arbitrary institution with a primarily social rather than individual mode of existence.[25]

185

Saussure relied on the idea of a "collective consciousness" in order to talk about the language system as a social phenomenon: "Static linguistics will be concerned with logical and psychological relationships between co-existent terms as they are perceived by the same collective consciousness (which moreover is mirrored by an individual consciousness—each of us has *langue* within us) and forming a system."[26] Here Saussure attempts to find a means of talking about the language system as something that is both social and holistic. In order for this model to work, the system of language has to be shared by members of the collective and mirrored in each individual's consciousness.

An analogous move is found in the thinking of Émile Durkheim, whom Harland described as sharing, with Saussure, "co-paternity" of the superstructuralist movement.[27] As Harland writes: "Durkheim views society as much more than the aggregate of its members. He argues for the existence of 'collective representations'" which are "exterior to individual minds" and "do not derive from them as such but from the association of minds."[28] In *The Division of Labor in Society* (1893), Durkheim wrote that "the totality of beliefs and sentiments common to the average citizens of the same society forms a determinate system which has its own life; one may call it the *collective* or *common consciousness*."[29] "In what medium," Harland asks, "can ideas, beliefs, and feelings reside if not in individual brains in individual bodies?" He explains that

> Durkheim envisaged *an analogy between the unity of society and the unity of thinking in the individual mind* . . . Durkheim did ultimately believe in a kind of social super-mind, hovering over and above the thinking of individual minds in the same way that the thinking of an individual mind hovers over and above the individual neural elements of the brain.[30]

Saussure's "collective consciousness"—a term which he did not describe in detail in his writings—is described in similar terms: the collective consciousness "mirrors" the individual consciousness.[31] Moreover, the similarities between the holism of Gestalt psychology and structuralism suggest an analogy between the operations of the individual perceptual system and that of a consciousness sustained by a collective. This idea is problematic and vague—or as Harland puts it, "embarrassingly mystical."[32] Yet it was essential to structuralist thinking in the 1920s and 1930s: the collective consciousness which maintains *la langue*, the shared "treasure" of the social group, is the source of the linguistic structure available to each individual. The idea of a collective consciousness was used by both Mukařovský and Bogatyrev, the two members of the Prague Linguistic Circle who did most to develop a cultural semiotics in the interwar period.[33]

THE WATERSHED MOMENT: 1928–1929

In *Dialogues* Jakobson recalled that "I followed Saussure with increasing insistence from the moment I became acquainted with his *Course*, which [Albert] Sechehaye sent to me in 1920 shortly after my arrival in Prague."[34] This reminiscence supports my argument that Jakobson's scholarship from the 1910s (Moscow Formalism) was not fundamentally informed by Saussure's ideas. However, other scholars have stressed the potential earlier influence of Serge Karcevski (Sergei Kartsevskii), a Russian linguist who had spent the 1910s studying in Geneva with Saussure's pupils before returning to Russia in the years 1917–19.[35] In 1956, Jakobson wrote that Karcevski "fired the young generation of Moscow linguists with the *Cours de linguistique générale*"; he is probably referring to Karcevski's presentation on "The System of the Russian Verb" to the Moscow Dialectological Commission on February 7, 1918 (at which Jakobson was present).[36] Karcevski's name does not, however, subsequently appear as a participant at any meeting of the Moscow Linguistic Circle. Scholars also note that Jakobson mentions Saussure by name, although in the context of a rather idiosyncratic reference, on the first page of his "Newest Russian Poetry."[37] It is thus clear that Jakobson had *some* knowledge of Saussure before he left Russia in 1920.

However, in his Moscow years Jakobson's work was overwhelmingly informed by his training in dialectology: in this period he repeated Shakhmatov's dictum that "only the language of every individual has a real existence; the language of the village, the city, the region, the nation is a known scholarly fiction."[38] He also concluded that it is impossible to posit phonetic "laws" that would describe the language of an entire group. As Jakobson concluded, "one cannot talk about the dialect of the village of Kostiunin, but only about a multiplicity of individual and short-term dialects: it is virtually impossible to speak about phonetic laws, but only about phonetic inclinations and tendencies."[39] Jakobson follows Neogrammarian dialectology by isolating innovations in Khlebnikov's poetry, offering these as "features" of his poetic "dialect" (by which Jakobson means idiolect) which could be picked up by other speakers. This is quite different from the Saussurean contention that the proper object of study is not individual speech, but rather the collectively shared system of language elements, defined by rule-bound interrelationships (i.e., not phonetics, but phonology).

It follows, then, that Jakobson could not immediately assimilate his Moscow training to the ideas coming out of Geneva. In his first linguistics monograph, *Remarks on the Phonological Evolution of Russian in Comparison with the Other Slavic Languages* (*Remarques sur l'évolution phonologique du russe comparée à celle des autres langues slaves*, 1929), Jakobson laid out his response to Saussure in full. In this book, Jakobson rejects

Chapter Five

the dialectology he was trained in and proposes a replacement: instead of tracing the geographic dispersal of a particular word or pronunciation, he suggests a teleological historical phonology that describes the evolution of *phonological systems*:

> Works that have appeared during the past decades in the field of linguistic geography have contributed much to our understanding of the spread of lexical features. However, as soon as we go from the domain of vocabulary to that of grammar or phonology, we see that the concept of a *system*, so clearly emphasized by Saussure and Fortunatov, claims its position as the cornerstone of linguistics. . . . Often, a grammatical or phonological isogloss, considered separately, is actually just a fiction, since features that seem identical in isolation are really not the same—that is, when considered as forming an integral part of a system.[40]

This book is a particularly important work in Jakobson's intellectual biography because it embodies both his reinterpretation of Saussure and his rejection of the linguistics in which he was trained. It is seen as "a corrective to the historical work of both the Neo-grammarians of the nineteenth century and Saussure's *Course in General Linguistics*."[41] Jakobson later characterized the years 1928–29 as "a moment of radical, worldwide reassessment [*peresmotr*] of methodology across the sciences."[42] This notion of radical "reassessment" underscores my argument regarding Jakobson's intellectual biography in this period. While in 1919 he claimed that theoretical abstractions are inevitably fictions, ten years later he argued the opposite—that atomizing comparative research produces "fiction" rather than facts.

An important publication of this time was the "Theses Presented to the First Congress of Slavic Philologists in Prague, 1929," which first presented the PLC's official methodological platform (structural functionalism) and research goals. The opening section characteristically pronounces that "no linguistic phenomenon can be understood without regard for the system to which it belongs."[43] The preparation of these "Theses" reportedly prompted a "transformation" of the Circle into a new kind of organization, which Jakobson described in April 1929 in a letter to Trubetskoi:

> An initiative core of the circle has now concluded that the circle in its function as a parliament of opinions . . . is a relic, and that it has to be transformed into a group, a party, which is tightly interlocked as far as scientific ideology is concerned. This process is taking place at present with much success . . . This transformation of the circle literally inspirited its members; in fact, I have never seen such a degree of enthusiasm in the Czechs at all.[44]

188

The Prague Linguistic Circle had been founded by Jakobson, along with the Czech linguist Vilém Mathesius, in 1926. The founding and early members included Bohumil Trnka, Bogatyrev, Jan Mukařovský, and Karcevski. The meetings between 1926 and 1929 were small in size and often took place in members' homes.[45] During this period the Circle did not keep records of its meetings, and there are almost no records of the Circle's activities in its archive from these years. Towards the end of the decade, as Jakobson suggests, the Circle became newly energized and coherent, having adopted an official program with which it would go public at the Congress. It was only in the year following this event that the PLC became an officially registered group with bylaws.[46] The first paragraph of the Circle's bylaws stipulated loyalty to the "structural functional method," stating that "the purpose of the PLC is to work towards progress in linguistic research on the basis of the functional structural method."[47] It was thus only at the end of the decade, in 1929–30, that the PLC emerged as an organization with a shared, publicly articulated commitment to advancing a structuralist theory of language.

A series of other coauthored statements which Jakobson worked on from 1927 to 1929 marked out the impact of structuralism across the domain formerly encompassed by philology: on linguistics, literature, and folklore. The first was a short statement: "Quelles sont les méthodes les mieux appropriées à un exposé complet et pratique de la phonologie d'une langue quelconque?" It was written in October 1927, co-signed by Trubetskoi and Karcevski, and distributed at the First International Linguistics Congress in 1928, held in The Hague.[48] "Quelles sont les méthodes" contrasts new developments prompted by Saussure's *Course* with Neogrammarian linguistics. As in Jakobson's 1929 *Remarks on the Phonological Evolution of Russian* and in the Prague school's "Theses," the systemic approach to language is promoted as a new cornerstone of linguistics. This treatise, along with another short statement, "The Concept of the Sound Law and the Teleological Criterion," and the full monograph of *Remarks on the Phonological Evolution of Russian* are placed at the beginning of the first volume of Jakobson's *Selected Writings* (1962). It appears that, in the 1960s, Jakobson understood these texts to be the starting point for his intellectual biography as a founder of structuralism.

Jakobson later recalled that his experience writing "Quelles sont les méthodes" with Trubetskoi and Karcevski prompted him to propose to Yuri Tynianov that they write a similar manifesto for literary studies, when the latter visited Prague in the winter of 1928–29.[49] This resulted in their well-known "Problems in the Study of Literature and Language" ("Problemy izucheniia literatury i iazyka"), which was published in the Soviet constructivist journal *Novyi LEF*. Jakobson also notes that at this same time he embarked on a third set of theses, with Petr Bogatyrev, "Towards the Problem of Separating Folkloristics and Literary Studies" ("K probleme razmezhevaniia fol'kloristiki i literaturovedeniia"). This statement was then elaborated into the longer, better-known article "Folklore as a Special Form of Creativity" ("Die Folklore als eine besondere Form des Schaffens," 1929).[50]

Taken together, these three manifesto statements share a common point of departure, with each calling for a methodological revolution in the study of language (phonology, literature, and folklore), informed by Saussure's distinction between *langue* and *parole*. In collaborating with Trubetskoi and Karcevski, Tynianov, and Bogatyrev, Jakobson appears to have been spearheading an effort to reconsider the old domain of philology through the new lens of structuralism. It was at the Slavic Congress in 1929, where the PLC presented its "Theses," that Jakobson used the term "structuralism" (*strukturalismus*) for the first time, characterizing it as part of a broader change occurring across the sciences (*vědy*):

> If we wanted to concisely characterize the leading idea of today's science in all its most diverse manifestations, we couldn't find a more suitable term than *structuralism*. Every collection of phenomena studied by contemporary science is discussed not as a mechanistic cluster, but as a structural whole, as a system, and the basic goal is to reveal its internal laws—static and evolutionary: not the external impulse, but the internal preconditions for evolution, not genesis in its mechanistic understanding, but function is the center of today's scientific interests.[51]

The structuralists' epistemological and methodological revolution entailed a departure from central assumptions of the philological paradigm: it replaced a psychological source of language structure (associationism) with a socially conceived concept of the collective consciousness, and it replaced the empiricist focus on individual, historical facts with an abstract system of elements as the true object of study. These core shifts were accompanied by a new rationale for disciplinary boundaries—which was used to carve up the formerly undifferentiated domain of philology. The concept of an internally defined system was used to articulate the concept of a boundary distinguishing literature from other kinds of discourse. We have seen this move in Trubetskoi's demarcation of phonology as a field distinct from phonetics. Unlike phonetics, phonology "needs to consider only *that aspect of sound which fulfills a specific function in the system of language*."[52] Likewise, Tynianov and Jakobson use the concept of a system to argue for the autonomy of literary studies:

The evolution of literature cannot be understood until the evolutionary problem ceases to be obscured by questions of episodic, nonsystemic origin, whether literary . . . or extraliterary. The literary and extraliterary material used in literature may be introduced into the orbit of scientific investigation only when it is considered from a functional point of view.[53]

Finally, Jakobson's statements coauthored with Bogatyrev argue that a line must be drawn between literature and folklore.

The previous chapters have argued that the non-differentiation between folklore and literature, facilitated by the category of *slovesnost'*, enabled the emergence of Russian Formalism. We have seen ramifications of this in the OPOIAZ Formalists' treatment of poetic texts as oral performances, and in the development of a poetic dialectology in the MLC. The watershed moment of the late 1920s signals a departure from the philological paradigm, however. Jakobson and Bogatyrev now argue that folklore and literature must be differentiated as distinct objects of study, defined by their own particular modes of being (*bytie*). They stress that *"there is a difference in the content of the concept 'the existence* [bytie] *of the literary work' and 'the existence* [bytie] *of the folkloric work,'"* and they explain that[54]

the work of folklore is extra-personal and has only a potential existence. It is only a complex of certain norms and impulses, a canvas of living tradition, which the performers animate with the embellishments of individual creativity, just as the creators of *parole* (in the Saussurean sense of the word) do in relation to *langue*. The literary work is objectified; it exists concretely, independently of the reader, and each individual reader turns directly to it.[55]

In "Folklore as a Special Form of Creativity" they summarize this point by stating that "a fundamental difference between folklore and literature is that folklore is set specifically towards *langue* [*die Einstellung auf die langue . . . ist*], while literature is set towards *parole*."[56] In both the theses and the article, Bogatyrev and Jakobson stress that a literary text can be ignored for generations (e.g., the writings of Comte de Lautréamont) but then rediscovered later, something impossible for folklore.[57] The "Folklore" article is notable as an early, and perhaps the first, extension of Saussure's categories of *langue* and *parole* beyond linguistics to the study of cultural phenomena. It also suggests that textuality is a defining feature of literature, which is a departure from Russian Formalist theory, which sought to theorize literature following the model of speech in dialogue. Bogatyrev and Jakobson are now arguing that folklore and literature need to be studied separately, since the former is collective and oral, and the latter is written and individual. This argument suggests a new priority on disciplinary divisions and boundaries, such as the boundary created by a discrete text, considered as a systemic whole. Jakobson and his collaborators' insistence that the methods of structuralism amount to a radical epistemological revolution cautions against the view that structuralism emerged from Formalist premises. The intellectual foundations of Russian Formalism and Czech structuralism were fundamentally incompatible: they were rooted in different epistemologies (empiricism vs. rationalism) and methodologies (inductive vs. deductive) and entailed different conceptions of the object of study, both in its boundaries (*slovesnost'* vs. literature as a field separate from folklore) and its medium (oral speech vs. texts).

FUNCTIONS AND STRUCTURES

While Jakobson and his coauthors—Tynianov, Trubetskoi, and Bogatyrev—used the same structuralist terminology, particularly "function" and "system," what they meant by these terms varied. Of particular significance is the term "function," which characterizes the nature of the system created by the functionally related elements. In hindsight, the most canonical definition was Trubetskoi's use of "function" to denote differentiation. For structuralist phonology, "function" was understood as follows:

> The signifier in the system of language consists of a number of elements whose *essential function is to distinguish themselves from each other*. . . . It is the task of phonology to study . . . in which way the discriminative elements (or marks) are related to each other, and the rules according to which they may be combined into words and sentences.[58]

Trubetskoi's understanding of structure and function generally follows Saussure, and articulates a central tenet of structuralist phonology. However, when we look at interwar structuralist literary and ethnographic theory, we find competing concepts of "function" in the 1920s and 1930s. Disentangling these different functionalisms allows us to clarify the theoretical writings of this period and to recover some less canonical branches of literary theory, ones that are further from post–World War II structuralism. In 1962, Jakobson noted that "during the last decades the terms 'structure' and 'function' have become the most equivocal and stereotyped words in the science of language." In particular, the "promiscuous" use of "function" with different meanings is a "source of confusion which makes certain pages of our time scarcely intelligible."[59]

A second concept of "function," found in the Formalists' earliest writings, is what Michael Silverstein describes as "user-focused functionalisms" in which "the 'functions' of language involve intentionalities, purposes, and strategic plans."[60] A user-oriented functionalism was a prominent feature of Russian Formalist discourse in the 1910s, especially in Lev Jakubinsky's early writings, including those published in the OPOIAZ *sborniki*. The concept of language "function" was also part of the discourse of the Moscow Linguistic Circle. Jakobson, for example, wrote in "The Newest Russian Poetry" that "poetry is language in its aesthetic function." Although he does not define these terms, one of the central aims of his 1919 study was to intervene in ongoing debates on the relationship between the emotional and poetic functions of language.[61] These references to user-oriented functions in the 1910s were part of the psychologistic understanding of language of the philological paradigm.

A psychological concept of function was influentially promoted by Baudouin de Courtenay (1845–1929).[62] To describe the Formalist understanding of "function" I will rely on Jakubinsky's work, since he developed this concept in the most detail. Jakubinsky studied linguistics under Baudouin de Courtenay at St. Petersburg University, and de Courtenay's psychological approach to phonetics (which he termed "psycho-phonetics") is reflected in the title of Jakubinsky's student essay "The Psychophonetic Zeros in Russian-Language Thought" (1911).[63] Jakubinsky's OPOIAZ publication "On the Sounds of Verse Language" ("O zvukakh stikhotvornogo iazyka") begins with the statement that "linguistic phenomena must be classified from the perspective of the goal with which the speaker uses his or her linguistic conceptions [*iazykovyimi predstavleniiami*] in any given situation."[64] The essay is famous for arguing for the autonomy of language in its poetic function, which Jakobson echoed in "The Newest Russian Poetry." Jakubinsky's understanding of "language" is not that of the structuralist *la langue*: he views it as the study of speech (something more like *parole*) in context. In a longer study, "On Dialogical Speech" ("O dialogicheskoi rechi," 1923), Jakubinsky explains that his object of study is "human speech *activity*" (*rechevaia deiatel'nost' cheloveka*). This "activity" needs to be studied in psychological and sociological terms. As Jakubinsky explains, linguistics needs to distinguish, in psychological terms, between "speech in the contexts of normal, pathological, and abnormal conditions."[65] From a sociological perspective, he argues, speech activity can be classified according to the "conditions of communication [*obshchenie*]" (in typical and unusual contexts); the "form of communication" (direct and indirect, monologic and dialogic); and the "goals of communication" (practical, artistic, indifferent or persuasive). Among the functions of language, Jakubinsky was primarily interested in the idea of a *poetic* function, a concept which he traces to the legacy of Wilhelm von Humboldt.

Jakubinsky's work on language function is consistent with the philological paradigm: the question of function pertains to the study of speech as an "activity" determined by particular psychological and social contexts. Moreover, he clarifies that claims about speech *functions* (e.g., practical, poetic, emotional) are separate from claims about the formal features of speech: "Certainly, when making distinctions in the domain of the 'purpose-oriented' [*tselovoi*], we are essentially distinguishing not between linguistic phenomena, but factors of these phenomena, and we cannot immediately give even a rough projection of these distinctions in the sphere of speech itself."[66] Jakubinsky's insistence on the centrality of dialogic speech influenced both Valentin Voloshinov (a student of his) and also possibly Bakhtin.[67] These thinkers share an assumption that speech in (dialogical) context is the linguist's proper object of study.

This is worth stressing because Jakobson's post–World War II articulation of the "functions" of language is different from the Formalist understanding of function, represented by Jakubinsky's work described above. In "Linguistics and Poetics" (1960), Jakobson famously argued that "language must be investigated in all the variety of its functions. . . . An outline of these functions demands a concise survey of the constitutive factors in *any* speech event, in *any* act of verbal communication."[68] Jakobson moves quickly from the concept of "function" to a universal communicative model. He was initially inspired by Karl Bühler's triangular organon model (1934), which consisted of three points: first person (addresser), second person (addressee), and third person (someone/thing spoken of).[69] Each point corresponds with a function: emotive, conative, referential. Jakobson uses a revised version of this universal model to propose a "scheme of functions" which "correspond" with the "fundamental factors" of communication.[70] His resulting six functions are the emotive, conative, referential, poetic, phatic, and metalingual. Jakobson thus assesses the function of an utterance by reference to the speaker's goals, but these are in turn defined by the communicative schema. While Jakubinsky's Formalist functionalism took *the individual speech act* as his object of study, Jakobson's post-1945 functionalism was built on a *universal* communicative *model*. (I return to this model in the last section of this chapter).

I will now turn to the concept of "function" as it was developed by the Prague school in the late 1920s and 1930s. In the late 1920s, Petr Bogatyrev and the Czech aesthetician Jan Mukařovský applied Saussure's concept of the linguistic sign to the study of contemporary art and culture.[71] Both men joined the Prague Linguistic Circle at its third meeting in December 1926, becoming its first two members who were not primarily linguists by training. Both can be seen as pioneers in the field of cultural semiotics, applying the Prague school's structural-linguistic platform to the study of material culture and the arts. Scholars frequently date the emergence of Prague school semiotics to 1934, and to the presentation of Mukařovský's seminal essay "L'Art comme fait sémiologique" at the International Philosophical Congress in Paris (September 1934).[72]

Mukařovský (1891–1975) began his career as a student of the aesthetician Otakar Zich at Charles University. One of his best-known works is *Aesthetic Function, Norm and Value as Social Facts* (*Estetická funkce, norma a hodnota jako sociální fakty*, 1936), in which he synthesizes the fields of aesthetics, structuralist semiotics, and sociology. Within the PLC, Mukařovský was chairman of the Circle's Commission for the Study of Poetic Language, and his writings on poetic language represented the PLC program on this subject.[73] Bogatyrev, who was a founder of the Moscow Linguistic Circle, moved to Czechoslovakia in 1921 as an employee and translator for the Soviet permanent representation in Czechoslovakia.[74] He was subsequently employed by the Moscow Literary Museum, and tasked with collecting literary and historical materials under the direction of V. Bonch-Bruevich.[75] He spent much of the 1920s conducting fieldwork in Subcarpathian Ruthenia (in the easternmost part of Czechoslovakia).[76] His first monograph, *Actes magiques, rites, et croyances en Russie Subcarpatique* (1929), sought to analyze the ethnographic data he had collected using a novel, "synchronic" approach.

Despite the differences in their areas of study—aesthetics as opposed to ethnography—Mukařovský and Bogatyrev approached structuralist semiotics in a similar way, relying on a set of shared ideas, which they developed in meetings of the PLC, and reading each other's work. Both were among the most frequent attendees of Circle meetings in the mid-1930s.[77] From their writings, it is clear that they were neither operating with a strictly differential concept of function (Trubetskoi) nor referring to a user-oriented functionalism focused on a speaker's communicative goals (Jakobson and Jakubinsky). Instead, they approached function in terms of the meaning of a cultural artifact (including art objects) for a particular social group. Bogatyrev first introduced the concept of function as an alternative to the historical genealogical study of popular belief:

> Usually scholars of folkloric [*narodnyi*] rituals and magical acts approach them from a historical perspective. In an effort to uncover their original form and original meaning they reconstruct the skeleton [*ostov*] of the ritual—that which in linguistics is called the Ur-form. Following the static or synchronic method, I have tried to focus on the actual *function* of rituals and magical acts in our time. When collecting material, I have tried to elicit explanations from peasants as to *what meaning* [*znachenie*] *they attribute to one or another ritual right now*.[78]

For example, Bogatyrev provides several different explanations of the ritual of placing a chain around the table on Christmas Eve. He notes that in Lozjans'kŷi it is said that "people put their feet on a chain so that they will be as strong as iron," but in Pryslop "the same rite . . . was explained as follows: 'Just as ferocious animals will not touch iron, they cannot attack the livestock!'" and in Jasinja the chain is fastened with a "padlock, so that all tongues will be fastened all year long."[79] Bogatyrev noted that these "interpretations are in constant motion, changing, merging, and growing as a result of the social context or the nature of the individual involved in them."[80] He sought to bring order to his data by applying James Frazier's "laws of magic"—that is, explanations (such as those cited above) adhere to either the "law of contact" or the "law of similarity." In other words, the two fundamental laws of association.

In his work in the 1930s, Bogatyrev developed a semiotic framework for the study of ethnography. Of central importance for him was the holistic model provided by Gestalt psychology. According to an obituary essay that Jakobson wrote for his colleague in 1971, this was a central facet of Bogatyrev's thinking: "It is indicative that in his [Bogatyrev's] doctoral orals of 1930 at Bratislava University . . . he pointed to Ehrenfels' idea of *Gestaltqualität* as the chief attainment of modern psychology."[81] Bogatyrev used Gestalt theory as a way of accounting for both the plurality and variability of his data, while also positing that these form a unitary structure. In "A Contribution to Structural Ethnography" ("Příspěvek k strukturální etnografii," 1931), Bogatyrev cites elicited explanations (functions of "beauty," "comfort," "ugliness," and "ungainliness" in relation to items of clothing) to demonstrate that the functions of an artifact are organized in relation to each other just as perceptions are organized in an individual's psyche:

> If a certain ethnographic phenomenon has several functions, this functional diversity leads us to the use of methods similar to the methods of structural psychology (Gestalt psychology). Let us agree on what we will mean by "structure." We will use [Kurt] Koffka's definition: "Such a co-occurrence of phenomena [*Zusammensein von Phänomenen*], in which each link [*Glied*] 'carries the other,' and in which each link has its own character only through and with the other, we will from now on call a structure."
>
> The term structure therefore contains the following two features:
>
> 1. A certain *plurality* and variability of parts or elements of a fact or phenomenon which is characterized by a structure, and at the same time
>
> 2. An *orderliness*, the mutual correlation of these elements, to which the given fact or phenomenon owes its integrity and unity.[82]

Bogatyrev combined this Gestalt concept of structure with a particular interpretation of the semiotic sign. Like other members of the Prague Linguistic

Circle, he followed Valentin Voloshinov's referential understanding of the sign. In Bogatyrev's 1937 book on folk costume, *Funkcie kroja na Moravskom Slovensku* (*The Functions of Folk Costume in Moravian Slovakia*), he quotes at length from Voloshinov's "Stylistics of Artistic Speech" ("Stilistika khudozhestvennoi rechi," 1930) where, in his discussion of "The Word and Its Social Function," Voloshinov describes the material sign. For example,

> we take a stone, paint it with lime, and place it on the boundary between two farms. That stone will take on a certain "meaning" [*znachenie*]. It will no longer simply be itself—a stone, a part of nature—it will have acquired another, new meaning [*smysl*]. It will refer [*ukazat'*] to something that is *beyond* itself. It will become a signal, a sign of definite and constant meaning; i.e., of the boundary between two portions of land.[83]

Bogatyrev used this referential understanding of the material sign to describe the regional meanings of details in elaborate Moravian folk costumes.

After describing the different elements of traditional folk costume, and their different functions, Bogatyrev concludes that all of these functions make up a structure of functions—understood as an "organic whole" or a "*unique* system." The system as a whole, he suggests, can be understood as a gestalt, with a *Gestaltqualität*. This *Gestaltqualität* of the costume is an emotional perception of "our costume," described by analogy with the feeling one has for a "mother tongue."[84] The content of the functions will be different for different towns, as in each case a sign refers to a particular social reality. As Voloshinov stresses: the sign "refers to something that is *beyond* itself," and is a "manifestation of something actually occurring in reality."[85] This interpretation of the sign was a significant aspect of Bogatyrev's structuralist ethnography, which has been described by Svetlana Sorokina as a "local approach" (*lokal'nyi podkhod*).[86] Bogatyrev sought to account for the particular cultural identities of the communities that he observed. For instance, he questions the assumption that "the conquest of urban dress [*kostium*] over rural will proceed in an unbroken band," and posits instead that there remain "individual islands, which preserve rural dress. After precisely noting these islands on the map, the next task is to explain the stable preservation of older forms of dress in particular places."[87] Bogatyrev assumes that cultural change is limited by the preexisting structures of thought that define a social unit. The "islands" that he identifies will, presumably, have their own collective structures of functions, and elucidating these will provide an answer as to why this collective behaves differently than its neighbors.

In a lecture delivered at Charles University, Mukařovský paraphrases Bogatyrev's work in order to explain his own understanding of the "sociology" of literature. Sociology is to be understood not just as the relationship between literature or other series and the concrete development of society . . . For now: sociology of a series as a collection of its relationships to all series possible. Many functions. These functions together create yet another structure, a structure of functions. Thus: *the sociology of a series [is] the development of the structure of its functions.* For clarification I turn your attention to P. Bogatyrev's article.[88]

Mukařovský, like Bogatyrev, was interested in the relationship between different social functions. Mukařovský in particular sought to use this framework to advance a sociological aesthetic theory. Both men stressed that the material, formal features of an object (e.g., a song, a poem, or an item of clothing) are not sufficient to determine its function for a group of people. One of Bogatyrev's best-known arguments was about rubber galoshes—a relatively new addition to peasants' wardrobes in the early twentieth century. He observed that some people wore galoshes not in rainy weather, but rather on holidays. He concluded that in these cases the galoshes had a predominantly aesthetic, rather than a practical function (of keeping feet dry). Bogatyrev concluded that "for the ethnographer studying the functions of costume, galoshes are just as interesting as the old-time lacquered boots or *pisany lapti* ('fancy' bast sandals), whose dominant function was, like that of the galoshes, aesthetic."[89]

Bogatyrev uses this example to stress that the isolated material artifact is not, for the structuralist ethnographer, the real object of study. Instead, it is the meanings of the object for a community. Mukařovský makes a similar point: "An active capacity for the aesthetic function is not a real property of an object, even if the object has been deliberately composed with the aesthetic function in mind. Rather, the aesthetic function manifests itself only under certain conditions, i.e., in a certain social context." For Mukařovský, the aesthetic function is distributed in the material world as a "sphere" which is "stabilized" by the collective.[90] Mukařovský argues that

> the aesthetic sphere develops as a whole and is, in addition, constantly related to those aspects of reality which, at a given point in time, do not exhibit the aesthetic function at all. Such unity and integrity are possible only if we assume a collective awareness which combines the ties among objects bearing the aesthetic function and which unifies mutually isolated individual states of awareness.[91]

The sphere of objects which carry the aesthetic function at a given point in time is thus diverse, but not without order. This order comes from the structure of the community's shared awareness, with functions—like beauty, comfort, and affordability—holistically interrelated. Like Bogatyrev, Mukařovský stresses that a structuralist, semiotic approach "must involve a particular time period and social entity." He points out that "collective awareness" is not a "psychological reality" but a "social fact . . . Collective awareness should not, however, be understood abstractly, i.e., without considering the concrete collective in which it is manifested."[92]

This semiotic model is relational in that the functions form a gestalt, a whole which is more than the sum of its parts. But the conceptual element of the system, the meaning that the signifier points to, is generated by a particular collective. Understood as social meanings, functions are not defined solely by their relationships with each other. That is, function in this case is not the function of differentiation, as it was for Trubetskoi. The Prague semioticians used the notion of a "structure of functions" within the holistic model provided by Gestalt psychology to elaborate the Saussurean or Durkheimian concept of a "collective consciousness." As Harland wrote of Durkheim, the Prague structuralists "envisaged an analogy between the unity of society and the unity of thinking in the individual mind."[93] This provided them with a concept of an interconnected structure (of social functions) that evolves over time in a way that is determined, in part, by the autonomous or imminent properties of a particular, historically conceived, collective consciousness.

Like Bogatyrev and Mukařovský, Yuri Tynianov argued that a system is a product of the "functions" of the elements which enter into that system. In "On Literary Evolution" ("O literaturnoi evoliutsii," 1927), he expands on the concepts of system and function in an effort to provide the field of literary history with a more reliable, scientific methodology. To do this, Tynianov argues: "it must be agreed that a literary work is a system, as is literature itself. Only after this basic agreement has been established is it possible to create a literary science which does not superficially examine diverse phenomena but studies them closely."[94] Tynianov proceeds by expanding on his preexisting research on the "elements of a work," considered as a system:

> The interrelationship [*sootnesennost'*] of each element with every other in a literary work and with the whole literary system as well may be called the constructional *function* of the given element.
>
> On close examination, such a function proves to be a complex concept. An element is on the one hand interrelated with similar elements in other works in other systems, and on the other hand it is interrelated with different elements within the same work. The former may be termed the *auto-function* and the latter, the *syn-function*.
>
> Thus, for example, the lexicon of a given work is interrelated with both the whole literary lexicon and the general lexicon of the language, as well as with other elements of that given work. These two components or functions operate simultaneously but are not of equal relevance.[95]

To clarify Tynianov's argument we can recall his book *The Problem of Verse Language* (1924), in which he argued that "lexical coloring" (*leksicheskaia okraska*) occurs within a "boundary," for example, in a poem (see chapter 3). A word in a poem can take on secondary meanings as a result of its relationship to other words in the poem. We saw him argue that in Pushkin's poem "To F. N. Glinka," "egoism" (a prosaic word) is "recolored" to become a "Greekism" due to its proximity to the word "ostracism." In his 1927 article Tynianov uses the terms "auto-" and "syn- function" to refer to the "interrelationships" (*sootnesennosti*) between words in a poem, and between words in a poem and words in the "general lexicon of the language." Although Tynianov suggests that the smaller system, that of the work, in which the auto-function prevails, is not of "equal relevance" because it works on top of other systems, he describes these systems as essentially the same in terms of their principles of operation and organization.

Tynianov is clearly not using "function" in the sense that Jakubinsky does, to indicate a speaker's intentional goals. His use of the term is also distinct from that of Bogatyrev and Mukařovský—as the social "meaning" of an artifact for a particular collective. Tynianov's use of "function" may be closest to Trubetskoi's, in that Tynianov often uses the term "difference" in connection with function; for example, "the very existence of a fact as literary depends on its differential quality, that is, on its interrelationship with both literary and extraliterary orders."[96] This use of difference, however, is not exactly the concept of "difference" proposed by Saussure and developed by Jakobson more rigorously after World War II. For Jakobson's structuralist phonology, the only function of a phonemic "feature," such as the "grave character" of /b/, is to indicate that /b/ is perceptually not the same as /d/ (which is characterized by the "feature" of "acute" sound).[97] Tynianov is instead describing an *interrelationship* based on the perception of *semantic* difference and similarity: a word in a poem is similar to other instances of its use, but it also has a secondary meaning due to its particular intra-poem relationships, which is what makes it different.

Svetlikova provides a convincing explanation of Tynianov's concept of a "system" by highlighting his reliance on Herbart's psychology. The central point of overlap is found in the description of a system as the "dynamic" product of a constant "battle" between its elements. Tynianov writes that "literature is a *dynamic verbal construction*. The demand for uninterrupted dynamics is the driving force behind literary evolution, for every dynamic system necessarily becomes automatized."[98] A poem is a dynamic system in the sense that the reader perceives a struggle between the auto- and syn- functions of the words in the poem. That is, the "prosaic" meaning of a word (its meaning in the general lexicon) can battle against the intra-poem meaning of the word, which can be imposed by rhythm. To return to the example from

Pushkin, the lines are "dynamic" as long as the reader perceives both the prosaic and poetic registers of the word "egoism," the latter deriving from its rhyme with "ostracism." Not only is the individual work of literature dynamic, but the entire domain of literature is in a constant state of dynamism and *"evolution, which is driven by struggle and shift [bor'ba i smena]."*[99]

Svetlikova argues that this concept of the dynamic system is based on a Herbartian understanding of consciousness. As Alan Kim explains, Herbart's psychological theory sought to explain how various mental

> representations mutually resolve each other to attain maximal unity . . . Two representations present in consciousness may either resemble each other or not. If the former, then they will merge into one, stronger representation, and unity will be attained in this way. If they differ, then they will struggle against each other, each trying to negate the other as far as possible.[100]

What, for Herbart, is the attainment of "unity" is for Tynianov the "automatization" of the system. Tynianov's interest in the perception of similarity and dissimilarity at the same time recalls Shklovsky's understanding of defamiliarization as based on parallelism, as described in chapter 3 ("In a parallelism what is important is the lack of convergence despite similarity").[101] Svetlikova writes, of Tynianov:

> The dynamic form of a single work is a product of the struggle between its elements. Describing this, Tynianov observes a strict correspondence with the psychological level that forms the stable . . . foundation of his system, the level of "struggle of representations." The dynamism of the Tynianovian concept, which has become so fruitful and attractive for later researchers, is connected to the fact that Tynianov speaks of the dynamics of the literary form based on ideas about the dynamics of mental processes and by analogy with them.[102]

The Herbartian basis is also clear in Tynianov's description of literary history. Svetlikova cites Boris Engel'gardt's description of Tynianov's model of literary development as evidence that his contemporaries understood that his history was based on an analogy with Herbartian consciousness. Describing Tynianov's ideas, Engel'gardt writes:

> Changes in literary schools and styles are not the crowding out of the familiar and old with newcomers from out of nowhere, but the exchange [*smena*] of the *older literary line*, that is, what is in the bright spot of public consciousness, for the *younger*, which was hitherto living in its dark spheres. Coming to the fore, these younger lines are, of course, undergoing significant changes, partly

under pressure from the adversary they are pushing out, which they almost never manage to overcome, and partly under the influence of allies, which are drawn from the distant past of a given literature or from the literature of neighboring countries in the process of its development [*razvertyvaniia*].[103]

Svetlikova notes that the phrases "bright spot of public consciousness" in opposition to "dark spheres" are references to Herbartian *Lichtspunkt des Bewusstseins* and *Verdunkelungspunkt des Bewusstseins*. The process that Engel'gardt describes recalls Herbart's description of consciousness as an area of awareness which can only, as Kim writes, accommodate a fraction of the "total number of cognitions, thoughts, or desires that *might* appear in our consciousness, given an appropriate stimulus." This other knowledge that is not present in consciousness resides below a threshold, or *limen*. Below this threshold, representations are inhibited but not inert; they rise and fall with regard to the threshold, a movement Herbart describes as "brightening" (*Erhellen*) and "dimming" (*Verdunkeln*). Svetlikova stresses that Herbart also describes the movement of representations within the "series" (*Vorstellungsreihen*) in which they are organized, using the verbs "develop" (*entwickeln*) or often "evolve" (*evolvieren*). Older representations reenter the light of consciousness from below the limit for different reasons: for example, when an occluding factor is removed, or in response to a new representation, or because it is connected to another representation that is moving upwards. As Kim summarizes, these processes "furnish the foundation for recollection and memory."

This model of consciousness has a number of clear correspondences with Tynianov's systemic model of literary history: elements are organized into evolving series within a dynamic system, which is divided into a small area illuminated by consciousness and a larger region in darkness. The similarity between the two models can be seen in the following passage from Tynianov's essay "Literary Fact" (1924): "*When a genre is in the process of disintegrating, it migrates from the center to the periphery, and a new phenomenon moves in from the minutiae of literature, its backwoods and lowlands* [zadvorkov i nizin], *and takes the previous genre's place at the center.*"[104] Unlike Bogatyrev and Mukařovský, Tynianov does not refer to a collective consciousness as the locus for the system of literature. However, like the Czech structuralists, he borrowed a model from psychology in order to imagine a social, collectively sustained system of values. One of Tynianov's most striking proposals is that literary scholars should conceive of "all literature" as a unitary system. His willingness to tackle such a vast field possibly indicates the influence of his teacher, Semen Vengerov (1855–1920), known for his ambitiously exhaustive bibliography of Russian writers and his legendary archive of two million filing cards with biographical information on

Russian writers. As Andy Byford writes of Vengerov, "nearly all his enterprises, whether bio-bibliographical, editorial, or literary-historical, had the aim of totally exhausting the field of 'literature.' His projects made sense only if nothing escaped knowledge."[105] Vengerov's archive of filing cards, and his dictionary, are of course not functional systems, but a mass of data. Yet, perhaps the organization of this material in Vengerov's mind was not entirely unlike Tynianov's proposed system of all literature.

The notion that the system of literature is based on a model developed for individual consciousness is relevant for understanding the place of the reader in this theory. Steiner points out that the study of literary reception is totally incompatible with systemic Formalism. For Tynianov, "the only legitimate object of literary studies is the self-regulating literary system. The perceiving subject is either treated as an appendix of this impersonal system or ignored." Steiner cites as evidence Tynianov's claim that "it is utterly impossible to separate the author of literature from the reader because they are essentially the same."[106] I would suggest that it is impossible to introduce diverse readers and writers, with different understandings of a text, into Tynianov's system because it is modeled on a singular consciousness. The model, as Svetlikova notes, is appealing in its dynamic evolution, but as a *coherent system* in evolution it cannot accommodate diverse perceiving subjects.

To summarize, interwar literary structuralism and semiotics (represented by Tynianov, Jakobson, Bogatyrev, and Mukařovský) integrated a holistic understanding of structure with the study of cultural history by developing models taken from psychology (Herbartian or Gestalt) and extrapolating a collective consciousness that is structured in the same way. They used psychological concepts of structure to describe the history of literature as systemic; this history is not arbitrarily dictated by extra-artistic forces (such as politics or economics), but is fundamentally shaped by the internal organization of the artistic domain (construed as a shared social system of perception). As Harland points out, the Durkheimian concept of a collective consciousness is problematic because it posits that there is a particular idea, some positive content, shared by all members of the collective.[107] It was this very interaction between positive content and system that appealed to the Russian and Czech interwar structuralists. Their systemic models allow for positive values, in that the concept of function that they were operating with was not purely a function of differentiation. Moreover, their use of the individual psyche as a model allows for the system to have a history of accrued contents (something like memories) which impact the subsequent development of the system. The idea of a "backwoods" or unconscious realm in which old forms reside allows previous meanings of a word (like inhibited representations, created by previous experiences) to remain accessible to the system. Forms, like memories, do not disappear but are relegated to a peripheral domain from which, given the right conditions, they can reemerge.

This was, as we have seen, a core concern of Veselovsky's historical poetics; he asked why some forms persist over time, or return into popular usage after a period of obscurity.[108] The younger generation turned to individual consciousness as a model for cultural history in an effort to explain this phenomenon. Even non-structuralist thinkers such as Shklovsky also used the individual psyche as a metaphor for describing the history of forms. In "Literature without a Plot" ("Literatura vne siuzheta," 1925), he states:

> Forbidden themes continue to exist outside canonized literature in the same way that the erotic anecdote has always existed and exists to this very day, or in the way that repressed desires exist in the psyche, occasionally appearing in dreams, sometimes unexpectedly for the dreamer.[109]

Shklovsky's thinking, as we know, was particularly close to Veselovsky's, and sought to refine the philological approach by looking for explanations for formal regularities in Freudian psychological universals. Shklovsky's reference to "repressed" themes of literary history very much fits with these tendencies. Shklovsky, however, did not describe literature as a system.

The turn to the concept of a collective consciousness in interwar structuralism was a way to attempt to answer old questions—how do verbal forms express the particular identity and needs of a collective—using a new deductive methodology. This becomes even clearer when we contrast these theories with those that were developed by post–World War II structuralism.

POST-1945 STRUCTURALISM

Post–World War II structuralism was similar to interwar structuralism in that both adopted a theory of language (and by extension culture) based on a holistic system, yet they differed in important ways. Interwar structuralism assumed a referential approach to semiotic meaning, described the evolution of a system as the interaction between that system and extra-systemic factors, and was committed to the study of linguistic variation and particular cultural identities. Post–World War II structuralism adopted an intrinsic concept of meaning, sought to describe culture in universalizing terms, and ultimately abandoned the effort to reconcile history and system. The source of these substantial differences can be traced to Jakobson's and others' adoption, in the late 1940s, of information theory as a new model for thinking about language.

Jürgen Van de Walle notes that information theory "resulted from the loose unification of two theories derived from engineering achievements of World War II: cybernetics and the 'Mathematical Theory of Communication.'"[110] Cybernetics was developed in New York in the 1940s by a heterogeneous group of researchers who were interested in systems, feedback, and teleology (the ability of feedback to direct systems toward a purpose). It was promoted by Norbert Wiener as a meta-discipline seeking to advance the study of "communication" conceived as a "behavior" that would transcend differences between "biological species and artificial machines."[111] Claude Shannon's seminal paper "A Mathematical Theory of Communication" (1948) provided information theory with a mathematical foundation, describing communication as the transmission of "information." Shannon defines communication as an "engineering" problem:

> The fundamental problem of communication is that of reproducing at one point either exactly or approximately a message selected at another point. Frequently the messages have meaning; that is, they refer to or are correlated according to some system with certain physical or conceptual entities. *These semantic aspects of communication are irrelevant to the engineering problem.* The significant aspect is that the actual message is one selected from a set of possible messages.[112]

According to Shannon's theory, "information" can be defined as one's freedom of choice when selecting a message. It can be measured using the unit of the "bit":

> Both Wiener and Shannon had defined the unit of information as "a choice between two equally probable simple alternatives." . . . In other words, the key concept of information was measured in terms of binary choices or BITS (a portmanteau of binary digits). For instance, the amount of information (or elementary choices) a card carries in a deck of 32 cards is 5 bits. That is to say, at most five yes/no questions are necessary to arrive at any card whatsoever in the set.[113]

There was disagreement regarding the scope of information theory's applicability. Whereas Shannon stressed that the binary code was *only* an engineering tool, to be used for measuring the capacity of a communication channel, others extended it to other domains, such as the workings of the human mind. Cybernetics was committed to developing a theory that would serve as a bridge between the behaviors of humans, nonhuman animals, and machines.

As Van de Walle and Bernard Geoghegan have documented, Jakobson was introduced to the work of Wiener and Shannon in the 1940s. Geoghegan stresses the role of the Rockefeller Foundation in the trajectory of Jakobson's career in the late 1940s. He cites a meeting held on December 22, 1949, between Jakobson and officers of the foundation as a turning point. A week before the meeting, Warren Weaver had mailed Jakobson a copy of "A Mathematical Theory of Communication."[114] Another turning point, noted by Van de Walle, was a conference of the Cybernetics Group, held in March 1948, where linguists (including Jakobson) were introduced to the relevance of the cybernetic approach.[115] Both scholars note Jakobson's early and enthusiastic reception of these ideas as documented in personal letters to Weaver, Wiener, and Charles Fahs (1949–50).[116] Jakobson began making references to cybernetics and to Shannon's ideas in his own work on language in the 1950s. His pursuit of this direction was facilitated by Rockefeller funding and by his appointment at MIT in 1951. In 1957 Jakobson helped establish a Center for Communications Sciences at MIT, which was affiliated with the Research Laboratory for Electronics. The center brought together linguists such as Jakobson and Morris Halle "with electrical engineers, including Gordon Brown, Jerome Wiesner, and Walter Rosenblith, as well as mathematicians, psychologists, logicians, and neurophysiologists. Their purpose was to study communication processes in both natural and man-made systems."[117]

This institutional environment impacted Jakobson's linguistic theory in two ways: first, the syntagmatic and paradigmatic *axes* which organize *la langue* were reinterpreted as *processes* of selection and combination; and second, the concept of function as the speaker's intention was replaced by an objective concept of function, based on the function of distinctiveness. The first reinterpretation meant that, rather than describing elements of language according to syntagmatic and paradigmatic relations (a concept which is a partial revision of the associationist and psychologistic understanding of language as organized in the individual's mind according to associations of similarity and contiguity), Jakobson describes a process in which a message is produced by concatenating elements, each of which is selected from a set of possible choices. This process is described using information theory, which was developed to make the transmission of signals from machine to machine (e.g., radio, telephone, television signals) more efficient. This process often involves a transmitter, which changes the initial message into a signal through a coding process, which is then decoded by the receiver.[118] Jakobson adopted both the model and terminology of information theory in his writings on language. In *Preliminaries to Speech Analysis*, coauthored with Gunnar Fant and Morris Halle, Jakobson explains that

Information Theory uses a sequence of binary selections as the most reasonable basis for the analysis of the various communication processes. It is an operational device imposed by the investigator upon the subject matter for pragmatic reasons. In the special case of speech, however, such a set of binary selections is inherent in the communication process itself as a constraint imposed by the code on the participants in the speech event, who could be spoken of as the *encoder* and the *decoder*.[119]

This statement reflects the fact that, after 1950, Jakobson used information theory to develop his intuition that phonemic features could be fully described in terms of binary oppositions. As Giorgio Graffi explains, Jakobson's innovation is that phonemes are

uniquely characterized by the presence or the absence of given "distinctive" features, respectively indicated with the signs + and –. Two such features are e.g. [± vocalic] and [± consonantal]: vocalic phonemes have the features [+vocalic] and [–consonantal]; consonantal ones the features [–vocalic] and [+consonantal] . . . According to binary theory, any phonemic opposition is to be represented as an opposition of features values: e.g., /p/ and /t/ are both [–compact], and such feature opposes them to /k/, which is [+compact], while they are different from each other since /p/ is [+grave] and /t/ [–grave]. These binary features (twelve in the earlier formulations of theory, fourteen in the final ones) are . . . assumed to be universal. In other words, the phonemes of any language cannot be constituted but by these features: cross-linguistic differences are accounted for by the fact that not all features occur in all languages, and that some phonemes can have a positive value in one language and the opposite value in another (e.g., /l/ is [+vocalic] in Czech, but [–vocalic] in Italian).[120]

In "Linguistics and Communication Theory" (1960), Jakobson explains that linguistic analysis has come to

resolve oral speech into a finite series of elementary informational units. These ultimate discrete units, the so-called "distinctive features," are aligned into simultaneous bundles termed "phonemes," which in turn are concatenated into sequences. Thus form in language has a manifestly granular structure and is subject to a quantal description.[121]

Jakobson goes on to speculate about the possibilities of not only measuring the amount of "phonemic information" encoded in the choices between binary distinctive features, but of extending the principle of binary oppositions to morphology so as to quantitatively measure "grammatical information":

Communication theory, after having mastered the level of phonemic information, may approach the task of measuring the amount of grammatical information, since the system of grammatical, particularly morphological categories, like the system of distinctive features, is ostensibly based on a scale of binary oppositions. Thus, for instance, 9 binary choices underlie over 100 simple and compound conjugational forms of an English verb which appear, for example, in combination with the pronoun I.[122]

Jakobson's enthusiasm for the potential of information theory or communication theory (these labels were used interchangeably in the 1950s) to "master" language on a grammatical level converged with a broader optimistic assessment of computational approaches to linguistics, described at the time as the problem of machine translation. As Viktor Zhivov explains, this phase of structuralism anticipated that computers would be able to fully ("grammatically") learn natural language:

> If for Saussure language was a metaphysical formation which was embodied in speech, then in the 1950s . . . language began to be perceived as a generative mechanism, as *a machine which could produce speech*. This machine worked according to formal rules which, as it then seemed, could be represented in almost mathematical formulas. At that time people began working on machine (computer) translation—not in the way this is done now, when the practical implementation of machine translation is based on stable combinations of words and the computer's capacities to instantaneously sort through and categorize millions of elements—but rather on a *fully "grammatical"* translation.[123]

Although, as Zhivov writes, these expectations were not borne out, they took on a second life in French structuralism, which extended these ideas, understood metaphorically, to the study of literature and culture.

As in Prague, after World War II structuralist linguistic theory was extended to the study of culture. However, the resulting French literary theory differed from interwar structuralism. A key difference was a new concept of "meaning" which emerged from the assimilation of structuralism to information theory. The subject of "meaning" was a point of contention in information theory. Shannon's 1948 paper was republished in 1949 with a general-audience paper by Weaver, which served as a preface. Notably, Weaver introduced Shannon's ideas by writing that

> the concept of information developed in this theory at first seems disappointing and bizarre—disappointing because it has nothing to do with meaning, and bizarre because it deals not with a single message but rather with the statistical character of a whole ensemble of messages . . . I think, however, that

these should be only temporary reactions; and that one should say, at the end, that this analysis has so penetratingly cleared the air that *one is now, perhaps for the first time, ready for a real theory of meaning.*[124]

Jakobson himself responded enthusiastically to Weaver's reframing of Shannon's information theory. In his 1960 talk, Jakobson cites Weaver's call for a "real theory of meaning," adding that now, finally, "linguists are gradually finding the way of tackling meaning . . . as an intrinsic linguistic topic, distinctly separate from the ontological problems of reference."[125] As he stresses, a theory of meaning compatible with information theory would have to be fully "intrinsic." Jakobson, however, did not spearhead this project. Van de Walle suggests that Jakobson's waning interest in the intersection between information theory and linguistics can be attributed to the success of Chomsky's generative grammar, which was explicitly not based on information theory.[126] Geoghegan summarizes that by the mid-1960s in the United States, the cybernetic project had "fallen into disrepair." The Rockefeller Foundation turned its efforts to other initiatives, "public diatribes by Shannon and other engineers against the popularization of information theory" meant that the field "narrowed its ranks to engineers focused on specialized mathematical analysis," Wiener fell into disrepute, and Jakobson's interests in the application of information theory shifted to molecular biology.[127]

However, as Geoghegan documents, "across the Atlantic, another cybernetics endured."[128] The effort to integrate Jakobson's information theory–informed, structuralist phonology into a full-fledged theory of meaning and culture was continued in France by Claude Lévi-Strauss, and then by French structuralism and post-structuralism (e.g., Roland Barthes, Jacques Lacan, Jacques Derrida). Lévi-Strauss was introduced to structuralism by Jakobson in 1942–43, when they met at the École Libre in New York and began attending each other's lectures. Lévi-Strauss, who returned to France in 1948, later recalled that he initially approached Jakobson for help on developing a notation system for Brazilian languages, but what he actually learned from him was "far more important: the revelation of structural linguistics."[129] In his 1945 article "Structural Analysis in Linguistics and in Anthropology," Lévi-Strauss articulated the expectation that "structural linguistics will certainly play the same renovating role with respect to the social sciences that nuclear physics, for example, has played for the physical sciences."[130]

However, although Lévi-Strauss consistently referred to the importance of "linguistics," the inspiration for his structural anthropology was really information theory (cybernetics). This is made clear in the proceedings of a Conference of Anthropologists and Linguists held at Indiana University in 1952, where Jakobson comments that:

> For the study of language in operation, linguistics has been strongly bul-
> warked by the impressive achievement of two conjoined disciplines—the
> mathematical theory of communication and information theory. Although
> communication engineering was not on the program of our Conference, it is
> indeed symptomatic that there was almost not a single paper uninfluenced by
> the works of Shannon and Weaver, of Wiener and Fano, or of the excellent
> London group. We have involuntarily discussed in terms specifically theirs, of
> encoders, decoders, redundancy, etc.[131]

Jakobson thus describes a conference held for "anthropologists and linguists"
at which the common ground between the fields was revealed to be information theory. This was evident in Lévi-Strauss's own presentation there. He
begins with the proposal that it "is obvious that we are entitled to affirm that
there should be some kind of relationship between language and culture,"
but concludes with the observation that what the two disciplines share is
"parallel ways of organizing the same data."[132] His presentation demonstrates
that kinship data can be broken down into primary elements ("atoms of kinship"), and he describes the relations between these atoms as a "system of
oppositions."[133] The organization system that he uses is that of information
theory. While Jakobson notes that information theory has been a constant
reference point, connecting the talks of the linguists and anthropologists,
Lévi-Strauss presents a particular interpretation of this fact: "We have not
been sufficiently aware of the fact that both language and culture are the
products of activities which are basically similar. I am now referring to this
uninvited guest which has been seated during this Conference beside us and
which is *the human mind.*"[134] For Lévi-Strauss, the broad applicability of
concepts derived from information theory is interpreted as evidence of universals of human thought. This would have been an interpretation shared,
at least in part, by Jakobson. Van de Walle describes Jakobson's synthesis of
information theory and linguistics as a process of psychologizing Shannon's
claims, and writes that "Jakobson was . . . relying on a model of the human
mind which was . . . based on a psychological interpretation of a communication process between machines."[135] Lévi-Strauss followed Jakobson in this
interpretation but pushed it further, to argue that "meaning" and "information" are ultimately interchangeable.

In *The Savage Mind,* Lévi-Strauss points to the "generalization" of
"information theory" to the domain of biology, and concludes that because
both human language and biological processes (such as the transmission of
information in DNA and RNA) bear "information," both are thus ultimately
"meaningful" in the same way. He argues that belief systems such as "totem-
ism" which treat "the sensible properties of the animal and plant kingdoms
as if they were the elements of a message" can be seen as having arrived at

the realizations "revealed to us only through very recent inventions: telecommunications, computers and electron microscopes."[136] The fact that the "savage" and "scientific" mind have crossed "paths" in this way, he concludes, is evidence that "the entire process of human knowledge . . . assumes the character of a closed system."[137] This conflation of the concepts of "information" and "meaning" is a fundamental and far-reaching feature of his structural anthropology.

Lévi-Strauss became a major source of inspiration for the French structuralist movement that emerged in the 1950s and 1960s, and he influenced the philosophy of Maurice Merleau-Ponty, Barthes's analyses of popular culture and myth, and Jacques Lacan's psychoanalytic theory. The growing interest in structuralism in France after World War II can be described as a "return" to Saussure.[138] However, even as writers like Lévi-Strauss, Barthes, and Lacan referred to Saussure, their understanding of concepts he introduced (e.g., the signifier and signified) was mediated by the linguistics of Jakobson, Émile Benveniste, or Louis Hjelmslev. This reception history was also impacted by Lévi-Strauss's commitment to, and promotion of, cybernetics in the 1940s and 1950s while serving as a director at UNESCO. Geoghegan notes: "Lévi-Strauss published articles and lectured widely on how cybernetic instruments and techniques could overcome the differences that divided scientific disciplines, ethnic groups, and the political sensibilities of capitalists and Communists."[139] He sought to advance the French adoption of the cybernetic model by attempting, unsuccessfully, to found in France a laboratory like Jakobson's Research Laboratory of Electronics at MIT. Lévi-Strauss did, however, with MIT funding, organize an interdisciplinary seminar on cybernetics in Paris in 1953. Attended by Jean Piaget, Lacan, and Benveniste, as well as physicists and mathematicians, the seminar covered "kinship and group exchange," "the structure of public opinion," "psychoanalysis considered as a process of communication," and "the study of myths as a special form of communications." While promoting an interdisciplinary cybernetic model, Lévi-Strauss influentially asserted that semantic "meaning" could be studied using Jakobson's system of binary oppositions for phonemic features.

In "Structural Analysis in Linguistics and in Anthropology," for example, Lévi-Strauss writes that "*like phonemes, kinship terms are elements of meaning*; like phonemes, they acquire meaning only if they are integrated into systems. 'Kinship systems,' like 'phonemic systems,' are built by the mind on the level of unconscious thought."[140] Ten years later, in another widely read article, "Structural Study of Myth" (1955), he writes that "the true constituent units of a myth are not the isolated relations but *bundles of such relations*, and it is only as bundles that these relations can be put to use and *combined so as to produce a meaning*."[141] Lévi-Strauss's extension of the principles of structuralist phonology into the domain of "meaning" was contested by linguists. In *Structuralist Anthropology* (1958), he responds to a critique by G. Gurvitch:

> When Gurvitch argues that structuralism has its place only in phonemics [i.e., phonology] and that it loses all meaning at the level of language in general, he is overlooking the structuralist contributions with respect to grammar, syntax, and even vocabulary, in the rich and variegated forms given to them by Benveniste, Hjelmslev, and especially Jakobson . . . In addition, the theoreticians of machine translation are in the process of laying the foundations of grammatical and lexical analysis, which belongs both to mathematics and to structuralism.[142]

This response lists the sources that Lévi-Strauss took as support for his extension of structuralist phonology to anthropology: Benveniste, Hjelmslev, Jakobson, and machine translation. Lévi-Strauss's reference to Benveniste and Hjelmslev highlights the influence of these two linguists on French structuralism. Both can be described as followers of Saussure who strove to make Saussure's proposals more logically consistent.

Both Benveniste and Hjelmslev reinterpreted Saussure's concept of signification (the mental content, or mental image, of the sign) so it would strictly follow Saussure's axiom that "in language there are only differences *and no positive terms*."[143] Both men developed a non-referential theory of signification, or "meaning," as solely a product of the function of differentiation. As Harland puts it, this is a "hermetic theory of language," according to which "meaning gets separated from objective things all together."[144] In *Problems in General Linguistics* (1966), Benveniste proposes that "the *meaning* of a linguistic unit is defined as its capacity to integrate a unit of a higher level":[145] "Thus /s/ has the status of a phoneme because it functions as the integrator of /-al/ in *salle* . . . of /-ivil/ in *civil*, etc. By virtue of the same relationship transposed to a still higher level, /sal/ is a sign because it functions as integrator in *salle a manger, salle de bains* . . ."[146] In sum, then, "when we say that a certain element of a language, long or short, has a meaning, we mean by this a certain property which this element possesses qua signifier: that of forming a unit which is distinctive, contrastive, delimited by other units, and identifiable for native speakers for whom this language is *language*."[147]

"Meaning" here is clearly defined as semiotic distinctiveness. In a 1969 article, "The Semiology of Language," Benveniste argued that semantics and semiotics are "two separate domains, each of which requires its own conceptual apparatus." Semantics is a specific domain of "meaning which is generated by *discourse*." Reference begins at the level of semantics, "while semiotics is in principle cut off and independent of all reference." Benveniste argued for a strict separation between semiotics and semantics: "In reality the world of the sign is closed. From the sign to the sentence there is no transition."[148] This separation was not followed by cultural and literary scholars such as Lévi-Strauss or Barthes. The view of "meaning" as an "integrating" function was amenable to metaphoric reinterpretation. As Jonathan Culler notes, "The notion that units of one level are to be recognized by their integrative capacity and that this capacity is their *sens* [meaning] has an intuitive validity in literary criticism, where the meaning of a detail is its contribution to a larger pattern."[149] The model could be extended on a metaphoric basis because it resembles hermeneutic reading practices.

Another influential effort to develop a Saussurean theory of "meaning" was found in Hjelmslev's *Prolegomena to a Theory of Language (Omkring sprogteoriens grundlaeggelse*, 1943), which laid out a program for the study of linguistics which he called "glossematics." Hjelmslev's theory was designed to be fully "immanent"—in contrast to other schools of linguistics which based themselves in some other field (psychology, sociology, logic, etc.). Like Benveniste, Hjelmslev specifies that, "from the basic point of view we have assumed . . . there exist no other perceivable meanings other than contextual meanings; any entity, and thus also any sign, is defined relatively, not absolutely, and only by its place in the context."[150] He seeks to demonstrate that "just as the expression plane can, through a functional analysis, be resolved into components with mutual relations . . . so also the content plane must be resolved by such an analysis into components with mutual relations that are smaller than the minimal sign-contents."[151] Harland summarizes Hjelmslev's effort in this way:

> The single word-meaning is unfolded out into a simultaneous multiplicity of semantic elements. Differentiation between word-meanings is no longer a matter of simple absolute boundaries, but a matter of sharing on some levels and differing on others. Thus we can recognize that the meaning of "mare" is similar to the meaning of "stallion" to the extent that both are equine, but different to the extent that "mare" is female whereas "stallion" is male. Or we can recognize that the meaning of "mare" is similar to the meaning of "ewe" to the extent that both are female, but different to the extent that "mare" is equine whereas "ewe" is ovine. In effect, two dividing lines cut out four word-meanings (mare, stallion, ewe, ram). A sufficiently complex system of dividing lines, so Hjelmslev believed, should make it possible to carry out Saussure's original program of describing meaning entirely in terms of differentiation.[152]

The outcome of this approach is that

> the units of language can now constitute themselves entirely in relation to one another and without relation to outside things. Even the units of meaning no longer conform to any independent natural units; before and apart

from language, there is only ever a shapeless mass of experience, a feature-less continuum.[153]

While Benveniste and Hjelmslev were not closely associated with American cybernetics, their extensions of Saussure's thought complemented the structuralism inspired by information theory.[154] Although Jakobson does not name Benveniste and Hjelmslev explicitly, it is possible that he had their work in mind when he asserted, in 1960, that linguists are tackling the question of meaning as an intrinsic linguistic topic. The impact of Benveniste and Hjelmslev on French structuralism is well known. Their work on differential "meaning" was central to Jacques Lacan's psychoanalytic theory, as well as Jacques Derrida's critique of Saussurean linguistics in *Of Grammatology* (1967).[155] The structuralism promoted by French scholars in the 1960s was a product of the particular interpretation and synthesis of these men's ideas. Culler presents this synthesis as a singular platform, which he refers to as "the Linguistic Foundation," thus potentially suggesting this interpretation is the one logical outcome of decades of linguistic research beginning with Saussure.[156]

In closing, I want to reiterate that the differential conception of "meaning" that was so central to French structuralism was not a feature of interwar structuralism. The Czech linguist Vladimír Skalička emphasized this in a 1948 article on the differences between (Hjelmslev's) Copenhagen structuralism and Prague structuralism. At stake is whether the two schools can rightfully be grouped together as "structuralist" linguistics.[157] Skalička points out that the schools diverge on a number of topics, including the concept of "function," the relationship between language and reality, and language variation. The Prague school defines function as a "goal," whereas Hjelmslev uses "function" in a sense closer to mathematical "dependence." The PLC's insistence on the social nature of linguistic "function," and thus the social basis of language (as opposed to Hjelmslev's fully immanent theory), is further reflected in Skalička's discussion of the relationship between the linguistic sign and extralinguistic reality: "We certainly cannot agree with the view that the extralinguistic world is an amorphous substance. [Bohuslav] Hávranek, for example, tells us that '(structuralist linguistics) understands language as a structure of linguistic signs, i.e., a primary series which is characterized within the realm of signs *by its direct relation to reality*.'"[158] Like Bogatyrev, Mukařovský relied on Voloshinov's referential conception of the "sign." In "Art as a Semiotic Fact" (1934), he writes:

> According to the usual definition, the sign is a sensory reality relating to another reality that it is supposed to evoke . . . Although there are signs not relating to any distinct reality, something is always referred to by the sign, and

this follows quite naturally from the fact that the sign must be understood in the same way by the one who expresses it and by the one who perceives it.[159]

Finally, Skalička argues, the Prague school is committed to the study of language variation. He describes Hjelmslev's theses first, and then contrasts these with Prague school linguistics:

The similarity of languages to each other is the principle of their structure. The diversity of languages is the implementation of this principle *in concreto*. All languages are shaped in principle in the same way, there are only differences in the details. . . . It is clear that Hjelmslev's views on this subject are diametrically opposed to ours here [in Prague]. When working on the problems of linguistic diversity, we always work with the opinion that individual languages have a direct relationship to reality. Individual languages try to capture reality as faithfully as possible, but they pursue this goal in different ways.[160]

Skalička concludes that "it is possible that Hjelmslev's school deserves the title of structuralism. But in this case the Prague school must find itself a new name."[161]

Post-1945 structuralism was thus distinct from Prague structuralism in its adoption of a mathematical rather than a social model—exemplified by Jakobson's binary distinctive features and the differential concept of "meaning" as the product of a fully immanent system. Interwar structuralism was characterized by an effort to reconcile the concept of a language system with cultural history. These differences are important, particularly in light of the argument that structuralist and post-structuralist theory is fundamentally ahistorical. Jameson's *Prison-House of Language* critiques French structuralist analyses of cultural history: "For the Structuralists the idea of a history of the objects or of the surface phenomena has been replaced with that of a history of models."[162] The problem with this approach, he argues, is that "the form of the model is in no way modified by the amount of empirical data available to it."[163] Because structuralism is ultimately unable "to do anything other than register pure differences," the "mutation" of the system in time is always only a "radical and meaningless shift from one internally coherent synchronic moment to another."[164] This describes postwar French structuralism better than it does interwar Czech structuralism.

The Czech structuralists adopted a positive (rather than a negative, strictly differential) concept of function and value, and insisted that signs have meaning as a result of their reference to a shared social reality. In their research, they sought to retain a focus on particular, historically situated meanings, while organizing these within a holistic system. This allowed them to describe cultures as "evolving" over time in a systemic manner. The interwar structuralists used the model of the individual psyche to imagine the interaction between intrinsic, systemic organizational principles and historical realities over time. The result was a semiotic theory of cultural history which sees this history as only partially determined by internal structural rules.[165] This is consistent with the historical importance of Romantic nationalism for Russian and Czech thinking about language. In the Herderian tradition, language is assumed to embody the "spirit" of a people. Recall Ľudovít Štúr's 1840 assertion that "language is . . . the surest sign of the essence and individuality of every nation. Just like an individual human being, the nation reveals its deepest inner self through language; it, so to speak, embodies its spirit in language."[166] Skalička asserts that Prague school linguistics is committed to the view that each language follows its own path, determined by individuals' efforts to capture the reality of their experiences as faithfully as possible. Unlike the post-1945 structuralism inspired by cybernetics, in the 1920s and 1930s structuralists believed that language is shaped by individuals' biographical-historical experiences. These seemingly unorthodox aspects of Czech structuralism have made it difficult to assimilate it into Anglo-American literary studies, which is considerably more familiar with French structuralism. Interwar structuralism is certainly not *as* lost a path as Jakobson's dialectological poetics, but it remains a relatively obscure branch of literary theory in comparison with French structuralism.

Formalism and Philology in the
Twenty-First Century

IN CONCLUSION, I will situate the arguments of this book in relation to two recent developments in literary studies: a "return to form" and a "return to philology." These returns are not in either case a call to reinstate earlier ideas, but are rather efforts to use the history of thought as a springboard for historically informed innovation in the field today.

RETURN TO FORM

In assessing calls for a "return to form" in English studies in the United States, the first thing to note is that this scholarship is far from unified. What *is* shared is a broad sense that literary studies in the United States have, in the last twenty years, paid insufficient attention to questions of "form." Susan Wolfson's introductory essay for a collection of new formalist essays published in 2000 characteristically asserts that "the readings for form that follow . . . show, if not consensus about what form means, covers, and implies, then a conviction of why it still has to matter."[1] The problem of what form "means" is complicated by fundamental divisions among the new formalists. At issue are the legacies of New Criticism and new historicism. Marjorie Levinson, in her summary article "What Is New Formalism?" (2007), divides the movement into two camps, defined by scholars' position on cultural studies (e.g., new historicism). "In short," she writes, "we have a new formalism that makes a continuum with new historicism and a backlash new formalism."[2] The proponents of a "backlash formalism," or "normative formalism," to use Levinson's terms, are described as

> those who campaign to bring back a sharp demarcation between history and art, discourse and literature, with form (regarded as the condition of aesthetic experience as traced to Kant . . .) the prerogative of art . . . Predictably, nor-

mative new formalism assigns to literature a special kind or concept of form, one that is responsible for a work's accession to literary status in the first place and that remains an integral property of the work.[3]

This description is close to the New Critical definition of form. The other strand of new formalism, which Levinson and others have referred to as "activist formalism," is differentiated from the first in that "these critics do not equate form with literariness."[4] They argue for a formalist theory that would not be tied to the specificity of art and would, instead, be historically grounded. As Ellen Rooney argues,

> Rather than confine or contain the concept of form . . . we should set it rigorously to work *in every interpretive practice that claims the name of reading* and thus rethink, reread, its multiple effectivity across social life. On this account, the sonnet is a form, as is kinship, the market, the *nouveau roman*, and the television sitcom. Literature or any particular canon can be conceived as a subset of the category of form, so that one might analyze the form of the canon of seventeenth-century poetry or of the neoslave narrative or explore the concept of "literary form" or the "popular" itself as a historically specific and shifting structure, which is of course not the same thing as suggesting that it does not "really" exist.[5]

Rooney suggests using "interpretive" reading practices to discover the formal qualities of a wide array of social institutions—the market, kinship, sonnets, and sitcoms. Caroline Levine's *Forms: Whole, Rhythm, Hierarchy, Network* (2015) likewise contains a program for an activist formalism. Like Levinson, she assumes that "traditional formalist analysis . . . meant interpreting all of the formal techniques of a text as contributing to an overarching *artistic whole*."[6] Her book, as she puts it, "makes a case for expanding our usual definition of form in literary studies to include patterns of sociopolitical experience"; and she accordingly opts for "a definition of form that is much broader than its ordinary usage in literary studies. Form, for our purposes, will mean all shapes and configurations, all ordering principles, all patterns of repetition and difference."[7] Of her book, she writes that "its method of tracking of shapes and arrangements is not confined to the literary text or to the aesthetic, *but it does involve a kind of close reading*, a careful attention to the forms that organize texts, bodies, and institutions."[8] For Levine and Rooney, as for the New Critics or "normative" new formalists, the identification of a "form" is the product of interpretative practices, often described as "close reading"; forms describe wholes, patterns, and arrangements observed in language and in culture. The distinction between the activists and the normative formalists is thus not methodological, but rather derives from a politically charged division, which is widely assumed to shape the field of literary studies more broadly. This is the disagreement as to whether forms can be studied on their own (often as works of art), or whether alternatively they must be considered in reference to the sociopolitical situations in which they are found.

This division has also been articulated using the terms "extrinsic" versus "intrinsic" criticism. These terms were popularized by New Criticism, particularly Warren and Wellek's *Theory of Literature* (1949)—a textbook that had "profound influence on the teaching of and research into literature at university level" in the United States in the 1950s and 1960s.[9] Their book divides the study of literature into an "extrinsic approach" (biography, psychology, society, ideas) and an "intrinsic" one (prosody, style, symbolism, myth, genre). This distinction was mapped onto a second opposition, between an "apolitical" or conservative stance and politically motivated, activist criticism. The New Critics emphatically rejected what they called "moral" criticism, particularly Marxist or Marxist-informed criticism.[10] They defended this political position by reference to their theory of intrinsic form, arguing that no statement of a poet's thought can be separated from the total communication of the poem as a complex whole. The legacy of this convergence between a conservative politics and intrinsic form is described by Derek Attridge:

> While there are no doubt those who favour the methods of close reading that dominated the mid-twentieth century, the demonstration of the complicity between those methods and unacceptable ethico-political assumptions has surely been too persuasive to allow a simple revival. Although there is more to learn from the best of the early formalist critics than has generally been allowed in recent decades, they also provide a clear lesson in the many hazards of a formalism that fails to take account of the situatedness of writers and readers, that treats works of literature as self-sufficient, organic wholes, and that allies evaluation with questionable human and social values.[11]

The importance of this intrinsic-extrinsic framework for contemporary thought about literary form is suggested by the fact that activist formalism operates with the assumption that if an *intrinsic* definition of form is inherently quietist, then an *extrinsic* definition of form is activist. As Levine writes of her own work, "the primary goal of this formalism is radical social change."[12]

The intrinsic versus extrinsic framework obscures the fact that the methodology of close reading, adopted by both camps, has resulted in a consensus regarding the concept of form across the divide. Form, both "inside" and "outside" of the text, is a product of close reading—of hermeneutic practices. For this reason, the acts of reading extrinsically or intrinsically can be construed as complementary practices. For example, Yopie Prins describes her work in English historical poetics (a movement closer to English new formalism than to Veselovsky's historical poetics) as responding to a "schematic division into two kinds of historical poetics—one practiced by cultural historians, who read from the outside in, and the other by literary critics, who read from the inside out."[13] Prins wants to bring the two together: "While we might be tempted to see these concerns in opposition, I believe that we cannot separate the practice of reading a poem from the histories and theories of reading that mediate our ideas about poetry. I am committed to a historical poetics that works recursively as a loop, reading simultaneously from inside out and from outside in."[14]

While this summary of new formalism does not do justice to the wide range of rigorous and subtle scholarship it has produced, I have highlighted the underlying opposition between intrinsic and extrinsic criticism because it allows us to see how lost paths within Russian Formalism provide an alternative approach to form—one that is neither intrinsic nor extrinsic, and which is, in fact, not an exclusively hermeneutic concept of form. New Criticism and Russian Formalism operated with very different concepts of "form." This fact has been obscured, due to the tendency to amalgamate Russian Formalism with New Criticism on the basis of an implied political allegiance shared by the two groups—one based on a shared opposition to extrinsic, that is, socially minded or Marxist criticism.[15] Mary Louise Pratt's critique of Russian Formalism and Czech structuralism makes reference to this perception:

> Regardless of their differences, there is no question that both structuralist poetics and New Criticism foster essentially the same exclusivist attitude toward the relation between literary discourse and our other verbal activities. This affinity no doubt accounts for the ease and enthusiasm with which structuralist poetics was received on this side of the Atlantic in the 1950s and 1960s.[16]

Pratt's critique responds to the Anglo-American reception of Russian Formalism, in the 1950s and 1960s, which consistently stressed the commonalities between Formalism and structuralism, and their compatibility with New Criticism.[17]

In order to reveal the aspects of Russian Formalism which speak to current concerns in twenty-first-century literary studies, the movement needs to be uncoupled from structuralism. I have sought to do this by reconstructing the premises of the philological paradigm: the adherence to a Humboldtian philosophy of language, to the comparative historical method, and to the assumption that the patterning observed in language is caused by language-external, sociopolitical, and psychological forces. I have demonstrated that different paths within Russian Formalism adopted these premises—albeit to different degrees—and that the theoretical core of Formalism was not structuralist, but derived from the concept of psychological parallelism. In the late 1910s and early 1920s, both Shklovsky's and Jakobson's theoretical programs derived from the philological paradigm: Shklovsky's psychological narrative theory and Jakobson's dialectological poetics both assumed that the sources of "formal" patterns in literary history were extralinguistic.

The concept of "form" within the philological paradigm provides an alternative to the new formalist concept of form as a product of close reading. The fundamental differences between Russian Formalism and New Criticism were indicated in a 1979 essay by René Wellek, where he defends New Criticism against the "charge" that it was a "formalist" movement: "In the writings of the New Critics the coherence of a poem is not studied in terms of form, as the label 'formalism' suggests. Actually the New Critics pay little attention to what is traditionally called the form of a poem." While they "inevitably pay some attention to the role of meter and stanzaic forms . . . the charge of formalism in any sense that is valid for the Russian school is completely off the mark. The New Critics are overwhelmingly concerned with *the meaning of a work of art*."[18] Cleanth Brooks, in "The Heresy of Paraphrase," clarifies what he means by the "structure" of a poem: it is not "the metrical pattern," or "the sequence of images," or the use of devices such as the "heroic couplet" or "mock-epic convention." Instead, it "is a structure of meanings, evaluations, and interpretations, and the principle of unity which informs it seems to be one of balancing and harmonizing connotations, attitudes, and meanings."[19] By contrast, I have argued that recurring devices such as couplets (parallelisms), meter, or generic conventions such as the mock-epic *could* all count as form for thinkers within the philological paradigm (i.e., Brik, Shklovsky, and Jakobson in the 1910s and early 1920s).

However, it is impossible to provide a single definition of "form" that would hold for all the Russian Formalists. One position results in what I will call "comparative form"—associated with comparative poetics. This assumes that a perceivable regularity found in discourse, such as a particular simile (e.g., arrows falling like rain), can be identified, across many texts, as instances of the same form (device). Another position assumes that no unit of a text can ever be abstracted from its context (the work) without a fundamental distortion. Tynianov pioneered the second position, and in doing so redefined form as something "dynamic"—as the result of the interaction between a text's dominant principle (*dominanta*) and the verbal material which is subjugated to it. While Tynianov's theory in many ways differs from that of the New Critics and the new formalists, his concept of dynamic form is like hermeneutic form in that it adopts a holistic and particularizing rather than a comparative understanding of form. Describing Tynianov's ideas, Petre Petrov writes that "for each literary text the analyst must establish anew the provenance of what constitutes form."[20]

The fundamental opposition that informed Russian literary theory at the turn of the twentieth century was different from the intrinsic-extrinsic divide that was central to English studies in the United States. For Russian theory, the critical opposition was between the treatment of a single text as a closed whole (hermeneutic analysis) and the comparison of multiple texts for formal similarities (comparative poetics). The latter was often defined in opposition to the hermeneutic approach to language. The comparative method presumes that it is possible to identify similar forms across texts regardless of the particular meanings that these forms have in their immediate contexts. The centrality of comparative poetics in the Russian philological tradition was encouraged by the tendency of scholars to study folklore alongside literary texts. In the nineteenth century these oral traditions were treated as anonymous, and contiguous with spoken language. The meanings of a folkloric text, or its component parts, were treated like denotative meanings in a shared lexicon. As we have seen Nekliudov argue, "folklore typically does not entail 'hermeneutic' difficulties and does not require particular effort on the part of the interpreter for understanding its texts: the many variants of oral communication present, as a rule, one meaning."[21] Work in folkloristics established a methodology (comparative poetics) for the study of literary works without reference to the biography or intentions of the author. As a result, studies of poetic devices followed a model provided by the study of oral speech. A device can travel from mouth to mouth (or from writer to writer) in the same way that a proverb does.

This is in contrast to the hermeneutic concept of form, which relies on the identification of a (textual) boundary within which *secondary* meanings can be established. It is these secondary meanings that are taken to be a work's form. Wellek, for example, describes New Critics as "formalists only in the sense that they insist on the organization of a work of art which prevents its becoming a simple communication."[22] The importance of hermeneutic form for English studies is manifest in the continued primacy of the "work" as the fundamental unit of analysis. Commenting on a seminal collection of new formalist articles in 2002, Mark Rasmussen argued that the commitment to the *"work"* as *"provid[ing] the initial context* for understanding the significance of any particular item in a text" is the one premise that none of the contributors "feel inclined to abandon, for the cost of such abandonment is the loss of what is most distinctive in the object of their study . . . whether that object [literature] is viewed primarily from a historical/cultural or a literary/aesthetic perspective."[23] This consensus as to the importance of the work as the non-debatable starting point for thinking about form is reflected in the new formalist emphasis on the inside/outside formulation—which is often stated as a contrast between New Criticism and cultural studies. This is unlike the Russian philological paradigm, which defined "form" as the result of a comparative procedure which requires disregarding the holistic unity of the text.

However, the definition of "form" in the philological paradigm rests not only on a comparative methodology, but on ideas drawn from associationist psychology. The thinkers in this paradigm operated with a bifurcated concept of "form" that relies on both comparative poetics and psychology. As a result, form is not considered to be solely a product of a particular, socially maintained system of meanings. On the one hand, the philological paradigm regards a form, such as a heroic couplet—a rhyming pair of lines in iambic pentameter—as a unit of discourse with particular social meanings. It is recognized to be a social fact—it circulates in a particular historical milieu where it is associated with particular ideas and social values. On the other hand, a rhymed couplet is also a product of universal features of human cognition (i.e., the laws of associationist psychology), namely the capacity to create associative links between similar sounds or concepts. Russian Formalist theory assumes that not only are devices products of cognitive rules, but the capacity to perceive a device—to make associative connections—is also potentially universal. A point of contrast can be found in the work on the history of lyric poetry which has been carried out by Virginia Jackson and Yopie Prins, of the English historical poetics group. Their work, in what is called lyrical studies, seeks to historicize concepts such as meter (e.g., the five iambic feet of a heroic couplet), rather than to treat these as "ideal" forms which can be assumed to be the same in different historical periods and contexts.[24] As noted by Adams, Calahan, and Hansen, the aim of this work is to "recover obscured metrical theories and methods of scansion before meter's twentieth-century abstraction into the dominant foot-substitution model."[25] Jackson and Prins thus historicize the concept of form; for them, form is determined by hermeneutic procedures and is considered a product of historical discourses.

The philological paradigm instead posits that form is a trans-historical category. For the Formalists closest to the philological paradigm (Shklovsky, Jakobson, Brik), a form had to be at some level explainable by reference to the psychological processes of association. As we have seen (in chapter 3), this meant that formal devices were all considered to be manifestations of parallelism (e.g., metaphor, sound repetitions). This limitation allows for a concept of form that persists over time and across verbal contexts. Comparative historical philology described the history of forms as a reservoir of cultural knowledge (*predanie*), as a loose collection of elements, not an interrelated system (e.g., *la langue*). Items in this fund, known as "devices," included topoi, metaphors, stock characters, metrical patterns, rhyme schemes, genres, plots, and so on. Shklovsky and Jakobson used this comparative concept of form as the basis for their theoretical innovations of the 1910s and early 1920s.

As we have seen (in chapter 2), one sphere of theoretical innovation was a reconceptualization of the concept of authorship as a performance. According to the Formalist theory developed by Shklovsky and other members of OPOIAZ, an author is not the individual owner or creator of a particular text, but someone who knows how to employ this cultural reservoir in a way that speaks to contemporaries—or as Brik would put it, "carries out the social command."[26] To do this requires knowledge of the "craft" of verbal creation: a familiarity with the reservoir of devices and an understanding of the social context. Within the Moscow Linguistic Circle (as described in chapter 4), the Formalists sought to bring rigor to the concept of traveling form by integrating poetic creativity into the study of dialectology: devices were not to be studied in the context of a particular text, but as they traveled outside of a poem, borrowed and adapted by other poets and non-poets. Poetic dialectology studied language as it is localized in the individual (the idiolect). Moscow Formalists were interested in the capacity of individuals to consciously introduce linguistic innovations. In the intensely politicized environment of the era, the study of how forms travel was viewed as akin to tracing the progress of an ideological battle. It was at the level of the individual that language was reshaping thought, and in the aggregate, the sociopolitical reality of the country.

In sum, the comparative concept of form is neither an intrinsic nor an extrinsic understanding of form—it is not a product of close reading (of either poetic or cultural texts). It is a genuine alternative, derived from the thought of a foreign era. This raises the question: What can we do now, in the twenty-first century, with a way of thinking about language that was a product of the nineteenth century, and was largely abandoned after World War II?

RETURN TO PHILOLOGY

Within recent work on the history of the humanities, there has been a surge of interest in philology. One example is James Turner's *Philology: The Forgotten Origins of the Modern Humanities* (2014), which surveys a range of scholarship that was, in the nineteenth century, covered by the framework of philology. One of Turner's central interests is the rise of disciplinarity. He suggests that a better understanding of philology could help us rearrange current disciplinary boundaries, which he describes as "cramping" mental "filters": "Sooner or later, the humanities disciplines must shift their shapes, even drastically shrink in number. The past does not prophesy the future. But perhaps some day humanistic scholarship will, once again, inhabit more wide-ranging academic divisions than it does today."[27] Sheldon Pollock's work, with collaborators, on *World Philology* (2015) places the history of the scholarly study of texts in a global context, their goal being to "rethink the very nature of the discipline, transhistorically and transculturally."[28] Nineteenth-century philology was a very broad field: current returns to "philology" thus may have little in common with each other. Yet the return to the "philological para-digm" in this book shares some of Turner's and Pollock's ambitions. Studying early twentieth-century philology reveals unfamiliar ways of thinking about scholarship in the humanities. Moreover, in my effort to make an eclipsed Russian paradigm of thought available to an English studies audience, I share Pollock's commitment to enriching literary studies through transcul-tural comparison.

The lost paths of Formalist scholarship that this book has traced are rooted in a forgotten conception of humanities studies—one which was grounded in the study of individual psychology, rather than in the hermeneu-tic method. R. Lanier Anderson's analysis of the German debate on the iden-tity of the "human sciences" (*Geisteswissenschaft*), which unfolded between the 1880s and 1910s, is instructive for contextualizing Russian literary stud-ies in this period. The debate was provoked by a positivist attempt to reform the human sciences on the model of the natural sciences. The positivist ap-proach was inspired by John Stuart Mill, who proposed that the study of human society, "the moral sciences," "should discover universal natural laws" which would be based on the "explanatory laws of individual psychology," namely the "simple laws of association governing . . . mental states."[29] That is, the social sciences should be grounded in associationist psychology—a posi-tion which is, at this point, familiar to us.

This positivist proposal was met with a number of important, non-positivist responses. The most influential of these was the neo-Kantian posi-tion, which Anderson describes as having won the debate, and advanced an understanding of humanistic knowledge which remains "in possession of the field" to this day. This neo-Kantian position was influentially articulated by Wilhelm Windelband and his student Heinrich Rickert in the 1890s and was based on an opposition between nomothetic and idiographic sciences; the former's "aim [was] to identify universal laws," while for the latter the "main cognitive aim is not law discovery, but the description of significant individual objects." The humanities are, in this view, an idiographic science; they explain and evaluate significant individual historical events, personali-ties, and cultural products. It is not subject matter that defines the humani-ties, but rather their method. Humanities scholars "appeal to values to pick out their objects, making objective, *factual* statements about those individuals' *relevance* to some value." In literary studies, the idiographic method is that of hermeneutics: the interpretation of significant texts in terms of their particular, holistic meanings. Beginning in the 1880s, the debate centered on the place of psychology in relation to the humanities. The neo-Kantian position, which won out, was the only major contending position which *did not* see psychology as the foundational *Geisteswissenschaft*—Windelband instead argued that psychology is a "natural science, incapable of accounting for the essentially valuable or significant objects of the human sciences."[30]

From the perspective of twenty-first-century literary studies in the Anglo-American academy, the Russian philological paradigm represents a path not taken. Instead of adopting the neo-Kantian, idiographic view of the humanities, Russian philologists prioritized the comparative method as the prerequisite for scholarliness (*nauchnost'*). The aim of this method was nomothetic—to discover general tendencies or even "laws." Moreover, the paradigm was psychologistic, assuming that the laws of psychology provide the foundation for the study of human culture (e.g., language, economics, philosophy). However, the Russian philological paradigm corresponds not so much with Mill's positivism but with the non-positivist, but still psychologistic, responses to positivism which were proposed in the late nineteenth century. Two such responses were mounted by Wilhelm Dilthey and Wilhelm Wundt. Wundt's proposal, which described a vision of the humanities based on *Völkerpsychologie*, is the closest to the Russian philological paradigm (recall that Potebnia and Veselovsky were students of Steinthal and Lazarus, whose *Völkerpsychologie* was the source of inspiration for Wundt). Like the Russian philological paradigm, Wundt divides the humanities into two fields: the comparative and interpretive study of culture expressed through social phenomena (language, myth, and ethical life); and the causal explanations of these phenomena via a theory grounded in the "laws of a naturalistic individual psychology."[31] The philological paradigm viewed the regular patterns, tendencies, and formal devices in verbal art as, ultimately, a product of human psychology. However, the real object of philological comparative poetics was not these psychological laws themselves, but the study of how these regularities interact with the history of culture. The bifurcated concept of form inherited by the Russian Formalists (and used to develop novel theories of authorship, narrative structure, and poetic dialectology) fit squarely within a conception of the humanities that was mainstream at the turn of the twentieth century, but largely forgotten today: the humanities viewed not in opposition to the natural sciences (as an idiographic science), but rather as connected to the natural sciences via a "bridge" provided by psychology.

This brings us to the "return to philology," which has been described as an effort to rethink the academic divisions established in the early twentieth century.[32] In the American academy we find contemporary literary scholars calling for a "return to philology" or a "return to form"—but does the Formalism of the philological paradigm provide ideas that are compatible with twenty-first-century priorities? While it is difficult to summarize a diverse field in a state of flux, some consensus can be found in what contemporary scholars are *against*. Julie Orlemanski characterizes the "return to philology" as two intertwined rejections of previous practices. The first is the "turn away from the linguistic turn," and the second is a "set of attitudes" which she calls "antihermeneutic."[33] The turn away from the linguistic turn refers to a rejection of structuralism and post-structuralism, starting in the 1990s.[34] It has been accompanied by the growth of an antihermeneutic attitude, which Orlemanski describes as a position which is "explicitly against the hallmarks of the hermeneutic tradition: against depth, consciousness, the primacy of language, humanism, interpretation, mediation, epistemology, and historicism." Instead of these values, she argues, scholars "have variously valorized surfaces, description, cognition, affect, materiality, nonhuman entities, the natural and social sciences, and speculative thought."[35] However, as Orlemanski and others have noted, even this antihermeneutic scholarship retains a hermeneutic practice, close reading, as its method. New formalism also belongs to this mode of thinking. Activist new formalists reject the humanist values of the New Critics, which included an evaluation of poetry as autonomous works of art. Levine, for example, argues that scholars should treat literary forms as no different from any other social form, such as an institutional timetable or an architectural form. However, the new formalists retain the hermeneutic practice of close reading as their method. One assessment, acknowledged by Orlemanski, is that the "disjunction between antihermeneutic *cris de coeur*, on the one hand, and ubiquitous hermeneutic practice, on the other, signals a kind of impasse in the field."[36]

While this conclusion is certainly far from unanimous, the appeal of philology in the twenty-first century reflects the perception of many that it is time to consider new ways of thinking about method, meaning, and even the epistemological foundations of the humanities. Of the return to philology, Orlemanski suggests that "one reason for its ongoing popularity is that philology returns us to the messy, changeable relationship of our discipline to language."[37] For those who are interested in finding "new" ideas in philology, this book can be read as a reconstruction of a lost theory of verbal form which is not structuralist, not hermeneutic, and which does not call for a strict boundary between artistic verbal forms and nonartistic (social) verbal forms. Moreover, it assumes that the history of these forms is determined by sociopolitical forces. It is thus compatible with some of the priorities of twenty-first-century literary studies. However, as I have stressed, this comparative concept of form is enabled by a particular understanding of language grounded in associationist psychology. Does this preclude its utility for twenty-first-century literary studies?

Certainly, the theoretical proposals of the philological paradigm cannot be uncritically adopted as ready tools one hundred years later. I will not attempt to assess the extent to which the psychologistic assumptions of the Russian Formalists are compatible with contemporary research in psychology. However, contemporary scholarship in linguistics and poetics suggests that the dusty old texts of nineteenth-century philology may in fact contain newly relevant research. Within the field of semantics, specialists have noted the overlap between the nineteenth-century interest in the psychological foundations of language and contemporary cognitivist research. Dirk Geeraerts has argued that "current developments in lexical semantics to a considerable extent constitute a return to the concerns of historical-philological semantics. Many of the older discussions on the subtleties of metaphor and metonymy or the psychological background of meaning in natural languages, then, could still be relevant for current discussions."[38] He writes that the historical-philological work from 1830 to 1930 produced

> a wealth of theoretical proposals and empirical descriptions. . . . Most of this has by now sunk into oblivion, however. In practical terms, the older monographs will be absent from all but the oldest and the largest academic libraries, and where they are available, there is likely to be a language barrier . . . As a result, some of the topics that were investigated thoroughly in the older tradition are later being reinvented rather than rediscovered.[39]

More generally, philological psychologism understood language (and literature) as phenomena which are not autonomous, specialized systems, but rather are manifestations of general psychological processes. This is a position that has been embraced, in new terms, by cognitive literary studies, a field which emerged in the 1990s. Peter Stockwell summarizes the "fundamental principles" of the method. The first of these is that "literary language is not in itself special or unique, though it is used in particular ways." This builds on the assumption, taken from cognitive linguistics, that "there is no special module in the brain for doing language, and no special module for literature. Understanding how we cognise our entire experience is the same understanding that allows us to account for literary reading."[40]

Like the scholarship by semanticists that Geeraerts describes as reinventing philological research, new work in cognitive poetics can echo the writings of Potebnia or Shklovsky. For example, Mark Turner's *The Literary Mind* (1996) can be compared to earlier research on what the philological paradigm called poetic thinking. Turner's arguments build on cognitive metaphor theory, which argues that there are "basic" cognitive metaphors,

Conclusion

such as "life is a journey," which are shared by many people, and which imperceptibly shape everyday thought and discourse. His book is devoted to what he describes as parabolic thinking: the transfer of meaning from one situation to another. This is for him a "root capacity of the everyday mind" which is "exploited by literary narrative, but is not exclusive to literature."[41] Literature accomplishes the blending of different conceptual spaces in a way that "wake[s] up the generic space" of a basic metaphor such as "life is a journey."[42] Turner's research interests thus retread, to some degree, Shklovsky's work on the way that "poetic thinking" (i.e., metaphoric thinking) shapes narrative structure. Both stress that literature can shake up a reader's entrenched, automatic associations by juxtaposing semantic spheres in a novel way.

Comparing cognitive poetics with the philological paradigm also allows us to see how these movements differ. Cognitive poetics is more closely allied with the natural sciences than Formalist poetics or Veselovsky's historical poetics were. In the last decades, the field of cognitive poetics has largely focused on the study of the individual's reading process. This leads away from the central concerns of the Russian philological paradigm with its focus on the *history* of verbal forms, which only partially reflects cognitive processes. The cognitive turn for poetics has meant a departure from the study of literary history. As Geeraerts observes for cognitive semantics, current research is unlike the philological study of language in that the psychological mechanisms such as metaphor and metonymy that were earlier studied in a diachronic perspective "are now primarily analyzed as synchronic phenomena."[43]

Like other twenty-first-century literary studies movements, cognitive poetics can be described as antihermeneutic. As Stockwell writes, "unlike literary criticism, cognitive poetics does not have to focus exclusively on minute differences between readings. Most readers, even from vaguely similar interpretative communities, tend to agree on readings of literature far more than they disagree." Instead, cognitive poetics "starts from a desire to account as rigorously as possible for effects and features that are fundamental to civilian readers. How does this make me feel? How do I know things about this character? Why is this text pacey or atmospheric?" Stockwell's appeal to the "civilian reader" is a way of asserting that the field is interested in discovering general laws. As he puts it, the field studies "readings" understood as "natural objects": "In scientific terms, readings are the data through which we can generalize patterns and principles across readers and texts."[44] In the turn away from the linguistic turn, literary scholars look to the natural and social sciences for methods that will allow for non-hermeneutic analyses of texts. Franco Moretti's use of the term "distant reading" to describe the use of algorithms to analyze digitized texts was intended to stress its polemical rejection of hermeneutic "close reading."[45] Some scholarship in the digital humanities describes its rationale explicitly by reference to philology.[46] Scholars in the digital humanities and classics have made use of the German *Wissenschaft* as a term for scholarship which does not distinguish between science and humanities research. They describe their work as "eWissenschaft" and "ePhilology"—designating practices distinctive to the digital environment.[47] Antihermeneutic scholarship inspired by new computer-assisted technologies questions the twentieth-century conception of the literary humanities, sometimes turning to a more distant past for alterative models.

The Russian philological paradigm presents a model for scholarship which eschews the disciplinary distinctions that emerged in the twentieth century, and offers a framework for thinking about humanities research which is *neither* that of the natural sciences nor the humanities, as those domains are constituted today. It was idiographic in the sense of the modern humanities; it studied textual artifacts in terms of culturally and historically determined semantic meanings. At the same time, it relied on nomothetic laws produced by psychological research and sought to generalize about tendencies, using concepts such as device, genre, and system. The way in which this paradigm negotiated between these two domains can serve as a source of ideas for innovative twenty-first-century literary theory.

This work has already begun. Veselovsky's historical poetics has, for the past decade, been the focus of an innovative recuperative project led by Boris Maslov and Ilya Kliger. Like other returns to philology, their research is motivated by the perception that historical poetics configures disciplinary knowledge in a way that can invigorate twenty-first-century literary studies. In the introduction to their coedited volume *Persistent Forms*, Kliger and Maslov write that historical poetics provides a way of "negotiating between . . . familiar oppositions" such as "theory vs. history; form vs. content; artistry vs. ideology; close reading vs. contextualization." The impasse created by these entrenched categorical oppositions can be surmounted by returning to an older reconfiguration of disciplinary knowledge: historical poetics, they argue, enables innovative research by "blending literary theory, history of poetic forms, cultural history, philosophy of history, and (often less overtly) philosophical aesthetics." Maslov and Kliger's priorities in their recuperation of the philological paradigm (for them, historical poetics) differ from those in this book. The role of associationist psychology for the paradigm is not a central focus of the studies in *Persistent Forms*. Instead, Maslov and Kliger foreground the "ties between philosophy, philology, and history established in [the] nineteenth-century European academy."[48]

The conceptual framework provided by the philological paradigm can be interpreted (for the twenty-first century) in different ways. I have described the paradigm as bifurcated, with one foot in associationist psychology and the other in comparative poetics. Maslov and Kliger work with other explanatory terms and references.[49] What our work shares, more broadly, is an effort to recover, and present for a contemporary audience, a lost Russian philological approach to the study of form. This book, along with the work on historical poetics is, in turn, part of a broader resurgence of interest in Russian Formalist theory within Slavic studies internationally, which has resulted in an array of new scholarship, scholarly collaborations, translations, and editions of the Formalists' texts in the last two decades (for details, see the introduction to this book). The real challenge, as I see it, for Slavists working on this legacy is to articulate how it can contribute to the development of literary studies, both inside and outside of our field, today. My own research has been motivated by the apparent collapse of the linguistic paradigm ("the turn against the linguistic turn") coupled with a puzzlement regarding those aspects of Russian Formalism that resist the explanations provided by canonical (structuralist) scholarship. My interest in the 1910s contains an echo of the Formalists' own nonlinear understanding of cultural history. Tynianov, for example, noted that in an effort to be novel, the poets of the twentieth century were coming to resemble those of the eighteenth: "Khlebnikov counters nineteenth-century verse culture with principles of construction that are, to a large extent, close to those of Lomonosov. This is not a regression to old forms; it is a struggle with the fathers, in which the grandson has come to resemble his grandfather."[50] The turn to a more distant past as a way of escaping the constraints of the more immediate past— this describes the return to philology in the wake of the linguistic paradigm.

Appendix

Saussurean structuralism followed three main tenets. The first of these is an adherence to a systemic understanding of language. A system is a structure in which a change to any part will change the whole.[1] As Giorgio Graffi puts it, within the system, "every linguistic unit can be defined only by virtue of the system of relations it has with the other units."[2] Saussure described language as made up of "signs"—that is, a unit, such as a word, which is understood to have two sides: the sound (the signifier) and the concept (signified). The system provides each sign with "value"; this value is "not intrinsic, but is simply the outcome of its differences from the other signs belonging to the system." According to Saussure, "In language there are only differences . . . differences *without positive terms*."[3] For example, he writes that

> modern French *mouton* can have the same signification as English *sheep* but not the same value, and this for several reasons, particularly because in speaking of a piece of meat ready to be served on the table, English uses *mutton* and not *sheep*. The difference in value between *sheep* and *mouton* is due to the fact that *sheep* has beside it a second term while the French word does not.[4]

The second tenet of structuralist thought I wish to stress is its view of language as an object of study fully autonomous from other fields, including psychology. Structuralists describe the linguistic system as a *social* construct. Saussure's *Course in General Linguistics* (1916) describes language by distinguishing between what he called *"langue"* and *"parole."* As Graffi summarizes:

> *Langue* is defined as the "social side" of language (*langage*). It is the common code shared by all the speakers belonging to a given linguistic community: it is "a storehouse filled by the members of a given community through their active use of speaking." What Saussure calls *parole*, "speaking," denotes both

(a) the usage of this common code by the different individuals and (b) the psycho-physical device which allows them to put such code into use.[5]

Structuralist linguistics, and the literary and cultural theory which built on this model, insisted that *langue* is the true object of the scholar's study.

The commitment to a strictly systemic, and social, understanding of language allowed the French structuralist and post-structuralist theorists, building on this model after the 1950s, to develop a philosophy of language that suggested a deterministic relationship between the social sign system and the individual who operates within it. This is the third tenet of structuralism. In his summary of these schools in *Superstructuralism* (1987), Richard Harland argues that they converge on two general positions: the "priority of Culture over Nature, and . . . a priority of Society over the Individual."[6] He writes:

> According to the Superstructuralists, we cannot live as human beings below the level of language categories and social meanings because it is language categories and social meanings which make us human in the first place. . . . This turns our usual picture of the world quite upside down. For language categories as social meanings are now the ultimate reality, coming before objective things and subjective ideas.[7]

The post–World War II structuralist philosophy of language thus presents a deterministic understanding of the relationship between the individual and this social system: the system precedes the individual; the individual cannot consciously attempt to alter it, and can only operate in the terms it allows.

Notes

INTRODUCTION

1. Julie Orlemanski, "Scales of Reading," *Exemplaria* 26, nos. 2–3 (2014): 226.

2. Michael S. Roth, "Ebb Tide," review of *Sublime Historical Experience*, by F. R. Ankersmit, *History and Theory* 46, no. 1 (February 2007): 66.

3. Orlemanski, "Scales," 225.

4. A series of recent publications, headed by Igor Pil'shchikov, are finally allowing for a better understanding of Moscow Formalism. Igor Pil'shchikov, "Zasedanie moskovskogo lingvisticheskogo kruzhka 1 iuniia 1919 g. i zarozhdenie stikhovedcheskikh kontseptsii O. Brika, B. Tomashevskogo i R. Iakobsona," *Revue des Études Slaves* 88, nos. 1–2 (2017): 151–75, https://doi.org/10.4000/res.956; Igor Pilshchikov and Andrei Ustinov, "Viktor Shklovskii v OPOIaZe i Moskovskom Lingvisticheskom Kruzhke (1919–1921 gg.)," *Wiener Slavistisches Jahrbuch*, n.s., 6 (2018): 176–206, https://doi.org/10.13173/wienslavjahr.6.2018.0176; Andrei Toporkov, "Russkie formalisty i izuchenie fol'klora: Folk'lornye temy na zasedaniiakh moskovskogo lingvisticheskogo kruzhka," in *Neizvestnye stranitsy russkoi fol'kloristiki*, ed. Andrei Toporkov (Moscow: Indrik, 2015), 38–56.

5. The archive includes the minutes of seventy-eight meetings held between 1918 and 1923.

6. Nina Kolesnikoff, "Russian Formalism," in *Encyclopedia of Contemporary Literary Theory: Approaches, Scholars, Terms*, ed. Irene Makaryk (Toronto: University of Toronto Press, 1993), 56.

7. Aage A. Hansen-Löve, *Der russische Formalismus: Methodologische Rekonstruktion seiner Entwicklung aus dem Prinzip der Verfremdung* (Vienna: Verlag der Österreichischen Akademie der Wissenschaften, 1978); Victor Erlich, *Russian Formalism: History—Doctrine*, 4th ed. (1955; The Hague: Mouton, 1980); Fredric Jameson, *The Prison-House of Language: A Critical Account of Structuralism and Russian Formalism* (Princeton, NJ: Princeton University Press, 1972); Peter Steiner, *Russian Formalism: A Metapoetics* (Ithaca, NY: Cornell University Press, 1984); Jurij Striedter, *Literary Structure, Evolution, and*

Value: Russian Formalism and Czech Structuralism Reconsidered (Cambridge, MA: Harvard University Press, 1989).

8. Ilona Svetlikova, *Istoki russkogo formalizma: Traditsiia psikhologizma i formal'naia shkola* (Moscow: Novoe literaturnoe obozrenie, 2005); Galin Tihanov, "Why Did Modern Literary Theory Originate in Central and Eastern Europe? (And Why Is It Now Dead?)," *Common Knowledge* 10, no. 1 (2004): 61–81; Galin Tihanov, *The Birth and Death of Literary Theory: Regimes of Relevance in Russia and Beyond* (Stanford, CA: Stanford University Press, 2019); Jan Levchenko, *Drugaia nauka: Russkie formalisty v poiskakh biografii* (Moscow: Izdatel'skii dom Vysshei shkoly ekonomiki, 2012).

9. Ilya Kalinin, "Formal'naia teoriia siuzheta: Strukturalistskaia fabula formalizma," *Novoe literaturnoe obozrenie*, no. 128 (April 2014), https://www.nlobooks.ru/magazines/novoe_literaturnoe_obozrenie/128_nlo_4_2014/article/11024/.

10. Erlich, *Russian Formalism*, 200; italics added.

11. Striedter, *Literary Structure*, 8, 11.

12. Boris Eikhenbaum, "The Theory of the Formal Method" (1927), in *Readings in Russian Poetics: Formalist and Structuralist Views*, ed. Ladislav Matejka and Krystyna Pomorska (Cambridge, MA: MIT Press, 1971), 3–37.

13. Jameson, *Prison-House*, 101.

14. Peter Steiner, "The Roots of Structuralist Esthetics," in *The Prague School: Selected Writings, 1929–1946*, ed. Peter Steiner (Austin: University of Texas Press, 1982), 208.

15. Steiner, "Roots," 211.

16. Steiner, *Russian Formalism*, 259.

17. Steiner, *Russian Formalism*, 23, 36.

18. Svetlikova, *Istoki*, 8 (my translation; if not otherwise noted, all translations are my own).

19. See also Sergei [Serguei] Oushakine [Ushakin], "'Ne vzletevshie samolety mechty': O pokolenii formal'nogo metoda," in *Formal'nyi metod: Antologiia russkogo modernizma*, vol. 1, *Sistemy*, ed. Serguei Oushakine (Moscow: Kabinetnyi uchenyi, 2016), 9–60.

20. Ferdinand de Saussure, *Course in General Linguistics*, trans. Roy Harris (LaSalle, IL: Open Court, 1986), 1.

21. Sheldon Pollock, "Future Philology? The Fate of a Soft Science in a Hard World," *Critical Inquiry* 35, no. 4 (Summer 2009): 934.

22. Alexander Veselovsky, "On the Methods and Aims of Literary History as a Science," trans. Harry Weber, *Yearbook of Comparative and General Literature* 16 (1967): 38; translation modified.

23. Dan Hunter, "No Wilderness of Single Instances: Inductive Inference in Law," *Journal of Legal Education* 48, no. 3 (September 1998): 369.

24. Veselovsky, "Methods," 38.

25. Cited in R. H. Robins, *A Short History of Linguistics*, 4th ed. (London: Longman, 1997), 188–89.

26. Jacob Grimm, *Teutonic Mythology*, trans. James Stallybrass (New York: Dover, 1966), 3:xxi–xxii.

27. Robins, *Short History*, 190.

28. Anna Morpurgo Davies, *Nineteenth-Century Linguistics*, vol. 4 of *History of Linguistics*, ed. Giulio Lepschy (London: Longman, 1998), 260.

29. Paul Kiparsky, "From Paleogrammarians to Neogrammarians," in *Studies in the History of Linguistics: Traditions and Paradigms*, ed. Dell Hymes (Bloomington: Indiana University Press, 1974), 331–45.

30. Morpurgo Davies, *Nineteenth-Century Linguistics*, 197.

31. Ilya Kliger and Boris Maslov, "Introducing Historical Poetics," in *Persistent Forms: Explorations in Historical Poetics*, ed. Kliger and Maslov (New York: Fordham University Press, 2015), 4, 17.

32. Alexander Veselovsky, "From the Introduction to Historical Poetics: Questions and Answers," in Kliger and Maslov, *Persistent Forms*, 39.

33. Robins, *Short History*, 166.

34. Cited in Andrew Wachtel, *Remaining Relevant after Communism: The Role of the Writer in Eastern Europe* (Chicago: University of Chicago Press, 2006), 13.

35. Ana Deumert, "Language, Culture, and Society," in *The Oxford Handbook of the History of Linguistics*, ed. Keith Allan (Oxford: Oxford University Press, 2013), 657.

36. Deumert, "Language," 657.

37. Cited in Deumert, "Language," 657.

38. Deumert, "Language," 657.

39. See Aleksandr Veselovskii, "Iazyk poezii i iazyk prozy," in *Izbrannoe: Istoricheskaia poetika*, by Veselovskii, ed. I. O. Shaitanov (St. Petersburg: Universitetskaia kniga, 2011), 377–417. On Veselovsky's use of the term "poetics," see Boris Maslov, "Oppozitsiia 'Vostok-Zapad' v istorii sravnitel'noi poetiki," *Arbor Mundi/Mirovoe drevo: International Journal of Theory and History of World Culture* 19 (2012): 72–94. This use of the term "poetics" is to be distinguished from the Anglo-American academic use of "poetics" to refer to techniques of lyrical composition.

40. Veselovsky, "Methods," 35.

41. Veselovsky, "Methods," 42.

42. Veselovskii, "Iazyk poezii," 390.

43. On the comparative method in folklore, see Kaarle Krohn, *Folklore Methodology* [*Die folkloristische Arbeitsmethode*, 1926] (Austin: University of Texas Press, 1971).

44. Veselovskii, *Izbrannoe*, 537.

45. Cited in Deumert, "Language," 657.

46. Veselovskii, *Izbrannoe*, 537–38.

47. For Jakobson's view of "verbal art" as a translation of *slovesnost'*, see Roman Jakobson, "Retrospect," in *Selected Writings* (The Hague: Mouton, 1966), 4:645.

48. Andy Byford, *Literary Scholarship in Late Imperial Russia: Rituals of Academic Institutionalisation* (London: Legenda, 2007), 32.

49. V. I. Dal', *Tolkovyi slovar' zhivogo velikorusskogo iazyka* (1880–82; Moscow: Izdatel'stvo russkyi iazyk, 1999), 4:222.

50. *Slovo*, like *logos* in Greek, has a broader meaning than the English term "word." The first four definitions of *slovo* given by Dal' are (1) the human capacity for speech; (2) a combination of sounds associated with a referent; (3) discussion, conversation; (4) a speech, sermon, or story.

51. See Byford, *Literary Scholarship*, 32–33.

52. Byford, *Literary Scholarship*, 37, 39.

53. Byford, *Literary Scholarship*, 34.

54. D. N. Ovsianiko-Kulikovskii, "Lingvisticheskaia teoriia proiskhozhdeniia iskusstva i evoliutsii poezii," in *Voprosy teorii i psikhologii tvorchestva*, ed. B. A. Lezin, 2nd ed. (Kharkov: Mirnyi trud, 1911), 1:21; second italics added.

55. Andy Byford, "Between Literary Education and Academic Learning: The Study of Literature at Secondary School in Late Imperial Russia (1860s–1900s)," *History of Education* 33, no. 6 (2004): 637–60.

56. Boris Tomashevskii, *Teoriia literatury: Poetika* (1931; Moscow: Aspekt, 1996), 22.

57. David Rodowick, *Elegy for Theory* (Cambridge, MA: Harvard University Press, 2014), 98.

58. This was the title of Osip Brik's paper, discussed on October 18, 1919. See Galina Barankova, "K istorii moskovskogo lingvisticheskogo kruzhka: Materialy iz Rukopisnogo otdela Instituta russkogo iazyka," in *Iazyk, Kul'tura, Gumanitarnoe znanie: Nauchnoe nasledie G. O. Vinokura i sovremennost'* (Moscow: Nauchnyi mir, 1999), 359–82.

59. Carol Any, *Boris Eikhenbaum: Voices of a Russian Formalist* (Stanford, CA: Stanford University Press, 1994), 3.

60. Boris Eikhenbaum, "O chtenii stikhov," *Zhizn' iskusstva*, no. 290 (November 12, 1919): 1.

61. Viktor Shklovsky, *Knight's Move* [*Khod konia*, 1923], trans. Richard Sheldon (Champaign, IL: Dalkey Archive, 2005), 19.

62. Tihanov, "Why Did," 76.

63. Eric Mandelbaum, "Associationist Theories of Thought," in *The Stanford Encyclopedia of Philosophy*, ed. Edward N. Zalta (Stanford, CA: Stanford University, Metaphysics Research Lab, Fall 2020), https://plato.stanford.edu/archives/fall2020/entries/associationist-thought/.

64. Svetlikova, *Istoki*, 21.

65. Svetlikova, *Istoki*, 21–22.

66. Svetlikova, *Istoki*, 35.

67. Svetlikova, *Istoki*, 39.

68. Svetlikova, *Istoki*, 40.

69. Mandelbaum, "Associationist Theories."

70. Mandelbaum, "Associationist Theories."

71. Alan Kim, "Johann Friedrich Herbart," in Zalta, *Stanford Encyclopedia of Philosophy* (Winter 2015), https://plato.stanford.edu/archives/win2015/entries/johann-herbart/.

72. Mikolaj Kruszewski, *Writings in General Linguistics: On Sound Alternation (1881) and Outline of Linguistic Science (1883)*, vol. 11 of *Amsterdam Classics in Linguistics: 1800–1925* (Philadelphia: John Benjamins, 1995), 100. Roman Jakobson recalled reading Krushevsky as a university student in 1914; see Jakobson and Krystyna Pomorska, *Dialogues* (Cambridge, MA: MIT Press, 1983), 126–27.

73. Kruszewski, *Writings*, 100.

74. This discussion may also recall Roman Jakobson's reference to similarity and contiguity associations in his writings on aphasia. For more on this see chapter 3.

75. Morpurgo Davies, *Nineteenth-Century Linguistics*, 203.

76. Morpurgo Davies, *Nineteenth-Century Linguistics*, 204.

77. In treating Tynianov's work in the context of "structuralism," I follow Striedter and others who distinguish between non-systemic and systemic Formalism. See Steiner, *Russian Formalism*, 32.

78. His ideas were particularly important for Soviet structuralism and the literary theory of Yuri Lotman. Tynianov's legacy was made the subject of a biennial conference series, the "Tynianov Readings" ("Tynianovskie chteniia"), beginning in 1982. The proceedings of these were published as *Tynianovskie sborniki* (1984–2018).

79. Viktor Shklovsky, "Art, as Device," trans. Alexandra Berlina, *Poetics Today* 36, no. 3 (September 2015): 161–63.

80. See Viktor Shklovskii, "Literatura vne 'siuzheta,' " in *O teorii prozy* (Moscow: Federatsiia, 1929; facsimile repr., Ann Arbor, MI: Ardis, 1985), 228.

81. Steiner, *Russian Formalism*, 57.

82. Alexei Kruchenykh, "Declaration of the Word as Such," in *Words in Revolution: Russian Futurist Manifestoes, 1912–1928*, ed. Anna Lawton, trans. Anna Lawton and Herbert Eagle (Washington, DC: New Academia, 2005), 67.

83. See N. A. Bogomolov, "K genezisu dikhotomii 'iazyk poeticheskii—iazyk prakticheskii,'" *Russkaia literatura*, no. 2 (2014): 250–56.

84. Stéphane Mallarmé, *Divagations*, trans. Barbara Johnson (Cambridge, MA: Harvard University Press, 2007), 210.

85. Mallarmé, *Divagations*, 211.

86. Maksim Shapir, "Iz istorii filologicheskoi nauki: Materialy po istorii lingvisticheskoi poetiki," *Izvestiia Akademii Nauk SSSR: Seriia literatury i iazyka* 50 (1991): 45.

87. Roman Jakobson, "Noveishaia russkaia poeziia—Nabrosok pervyi: Postupy k Khlebnikovu," in *Selected Writings*, 5:330, 319; italics added.

88. Deumert, "Language," 657.

89. Svetlikova, *Istoki*, 80, 82.

90. Roman Jakobson, *My Futurist Years*, ed. Bengt Jangfeldt and Stephen Rudy, trans. Stephen Rudy (New York: Marsilio, 1997), 195; translation modified. Jakobson uses the term *ustanovka* and indicates that this is a translation of *Einstellung*. In another essay published in the same year, "Futurizm" [Futurism] (1919), he specifies that *ustanovka* is a "psychological term."

91. Shklovskii, *O teorii prozy*, 79.

92. Svetlikova, *Istoki*, 85.

93. Shklovsky, "Art, as Device," 158–59; italics added.

94. Shklovsky, *Knight's Move*, 130.

95. Bengt Jangfeldt, *Mayakovsky: A Biography*, trans. Harry D. Watson (Chicago: University of Chicago Press, 2014), 151.

96. Jakobson, *My Futurist Years*, 280–81, 29.

97. Peter Steiner, "'Which Side Are You On, Boy?' Roman Iakobson v Prage mezhvoennogo perioda," *Slovo.ru: Baltiiskii aktsent* 9, no. 1 (2018): 13–28.

98. Any, *Boris Eikhenbaum*, 3, 11–12.

99. Kliger and Maslov, "Introducing Historical Poetics," 13.

100. Ewa Thompson, "Formalism," in *Handbook of Russian Literature*, ed. Victor Terras (New Haven, CT: Yale University Press, 1985), 152.

101. Andy Byford, "The Rhetoric of Aleksandr Veselovskii's 'Historical Poetics' and the Autonomy of Academic Literary Studies in Late Imperial Russia," *Slavonica* 11, no. 2 (2005): 128.

102. Eikhenbaum, "Theory of the Formal Method," 33.

103. Jakobson, *My Futurist Years*, 179.

104. Kliger and Maslov, "Introducing Historical Poetics," 10.

105. See Jessica Merrill, "The North American Reception of Russian Formalism," in *Literary Theory between East and West: Transcultural and Transdisciplinary Movements from Russian Formalism to Cultural Studies*, ed. Michał Mrugalski, Schamma Schahadat, Danuta Ulicka, and Irina Wutsdorff (Walter de Gruyter, forthcoming). I return to the Anlgophone reception of Russian Formalism in the conclusion.

106. Mary Louise Pratt, *Toward a Speech Act Theory of Literary Discourse* (Bloomington: Indiana University Press, 1977), xii, xvi–xix, 68.

107. Terry Eagleton, *Literary Theory: An Introduction*, 2nd ed. (Minneapolis: University of Minnesota Press, 1996), 2.

108. Eagleton, *Literary Theory*, 4.

109. Roman Jakobson, *O cheshskom stikhe preimushchestvenno v sopostav-lenii s russkim* (1923; Providence, RI: Brown University Press, 1969), 16–17. See also Jakobson, *Formal'naia shkola i sovremennoe russkoe literaturovedenie*, ed. Tomash Glants (1935; Moscow: Iazyki slavianskikh kul'tur, 2011), 72, 63.

110. See Vladimir Maiakovskii and Osip Brik, "Nasha slovesnaia rabota," *LEF*, no. 1 (March 1923): 40–41; and Boris Eikhenbaum, "Osnovnye stilevye tendentsii v rechi Lenina," *LEF*, no. 1[5] (1924): 57–70.

CHAPTER 1

1. See Eagleton, *Literary Theory*, ix–5.

2. Viktor Shklovskii, "Potebnia" (1916), in *Poetika: Sborniki po teorii po-eticheskogo iazyka*, vol. 3 (Petrograd: OPOIaZ, 1919); and Shklovskii, "Sviaz' siu-zhetoslozheniia s obshchimi priemami stilia," in *O teorii prozy*.

3. Given at the Moscow Linguistic Circle on September 23, 1919. Later published as Roman Jakobson, "Briusovskaia stikhologiia i nauka o stikhe," in *Nauchnye izvestiia Akademicheskogo tsentra Narkomprosa, Sbornik 2, Filoso-fiia, literatura, iskusstvo* (Moscow: Gosudarstvennoe izdatel'stvo, 1922), 222–40. See S. I. Gindin, "Kak moskovskii lingvisticheskii kruzhok voeval s Briusovym i Potebnei," *Novoe literaturnoe obozrenie*, no. 4 (2007): 70–78.

4. Erlich, *Russian Formalism*, 23–31.

5. Eikhenbaum, "Theory of the Formal Method," 6.

6. Thomas Kuhn, *The Structure of Scientific Revolutions* (1962; Chicago: University of Chicago Press, 1996).

7. James Turner, *Philology: The Forgotten Origins of the Modern Humani-ties* (Princeton, NJ: Princeton University Press, 2015), xii–xiv.

8. Morpurgo Davies, *Nineteenth-Century Linguistics*, 152–54.

9. R. Steven Turner, "The Prussian Universities and the Concept of Re-search," *Internationales Archiv für Sozialgeschichte der deutschen Literatur* 5 (1980): 87; R. Steven Turner, "Historicism, *Kritik*, and the Prussian Professori-ate," in *Philologie und Hermeneutik im 19. Jahrhundert II*, ed. Mayotte Bollack, Heinz Wismann, and Theodor Lindken (Göttingen: Vandenhoeck & Ruprecht, 1983), 465.

10. Turner, "Historicism," 476.

11. John Edwin Sandys, *A History of Classical Scholarship* (New York: Haf-ner, 1964), 3:50–54.

12. Tuska Benes, *In Babel's Shadow: Language, Philology, and the Nation in Nineteenth-Century Germany* (Detroit, MI: Kritik, 2008), 163.

13. Benes, *In Babel's Shadow*, 163.

14. Sebastiano Timpanaro, *The Genesis of Lachmann's Method* (Chicago: University of Chicago Press, 2005), 43.

15. Sandys, *History*, 3:130–31.

16. Bernard Cerquiglini, *In Praise of the Variant: A Critical History of Philology* (Baltimore, MD: Johns Hopkins University Press, 1999), 1–12.

17. Sandys, *History*, 3:99.

18. In Kurt Mueller-Vollmer, ed., *The Hermeneutics Reader: Texts of the German Tradition from the Enlightenment to the Present* (New York: Continuum, 1994), 132.

19. In Mueller-Vollmer, *Hermeneutics Reader*, 135.

20. See Robins, *Short History*, 191–92.

21. Grimm, *Teutonic Mythology*, xxi–xxii.

22. Cited in Bernard Cohen, "Analogy, Homology, and Metaphor in the Interactions between the Natural Sciences and the Social Sciences, Especially Economics," in *Non-Natural Science: Reflecting on the Enterprise of More Heat Than Light*, ed. Neil De Marchi (Durham, NC: Duke University Press, 1993), 17.

23. William Hansen, "Mythology and Folklore Typology: Chronicle of a Failed Scholarly Revolution," *Journal of Folklore Research* 34, no. 3 (1997): 275–80.

24. Benes, *In Babel's Shadow*, 115, 140. For more detail, see also 152–53, 157.

25. Jacob Grimm accepted a university position at Göttingen in 1829. On the power of classical philologists in the German academy, see Turner, "Historicism," 462.

26. Benes, *In Babel's Shadow*, 121.

27. See Gerald Graff, *Professing Literature: An Institutional History* (Chicago: University of Chicago Press, 1987), 63.

28. Graff, *Professing Literature*, 73.

29. See Nicholas Hans, *History of Russian Educational Policy (1701–1917)* (New York: Russell and Russell, 1964), 67.

30. Byford, *Literary Scholarship*, 14, 16.

31. Cited in R. D. Anderson, *European Universities from the Enlightenment to 1914* (Oxford: Oxford University Press, 2004), 244–45.

32. See Byford, *Literary Scholarship*, 15. On secondary schools, see Byford, "Literary Education."

33. It should be noted, however, that the study of the classics was favored by authorities in Russia, as in Germany. Byford, "Literary Education," 648, 645.

34. Petr Nikolaev, *Akademicheskie shkoly v russkom literaturovedenii* (Moscow: Nauka, 1975).

35. Byford, *Literary Scholarship*, 29; see also 92, 94.

36. Buslaev didn't use the term "folklore." See Andrei Toporkov, *Teoriia mifa v russkoi filologicheskoi nauke XIX veka* (Moscow: Indrik, 1997), 100.

37. Nikolaev, *Akademicheskie shkoly*, 61.

38. Nikolaev, *Akademicheskie shkoly*, 27.

39. Toporkov, *Teoriia mifa*, 76–77.

40. Fedor Buslaev, *Prepodavanie otechestvennogo iazyka* (Moscow: Prosveshchenie, 1992), 78.

41. Toporkov, *Teoriia mifa*, 103.

42. Roman Jakobson and Petr Bogatyrev, "K probleme razmezhevaniia fol'kloristiki i literaturovedeniia" (1931), in Jakobson, *Selected Writings*, 4:16–18.

43. Turner, *Philology*, 136.

44. Thomas Seifrid, *The Word Made Self: Russian Writings on Language, 1860–1930* (Ithaca, NY: Cornell University Press, 2005), 29–30.

45. Holger Pedersen, *The Discovery of Language: Linguistic Science in the Nineteenth Century*, trans. John Spargo (Bloomington: Indiana University Press, 1959), 251.

46. Wilhelm von Humboldt, *On Language: On the Diversity of Human Language Construction and Its Influence on the Mental Development of the Human Species*, ed. Michael Losonsky, trans. Peter Heath (Cambridge: Cambridge University Press, 1999), 49; italics in original.

47. Robins, *Short History*, 200.

48. See Henry Hoenigswald, "On the History of the Comparative Method," *Anthropological Linguistics* 5 (1963): 1–11. On the textuality of Grimm's linguistic theory, see Robins, *Short History*, 198–99.

49. Alan Dundes, "The Devolutionary Premise in Folklore Theory," *Journal of the Folklore Institute* 6 (1969): 7.

50. Boris Maslov, "Comparative Literature and Revolution, or the Many Arts of (Mis)Reading Alexander Veselovsky," *Compar(a)ison: An International Journal of Comparative Literature* 2 (2008 [2013]): 113.

51. Toporkov, *Teoriia mifa*, 289.

52. Cited in Toporkov, *Teoriia mifa*, 290–91; italics added.

53. See Veselovsky's autobiographical essay in A. N. Pypin, *Istoriia russkoi etnografii* (St. Petersburg: Tip. M. M. Stasiulevicha, 1891), 2:423–27.

54. Craig Brandist, "The Rise of Soviet Sociolinguistics from the Ashes of Völkerpsychologie," *Journal of the History of the Behavioral Sciences* 42, no. 3 (Summer 2006): 262.

55. John Fizer, *Alexander A. Potebnja's Psycholinguistic Theory of Literature: A Metacritical Inquiry* (Cambridge, MA: Harvard Ukrainian Research Institute and Harvard University Press, 1988), 43.

56. Kim, "Johann Friedrich Herbart."

57. Ivan Kalmar, "The Völkerpsychologie of Lazarus and Steinthal and the Modern Concept of Culture," *Journal of the History of Ideas* 48, no. 4 (October–December 1987): 679.

58. Cited in Kalmar, "Völkerpsychologie," 678.

59. See Byford, *Literary Scholarship*, 15.

60. Nikolaev, *Akademicheskie shkoly*, 138, 147.

61. Cited in Brandist, "Rise," 262.

62. Fizer, *Potebnja's Psycholinguistic Theory*, 43.

63. See Shklovsky, "Art, as Device."

64. Fizer, *Potebnja's Psycholinguistic Theory*, 43.

65. Aleksandr Potebnia, *Iz zapisok po teorii slovesnosti* (1905; The Hague: Mouton, 1970), 97.

66. Veselovskii, *Izbrannoe*, 83.

67. Potebnia, *Iz zapisok*, 100–101.

68. Cited in Fizer, *Potebnja's Psycholinguistic Theory*, 43.

69. Veselovskii, "Iazyk poezii," 384–85.

70. Veselovskii, *Izbrannoe*, 385.

71. Veselovskii, *Izbrannoe*, 537.

72. Veselovsky, "Methods," 35; translation modified.

73. On Veselovsky and genre, see Boris Maslov, "Metapragmatics, Toposforschung, Marxist Stylistics: Three Extensions of Veselovsky's Historical Poetics," in Kliger and Maslov, *Persistent Forms*, 130–39.

74. Yuri Tynianov, "On Literary Evolution," in *Permanent Evolution: Selected Essays on Literature, Theory and Film*, trans. and ed. Ainsley Morse and Philip Redko (Boston: Academic Studies, 2019), 267.

75. N. K. Dmitrenko, *A. A. Potebnia—sobiratel' i issledovatel' fol'klora* (Kiev: Znanie, 1985), 16, 12.

76. Cited in Dmitrenko, *Potebnia*, 6.

77. Potebnia, *Iz zapisok*, 123.

78. See Pypin, *Istoriia*, 2:423–25.

79. René Wellek, *A History of Modern Criticism: 1750–1950*, vol. 4, *The Later Nineteenth Century* (London: Jonathan Cape, 1966), 278–79.

80. Tatiana Ivanova, *Istoriia russkoi fol'kloristiki XX veka: 1900–pervaia polovina 1941 gg.* (St. Petersburg: Dmitrii Bulanin, 2009), 154.

81. Boris Kazanskii, "Ideia istoricheskoi poetiki," in *Poetika: Sbornik statei* (Leningrad: Akademia, 1926), 1:7; italics in original.

82. Roman Jakobson, postscript to Osip Brik, *Two Essays on Poetic Language* (Ann Arbor: University of Michigan, Dept. of Slavic Languages and Literatures, 1964), 78.

83. Jakobson, postscript to Brik, *Two Essays*, 78–79.

84. Svetlikova, *Istoki*, 136–39.

85. Viktor Shklovsky, *Third Factory* (1926), trans. Richard Sheldon (Ann Arbor, MI: Ardis, 1977), 36.

86. Roman Jakobson, "Noveishaia russkaia poeziia," in *Selected Writings*, 5:301.

87. Shklovskii, "Sviaz' siuzhetoslozheniia," in *O teorii prozy*, 22.

88. Shklovsky, "Art, as Device," 157.

89. L. P. Iakubinskii, "O zvukakh stikhotvornogo iazyka," in *Izbrannye raboty: Iazyk i ego funktsionirovanie*, ed. A. A. Leont'ev (Moscow: Nauka, 1986), 163; italics and parenthesis in original.

90. Brik, *Two Essays*, 4.

91. Brik, *Two Essays*, 7, 9.

92. Jakobson, "Noveishaia russkaia poeziia," 5:304.

93. Shklovskii, *O teorii prozy*, 33.

94. Shklovskii, *O teorii prozy*, 37.

95. Shklovskii, *O teorii prozy*, 64.

96. Tomashevskii, *Teoriia literatury*, 25; italics in original.

97. Any, *Boris Eikhenbaum*, 64.

98. Any, *Boris Eikhenbaum*, 14–19, 32, 46.

99. Svetlikova, *Istoki*, 136.

100. On Vengerov, see Mark Gamsa, "Two Million Filing Cards: The Empirical-Biographical Method of Semen Vengerov," *History of Humanities* 1, no. 1 (2016): 129–53.

101. Catherine Depretto, *Le Formalisme en Russie* (Paris: Institut d'Études Slaves, 2009), 68–70.

102. Roman Jakobson, "Iurii Tynianov v Prage," in *Selected Writings*, 5:560. Tynianov's name is not included in a list of members published in October 1919. See [Viktor Shklovskii], "Izuchenie teorii poeticheskogo iazyka," *Zhizn' iskusstva*, no. 273 (October 21, 1919): 2. This article lists the following members: Sergei Bernshtein, Aleksandra Veksler, B. A. Larin, V. A. Piast, E. G. Polonskaia, Piotrovsky, M. Slonimsky, Boris Eikhenbaum, Viktor Shklovsky, V[ladimir]. B. Shklovsky, Lev Iakubinsky. It provides the following address for OPOIAZ: Nadezhdinskaia 33, apt. 7.

103. Tynianov, *Permanent Evolution*, 49.

104. Boris Eikhenbaum, *The Young Tolstoy* (1922), trans. Gary Kern (Ann Arbor, MI: Ardis, 1972), 67.

105. Eikhenbaum, *Young Tolstoy*, 11.

106. Tihanov, "Why Did," 76.

107. Eikhenbaum, *Young Tolstoy*, 4; translation modified.

108. Dal', *Tolkovyi slovar'*, 4:222.

109. See V. V. Ivanov and B. N. Toporov, "Vklad R. O. Iakobsona v slavianskie i indoevropeiskie fol'klornye i mifologicheskie issledovaniia," in *Roman Jakobson: Echoes of His Scholarship*, ed. Daniel Armstrong and C. H. van Schooneveld (Berlin: De Gruyter, 1977), 163–84; Lyubomira D. Parpulova, Charles E. Gribble, and James O. Bailey, "Obituary: Roman Jakobson (1896–1982)," *Journal of American Folklore* 97, no. 383 (1984): 57–60.

110. Jakobson, *Selected Writings*, 4:637.

111. Jakobson, *My Futurist Years*, 47. This comes from a tape-recorded conversation with Bengt Jangfeldt in 1977.

112. Jakobson, *My Futurist Years*, 30.

113. Shklovsky, *Third Factory*, 12.

114. Shklovsky, *Third Factory*, 17.

115. Sources differ as to how long Shklovsky remained at St. Petersburg University. Some sources suggest less than one year, others three years. Emily Finer, *Turning into Sterne: Viktor Shklovskii and Literary Reception* (Leeds, UK: Legenda, 2010), 10.

116. Steiner, *Russian Formalism*, 53, 63.

117. Viktor Shklovskii, "Aleksandr Veselovskii—Istorik i teoretik," *Oktiabr'* 12 (1947): 182.

118. Maslov, "Comparative Literature," 101–29.

119. Viktor Shklovsky, *A Sentimental Journey: Memoirs 1917–1922*, trans. Richard Sheldon (Ithaca, NY: Cornell University Press, 1984), 147, 153.

120. Shklovsky, *Sentimental Journey*, 151.

121. Shklovskii, *O teorii prozy*, 50–54.

122. Roman Jakobson, *Formalistická škola a dnešní literární věda ruská: Brno 1935*, ed. Tomáš Glanc (Prague: Academia, 2005), 14.

123. One exception is Heda Jason, "Precursors of Propp: Formalist Theories of Narrative in Early Russian Ethnopoetics," *PTL: A Journal for Descriptive Poetics and Theory of Literature* 3 (1977): 471–516.

124. Andrei Toporkov, "Rannye stat'i V. B. Shklovskogo i uchebnik M. N. Speranskogo *Russkaia ustnaia slovesnost*," *Izvestiia RAN: Seriia literatury i iazyka* 75, no. 2 (2016): 60–65.

125. Roman Jakobson and Petr Bogatyrev, *Slavianskaia filologiia v Rossii za gody voiny i revoliutsii* (Berlin: OPOIaZ, 1923), 38.

126. Mikhail Speransky, *Russkaia ustnaia slovesnost'* (1917; repr. The Hague: Mouton, 1969), 145–48.

127. Toporkov, "Rannye stat'i," 64–65. B. Kazanskii makes a similar point in "Ideia istoricheskoi poetiki," 7–8.

128. Cited in Kalmar, "Völkerpsychologie," 678.

129. James von Geldern, *Bolshevik Festivals, 1917–1920* (Berkeley: University of California Press, 1993), 103–33.

130. Shklovsky, *Knight's Move*, 30; translation modified.

CHAPTER 2

1. Osip Brik, "T. n. formal'nyi metod," *LEF*, no. 1 (1923): 213.

2. Jakobson, *My Futurist Years*, 184.

3. Daniel Rancour-Laferriere, "Why the Russian Formalists Had No Theory of the Literary Person," *Wiener Slawistischer Almanach* 31 (1992): 327.

4. Rancour-Laferriere, "Russian Formalists," 334.

5. Anthony Giddens, "Structuralism, Post-Structuralism, and the Produc-

tion of Culture," in *Social Theory Today*, ed. Jonathan H. Turner and Anthony Giddens (Stanford, CA: Stanford University Press, 1987), 205–7.

6. Roland Barthes, "The Death of the Author," in *Image, Music, Text*, trans. Stephen Heath (New York: Hill and Wang, 1977), 142.

7. Cited in Richard Harland, *Superstructuralism: The Philosophy of Structuralism and Post-Structuralism* (London: Routledge, 1987), 127–28.

8. Cited in Deumert, "Language," 658.

9. Boris Eikhenbaum, *Skvoz' literaturu: Sbornik statei* (The Hague: Mouton, 1962), 156.

10. Tamara Khmel'nitskaia, "Emkost' slova," in *Vospominaniia o Iu. N. Tynianove: Portrety i vstrechi*, ed. V. A. Kaverin (Moscow: Sovetskii pisatel', 1983), 122.

11. Viktor Shklovskii, "Kollektivnoe tvorchestvo," in *Gamburgskii schet: Stat'i—vospominaniia—esse (1914–1933)*, ed. A. Iu. Galushkin and A. P. Chudakov (Moscow: Sovetskii pisatel', 1990), 89.

12. Tzvetan Todorov, "Structuralism and Literature," in *Approaches to Poetics: Selected Papers from the English Institute*, ed. Seymour Chatman (New York: Columbia University Press, 1973), 158; italics added.

13. R. Lanier Anderson, "The Debate over the Geisteswissenschaften in German Philosophy," in *The Cambridge History of Philosophy 1870–1945*, ed. Thomas Baldwin (Cambridge: Cambridge University Press, 2003), 228–29.

14. S. Iu. Nekliudov, *Temy i variatsii* (Moscow: Indrik, 2016), 13.

15. Potebnia, *Iz zapisok*, 142.

16. Potebnia, *Iz zapisok*, 143.

17. Toporkov, *Teoriia mifa*, 103.

18. Howell dates the rise of "performer studies" to 1908–18; see Dana Howell, *The Development of Soviet Folkloristics* (New York: Garland, 1992), 13.

19. Ivanova, *Istoriia*, 187; on this approach, see also 186–92, 397–404.

20. Howell, *Development*, 22.

21. James Bailey and Tatiana Ivanova, "The Russian Oral Epic Tradition: An Introduction," in *An Anthology of Russian Folk Epics* (New York: M. E. Sharpe, 1998), xviii.

22. Howell, *Development*, 35–37.

23. These included Nikolai Onchukov's 650-page *Sievernyia skazki: Arkhangel'skaia i Olonetskaia gg.* (1908); Zelenin's two studies, each more than 600 pages, *Velikorusskiia skazki Permskoi gubernii* (1914) and *Velikorusskiia skazki Viatskoi gubernii* (1915); and Yuri and Boris Sokolov's 1,500-page *Skazki i pesni Belozerskogo kraia* (1915).

24. Cited in Howell, *Development*, 36; translation modified.

25. Howell, *Development*, 26; Ivanova, *Istoriia*, 187–88.

26. Mark Azadovskii, *A Siberian Tale Teller*, trans. James Dow (Austin: University of Texas Press, 1974), 30, 27, 25, 39, 41, 44, 11, 12 (italics added), 13.

27. Cited in Howell, *Development*, 36.

28. Ivanova, *Istoriia*, 397.

29. Kazanskii, "Ideia," 8; italics added.

30. Roman Jakobson, "Petr Bogatyrev (29.I.93–18.VIII.71): Expert in Transfiguration," in *Sound, Sign and Meaning: Quinquagenary of the Prague Linguistic Circle*, ed. L. Matejka (Ann Arbor: University of Michigan Press, 1976), 37.

31. Jakobson and Pomorska, *Dialogues*, 15.

32. Edward J. Brown, *Mayakovsky: A Poet in the Revolution* (Princeton, NJ: Princeton University Press, 2016), 205–6.

33. Cited in Brown, *Mayakovsky*, 204.

34. Vladimir Mayakovsky, *Selected Poems*, Translated by James H. McGavran III (Evanston: Northwestern University Press, 2013), 196.

35. Vladimir Maiakovskii, "150 000 000. Poema" (1921), in *Polnoe sobranie sochinenii v 13 tomakh* (Moscow: Khudozhestvennaia literatura, 1956), 2:115.

36. Lynn Mally, *Culture of the Future: The Proletkult Movement in Revolutionary Russia* (Berkeley: University of California Press, 1990), xix; see also xviii.

37. Mally, *Culture*, 24–25, 4. The Vpered group was made up of members of the Left Bolshevik faction (Alexander Bogdanov, Anatoli Lunacharsky, and Maxim Gorky), which sought to reinterpret Marxist theory so as to give ideology and culture a more creative and central role.

38. N. Verner, A. Bogdanov, V. Bazarov, A. Lunacharsky, and M. Gorky, *Ocherki filosofii kollektivizma* (St. Petersburg: Znanie, 1909), 5; italics in original.

39. Aleksandr Bogdanov, *O proletarskoi kul'ture 1904–1924* (Leningrad: Kniga, 1924), 197.

40. Mally, *Culture*, 147, 148.

41. Lynn Mally, "Egalitarian and Elitist Visions of Cultural Transformation," in *Culture et révolution*, ed. Marc Ferro and Sheila Fitzpatrick (Paris: Éditions de l'École des Hautes Études en Sciences Sociales, 1989), 137.

42. Mally, "Egalitarian," 141–42.

43. Mally, "Egalitarian," 141–42.

44. Cited in Howell, *Development*, 33.

45. Gorky, in Verner et al., *Ocherki*, 350.

46. Malcolm Bradbury and James McFarlane, *Modernism: 1890–1930* (London: Penguin Books, 1991), 27.

47. Jeffrey Brooks, "The Breakdown in Production and Distribution of Printed Material," in *Bolshevik Culture: Experiment and Order in the Russian Revolution*, ed. Abbott Gleason, Peter Kenez, and Richard Stites (Bloomington: Indiana University Press, 1989), 152.

48. Brooks, "Breakdown," 165, 153.

49. Eikhenbaum, "O chtenii stikhov," 1.

50. Martha Hickey, *The Writer in Petrograd and the House of Arts* (Evanston, IL: Northwestern University Press, 2009), 176.

51. Hickey, *Writer*, 179.

52. Sergei Bernshtein, "Zvuchashchaia khudozhestvennaia rech' i ee izuche-nie," in *Poetika: Sbornik statei,* Vremennik Otdela slovesnykh iskusstv (Lenin-grad: Akademia, 1926), 1:42.

53. See also Peter Brang, *Das klingende Wort: Zu Theorie und Geschichte der Deklamationskunst in Russland* (Vienna: Verlag der Österreichischen Akademie der Wissenschaften, 1988); V. V. Feshchenko, *Zhivoe slovo: Logos—golos—dvizhenie—zhest: Sbornik statei i materialov* (Moscow: Novoe literaturnoe obozrenie, 2015).

54. Brooks, "Breakdown," 165.

55. Raffaella Vassena, "K rekonstruktsii istorii i deiatel'nosti instituta zhi-vogo slova (1918–1924)," *Novoe literaturnoe obozrenie,* no. 4 (2007): 82.

56. Stephen Kotkin, *Stalin,* vol. 1: *Paradoxes of Power, 1878–1928* (New York: Penguin, 2015), 227–32.

57. Vassena, "K rekonstruktsii istorii," 85, 84.

58. Vassena, "K rekonstruktsii istorii," 83.

59. Sergei Bernshtein, "Golos Bloka" (1921), in *Blokovskii sbornik,* vol. 2 (Tartu: Tartuskii gosudarstvennyi universitet, 1972).

60. Boris Eikhenbaum, *Melodika russkogo liricheskogo stikha* (St. Peters-burg: OPOIaZ, 1922), 12.

61. Yuri Tynianov, *Poetika, Istoriia literatury, Kino,* ed. E. A. Toddes, A. P. Chudakov, and M. O. Chudakova (Moscow: Nauka, 1977), 491.

62. Vassena, "K rekonstruktsii istorii," 79–95; Bernshtein, "Golos," 455.

63. Aage A. Hansen-Löve [Oge A. Khansen-Leve], *Russkii formalizm: Metodologicheskaia rekonstruktsiia razvitiia na osnove printsipa ostraneniia,* trans. S. A. Romashko (Moscow: Iazyki russkoi kul'tury, 2001), 102–3.

64. Wilhelm Wundt, *Völkerpsychologie: Eine Untersuchung der Entwick-lungsgesetze von Sprache, Mythus und Sitte,* vol. 1, *Die Sprache* (Leipzig: Wilhelm Engelmann, 1904), 333.

65. F. N. Hales, review of *Volkerpsychologie,* by Wilhelm Wundt, *Mind,* n.s., 12, no. 46 (April 1903): 243.

66. Shklovskii, *Gamburgskii schet,* 56. See also Amy Mandelker, "Russian Formalism and the Objective Analysis of Sound in Poetry," *Slavic and East European Journal* 27, no. 3 (Autumn 1983): 331.

67. Steven Cassedy, *Flight from Eden: The Origins of Modern Literary Criticism and Theory* (Berkeley: University of California Press, 1990), 39–64.

68. Mel Gordon and Alma Law, "Eisenstein's Early Work in Expressive Be-havior: The Montage of Movement," *Millennium Film Journal,* no. 3 (Winter/Spring 1979): 28.

69. Sergei Eisenstein and Sergei Tretyakov, "Expressive Movement," trans. Alma H. Law, *Millennium Film Journal,* no. 3 (Winter/Spring 1979): 36–37; ital-ics added.

70. Eisenstein and Tretyakov, "Expressive Movement," 37.

71. See Vladimir Shklovskii, "Deklamatsiia Bloka," *Zhizn' iskusstva*, no. 18 (May 8, 1922): 2.

72. Julian Graffy, *Gogol's The Overcoat* (London: Bristol Classical Press, 2000), 102–20.

73. Boris Eikhenbaum, "How Gogol's 'Overcoat' Is Made," in *Dostoevsky and Gogol: Texts and Criticism*, ed. Priscilla Meyer and Stephen Rudy (Ann Arbor, MI: Ardis, 1979), 119; italics in original.

74. Boris Eikhenbaum, *Literatura: Teoriia, kritika, polemika* (Leningrad: Priboi, 1927), 250–64.

75. Eikhenbaum, "Gogol's Overcoat," 121.

76. Eikhenbaum, "Gogol's Overcoat," 121–22.

77. Eikhenbaum, "Gogol's Overcoat," 130.

78. Any, *Eikhenbaum*, 56, 65.

79. Eikhenbaum, "Gogol's Overcoat," 131.

80. Eikhenbaum, "Gogol's Overcoat," 127.

81. Jakobson and Pomorska, *Dialogues*, 125–26.

82. Tynianov, *Permanent Evolution*, 80.

83. Michael Burke, "Rhetoric and Persuasion," in *The Cambridge Encyclopedia of the Language Sciences*, ed. Patrick Colm Hogan (Cambridge: Cambridge University Press, 2011), 716.

84. See Ilya Kalinin, "How Lenin's Language Was Made: Russian Formalists on the Material of History and Technique of Ideology," in *Words, Bodies, Memory: A Festschrift in Honor of Irina Sandomirskaia*, ed. Lars Kleberg, Tora Lane, and Marcia Sá Cavalcante Schuback (Stockholm: Elanders, 2019), 335–46; and Samuel D. Eisen, "Whose Lenin Is It Anyway? Viktor Shklovsky, Boris Eikhenbaum and the Formalist-Marxist Debate in Soviet Cultural Politics (A View from the Twenties)," *Russian Review* 55, no. 1 (January 1996): 65–79.

85. Eikhenbaum, "Osnovnye stilevye tendentsii," 64.

86. Any, *Eikhenbaum*, 66.

87. Viktor Shklovskii, "Lenin, kak dekanonizator," *LEF*, no. 1[5] (1924): 55–56. Compare to "Art, as Device," 163, and *O teorii prozy*, 79.

88. Translation cited from Any, *Eikhenbaum*, 78.

89. Any, *Eikhenbaum*, 78.

90. Cited from Steiner, *Russian Formalism*, 104.

91. Any, *Eikhenbaum*, 61.

92. Steiner, *Russian Formalism*, 111.

93. Tynianov, *Permanent Evolution*, 78.

94. Tynianov, *Permanent Evolution*, 104.

95. Richard Sheldon, "Viktor Borisovich Shklovsky: Literary Theory and Practice: 1914–1930" (PhD diss., University of Michigan, 1966), 24.

96. Richard Sheldon, *Viktor Shklovsky: An International Bibliography of Works by and about Him* (Ann Arbor, MI: Ardis, 1977).

97. Shklovsky, *Knight's Move*, 3.

98. Sheldon, "Viktor Borisovich Shklovsky," 31, 39. Viktor Shklovskii, "Nachatki grammoty," in *Gamburgskii schet*, 376–78.

99. Sheldon, *Viktor Shklovsky*.

100. Shklovsky's analyses were impacted by his association with Gorky's "World Literature" publishing house. See Jessica Merrill, "The Role of Folklore Study in the Rise of Russian Formalist and Czech Structuralist Literary Theory" (PhD diss., University of California, Berkeley, 2012), 26–30.

101. Finer, *Turning into Sterne*, 13–14, 10.

102. Shklovskii, *Gamburgskii schet*, 103.

103. Viktor Shklovskii, "Retsenziia na etu knigu," in *Gamburgskii schet*, 381.

104. Shklovskii, *Gamburgskii schet*, 226.

105. Viktor Shklovsky, *ZOO, or Letters Not about Love* (1923), trans. Richard Sheldon (Ithaca, NY: Cornell University Press, 1971), xxvii.

106. Shklovskii, *Gamburgskii schet*, 289.

107. Konstantin Fedin, "Melok na shube," *Zhizn' iskusstva*, no. 792–97 (August 2–7, 1921): 2–3.

108. Shklovskii, *Gamburgskii schet*, 84.

109. Ilya Kalinin, "History as the Art of Articulation," *Social Sciences* 37, no. 1 (2006): 46–47.

110. Shklovsky, *Knight's Move*, 117.

111. Cited from Shklovskii, *O teorii prozy*, 26–27; italics in original.

112. Cited in Haun Saussy, *The Ethnography of Rhythm: Orality and Its Technologies* (New York: Fordham University Press, 2016), 22. Note that Rybnikov stresses variation in tradition, while Paulhan stresses fixity.

113. Albert Lord, *The Singer of Tales* (Cambridge, MA: Harvard University Press, 1981), 20.

114. Shklovskii, *Gamburgskii schet*, 89.

115. Shklovskii, *Gamburgskii schet*, 88–89. Shklovsky reiterates Veselovsky's claim that the "schematism" observed in older, formulaic genres will continue to hold for contemporary literature if it is viewed with greater perspective.

116. Cited in Sheldon, "Viktor Borisovich Shklovsky," 38.

117. Shklovskii, *Gamburgskii schet*, 56.

118. Brik, "T. n. formal'nyi metod," 213.

119. Richard Sherwood, "Translation from *LEF* with an Introduction," *Screen* 12, no. 4 (Winter 1971): 43, 44; translation modified.

120. Shklovskii, *Gamburgskii schet*, 106.

121. Tynianov, *Poetika*, 568. The book came out with the title *Archaists and Innovators* (*Arkhaisty i novatory*).

122. Shklovskii, *O teorii prozy*, 227.

123. Cited in Khmel'nitskaia, "Emkost' slova," 124.

124. Sheldon, "Viktor Borisovich Shklovsky," 30.

125. Manfred Hildermeier, "Neopopulism and Modernization: The Debate on Theory and Tactics in the Socialist Revolutionary Party, 1905–14," *Russian Review* 34, no. 4 (October 1975): 453–75.

126. Kotkin, *Stalin*, 1:243.

127. Leon Trotsky, *Literature and Revolution* (Ann Arbor: University of Michigan Press, 1960), 222–23.

128. Sheila Fitzpatrick, "The Bolsheviks' Dilemma: Class, Culture, and Politics in the Early Soviet Years," *Slavic Review* 47, no. 4 (Winter 1988): 601.

129. Fitzpatrick, "Bolsheviks' Dilemma," 602.

130. Shklovskii, *Gamburgskii schet*, 88.

131. *Bol'shaia sovetskaia entsiklopediia*, ed. Otto Schmidt (Moscow: Sovetskaia entsiklopediia, 1933), 27:641. On Shklovsky's essay, see Karl Maurer, "Kollektivnoe Tvorchestvo—Kollektives Schaffen," *Poetica: Zeitschrift für Sprach- und Literaturwissenschaft* 1 (1967): 98–108.

132. Viktor Shklovskii, "Kollektivnoe tvorchestvo," in *Gamburgskii schet*, 89.

133. Shklovsky, *Knight's Move*, 8, 22.

134. Shklovsky, *Sentimental Journey*, 232.

135. Shklovskii, *Gamburgskii schet*, 40.

136. Shklovskii, *O teorii prozy*, 24.

137. See Robert Sayre and Michael Löwy, "Figures of Romantic Anti-Capitalism," *New German Critique*, no. 32 (Spring–Summer 1984): 42–92.

138. Walter Benjamin, *Illuminations*, ed. Hannah Arendt, trans. Harry Zohn (New York: Harcourt, Brace and World, 1968), 91–92.

139. Ilya Kalinin, "Ot poniatiia 'sdelannost'' k tekhnologii 'literaturnogo remesla' Viktor Shklovskii i sotsialisticheskii formalizm," *Translit: Literaturno-kriticheskii al'manakh*, no. 6/7 (2010): 18–21, 23. See also Galin Tihanov, "The Politics of Estrangement: The Case of the Early Shklovsky," *Poetics Today* 26 (2005): 665–96.

140. Jan Levchenko, *Istoriia i fiktsiia v tekstakh V. Shklovskogo i B. Eikhenbauma v 1920-e gg.* (Tartu: Tartu University Press, 2003), 10.

141. Levchenko, *Istoriia*, 7.

142. Cited in Any, *Eikhenbaum*, 102.

143. Levchenko, *Istoriia*, 119.

CHAPTER 3

1. Translation from Byford, "Rhetoric," 128; translation modified; originally from: Aleksandr Veselovskii, "Istoriia ili teoriia romana?" in A. N. Veselovskii,

Izbrannye stat'i, ed. M. P. Alekseev (Leningrad: Khudozhestvennaia literatura, 1939), 23. Veselovsky refers here to the German novelist Friedrich Spielhagen.

2. Veselovsky, "From the Introduction," 45–46.

3. Erlich, *Russian Formalism*, 9, 30, 172, 173, 195.

4. Viktor Shklovskii, "Ornamental'naia proza," in *O teorii prozy*, 211; italics in original.

5. Shklovsky, *Sentimental Journey*, 60.

6. Svetlikova, *Istoki*, 100–111.

7. William Edward Morris and Charlotte R. Brown, "David Hume," in Zalta, *Stanford Encyclopedia of Philosophy* (Spring 2021), https://plato.stanford.edu/archives/spr2021/entries/hume/.

8. Roman Jakobson, "Two Aspects of Language and Two Types of Aphasic Disturbances," in *Language in Literature*, ed. Krystyna Pomorska and Stephen Rudy (Cambridge, MA: Belknap Press of Harvard University Press, 1987), 113.

9. On the place of associationist theories in relation to cognitive science, see Robert Harnish, *Minds, Brains, Computers: An Historical Introduction to the Foundations of Cognitive Science* (Malden, MA: Blackwell, 2002), 15–35.

10. Aleksandr Veselovskii, "Opredeleniia poezii," in *Izbrannoe*, 120.

11. Veselovskii, *Izbrannoe*, 120.

12. Veselovskii, *Izbrannoe*, 120.

13. Veselovskii, *Izbrannoe*, 401.

14. Shklovsky, *Knight's Move*, 70.

15. See also Boris Maslov, "Lyric Universality," in *Cambridge Companion to World Literature*, ed. B. Etherington and J. Zimbler (Cambridge: Cambridge University Press, 2018), 133–48.

16. Veselovsky also develops the central ideas in this study in "From Lectures on the History of the Lyric and Drama" ("Iz lektsii po istorii liriki i dramy," 1882–83), "The Language of Poetry and Language of Prose" ("Iazyk poezii i iazyk prozy," 1899), and "The Poetics of Plots" ("Poetika siuzhetov," 1913).

17. Tatiana Ivanova, "Tiander K. F.," in Toporkov, *Neizvestnye stranitsy*, 544.

18. Cited from Lord, *Singer*, 57; translation modified.

19. See *Oral Tradition* 31, no. 2 (2017), special issue on "Parallelism in Verbal Art and Performance," ed. M. Frog and Lotte Tarkka.

20. Veselovskii, *Izbrannoe*, 426, 427.

21. Aleksandr Veselovskii, "Iz lektsii po istorii liriki i dramy," in *Istoricheskaia poetika*, ed. V. M. Zhirmunskii (Leningrad: Khudozhestvennaia literatura, 1940), 400.

22. Veselovskii, *Izbrannoe*, 417; italics in original.

23. Veselovskii, *Izbrannoe*, 425–437; citation is from 437.

24. Veselovskii, *Izbrannoe*, 424–25; italics added.

25. Veselovskii, *Izbrannoe*, 443.

26. Brik, *Two Essays*, 3; italics added. On Brik's "Sound Repetition," see Svetlikova, *Istoki*, 132–39.

27. Brik, *Two Essays*, 4.

28. Brik, *Two Essays*, 4.

29. John Dienhart, "A Linguistic Look at Riddles," *Journal of Pragmatics* 31 (1998): 106.

30. Svetlikova, *Istoki*, 87–92.

31. Cited from Craig Cairns, *Associationism and the Literary Imagination, 1739–1939* (Edinburgh: Edinburgh University Press, 2006), 23.

32. Kruszewski, *Writings*, 100.

33. Kruszewski, *Writings*, 100.

34. Sergei Eisenstein, "A Dialectic Approach to Film Form," in *Film Form: Essays in Film Theory*, trans. Jay Leyda (New York: Harcourt Brace Jovanovich, 1949), 57, 60.

35. Cited in Jakobson, *My Futurist Years*, 177.

36. Aleksei Kruchenykh, "New Ways of the Word," in Lawton, *Words in Revolution*, 75, 73.

37. On the term *"riad,"* see Svetlikova, *Istoki*, 116–18.

38. Shklovskii, *O teorii prozy*, 79; italics added.

39. Jakobson, *My Futurist Years*, 178.

40. Tynianov, *Poetika*, 502.

41. Svetlikova, *Istoki*, 102.

42. Yuri Tynianov, *The Problem of Verse Language*, ed. and trans. Michael Sosa and Brent Harvey (Ann Arbor, MI: Ardis, 1981), 57, 74; italics in original.

43. Cited in Tynianov, *Problem*, 110.

44. Tynianov, *Problem*, 110; translation modified.

45. Shklovskii, *O teorii prozy*, 44, 41, 51; italics added.

46. Jakobson and Pomorska, *Dialogues*, 100.

47. Jakobson, *My Futurist Years*, 200; translation modified.

48. See also Grigorii Vinokur, "Moskovskii lingvisticheskii kruzhok," in *Nauchnye izvestiia: Akademicheskii tsentr Narkomprosa, Sbornik 2, Filosofiia, literatura, iskusstvo* (Moscow: Gosudarstvennoe izdatel'stvo, 1922), 289.

49. Jakobson and Pomorska, *Dialogues*, 102.

50. Jakobson and Pomorska, *Dialogues*, 102–3.

51. Cited from Roman Jakobson, "Grammatical Parallelism and Its Russian Facet," *Language* 42, no. 2 (April–June 1966): 407–8.

52. Michael Riffaterre, "Describing Poetic Structures: Two Approaches to Baudelaire's 'Les Chats'" (1966), in *Reader-Response Criticism: From Formalism to Post-Structuralism*, ed. Jane Tompkins (Baltimore, MD: Johns Hopkins University Press, 1980), 31.

53. Jakobson, "Grammatical Parallelism," 413.

54. "Protokol zasedaniia Moskovskogo Lingvisticheskogo Kruzhka ot 19

dekabria 1919 goda," Moskovskii lingvisticheskii kruzhok [Moscow Linguistic Circle] Archive, fond 20, ed. khr. 2, no. 19, list [page] 521, Institut russkogo iazyka imeni V. V. Vinogradova (IRIa) [V. V. Vinogradov Institute of Russian Language], Otdel rukopisei [Manuscript Division], Rossiiskaia Akademiia nauk [Russian Academy of Sciences], Moscow; hereafter cited as IRIa. See also Boris Gasparov, "Futurism and Phonology: Futurist Roots of Jakobson's Approach to Language," in *Jakobson entre l'est et l'ouest 1915–1939*, ed. Françoise Gadet and Patrick Sériot (Lausanne: Université de Lausanne, 1997), 113–16.

55. Jakobson, "Two Aspects," in *Language in Literature*, 95–120.

56. Hugh Buckingham, "Aristotle's Functional Association Psychology: The Syntagmatic and the Paradigmatic Axes in the Neurolinguistics of Roman Jakobson and Alexander Luria; An Anatomical and Functional Quagmire," *Aphasiology* 24, no. 3 (2010): 402.

57. For example: Rad Borislavov, " 'I Know What Motivation Is': The Politics of Emotion and Viktor Shklovskii's Sentimental Rhetoric," *Slavic Review* 74, no. 4 (Winter 2015): 785–807; Svetlana Boym, "Poetics and Politics of Estrangement: Victor Shklovsky and Hannah Arendt," *Poetics Today* 26, no. 4 (Winter 2005): 581–611; Carlo Ginzburg, "Making Things Strange: The Prehistory of a Literary Device," *Representations*, no. 56 (Autumn 1996): 8–28; Anne Dwyer, "Standstill as Extinction: Viktor Shklovsky's Poetics of and Politics of Movement in the 1920s and 1930s," *PMLA* 131, no. 2 (2016): 269–88; Tihanov, "Politics"; Il'ya Kalinin, "Viktor Shklovskii kak priem," in *Formal'nyi metod: Antologiia russkogo modernizma*, vol. 1, *Sistemy*, ed. Sergei Ushakin [Oushakine] (Moscow: Kabinetnyi uchenyi, 2016), 63–106.

58. Tomashevskii, *Teoriia literatury*, 180–82.

59. Shklovskii, *O teorii prozy*, 203, 204.

60. Shklovskii, *O teorii prozy*, 33–35.

61. Shklovskii, *O teorii prozy*, 36.

62. Veselovskii, *Izbrannoe*, 538; italics added.

63. Veselovskii, *Izbrannoe*, 449, 460–61.

64. Vladimir Propp, *Morphology of the Folktale*, trans. Laurence Scott, 2nd ed. (Austin: University of Texas Press, 1968), 39–43.

65. Tomashevskii, *Teoriia literatury*, 182, 183.

66. For an extension of Shklovsky's approach, see Yuri Lotman, *The Structure of the Artistic Text*, trans. Ronald Vroon (Ann Arbor: University of Michigan Press, 1977), 217–38.

67. Viktor Shklovskii, "Siuzet u Dostoevskogo," *Letopis' Doma literatorov*, no. 4 (1921): 4–5.

68. Shklovskii, "Siuzet," 4.

69. Shklovskii, "Siuzet," 4.

70. Cited in Shklovskii, *O teorii prozy*, 37.

71. Shklovskii, *O teorii prozy*, 80.

72. Shklovskii, "Siuzet," 4.

73. Viktor Shklovskii, "Literatura vne 'siuzheta,' " in *O teorii prozy*, 239.

74. Shklovskii, *O teorii prozy*, 81, 83, 68.

75. Shklovskii, *O teorii prozy*, 68, 72.

76. Aristotle, *Poetics*, trans. S. H. Butcher, 3rd ed. (London: Macmillan, 1902), part 22, p. 83, https://hdl.handle.net/2027/hvd.32044010427722.

77. Shklovskii, *O teorii prozy*, 75, 146.

78. Shklovskii, "Siuzet," 5.

79. Shklovskii, *O teorii prozy*, 154.

80. Shklovskii, "Siuzet," 5.

81. On Freud's reception in Russia, see Alexander Etkind, *Eros of the Impossible: The History of Psychoanalysis in Russia* (Boulder, CO.: Westview, 1997); Martin Miller, *Freud and the Bolsheviks: Psychoanalysis in Imperial Russia and the Soviet Union* (New Haven, CT: Yale University Press, 1998).

82. On Shklovsky and Freud, see Eric Naiman, "Shklovsky's Dog and Mulvey's Pleasure: The Secret Life of Defamiliarization," *Comparative Literature* 50, no. 4 (1998): 333–52; Il'ya Kalinin, "Istoriia literatury kak Familienroman (russkii formalizm mezhdu Edipom i Gamletom)," *Novoe literaturnoe obozrenie* 4 (2006): 64–83.

83. Sigmund Freud, *Collected Papers*, ed. Joan Riviere (New York: Basic Books, 1959), 4:69.

84. Robert Holt, "Beyond Vitalism and Mechanism: Freud's Concept of Psychic Energy," in *Science and Psychoanalysis*, vol. 11, *The Ego*, ed. Jules Masserman (New York: Grune and Stratton, 1967), 14–20.

85. Allan Rosenblatt and James Thickstun, "A Study of the Concept of Psychic Energy," *International Journal of Psycho-Analysis* 51 (1970): 266.

86. Herbert Marcuse, *Eros and Civilization: A Philosophical Inquiry into Freud* (1956; London: Routledge, 1998), 27.

87. Peter Brooks, *Reading for the Plot: Design and Intention in Narrative* (New York: Vintage, 1985), 37.

88. Kalinin, "Istoriia," 77–81. A portion of Freud's *Interpretation of Dreams* appeared in Russian in 1904 (Miller, *Freud*, 181n13).

89. Shklovskii, *O teorii prozy*, 57–58.

90. Shklovskii, *O teorii prozy*, 147, 150. Shklovsky discusses literary texts which he cannot cite, because he does not have a copy on hand.

91. Sigmund Freud, *The Interpretation of Dreams*, trans. Joyce Crick, ed. Ritchie Robertson (Oxford: Oxford University Press, 1999), 201.

92. Marcuse, *Eros*, 58.

93. Shklovsky cites riddles from folklore collections published by D. N. Savodnikov, P. N. Rybnikov, E. R. Romanov, N. E. Onchukov, and D. K. Zelenin. These examples were not included in the first version of the article, published in *Sborniki po teorii poeticheskogo iazyka*, vol. 2 (Petrograd: OPOIaZ, 1917), 3–14.

94. Shklovskii, *O teorii prozy*, 69.

95. This chapter first appeared in *Theory of Prose* (1925) as "The Mystery Novel" ["Roman tain"]. It includes a section that was published as "Tekhnika roman tain" in *LEF* 4 (1924).

96. Shklovskii, *O teorii prozy*, 143; italics in original.

97. Veselovskii, *Izbrannoe*, 480.

98. Roger Abrahams and Alan Dundes, "Riddles," in *Folklore and Folklife: An Introduction*, ed. Richard Dorson (Chicago: University of Chicago Press, 1972), 140.

99. Shklovskii, *O teorii prozy*, 150.

100. Shklovskii, *O teorii prozy*, 13.

101. Shklovsky, *Knight's Move*, 13, 14; translation modified.

102. Shklovskii, *O teorii prozy*, 20.

103. See Marcuse, *Eros*, 38.

104. Shklovskii, *O teorii prozy*, 52.

105. Viktor Shklovskii, "O poezii," in *Gamburgskii schet*, 56.

106. Shklovskii, *O teorii prozy*, 5

107. Levchenko, *Drugaia nauka*, 115, 89, 94.

108. The Studio, which opened in February 1919, was part of Gorky's "Vsemirnaia literatura" project. See A. D. Zaidman, "Literaturnye studii 'Vsemirnoi literatury' i 'Doma iskusstv' (1919–1921 gody)," *Russkaia literatura* 1 (1973): 143; and Shklovsky, *Sentimental Journey*, 186.

109. See Cristina Vatulescu, "The Politics of Estrangement: Tracking Shklovsky's Device through Literary and Policing Practices," *Poetics Today* 27, no. 1 (Spring 2006): 35–66.

110. Shklovsky, *ZOO,* 104.

111. See Jakobson, *My Futurist Years*, 111–41.

112. Il'ya Kalinin, "Viktor Shklovskii versus Roman Jakobson: Voina iazykov," in *Vestnik Sankt-Peterburgskogo universiteta* 9, no. 3 (2016): 55–63. See also Aleksandr Galushkin, ed., "Viktor Shklovskii i Roman Iakobson: Perepiska (1922–1956)," in *Roman Iakobson: Teksty, dokumenty, issledovaniia*, ed. H. Beran [Henryk Baran] and S. I. Gindin (Moscow: Rossiiskii gosudarstvennyi gumanitarnyi institut, 1999), 104–35.

113. Cited in Vladimir Berezin, *Viktor Shklovskii* (Moscow: Molodaia gvardiia, 2014), 193.

114. Borislavov, " I Know, " 804.

115. Shklovsky, *ZOO,* 64.

116. Shklovsky, *ZOO,* 4. Shklovsky is referring to the erotic and anticlerical folktales that Alexander Afanas'ev published anonymously in Geneva in 1872.

117. Shklovsky, *ZOO,* 103–4; translation modified.

118. Shklovsky, *ZOO,* 64.

119. Shklovsky, *ZOO,* 35.

120. Compare Shklovsky's commentary on an erotic folk custom, cited as an instance of the "device of deceleration," in *O teorii prozy*, 53.

121. Shklovsky, *Knight's Move*, 3.

CHAPTER 4

1. Jakobson arrived in Czechoslovakia on July 10, 1920. See Steiner, "Which Side," 14.

2. Cited from Brandist, "Rise," 264.

3. Eikhenbaum, "Theory of the Formal Method," 35n1.

4. These three works were all published by OPOIaZ as part of the "Sborniki po teorii poeticheskogo iazyka" series, numbers 4–6, in St. Petersburg and Berlin: Eikhenbaum, *Melodika russkogo liricheskogo stikha*; Jakobson, *O cheshskom stikhe preimushchestvenno v sopostavlenii s russkim*; Bogatyrev, *Cheshskii kukol'nyi i russkii narodnyi teatr*. There was also a virtual number 4 *Siuzhet* (1921), which was published as five separate pamphlets rather than as a single volume.

5. Tynianov, *Poetika*, 504.

6. On the MLC and its research activities, see Roman Iakobson [Jakobson], "Moskovskii lingvisticheskii kruzhok," ed. Maksim Shapir, *Philologica* 3, no. 5/7 (1996): 361–80; Ladislav Matejka, "The Sociological Concerns of the Moscow Linguistic Circle," in *Language, Poetry and Poetics: The Generation of the 1890s; Jakobson, Trubetzkoy, Majakovskij*, ed. Krystyna Pomorska et al. (Berlin: Mouton de Gruyter, 1987), 307–12; Barankova, "K istorii moskovskogo lingvisticheskogo kruzhka"; Toporkov, "Russkie formalisty"; Aleksandr Dmitriev, "Kak sdelana 'formal'no-filosofskaia shkola' (ili pochemu ne sostoialsia moskovskii formalizm?)," in *Issledovaniia po istorii russkoi mysli*, ed. Modest Kolerov and Nikolai Plotnikov, Ezhegodnik 2006–2007, vol. 8 (Moscow: Modest Kolerov, 2009), 70–95; and Tomash Glants and Igor' Pil'shchikov, "Russkie formalisty kak nauchnoe soobshchestvo," in *Epokha ostraneniia: Russkii formalizm i sovremennoe gumanitarnoe znanie* (Moscow: Novoe literaturnoe obozrenie, 2017), 85–102.

7. Cited in Glants and Pil'shchikov, "Russkie formalisty," 90.

8. Maksim Shapir, introduction to Jakobson, "Moskovskii lingvisticheskii kruzhok," 361–63. The earliest date of a recorded meeting is February 7, 1918. This corresponds roughly with the official registry of the Circle as a legal entity, with an official stamp, in the fall of 1918, when it was included in the network of state institutions (Glavnauka Narkompros) and began receiving subsidies from the state budget.

9. IRIa, fond 20, ed. khr. 2.II, no. 18: "Protokol zasedaniia MLK ot 9 dekabria 1919 g.," list 57.

10. On this society, see E. V. Pomerantseva, "Komissiia po narodnoi slovesnosti

Obshchestva liubetelei estestvoznaniia antropologii i etnografii (1911–1926)," *Ocherki istorii russkoi etnografii folkloristiki i antropologii* 2 (1963): 197–206.

11. He was replaced with Aleksei Shakhmatov. See Shapir, introduction to Jakobson, "Moskovskii lingvisticheskii kruzhok," 361.

12. The three honorary members of the MLC, Dmitri Ushakov, Nikolai Durnovo, and Viktor Porzhezinsky, were also members of the MDC.

13. These nine were G. O. Vinokur, G. G. Dinges, V. N. Kamenev, S. O. Kartsevsky, M. N. Peterson, Y. M. Sokolov, B. V. Shergin, M. M. Kenigsberg, and S. Ia. Maze. The others who joined during this period were L. I. Vazilevich, S. P. Bobrov, S. M. Bondi, O. M. Brik, F. M. Vermel', B. V. Gornung, I. L. Kan, B. O. Kushner, V. V. Mayakovsky, V. I. Neishtadt, B. V. Tomashevsky, E. M. Shilling, Vlad. B. Shklovsky, Vikt. B. Shklovsky, B. I. Iarkho, S. I. Bernshtein, A. I. Romm, and G. G. Shpet.

14. Pomerantseva, "Komissiia," 200.

15. There were fewer senior scholars who belonged to both groups; only N. V. Vasil'ev regularly contributed to both commissions. Durnovo and Ushakov occasionally attended meetings of the Commission for Folklore Study.

16. N. S. Trubetzkoy, *Principles of Phonology*, trans. Christiane A. M. Baltaxe (1939; Berkeley: University of California Press, 1969), 309.

17. Roman Jakobson, ed., *N. S. Trubetzkoy's Letters and Notes* (The Hague: Mouton, 1975), 1.

18. Fol'klornyi arkhiv, "Komissiia po narodnoi slovesnosti" [Folkloric Archive, "Commission for Folklore Study"], fond 23, ed. khr. 1, Gosudarstvennyi muzei istorii rossiiskoi literatury imeni V. I. Dalia (GMIRLI) [V. I. Dal' State Museum of the History of Russian Literature], Moscow; hereafter cited as GMIRLI. The minutes of meetings of this society show that Bogatyrev joined on April 21, 1914, and Jakobson joined on November 29, 1914. The Commission for Folklore Study stopped meeting regularly in the spring of 1917; both Jakobson and Bogatyrev attended virtually every meeting held between 1915 and 1917. Trubetskoi joined earlier on November 14, 1911, and attended less regularly.

19. Jakobson, *My Futurist Years*, 31; Milan Leshchak and Svetozar Shvedlik, "Razgovor na proshchanie," in *Petr Grigor'evich Bogatyrev: Vospominaniia, Dokumenty, Stat'i*, ed. L. P. Solntseva (St. Petersburg: ALETEII, 2002), 47.

20. On Shpet, see Tihanov, *Birth and Death*, 68–96.

21. Boris Gornung, "Hermes," in *Pokhod vremeni*, vol. 2, *Stat'i i esse* (Moscow: RGGU 2001), 206.

22. Dmitriev, "Kak sdelana," 89–90.

23. The MLC met in apartment number 10; Mayakovsky lived in apartment 12.

24. The first meeting Brik attended (and when he was elected a member of the MLC) was April 12, 1919; the last was June 9, 1922. See Barankova, "K istorii moskovskogo lingvisticheskogo kruzhka," 363; Dmitriev, "Kak sdelana," 84.

25. Glants and Pil'shchikov, "Russkie formalisty," 87.

26. IRIa, fond 20, ed. khr. 13: "Ob"iasnitel'naia zapiska k smete Moskovsk-ogo lingvisticheskogo kruzhka," list 340.

27. IRIa, fond 20, ed. khr. 2.II, no. 12: "Protokol zasedaniia MLK ot 1 sen-tiabria 1919 g."; published as Galina Barankova, "Siuzhet v kinematografe: Po materialam Moskovskogo lingvisticheskogo kruzhka," *Literaturnoe obozrenie* 3 (1997): 81–84. Shklovsky's personal archive contains a table of contents for a *Sbornik* which would include contributions from both OPOIaZ and MLC members: see V. B. Shklovskii Archive, fond 562, op. 1, ed. khr. 378, Rossiiskii gosu-darstvennyi arkhiv literatury i iskusstva [Russian State Archive of Literature and Art], Moscow; hereafter cited as RGALI.

28. Jakobson and Bogatyrev, *Slavianskaia filologiia*, 31.

29. Barankova, "Siuzhet v kinematografe," 82.

30. L. P. Iakubinskii, "Skoplenie odinakovykh plavnykh v prakticheskom i poeticheskom iazykakh," in Leont'ev, *Izbrannye raboty*, 180. "Dissimilation" re-fers to processes which result in two sounds becoming less alike in articulatory or acoustic terms. The resulting sequence is easier to articulate and distinguish.

31. However, in this article Jakubinsky also mentions that this tendency (i.e., the dissimilation of liquid sounds) is absent in the speech of children or the men-tally ill (Iakubinskii, *Izbrannye raboty*, 181).

32. IRIa, fond 20, ed. khr. 2.II: "Protokol zasedaniia MLK ot 12 aprelia 1919 g. Doklad O. M. Brika 'O poeticheskom epitete,'" list 19b.

33. As mentioned in the introduction, Jakobson later explicitly rejected Jakubinsky's argument regarding the dissimilation of liquids in verse on em-pirical grounds. See Jakobson, *O cheshskom stikhe*, 16–17.

34. Brik and Mayakovsky wrote: "We do not want to distinguish between poetry, prose, and practical language. We recognize only a single linguistic mate-rial, and we will process it according to today's methods" ("Our Linguistic Work" ["Nasha slovesnaia rabota"], *LEF*, no. 1 [1923]; cited from Lawton, *Words in Revolution*, 202).

35. A draft of the study can be found in RGALI, fond 611, "Gosudarst-vennoe izdatel'stvo RSFSR," op. 1, ed. khr. 107, "Iakobson, Roman Osipovich, 'Sovremennaia russkaia poeziia: Viktor Khlebnikov.'" For Jakobson's description of his work with Khlebnikov on the latter's poetry in 1919, see *My Futurist Years*, 56–60.

36. Shapir, "Iz istorii filologicheskoi nauki," 44.

37. Jakobson, *Selected Writings*, 5:301.

38. Jakobson, *Selected Writings*, 5:301.

39. Shapir, "Iz istorii filologicheskoi nauki," 46.

40. Aleksei Shakhmatov, *Ocherk sovremennogo russkogo literaturnogo ia-zyka*, 4th ed. (1913; Moscow: Gosudarstvennoe uchebno-pedagogicheskoe izda-tel'stvo Narkomprosa RSFSR, 1941), 59.

41. See Jakobson, *My Futurist Years*, 34–35. Correspondence between Jakobson and Shakhmatov in Jindřich Toman, *Letters and Other Materials from the Moscow and Prague Linguistic Circles: 1912–1945* (Ann Arbor: Michigan Slavic Publications, 1994), 36–38.

42. Cited in Jakobson, "Two Aspects," in *Language in Literature*, 104.

43. Roland Barthes, *Elements of Semiology* (1964), trans. Annette Lavers and Colin Smith (New York: Hill and Wang, 1977), 21.

44. J. K. Chambers and Peter Trudgill, *Dialectology*, 2nd ed. (Cambridge: Cambridge University Press, 2004), 15.

45. IRIa, fond 20, ed. khr. 2.II: "Protokol zasedaniia MLK ot 12 aprelia 1919 g.," list 19b.

46. Veselovskii, *Izbrannoe*, 387.

47. Veselovskii, *Izbrannoe*, 387; italics added.

48. Jakobson, *Formalistická škola*, 53. See also Jakobson, *O cheshskom stikhe*, 12.

49. Korsh would have had ample opportunity to influence Jakobson before 1915, however, since he taught at the Lazarev Institute of Eastern Languages, where Jakobson studied from 1903 to 1914.

50. Fedor Korsh, *Vvedenie v nauku o slavianskom stikhoslozhenii: O russkom narodnom stikhoslozhenii* (1901; Moscow: LIBROKOM, 2012), 132–33.

51. See Barankova, "K istorii moskovskogo lingvisticheskogo kruzhka," 366, 369.

52. "Zasedanie 25 aprelia 1919 g.," in Toporkov, *Neizvestnye stranitsy*, 88.

53. IRIa, fond 20, ed. khr. 2.II, no. 17: "Protokol zasedaniia MLK ot 25 oktiabria 1919 g. Doklad O. M. Brika 'Chetyrekhstopnyi khorei s daktilicheskimi okonchaniiami,'" list 75.

54. Jindřich Toman, *The Magic of a Common Language: Jakobson, Mathesius, Trubetzkoy, and the Prague Linguistic Circle* (Cambridge, MA: MIT Press, 1995), 12; Jakobson cited in Toman, 12.

55. Jakobson, *Selected Writings*, 5:301.

56. One exception is Toman, *Magic*, 13–14.

57. Shapir, "Iz istorii filologicheskoi nauki," 45.

58. See Jakobson, "Briusovskaia stikhologiia," 235.

59. IRIa, fond 20, ed. khr. 2.II, no. 11: "Protokol zasedaniia MLK ot 28 iiunia 1919 g. Doklad S. P. Bobrova 'Ob ustanovlenii vliianii,'" list 62.

60. Jakobson and Bogatyrev, *Slavianskaia filologiia*, 12; N. N. Durnovo, "Vvedenie: Perekhodnye govory," in *Dialektologicheskaia razyskaniia v oblasti velikorusskikh govorov*, part 1, issue 1, *Iuzhnovelikorusskoe narechie* (Moscow: Sinodal'naia tipografiia, 1917), 1–13.

61. Walt Wolfram and Natalie Schilling-Estes, "Dialectology and Linguistic Diffusion," in *The Handbook of Historical Linguistics*, ed. Brian Joseph and Richard Janda (Malden, MA: Blackwell, 2003), 721.

62. On Shakhmatov's place in the history of the discipline, see S. S. Vysotskii, "Razvitie russkoi dialektologii v kontse XIX v. i v nachale XX v.," in *Istoriia russkoi dialektologii*, ed. B. V. Gornung (Moscow: Izdatelstvo Akademii nauk SSSR, 1961), 40–66; Aleksei Shakhmatov, *Russkaia dialektologiia: Lektsii* (St. Petersburg: Fakul'tet filologii i iskusstv SPbGU, 2010), 28; italics added.

63. Durnovo, "Vvedenie," 5.

64. Wolfram and Schilling-Estes, "Dialectology," 714. The reference is to Everett Rogers, *Diffusion of Innovations* (New York: Free Press, 1962).

65. Wolfram and Schilling-Estes, "Dialectology," 724.

66. Shakhmatov, *Ocherk*, 65.

67. Toman, *Magic*, 11.

68. Roman Jakobson, review of "Opyt dialektologicheskoi karty russkogo iazyka v Evrope," by N. N. Durnovo, N. N. Sokolov, and D. N. Ushakov, *Etnograficheskoe obozrenie* 1–2 (1916): 102–7 (signed R. Ia.). See also Toman, *Letters*, 76–79.

69. Jakobson and Bogatyrev, *Slavianskaia filologiia*, 12; italics added.

70. Roman Jakobson, "Fonetika odnogo severno-velikorusskogo govora s namechaiushcheisia perekhodnost'iu" (written 1916; pub. 1927), in *Selected Writings*, 1:573.

71. IRIa, fond 20, ed. khr. 2.II: "Protokol zasedaniia MLK ot 12 aprelia 1919 g.," list 19b.

72. Roman Jakobson, "The Concept of the Sound Law and the Teleological Criterion" (1928), in *Selected Writings*, 1:2.

73. Morpurgo Davies, *Nineteenth-Century Linguistics*, 232.

74. Robins, *Short History*, 211–12.

75. Deumert, "Language," 658–59.

76. Ivanova, "Istoriia," 22–23.

77. "Bogatyrev's account of the investigations of the dialect and oral tradition in the Vereya district, 1915," Roman Jakobson Papers, MC 72, box 7, folders 2–3, page 13b, Massachusetts Institute of Technology, Department of Distinctive Collections, Cambridge, MA (hereafter cited as MIT). Jakobson and Bogatyrev were accompanied by Nikolai Jakovlev, a fellow member of both the Commission for Folklore Study and the MLC.

78. MIT, MC 72, box 31, folder 25: "Dialectological field notes, c. 1915–17."

79. See "Kratkii ocherk deiatel'nosti Postoiannoi Komissii po Dialektologii Russkogo Iazyka za 12 let (ianvar' 1914 g.–ianvar' 1926 g.)," *Trudy Komissii po Dialektologii Russkogo Iazyka* 9 (1927): 1–12; and "Khronika: Otchet' o deiatel'nosti Etnograficheskogo Otdela i ego Komissii za 1915/16 god," *Etnograficheskoe obozrenie* 3–4 (1915): 145–51.

80. MIT, MC 72, box 7, folders 2–3: "Bogatyrev's account," page 14a.

81. Sheila Fitzpatrick, *The Russian Revolution*, 3rd. ed. (Oxford: Oxford University Press, 2008), 18.

82. Roman Jakobson, "Fonetika," in *Selected Writings*, 1:610–12.

83. Jakobson, *Selected Writings*, 1:573.

84. GMIRLI, fond 23, ed. khr. 1: "Protokol zasedaniia Komissii po narodnoi slovesnosti 16-ogo oktiabria 1915 goda," listy 53a–54b.

85. MIT, MC 72, box 7, folders 2 and 3: "Bogatyrev's account," pages 15b, 16b.

86. Shakhmatov, *Russkaia dialektologiia*, 28; italics added.

87. Shklovsky's talk was called "The Place of Futurism in the History of Language," published as "Voskreshenie slova" (1914); see *Gamburgskii schet*, 486.

88. Krystyna Pomorska, *Russian Formalism and Its Poetic Ambiance* (The Hague: Mouton, 1968), 7.

89. Peter Bürger, "Avant-Garde and Neo-Avant-Garde: An Attempt to Answer Certain Critics of 'Theory of the Avant-Garde,'" trans. Bettina Brandt and Daniel Purdy, *New Literary History* 41, no. 4 (Autumn 2010): 696.

90. Bürger, "Avant-Garde," 696.

91. Velimir Khlebnikov, "Bukva kak takovaia," in *Sobranie sochinenii v shesti tomakh*, vol. 6, part 1, *Stat'i (Nabroski), uchenye trudy vozzvaniia, otkrytye pis'ma, vystupleniia 1904–1922*, ed. P. B. Duganov (Moscow: IMLI RAN, Nasledie, 2005), 339, 438. This manifesto also uses the neologism *rechaz'* to refer to the poet.

92. Jakobson, *My Futurist Years*, 16.

93. Jakobson, *My Futurist Years*, 16; Jakobson, "Retrospect," in *Selected Writings*, 4:640.

94. Gornung, "Hermes," 206–7.

95. IRIa, fond 20, ed. khr. 2.II, no. 20: "Protokol zasedaniia MLK ot 23 dekabria 1919 g. Doklad O. M. Brika 'Problema proletarskoi poezii,'" list 55. "Proletariat" is crossed out and replaced with "folk."

96. Shapir, "Iz istorii filologicheskoi nauki," 49–50.

97. P. N. Medvedev, *Formalizm i formalisty* (1934; Ann Arbor, MI: University Microfilms International, 1981), 78–79.

98. Benedikt Livshits, *Polutoraglazyi strelets: Vospominaniia* (1933; Moscow: Khudozhestvennaia literatura, 1991), 176–77. On Marinetti in Russia, see Harsha Ram, "Futurist Geographies: Uneven Modernities and the Struggle for Aesthetic Autonomy: Paris, Italy, Russia, 1909–1914," in *The Oxford Handbook of Global Modernisms*, ed. Mark Wollaeger and Matt Eatough (New York: Oxford University Press, 2012), 313–40.

99. Vladimir Maiakovskii, "V. V. Khlebnikov" (1922), in *Polnoe sobranie sochinenii v 13 tomakh* (Moscow: Khudozhestvennaia literatura, 1959), 12:23.

100. Cited from Deumert, "Language," 661–62.

101. IRIa, ed. khr. 2.II, no. 19: "Protokol zasedaniia MLK ot 19 dekabria 1919 g. Doklad B. O. Kushnera, 'O iazykakh malykh narodnostei i iazykovoi politike,'" list 52. Boris Kushner (1888–1937) was a linguist and founding member

of OPOIaZ who joined the MLC in 1919. His presentation apparently addressed contemporary tendencies towards linguistic homogeneity.

102. Robins notes that Vossler was inspired by Neogrammarian linguistics as well as by Humboldt. See Robins, *Short History*, 213, 214.

103. Robins, *Short History*, 214.

104. IRIa, ed. khr. 2.II, no. 19: "Protokol zasedaniia MLK ot 19 dekabria 1919 g.," listy 52, 53; italics added.

105. IRIa, fond 20, ed. khr. 13: "Ob"iasnitel'naia zapiska," listy 340–42; quotes are from list [page] 341. The MLC also offered expertise in the form of "criticism" (*kritika*), including a "thorough criticism of existing educational plans" and "sober linguistic criticism" of the approach to literary studios.

106. IRIa, fond 20, ed. khr. 13: "Ob"iasnitel'naia zapiska," listy 340–42; quotation is from list 341. See also M. Iu. Sorokina, "Emigrant no. 1017: Roman Iakobson v moskovskikh arkhivakh," *Ezhegodnik Doma russkogo zarubezh'ia im. Aleksandra Solzhenitsyna* (2016): 86–91.

107. Roman Jakobson, "Vliv revoluce na ruský jazyk (Poznámky ke knize André Mazona, Lexique de la guerre et de la révolution ne Russie)," *Nové Atheneum* 2 (1920–21): 204 (article dated "October 1920").

108. Trotsky, *Literature and Revolution*, 133; italics added.

109. Trotsky, *Literature and Revolution*, 133; italics added.

110. Grigorii Vinokur, *Filologicheskie issledovaniia: Lingvistika i poetika*, ed. G. V. Stepanov and V. P. Neroznak (Moscow: Nauka, 1990), 17.

111. Vinokur, *Filologicheskie issledovaniia*, 17.

112. Vinokur, *Filologicheskie issledovaniia*, 16.

113. Maiakovskii, "V. V. Khlebnikov," 23.

114. Roman Jakobson, "What Is Poetry?" trans. Michael Heim, in *Selected Writings*, 3:749.

115. Roman Jakobson, "Co je poezie?/Was ist Poesie?" in *Texte der russischen Formalisten*, vol. 2, *Texte zur Theorie des Verses und der poetischen Sprache*, ed. Wolf-Dieter Stempel (Munich: Fink, 1972), 414–16. This ending is not included in the English translation of the article.

116. Jakobson, "Fonetika," in *Selected Writings*, 1:573.

117. Jakobson, "What Is Poetry?" in *Selected Writings*, 3:750.

118. Jakobson, *Language in Literature*, 64.

119. Shklovskii, "Lenin," 55.

120. Eikhenbaum, "Osnovnye stilevye tendentsii," 59.

121. Kotkin, *Stalin*, 1:260; see also 280.

122. MIT, MC 72, box 7, folders 2 and 3: "Bogatyrev's account," page 28b.

123. MIT, MC 72, box 7, folders 2 and 3: "Bogatyrev's account," page 30a.

124. IRIa, fond 20, ed. khr. 3, no. 1: "Protokol zasedaniia MLK ot fevralia 1920 g."; no. 10: "Protokol zasedaniia MLK ot 11 avgusta 1920 g."; no. 11: "Protokol zasedaniia MLK ot 19 avgusta 1920 g."

125. Antoine Meillet, *The Comparative Method in Historical Linguistics* (1922), trans. Gordon Ford, Jr. (Paris: Librairie Honoré Champion, 1967), 24.

126. Wolfram and Schilling-Estes, "Dialectology," 715.

127. Wolfram and Schilling-Estes, "Dialectology," 713.

128. Yuri Tynianov and Roman Jakobson, "Problems in the Study of Literature and Language," in Matejka and Pomorska, *Readings in Russian Poetics*, 79.

129. IRIa, fond 20, ed. khr. 13: "Ob"iasnitel'naia zapiska," list 341.

130. Sorokina, "Emigrant," 85.

131. Glants and Pil'shchikov, "Russkie formalisty," 87.

132. IRIa, fond 20, ed. khr. 13: "Ob"iasnitel'naia zapiska," list 342.

133. Sorokina, "Emigrant," 85–86.

134. IRIa, fond 20, ed. khr. 13: "Ob"iasnitel'naia zapiska," list 341.

135. Jakobson, "Vliv revoluce na ruský jazyk," 113n1. Jakobson's article was discussed in the MLC in March 1922; see Barankova, "K istorii," 372.

136. Jakobson, "Vliv revoluce na ruský jazyk," 254.

137. Jakobson, "Vliv revoluce na ruský jazyk," 253.

138. Jakobson, "Vliv revoluce na ruský jazyk," 252–53, 255.

139. Viktor Shklovskii, "K teorii komicheskogo," *Epopea* 3 (December 1922): 61.

140. The minutes of these meetings have been published in "Fol'klornye temy na zasedaniiakh Moskovskogo lingvisticheskogo kruzhka," in Toporkov, *Neizvestnye stranitsy*, 91–114.

141. Toporkov, *Neizvestnye stranitsy*, 93, 94.

142. Toporkov, *Neizvestnye stranitsy*, 95.

143. The membership of the MLC also included other scholars with German or Jewish names: Boris Iarkho, Maksim Kennigsberg, Vladimir Neishtadt, Boris Gornung, and E. M. Shilling. Of those that joined before 1921, also: S. M. Bondi, G. G. Dinges, I. L. Kan, B. O. Kushner, S. I. Bernshtein, S. Ia. Maze, A. I. Romm, and G. G. Shpet. The leading OPOIAZ Formalists—Shklovsky, Tynianov, and Eikhenbaum—also came from Jewish families.

144. Jakobson and Bogatyrev, *Slavianskaia filologiia*, 31.

145. Jakobson, "Retrospect," in *Selected Writings*, 4:643–44.

146. MIT, MC 72, box 7, folders 2 and 3: "Bogatyrev's account," page 27b.

CHAPTER 5

1. Cited in Toman, *Magic*, 154, 156.

2. Jameson, *Prison-House*, 104–5.

3. Roman Jakobson, *Remarks on the Phonological Evolution of Russian in Comparison with the Other Slavic Languages* (1929), trans. Ronald F. Feldstein (Cambridge, MA: MIT Press, 2018), 164–65.

4. Ernst Cassirer, "Structuralism in Modern Linguistics," in *Aufsätze und Kleine Schriften* (Hamburg: Felix Meiner Verlag, 2007), 319.

5. Roman Jakobson, "Principles of Historical Phonology," in *A Reader in Historical and Comparative Linguistics*, ed. Allan Keiler (New York: Holt, Rinehart and Winston, 1971), 122.

6. Mitchell Ash, *Gestalt Psychology in German Culture, 1890–1967: Holism and the Quest for Objectivity* (Cambridge: Cambridge University Press, 1998), 88, 105.

7. Ash, *Gestalt Psychology*, 125, 127.

8. John Anderson and Gordon Bower, *Human Associative Memory* (Washington, DC: V. H. Winston and Sons, 1973), 48.

9. Ash, *Gestalt Psychology*, 122.

10. Cited in Anderson and Bower, *Human Associative Memory*, 47.

11. Anderson and Bower, *Human Associative Memory*, 48.

12. Ash, *Gestalt Psychology*, 123–24, 132.

13. Saussure, *Course*, 112.

14. Cited in Zellig Harris, *Papers in Structural and Transformational Linguistics* (Dordrecht: Springer, 1970), 707.

15. Harris, *Papers*, 706, 707.

16. Trubetzkoy, *Principles*, 11; italics in original.

17. Roman Jakobson, "The Dominant," in Matejka and Pomorska, *Readings in Russian Poetics*, 85; italics added.

18. Jakobson, "Co je poezie," 410.

19. Toman, *Magic*, 168–69.

20. Saussure, *Course*, 13.

21. The quote is from William Whitney, cited in Noam Chomsky, *Current Issues in Linguistic Theory* (1969; The Hague: De Gruyter Mouton, 2010), 22.

22. Chomsky, *Current Issues*, 23.

23. Trubetzkoy, *Principles*, 12; italics added.

24. John E. Joseph, "The Unconscious and the Social in Saussure," *Historiographia Linguistica* 27, nos. 2/3 (2000): 327.

25. Joseph, "Unconscious," 324.

26. Cited in Joseph, "Unconscious," 317n22.

27. Harland, *Superstructuralism*, 20.

28. Harland, *Superstructuralism*, 20–21.

29. Émile Durkheim, *The Division of Labor in Society*, trans. George Simpson (Glencoe, IL: Free Press, 1933), 79.

30. Harland, *Superstructuralism*, 24; italics added.

31. On Saussure and Durkheim, see W. Doroszewski, "Quelque remarques sur les rapports de la sociologie et de la linguistique: Durkheim et F. de Saussure," *Journal de Psychologie* 80 (1932): 82–91.

32. Harland, *Superstructuralism*, 24.

33. See Jan Mukařovský, "Art as Semiotic Fact" (1936), in *Structure, Sign, and Function: Selected Essays*, trans. and ed. John Burbank and Peter Steiner (New Haven, CT: Yale University Press, 1978), 81–88; and Jan Mukařovský, *Aesthetic Function, Norm and Value as Social Facts* (1936), trans. Mark Suino (Ann Arbor: Michigan Slavic Contributions, 1970), 20. Mukařovský's terms are "la conscience collective" and "kolektivní vědomí," translated as "social consciousness" and "collective awareness."

34. Jakobson and Pomorska, *Dialogues*, 41. On the reception of Saussure in Russia, see W. Keith Percival, "Roman Jakobson and the Birth of Linguistic Structuralism," *Sign Systems Studies* 39, no. 1 (2011): 236–62; and Ekaterina Velmezova, "On the Early Stages of the Reception of the Saussurean Concept of *Semiology* in Russia," *Cahiers de l'ILSL*, no. 57 (2018): 165–78.

35. Tynianov, *Poetika*, 522–23.

36. Roman Jakobson, "Sergej Karcevskij," in *Selected Writings*, 2:518.

37. See Percival, "Roman Jakobson," 241–42.

38. Shakhmatov, *Ocherk*, 59.

39. Jakobson, *Selected Writings*, 1:573.

40. Jakobson, *Remarks*, 159; italics in original.

41. Ronald Feldstein, "Translator's Foreword," in Jakobson, *Remarks*, xiv.

42. Jakobson, "Iurii Tynianov v Prage," in *Selected Writings*, 5:563.

43. In Steiner, *Prague School*, 5.

44. Cited in Toman, *Magic*, 154.

45. See Toman, *Magic*, 103–37.

46. Toman, *Magic*, 153–55.

47. Toman, *Magic*, 155.

48. Jakobson, *Selected Writings*, 1:3–7.

49. Jakobson, "Iurii Tynianov v Prage," in *Selected Writings*, 5:563.

50. Jakobson and Bogatyrev, "K probleme razmezhevaniia"; Petr Bogatyrev and Roman Jakobson, "Folklore as a Special Form of Creativity," trans. Manfred Jacobson, in Steiner, *Prague School*, 32–46.

51. Roman Jakobson, "Romantické všeslovanství—nová slavistika," *Čin* 1, no. 1 (October 31, 1929): 11; italics in original.

52. Trubetzkoy, *Principles*, 11.

53. Tynianov and Jakobson, "Problems," 78.

54. Jakobson and Bogatyrev, "K probleme razmezhevaniia," 17; italics in original.

55. Bogatyrev and Jakobson, "Folklore," 38; translation modified.

56. Bogatyrev and Jakobson, "Folklore," 39.

57. For a similar argument, see Nekliudov, *Temy i variatsii*, 7–22. On modes of being and literature, see René Wellek and Austin Warren, *Theory of Literature* (1949; New York: Harcourt, Brace, 1956), 143, 156.

58. Trubetzkoy, *Principles*, 10; italics added.

59. Roman Jakobson, "Efforts toward a Means-Ends Model of Language in Interwar Continental Linguistics," in *Selected Writings*, 2:526.

60. Michael Silverstein, "Functions," *Journal of Linguistic Anthropology* 9, no. 1/2 (June 1999): 76.

61. Jakobson, *Selected Writings*, 5:304–5; for quote, see 305.

62. Jakobson, "Efforts," in *Selected Writings*, 2:524.

63. "Psychophonetic" is de Courtenay's term. See E. F. K. Koerner, "Jan Baudouin de Courtenay: His Place in the History of Linguistic Science," *Canadian Slavonic Papers / Revue Canadienne des Slavistes* 14, no. 4 (Winter 1972): 669.

64. Iakubinskii, *Izbrannye raboty*, 163.

65. Iakubinskii, *Izbrannye raboty*, 17 (italics added), 18.

66. Iakubinskii, *Izbrannye raboty*, 25.

67. See Dóris de Arruda C. da Cunha, "On Dialogic Speech: Convergences and Divergences between Jakubinskij, Bakhtin and Voloshinov," *Revista Conexão Letras* 11, no. 16 (2016): 52–69.

68. Jakobson, *Language in Literature*, 66; italics added.

69. See Karl Bühler, *Sprachtheorie: Die Darstellungsfunktion der Sprache* (Jena: Fischer, 1934).

70. Jakobson, *Language in Literature*, 71.

71. On Prague semiotics, see Peter Steiner and Bronislava Volek, "Semiotics in Bohemia in the 19th and Early 20th Century," in *The Sign: Semiotics around the World*, ed. Richard Weld Bailey, Ladislav Matejka, and Peter Steiner (Ann Arbor: Michigan Slavic Publications, 1978), 206–26.

72. See František Galan, *Historic Structures: The Prague School Project, 1928–1946* (Austin: University of Texas Press, 1985), 82; Steiner, "Roots," 177; Striedter, *Literary Structure*, 116.

73. See Merrill, "Role of Folklore Study," 175–76; Jan Mukařovský, "On Poetic Language," in *The Word and Verbal Art: Selected Essays*, trans. and ed. John Burbank and Peter Steiner (New Haven, CT: Yale University Press, 1977), 1–64; Prague Linguistic Circle, "Theses Presented to the First Congress of Slavic Philologists in Prague, 1929," in Steiner, *Prague School*, 15–18.

74. Leshchak and Shvedlik, "Razgovor," 43; and Svetlana Sorokina, "Funktsional'no-struktural'nyi metod P. G. Bogatyreva," introduction to *Funktsional'no-struktural'noe izuchenie fol'klora*, by Petr Bogatyrev, ed. Svetlana Sorokina (Moscow: IMLI RAN, 2006), 25.

75. Leshchak and Shvedlik, "Razgovor," 46.

76. Klaas-Hinrich Ehlers, "Petr G. Bogatyrev: Leben und Werk im wissenschaftlichen Kontext der 1920er und 1930er Jahre und in späterer Rezeption," introduction to *Funktional-strukturale Ethnographie in Europa*, by Petr Bogatyrev, ed. K. Ehlers and M. Nekula (Heidelberg: Universitätsverlag Winter, 2011), 24.

77. "Zápisy o schůzích" [Minutes of meetings], fond Pražský lingvistický kroužek (PLK) [Prague Linguistic Circle], kart. 1, i. č. 7, Masarykův ústav a Archiv Akademie věd České republiky (MÚA AV ČR) [Masaryk Institute and Archives of the Academy of Sciences of the Czech Republic], Prague. See also Merrill, "Role of Folklore Study," 185.

78. Petr Bogatyrev, "Etnograficheskie poezdki v podkarpatskuiu Rus': Opyt staticheskogo issledovaniia," in *Funktsional'no-struktural'noe izuchenie fol'klora*, 74; italics added.

79. Petr Bogatyrev, *Vampires in the Carpathians: Magical Acts, Rites, and Beliefs in Subcarpathian Rus'* (1929), trans. Stephen Reynolds and Patricia Krafcik (New York: Columbia University Press 1998), 9.

80. Bogatyrev, *Vampires*, 13.

81. Jakobson, "Petr Bogatyrev," 37.

82. Petr Bogatyrev, *Souvislosti tvorby: Cesty k struktuře lidové kultury a divadla*, ed. Jaroslav Kolár (Prague: Odeon, 1971), 66.

83. Valentin Voloshinov, "Stilistika khudozhestvennoi rechi: Stat'ia tret'ia: Slovo i ego sotsial'naia funktsiia," *Literaturnaia ucheba* 5 (1930): 45. See Petr Bogatyrev, *The Functions of Folk Costume in Slovakia* (1937), trans. Richard Crum (The Hague: Mouton, 1971), 80.

84. Bogatyrev, *Functions*, 100 (italics added), 95, 96.

85. Voloshinov, cited in Bogatyrev, *Functions*, 81.

86. Sorokina, "Funktsional'no-struktural'nyi metod," 15.

87. Bogatyrev, *Funktsional'no-struktural'noe izuchenie fol'klora*, 82.

88. Jan Mukařovský, *Básnická sémantika: Univerzitní přednášky Praha—Bratislava*, ed. Miroslav Procházka (Prague: Vydavatelství Karolinum, 1995), 140; italics added.

89. Bogatyrev, *Functions*, 101.

90. Mukařovský, *Aesthetic Function*, 3, 18.

91. Mukařovský, *Aesthetic Function*, 19.

92. Mukařovský, *Aesthetic Function*, 5, 19, 20.

93. Harland, *Superstructuralism*, 24.

94. Yuri Tynianov, "On Literary Evolution," in Matejka and Pomorska, *Readings in Russian Poetics*, 67.

95. Tynianov, "On Literary Evolution," 68; italics in original.

96. Tynianov, "On Literary Evolution," 69.

97. See Roman Jakobson, C. Gunnar M. Fant, and Morris Halle, *Preliminaries to Speech Analysis: The Distinctive Features and Their Correlates* (Cambridge, MA: MIT Press, 1967), 9.

98. Yuri Tynianov, "Literary Fact," in *Permanent Evolution*, 160; italics in original.

99. Tynianov, *Permanent Evolution*, 157.

100. Kim, "Johann Friedrich Herbart."

101. Shklovskii, *O teorii prozy*, 20.

102. Svetlikova, *Istoki*, 123.

103. Boris Engel'gardt, *Formal'nyi metod v istorii literatury* (Leningrad: Academia, 1927), 104; italics in original.

104. Tynianov, *Permanent Evolution*, 156; italics in original. Compare Mukařovský, *Aesthetic Function*, 58.

105. Andy Byford, "S. A. Vengerov: The Identity of Literary Scholarship in Late Imperial Russia," *Slavonic and East European Review* 81, no. 1 (January 2003): 9–10.

106. Steiner, *Russian Formalism*, 136–37.

107. Harland, *Superstructuralism*, 24–25.

108. This Veselovskian question was developed, using an explicitly non-structuralist theory of language, by Mikhail Bakhtin. Particularly relevant to my argument in this chapter is Bakhtin's concept of "heteroglossia" (*raznorechie*), as articulated in *Discourse in the Novel* (*Slovo v romane*, 1930–34), in Bakhtin, *The Dialogic Imagination: Four Essays*, ed. Michael Holquist, trans. Caryl Emerson and Michael Holquist (Austin: University of Texas Press, 1981); see especially 262–63, 288–98. See also Ilya Kliger, "On 'Genre Memory' in Bakhtin," in Kliger and Maslov, *Persistent Forms*, 229.

109. Shklovskii, *O teorii prozy*, 229.

110. Jürgen Van de Walle, "Roman Jakobson, Cybernetics and Information Theory: A Critical Assessment," *Folia Linguistica Historica* 29 (2008): 89.

111. Van de Walle, "Roman Jakobson," 90.

112. Claude E. Shannon and Warren Weaver, *The Mathematical Theory of Communication* (Urbana: University of Illinois Press, 1964), 31; italics added.

113. Van de Walle, "Roman Jakobson," 110.

114. Bernard Geoghegan, "From Information Theory to French Theory: Jakobson, Lévi-Strauss, and the Cybernetic Apparatus," *Critical Inquiry* 38, no. 1 (Autumn 2011): 109.

115. Van de Walle, "Roman Jakobson," 91, 94.

116. Weaver was chairman of the Natural Sciences Division at the Rockefeller Foundation. Fahs was the director of the Humanities Division.

117. Stephen Rudy, "Roman Jakobson: A Brief Chronology," MIT, MC 72, page 21, https://archivesspace.mit.edu/repositories/2/archival_objects/164721.

118. Shannon and Weaver, *Mathematical Theory*, 34.

119. Jakobson, Fant, and Halle, *Preliminaries*, 9; italics in original.

120. Giorgio Graffi, "European Linguistics since Saussure," in *The Oxford Handbook of the History of Linguistics*, ed. Keith Allan (Oxford: Oxford University Press, 2013), 480.

121. Jakobson, *Selected Writings*, 2:570.

122. Jakobson, *Selected Writings*, 2:577.

123. Viktor Zhivov, "Moskovsko-Tartuskaia semiotika: Ee dostizheniia i ee ogranicheniia," *Novoe literaturnoe obozrenie*, no. 98 (2009): 15; italics added.

124. Shannon and Weaver, *Mathematical Theory*, 27; italics added.

125. Roman Jakobson, "Linguistics and Communication Theory," in *Selected Writings*, 2:577. Compare Geoghegan, "Information Theory," 110.

126. Van de Walle, "Roman Jakobson," 96.

127. Geoghegan, "Information Theory," 123.

128. Geoghegan, "Information Theory," 124.

129. Claude Lévi-Strauss, preface to *Six Lectures on Sound and Meaning*, by Roman Jakobson, trans. John Mepham (Cambridge, MA: MIT Press, 1978), xi.

130. Claude Lévi-Strauss, *Structural Anthropology* (1945), trans. Claire Jacobson and Brooke Grundfest (New York: Basic Books, 1963), 33.

131. Claude Lévi-Strauss, Roman Jakobson, C. F. Voegelin, and Thomas A. Sebok, *Results of the Conference of Anthropologists and Linguists* (Baltimore, MD: Waverly, 1953), 13.

132. Lévi-Strauss et al., *Results*, 4, 5.

133. Lévi-Strauss et al., *Results*, 7.

134. Lévi-Strauss et al., *Results*, 4; italics in original.

135. Van de Walle, "Roman Jakobson," 115.

136. Claude Lévi-Strauss, *The Savage Mind*, trans. George Weidenfeld (Chicago: University of Chicago Press, 1966), 268.

137. Lévi-Strauss, *Savage Mind*, 269.

138. Steven Ungar, "Saussure, Barthes and Structuralism," in *The Cambridge Companion to Saussure*, ed. Carol Sanders (Cambridge: Cambridge University Press, 2004), 157.

139. Geoghegan, "Information Theory," 117.

140. Lévi-Strauss, *Structural Anthropology*, 34.

141. Lévi-Strauss, *Structural Anthropology*, 211; first italics in original, second italics added.

142. Lévi-Strauss, *Structural Anthropology*, 331.

143. Saussure, *Course*, 118.

144. Harland, *Superstructuralism*, 88, 79.

145. Émile Benveniste, *Problems in General Linguistics*, trans. Mary Meek (Coral Gables, FL: University of Miami Press, 1971), 107.

146. Benveniste, *Problems*, 106.

147. Benveniste, *Problems*, 108.

148. Benveniste, cited from Winfried Nöth, *Handbook of Semiotics* (Bloomington: Indiana University Press, 1990), 104–5.

149. Jonathan Culler, *Structuralist Poetics: Structuralism, Linguistics and the Study of Literature* (London: Routledge and Kegan Paul, 1975), 13.

150. Louis Hjelmslev, *Prolegomena to a Theory of Language*, trans. Francis Whitfield (Madison: University of Wisconsin Press, 1963), 45.

151. Hjelmslev, *Prolegomena*, 67.

152. Harland, *Superstructuralism*, 86–87. This example is discussed in Hjelmslev, *Prolegomena*, 70.

153. Harland, *Superstructuralism*, 88.

154. See Geoghegan, "Information Theory," 109, 112.

155. Geoffrey Bennington, "Saussure and Derrida," in Sanders, *Cambridge Companion to Saussure*, 196–97.

156. Culler, *Structuralist Poetics*, 3–31.

157. Vladimír Skalička, "Kodaňský strukturalismus a pražská škola," *Slovo a slovesnost* 10, no. 3 (1948): 135–42.

158. Skalička, "Kodaňský strukturalismus," 140; italics added.

159. Mukařovský, "Art as Semiotic Fact," 84.

160. Skalička, "Kodaňský strukturalismus," 141.

161. Skalička, "Kodaňský strukturalismus," 141.

162. Jameson, *Prison-House*, 129.

163. Jameson, *Prison-House*, 194.

164. Jameson, *Prison-House* 194.

165. Jakobson, *Remarks*, 160. See also Tynianov and Jakobson, "Problems."

166. Cited in Wachtel, *Remaining Relevant,* 13.

CONCLUSION

1. Susan J. Wolfson, "Reading for Form," *Modern Language Quarterly* 61 (2000): 9.

2. Marjorie Levinson, "What Is New Formalism?" *PMLA* 122, no. 2 (2007): 559.

3. Levinson, "What Is New Formalism?" 559, 560.

4. Levinson, "What Is New Formalism?" 559.

5. Ellen Rooney, "Form and Contentment," *MLQ: Modern Language Quarterly* 61, no. 1 (March 2000): 35; italics added.

6. Caroline Levine, *Forms: Whole, Rhythm, Hierarchy, Network* (Princeton, NJ: Princeton University Press, 2015), 1; see also 111; italics added.

7. Levine, *Forms*, 2, 3.

8. Levine, *Forms*, 23; italics added.

9. C. J. van Rees, "'Theory of Literature' Viewed as a Conception of Literature: On the Premises Underlying Wellek and Warren's Handbook," *Poetics* 13 (1984): 504.

10. Graff, *Professing Literature*, 150.

11. Derek Attridge, "A Return to Form?" *Textual Practice* 22, no. 3 (2008): 567.

12. Levine, *Forms*, 18.

13. Yopie Prins, "What Is Historical Poetics?" *Modern Language Quarterly* 77, no. 1 (March 2016): 14. English historical poetics is described as a "strain" of new formalism in V. Joshua Adams, Joel Calahan, and Michael Hansen, "Reading Historical Poetics," *Modern Language Quarterly* 77, no. 1 (March 2016): 4.

14. Prins, "What Is Historical Poetics?" 14.

15. See Merrill, "North American Reception."

16. Pratt, *Speech Act Theory*, xiv–xv.

17. See Erlich, *Russian Formalism*, 275; and Lee T. Lemon and Marion J. Reis, introduction to *Russian Formalist Criticism: Four Essays*, ed. Lemon and Reis (Lincoln: University of Nebraska Press, 1965), ix–xvii.

18. René Wellek, "The New Criticism: Pro and Contra," *Critical Inquiry* 4, no. 4 (Summer 1978): 618; italics added.

19. Cleanth Brooks, *The Well Wrought Urn: Studies in the Structure of Poetry* (New York: Harcourt, Brace and World, 1947), 195.

20. Petre Petrov, "Form," in *The Encyclopedia of Literary and Cultural Theory*, vol. 1: *Literary Theory from 1900 to 1966: A–Z*, ed. Michael Ryan (Hoboken, NJ: Wiley, 2011), https://doi.org/10.1002/9781444337839.wbelctv1f003.

21. Nekliudov, *Temy i variatsii*, 13.

22. Wellek, "New Criticism," 618.

23. Mark David Rasmussen, "Introduction: New Formalisms?" in *Renaissance Literature and Its Formal Engagements*, ed. Mark Rasmussen (New York: Palgrave, 2002), 8; italics in original.

24. Virginia Jackson and Yopie Prins, "Lyrical Studies," *Victorian Literature and Culture* 27, no. 2 (1999): 529.

25. Adams, Calahan, and Hansen, "Reading Historical Poetics," 6.

26. Osip Brik, "The So-Called 'Formal Method,'" in Sherwood, "Translation from *LEF*," 43, 44; translation modified.

27. Turner, *Philology*, 383, 386.

28. Sheldon Pollock, introduction to *World Philology*, ed. Sheldon Pollock, Benjamin A. Elman, and Ku-ming Kevin Chang (Cambridge, MA: Harvard University Press, 2015), 6.

29. Anderson, "Debate," 222.

30. Anderson, "Debate," 231, 226, 228 (italics in original), 226.

31. Anderson, "Debate," 227.

32. See Julie Orlemanski, "Philology and the Turn Away from the Linguistic Turn," *Florilegium* 32 (2015): 157–81.

33. See Orlemanski, "Philology"; and Julie Orlemanski, "Scales of Reading," *Exemplaria* 26, nos. 2–3 (2014): 226.

34. Orlemanski, "Philology," 172.

35. Orlemanski, "Scales," 226.

36. Orlemanski, "Scales," 227.

37. Orlemanski, "Philology," 174.

38. Dirk Geeraerts, *Theories of Lexical Semantics* (Oxford: Oxford University Press, 2010), 42.

39. Geeraerts, *Theories*, 1.

40. Peter Stockwell, *Cognitive Poetics: An Introduction*, 2nd. ed. (London: Routledge 2020), 12.

41. Mark Turner, *The Literary Mind: The Origins of Thought and Language* (New York: Oxford University Press, 1996), 5.

42. Turner, *Literary Mind*, 91.

43. Geeraerts, *Theories*, 203.

44. Stockwell, *Cognitive Poetics*, 11, 3.

45. Franco Moretti, "Conjectures on World Literature," *New Left Review* 1 (January–February 2000): 57.

46. See Daniel Shore, *Cyberformalism: Histories of Linguistic Forms in the Digital Archive* (Baltimore, MD: Johns Hopkins University Press, 2018), 27.

47. Gregory Crane, Brent Seales, and Melissa Terras, "Cyberinfrastructure for Classical Philology," *Digital Humanities Quarterly* 3, no. 1 (2009): 8–11, http://www.digitalhumanities.org/dhq/vol/3/1/000023/000023.html.

48. Kliger and Maslov, "Introducing Historical Poetics," 1, 21.

49. Maslov, "Metapragmatics," 134, 145; and also Maslov, "Lyric Universality," 134; Kliger, "Genre Memory," 239.

50. Tynianov, *Permanent Evolution*, 195.

APPENDIX

1. Carol Sanders, "Structuralism," in *The Cambridge Encyclopedia of the Language Sciences*, ed. Patrick Colm Hogan (Cambridge: Cambridge University Press, 2011), 811.

2. Graffi, "European Linguistics," 470–71.

3. Cited in Graffi, "European Linguistics," 472.

4. Cited in Graffi, "European Linguistics," 472.

5. Graffi, "European Linguistics," 471.

6. Harland, *Superstructuralism*, 9.

7. Harland, *Superstructuralism*, 68.

Bibliography

ARCHIVES CONSULTED

Fol'klornyi arkhiv, "Komissiia po narodnoi slovesnosti" [Folkloric Archive, "Commission for Folklore Study"]. Gosudarstvennyi muzei istorii rossiiskoi literatury imeni V. I. Dalia (GMIRLI) [V. I. Dal' State Museum of the History of Russian Literature]. Moscow. https://goslitmuz.ru/. Cited in the notes as GMIRLI.

Fond Pražský lingvistický kroužek (PLK) [Prague Linguistic Circle]. Masarykův ústav a Archiv Akademie věd České republiky (MÚA AV ČR) [Masaryk Institute and Archives of the Academy of Sciences of the Czech Republic]. Prague. https://www.mua.cas.cz/cs/fondy-a-sbirky-archivu-akademie-ved -ceske-republiky-633.

Moskovskii lingvisticheskii kruzhok [Moscow Linguistic Circle] Archive. Fond 20. Institut russkogo iazyka imeni V. V. Vinogradova (IRIa) [V. V. Vinogradov Institute of Russian Language]. Otdel lingvisticheskogo istochnikove-deniia i istorii russkogo literaturnogo iazyka, Otdel rukopisei [Dept. of Linguistic Source Studies and the History of the Russian Literary Language, Manuscript Division]. Rossiiskaia Akademiia nauk [Russian Academy of Sciences]. Moscow. http://www.ruslang.ru/. Cited in the notes as IRIa.

Roman Jakobson Papers. MC 72. Massachusetts Institute of Technology, Department of Distinctive Collections, Cambridge, MA. https://archivesspace .mit.edu/repositories/2/resources/633. Cited in the notes as MIT.

Rossiiskii gosudarstvennyi arkhiv literatury i iskusstva (RGALI) [Russian State Archive of Literature and Art]. Moscow. https://rgali.ru/. Cited in the notes as RGALI.

WORKS CITED

Abrahams, Roger, and Alan Dundes. "Riddles." In *Folklore and Folklife: An Introduction*, edited by Richard Dorson, 129–45. Chicago: University of Chicago Press, 1972.

Adams, V. Joshua, Joel Calahan, and Michael Hansen. "Reading Historical Poetics." *Modern Language Quarterly* 77, no. 1 (March 2016): 1–12.

Anderson, John, and Gordon Bower. *Human Associative Memory*. Washington, DC: V. H. Winston and Sons, 1973.

Anderson, R. D. *European Universities from the Enlightenment to 1914*. Oxford: Oxford University Press, 2004.

Anderson, R. Lanier. "The Debate over the Geisteswissenschaften in German Philosophy." In *The Cambridge History of Philosophy 1870–1945*, edited by Thomas Baldwin, 221–34. Cambridge: Cambridge University Press, 2003.

Any, Carol. *Boris Eikhenbaum: Voices of a Russian Formalist*. Stanford, CA: Stanford University Press, 1994.

Aristotle. *Poetics*. Translated by S. H. Butcher. 3rd ed. London: Macmillan, 1902. https://hdl.handle.net/2027/hvd.32044010427722.

Ash, Mitchell. *Gestalt Psychology in German Culture, 1890–1967: Holism and the Quest for Objectivity*. Cambridge: Cambridge University Press, 1998.

Attridge, Derek. "A Return to Form?" *Textual Practice* 22, no. 3 (2008): 563–75.

Azadovskii, Mark. *A Siberian Tale Teller*. 1926. Translated by James Dow. Austin: University of Texas Press, 1974.

Bailey, James, and Tatiana Ivanova. "The Russian Oral Epic Tradition: An Introduction." In *An Anthology of Russian Folk Epics*. New York: M. E. Sharpe, 1998.

Bakhtin, Mikhail. *The Dialogic Imagination: Four Essays*. Edited by Michael Holquist. Translated by Caryl Emerson and Michael Holquist. Austin: University of Texas Press, 1981.

Barankova, Galina. "K istorii moskovskogo lingvisticheskogo kruzhka: Materialy iz Rukopisnogo otdela Instituta russkogo iazyka." In *Iazyk, Kul'tura, Gumanitarnoe znanie: Nauchnoe nasledie G. O. Vinokura i sovremennost'*, 359–82. Moscow: Nauchnyi mir, 1999.

———. "Siuzhet v kinematografe: Po materialam Moskovskogo lingvisticheskogo kruzhka." *Literaturnoe obozrenie* 3 (1997): 81–84.

Barthes, Roland. "The Death of the Author." In *Image, Music, Text*, translated by Stephen Heath, 142–48. New York: Hill and Wang, 1977.

———. *Elements of Semiology*. 1964. Translated by Annette Lavers and Colin Smith. New York: Hill and Wang, 1977.

Belyi, Andrei. *Glossolalie: Poem über den Laut. Glossolalia: A Poem about Sound. Glossolaliia: Poema o zvuke*. Translated by Thomas R. Beyer, Jr. and Maka Kandelaki. Dornach, Switz.: Pforte, 2003.

Benes, Tuska. *In Babel's Shadow: Language, Philology, and the Nation in Nineteenth-Century Germany*. Detroit, MI: Kritik, 2008.

Benjamin, Walter. *Illuminations*. Edited by Hannah Arendt. Translated by Harry Zohn. New York: Harcourt, Brace and World, 1968.

Bennington, Geoffrey. "Saussure and Derrida." In Sanders, *Cambridge Companion to Saussure*, 186–202.

Benveniste, Émile. *Problems in General Linguistics*. Translated by Mary Meek. Coral Gables, FL: University of Miami Press, 1971.

Berezin, Vladimir. *Viktor Shklovskii*. Moscow: Molodaia gvardiia, 2014.

Bernshtein, Sergei. "Golos Bloka." 1921. In *Blokovskii sbornik*, vol. 2. Tartu: Tartuskii gosudarstvennyi universitet, 1972.

———. "Zvuchashchaia khudozhestvennaia rech' i ee izuchenie." In *Poetika: Sbornik statei*, 1:41–53. Vremennik Otdela slovesnykh iskusstv. Leningrad: Gosudarstvennyi institut istorii iskusstv; Akademia, 1926.

Bogatyrev, Petr. *Cheshskii kukol'nyi i russkii narodnyi teatr*. Berlin: OPOIaZ, 1923.

———. *The Functions of Folk Costume in Slovakia*. 1937. Translated by Richard Crum. The Hague: Mouton, 1971.

———. *Funktsional'no-struktural'noe izuchenie fol'klora: Maloizvestnye i neopublikovannye raboty*. Edited by Svetlana Sorokina. Moscow: IMLI RAN, 2006.

———. *Souvislosti tvorby: Cesty k struktuře lidové kultury a divadla*. Edited by Jaroslav Kolár. Prague: Odeon, 1971.

———. *Vampires in the Carpathians: Magical Acts, Rites, and Beliefs in Subcarpathian Rus'*. 1929. Translated by Stephen Reynolds and Patricia Krafcik. New York: Columbia University Press, 1998.

Bogatyrev, Petr, and Roman Jakobson. "Folklore as a Special Form of Creativity." Translated by Manfred Jacobson. In Steiner, *Prague School*, 32–46.

Bogdanov, Aleksandr. *O proletarskoi kul'ture 1904–1924*. Leningrad: Kniga, 1924.

Bogomolov, N. A. "K genezisu dikhotomii 'iazyk poeticheskii—iazyk prakticheskii.'" *Russkaia literatura*, no. 2 (2014): 250–56.

Borislavov, Rad. "'I Know What Motivation Is': The Politics of Emotion and Viktor Shklovskii's Sentimental Rhetoric." *Slavic Review* 74, no. 4 (Winter 2015): 785–807.

Boym, Svetlana. "Poetics and Politics of Estrangement: Victor Shklovsky and Hannah Arendt." *Poetics Today* 26, no. 4 (Winter 2005): 581–611.

Bradbury, Malcolm, and James McFarlane. *Modernism: 1890–1930*. London: Penguin Books, 1991.

Brandist, Craig. "The Rise of Soviet Sociolinguistics from the Ashes of Völkerpsychologie." *Journal of the History of the Behavioral Sciences* 42, no. 3 (Summer 2006): 261–77.

Brang, Peter. *Das klingende Wort: Zu Theorie und Geschichte der Deklamationskunst in Russland*. Vienna: Verlag der Österreichischen Akademie der Wissenschaften, 1988.

Brik, Osip. "T. n. formal'nyi metod." *LEF*, no. 1 (1923): 213–15.

———. *Two Essays on Poetic Language*. Postscript by Roman Jakobson. Ann Arbor: University of Michigan, Dept. of Slavic Languages and Literatures, 1964.

Brooks, Cleanth. "The Heresy of Paraphrase." In *The Well Wrought Urn: Studies in the Structure of Poetry*. New York: Harcourt, Brace and World, 1947.

Brooks, Jeffrey. "The Breakdown in Production and Distribution of Printed Material." In *Bolshevik Culture: Experiment and Order in the Russian Revolution*, edited by Abbott Gleason, Peter Kenez, and Richard Stites, 151–74. Bloomington: Indiana University Press, 1989.

Brooks, Peter. *Reading for the Plot: Design and Intention in Narrative*. New York: Vintage, 1985.

Brown, Edward J. *Mayakovsky: A Poet in the Revolution*. Princeton, NJ: Princeton University Press, 2016.

Buckingham, Hugh. "Aristotle's Functional Association Psychology: The Syntagmatic and the Paradigmatic Axes in the Neurolinguistics of Roman Jakobson and Alexander Luria; An Anatomical and Functional Quagmire." *Aphasiology* 24, no. 3 (2010): 395–403.

Bürger, Peter. "Avant-Garde and Neo-Avant-Garde: An Attempt to Answer Certain Critics of 'Theory of the Avant-Garde.'" Translated by Bettina Brandt and Daniel Purdy. *New Literary History* 41, no. 4 (Autumn 2010): 695–715.

Burke, Michael. "Rhetoric and Persuasion." In *The Cambridge Encyclopedia of the Language Sciences*, edited by Patrick Colm Hogan, 715–17. Cambridge: Cambridge University Press, 2011.

Buslaev, Fedor. *Prepodavanie otechestvennogo iazyka*. Moscow: Prosveshchenie, 1992.

Byford, Andy. "Between Literary Education and Academic Learning: The Study of Literature at Secondary School in Late Imperial Russia (1860s–1900s)." *History of Education* 33, no. 6 (2004): 637–60.

———. *Literary Scholarship in Late Imperial Russia: Rituals of Academic Institutionalisation*. London: Legenda, 2007.

———. "The Rhetoric of Aleksandr Veselovskii's 'Historical Poetics' and the Autonomy of Academic Literary Studies in Late Imperial Russia." *Slavonica* 11, no. 2 (2005): 115–32.

———. "S. A. Vengerov: The Identity of Literary Scholarship in Late Imperial Russia." *Slavonic and East European Review* 81, no. 1 (January 2003): 1–31.

Cairns, Craig. *Associationism and the Literary Imagination, 1739–1939*. Edinburgh: Edinburgh University Press, 2006.

Cassedy, Steven. *Flight from Eden: The Origins of Modern Literary Criticism and Theory*. Berkeley: University of California Press, 1990.

Cassirer, Ernst. "Structuralism in Modern Linguistics." In *Aufsätze und Kleine Schriften*, 299–320. Hamburg: Felix Meiner Verlag, 2007.

Cerquiglini, Bernard. *In Praise of the Variant: A Critical History of Philology*. Baltimore, MD: Johns Hopkins University Press, 1999.

Chambers, J. K., and Peter Trudgill. *Dialectology*. 2nd ed. Cambridge: Cambridge University Press, 2004.

Chomsky, Noam. *Current Issues in Linguistic Theory*. 1969. The Hague: De Gruyter Mouton, 2010.

Cohen, Bernard. "Analogy, Homology, and Metaphor in the Interactions between the Natural Sciences and the Social Sciences, Especially Economics." In *Non-Natural Science: Reflecting on the Enterprise of More Heat Than Light*, edited by Neil De Marchi, 7–44. Durham, NC: Duke University Press, 1993.

Crane, Gregory, Brent Seales, and Melissa Terras. "Cyberinfrastructure for Classical Philology." *Digital Humanities Quarterly* 3, no. 1 (2009): 1–78. http://www.digitalhumanities.org/dhq/vol/3/1/000023/000023.html.

Culler, Jonathan. *Structuralist Poetics: Structuralism, Linguistics and the Study of Literature*. London: Routledge and Kegan Paul, 1975.

Cunha, Dóris de Arruda Carneiro da. "On Dialogic Speech: Convergences and Divergences between Jakubinskij, Bakhtin and Voloshinov." *Revista Conexão Letras* 11, no. 16 (2016): 52–69.

Depretto, Catherine. *Le Formalisme en Russie*. Paris: Institut d'Études Slaves, 2009.

Deumert, Ana. "Language, Culture, and Society." In *The Oxford Handbook of the History of Linguistics*, edited by Keith Allan, 655–73. Oxford: Oxford University Press, 2013.

Dienhart, John. "A Linguistic Look at Riddles." *Journal of Pragmatics* 31 (1998): 95–125.

Dmitrenko, N. K. *A. A. Potebnia—sobiratel' i issledovatel' fol'klora*. Kiev: Znanie, 1985.

Dmitriev, Aleksandr. "Kak sdelana 'formal'no-filosofskaia shkola' (ili pochemu ne sostoialsia moskovskii formalizm?)." *Issledovaniia po istorii russkoi mysli*, edited by Modest Kolerov and Nikolai Plotnikov, 70–95. Ezhegodnik 2006–2007, vol. 8. Moscow: Modest Kolerov, 2009.

Doroszewski, W. "Quelque remarques sur les rapports de la sociologie et de la linguistique: Durkheim et F. de Saussure." *Journal de Psychologie* 80 (1932): 82–91.

Dundes, Alan. "The Devolutionary Premise in Folklore Theory." *Journal of the Folklore Institute* 6 (1969): 7.

Durkheim, Émile. *The Division of Labor in Society*. Translated by George Simpson. Glencoe, IL: Free Press, 1933.

Durnovo, N. N. "Vvedenie: Perekhodnye govory." In *Dialektologicheskaia razyskaniia v oblasti velikorusskikh govorov*. Part 1, issue 1, *Iuzhnovelikorusskoe narechie*, 1–13. Moscow: Sinodal'naia tipografiia, 1917.

Dwyer, Anne. "Standstill as Extinction: Viktor Shklovsky's Poetics of and Politics of Movement in the 1920s and 1930s." *PMLA* 131, no. 2 (2016): 269–88.

Eagleton, Terry. *Literary Theory: An Introduction*. 2nd ed. Minneapolis: University of Minnesota Press, 1996.

Ehlers, Klaas-Hinrich. "Petr G. Bogatyrev: Leben und Werk im wissenschaftlichen Kontext der 1920er und 1930er Jahre und in späterer Rezeption." Introduction to *Funktional-strukturale Ethnographie in Europa*, by Petr Bogatyrev, edited by K. Ehlers and M. Nekula, 19–53. Heidelberg: Universitätsverlag Winter, 2011.

Eikhenbaum, Boris. "How Gogol's 'Overcoat' Is Made." In *Dostoevsky and Gogol: Texts and Criticism*, edited by Priscilla Meyer and Stephen Rudy, 119–36. Ann Arbor, MI: Ardis, 1979.

———. "Illiuziia skaza." In *Skvoz' literaturu: Sbornik statei*, 152–56. The Hague: Mouton, 1962.

———. *Literatura: Teoriia, kritika, polemika*. Leningrad: Priboi, 1927.

———. *Melodika russkogo liricheskogo stikha*. St. Petersburg: OPOIaZ, 1922.

———. "O chtenii stikhov." *Zhizn' iskusstva*, no. 290 (November 12, 1919): 1.

———. "Osnovnye stilevye tendentsii v rechi Lenina." *LEF*, no. 1[5] (1924): 57–70.

———. "The Theory of the Formal Method." 1927. In Matejka and Pomorska, *Readings in Russian Poetics*, 3–37.

———. *The Young Tolstoy*. 1922. Translated by Gary Kern. Ann Arbor, MI: Ardis, 1972.

Eisen, Samuel D. "Whose Lenin Is It Anyway? Viktor Shklovsky, Boris Eikhenbaum and the Formalist-Marxist Debate in Soviet Cultural Politics (A View from the Twenties)." *Russian Review* 55, no. 1 (January 1996): 65–79.

Eisenstein, Sergei. *Film Form: Essays in Film Theory*. Edited and translated by Jay Leyda. New York: Harcourt Brace Jovanovich, 1949.

Eisenstein, Sergei, and Sergei Tretyakov. "Expressive Movement." Translated by Alma H. Law. *Millennium Film Journal*, no. 3 (Winter/Spring 1979): 30–38.

Engel'gardt, Boris. *Formal'nyi metod v istorii literatury*. Leningrad: Academia, 1927.

Erlich, Victor. *Russian Formalism: History—Doctrine*. 1955. 4th ed. The Hague: Mouton, 1980.

Etkind, Alexander. *Eros of the Impossible: The History of Psychoanalysis in Russia*. Boulder, CO: Westview, 1997.

Fedin, Konstantin. "Melok na shube." *Zhizn' iskusstva*, nos. 792–97 (August 2–7, 1921): 2–3.

Feshchenko, V. V. *Zhivoe slovo: Logos–golos–dvizhenie–zhest. Sbornik statei i materialov*. Moscow: Novoe literaturnoe obozrenie, 2015.

Finer, Emily. *Turning into Sterne: Viktor Shklovskii and Literary Reception*. Leeds, UK: Legenda, 2010.

Fitzpatrick, Sheila. "The Bolsheviks' Dilemma: Class, Culture, and Politics in the Early Soviet Years." *Slavic Review* 47, no. 4 (Winter 1988): 599–613.

———. *The Russian Revolution*. 3rd. ed. Oxford: Oxford University Press, 2008.

Fizer, John. *Alexander A. Potebnja's Psycholinguistic Theory of Literature: A Metacritical Inquiry*. Cambridge, MA: Harvard Ukrainian Research Institute and Harvard University Press, 1988.

Freud, Sigmund. *Collected Papers*. Edited by Joan Riviere. New York: Basic Books, 1959.

———. *The Interpretation of Dreams*. Translated by Joyce Crick. Edited by Ritchie Robertson. Oxford: Oxford University Press, 1999.

Galan, František. *Historic Structures: The Prague School Project, 1928–1946*. Austin: University of Texas Press, 1985.

Galushkin, Aleksandr, ed. "Viktor Shklovskii i Roman Iakobson: Perepiska (1922–1956)." In *Roman Iakobson: Teksty, dokumenty, issledovaniia*, edited by Henryk Baran [H. Beran] and S. I. Gindin, 104–35. Moscow: Rossiiskii gosudarstvennyi gumanitarnyi institut, 1999.

Gamsa, Mark. "Two Million Filing Cards: The Empirical-Biographical Method of Semen Vengerov." *History of Humanities* 1, no. 1 (2016): 129–53.

Gasparov, Boris. "Futurism and Phonology: Futurist Roots of Jakobson's Approach to Language." In *Jakobson entre l'est et l'ouest 1915–1939*, edited by Françoise Gadet and Patrick Sériot, 109–29. Lausanne: Université de Lausanne, 1997.

Geeraerts, Dirk. *Theories of Lexical Semantics*. Oxford: Oxford University Press, 2010.

Geldern, James von. *Bolshevik Festivals, 1917–1920*. Berkeley: University of California Press, 1993.

Geoghegan, Bernard. "From Information Theory to French Theory: Jakobson, Lévi-Strauss, and the Cybernetic Apparatus." *Critical Inquiry* 38, no. 1 (Autumn 2011): 96–126.

Giddens, Anthony. "Structuralism, Post-Structuralism and the Production of Culture." In *Social Theory Today*, edited by Jonathan H. Turner and Anthony Giddens, 195–223. Stanford, CA: Stanford University Press, 1987.

Gindin, S. I. "Kak moskovskii lingvisticheskii kruzhok voeval s Briusovym i Potebnei." *Novoe literaturnoe obozrenie*, no. 4 (2007): 70–78.

Ginzburg, Carlo. "Making Things Strange: The Prehistory of a Literary Device." *Representations*, no. 56 (Autumn 1996): 8–28.

Glants, Tomash, and Igor' Pil'shchikov. "Russkie formalisty kak nauchnoe soobshchestvo." In *Epokha ostraneniia: Russkii formalizm i sovremennoe gumanitarnoe znanie*, edited by Jan Levchenko and Igor' Pil'shchikov, 85–102. Moscow: Novoe literaturnoe obozrenie, 2017.

Gordon, Mel, and Alma Law. "Eisenstein's Early Work in Expressive Behavior: The Montage of Movement." *Millennium Film Journal*, no. 3 (Winter/Spring 1979): 25–29.

Gornung, Boris. "Hermes." In *Pokhod vremeni*. Vol. 2, *Stat'i i esse*. Moscow: RGGU 2001.

Graff, Gerald. *Professing Literature: An Institutional History*. Chicago: University of Chicago Press, 1987.

Graffi, Giorgio. "European Linguistics since Saussure." In *The Oxford Handbook of the History of Linguistics*, edited by Keith Allan, 469–84. Oxford: Oxford University Press, 2013.

Graffy, Julian. *Gogol's The Overcoat*. London: Bristol Classical Press, 2000.

Grimm, Jacob. *Teutonic Mythology*, vol. 3. Translated by James Stallybrass. New York: Dover, 1966.

Hales, F. N. Review of *Volkerpsychologie: Eine Untersuchung der Entwicklungsgesetze von Sprache, Mythus und Sitte*, by Wilhelm Wundt. *Mind*, n.s., 12, no. 46 (April 1903): 239–45.

Hans, Nicholas. *History of Russian Educational Policy (1701–1917)*. New York: Russell and Russell, 1964.

Hansen, William. "Mythology and Folklore Typology: Chronicle of a Failed Scholarly Revolution." *Journal of Folklore Research* 34, no. 3 (1997): 275–80.

Hansen-Löve, Aage A. *Der russische Formalismus: Methodologische Rekonstruktion seiner Entwicklung aus dem Prinzip der Verfremdung*. Vienna: Verlag der Österreichischen Akademie der Wissenschaften, 1978.

———. [Oge A. Khansen-Leve]. *Russkii formalizm: Metodologicheskaia rekonstruktsiia razvitiia na osnove printsipa ostraneniia*. Translated by S. A. Romashko. Moscow: Iazyki russkoi kul'tury, 2001.

Harland, Richard. *Superstructuralism: The Philosophy of Structuralism and Post-Structuralism*. London: Routledge, 1987.

Harnish, Robert. *Minds, Brains, Computers: An Historical Introduction to the Foundations of Cognitive Science*. Malden, MA: Blackwell, 2002.

Harris, Zellig. *Papers in Structural and Transformational Linguistics*. Dordrecht: Springer, 1970.

Hickey, Martha. *The Writer in Petrograd and the House of Arts*. Evanston, IL: Northwestern University Press, 2009.

Hildermeier, Manfred. "Neopopulism and Modernization: The Debate on Theory and Tactics in the Socialist Revolutionary Party, 1905–14." *Russian Review* 34, no. 4 (October 1975): 453–75.

Hjelmslev, Louis. *Prolegomena to a Theory of Language*. Translated by Francis Whitfield. Madison: University of Wisconsin Press, 1963.

Hoenigswald, Henry. "On the History of the Comparative Method." *Anthropological Linguistics* 5 (1963): 1–11.

Holt, Robert. "Beyond Vitalism and Mechanism: Freud's Concept of Psychic Energy." In *Science and Psychoanalysis*. Vol. 11, *The Ego*, edited by Jules Masserman, 1–41. New York: Grune and Stratton, 1967.

Howell, Dana. *The Development of Soviet Folkloristics*. New York: Garland, 1992.

Humboldt, Wilhelm von. *On Language: On the Diversity of Human Language Construction and Its Influence on the Mental Development of the Human Species*. Edited by Michael Losonsky. Translated by Peter Heath. Cambridge: Cambridge University Press, 1999.

Hunter, Dan. "No Wilderness of Single Instances: Inductive Inference in Law." *Journal of Legal Education* 48, no. 3 (September 1998): 365–401.

Iakubinskii [Jakubinksy], L. P. *Izbrannye raboty: Iazyk i ego funktsionirovanie*. Edited by A. A. Leont'ev. Moscow: Nauka, 1986.

Ivanov, V. V., and B. N. Toporov. "Vklad R. O. Iakobsona v slavianskie i indo-evropeiskie fol'klornye i mifologicheskie issledovaniia." In *Roman Jakobson: Echoes of His Scholarship*, edited by Daniel Armstrong and C. H. van Schooneveld, 163–84. Berlin: De Gruyter, 1977.

Ivanova, Tatiana. *Istoriia russkoi fol'kloristiki XX veka: 1900–pervaia polovina 1941 gg*. St. Petersburg: Dmitrii Bulanin, 2009.

———. "Tiander K. F." In Toporkov, *Neizvestnye stranitsy russkoi fol'kloristiki*, 540–45.

Jackson, Virginia, and Yopie Prins. "Lyrical Studies." *Victorian Literature and Culture* 27, no. 2 (1999): 521–30.

Jakobson [Iakobson], Roman. "Briusovskaia stikhologiia i nauka o stikhe." In *Nauchnye izvestiia Akademicheskogo tsentra Narkomprosa. Sbornik 2, Filosofiia, literatura, iskusstvo*, 222–40. Moscow: Gosudarstvennoe izdatel'stvo, 1922.

———. "Co je poezie?/Was ist Poesie?" In *Texte der russischen Formalisten*. Vol. 2, *Texte zur Theorie des Verses und der poetischen Sprache*, edited by Wolf-Dieter Stempel, 392–417. Munich: Fink, 1972.

———. "The Dominant." In Matejka and Pomorska, *Readings in Russian Poetics*, 82–87.

———. *Formalistická škola a dnešní literární věda ruská: Brno 1935*. Edited by Tomáš Glanc. Prague: Academia, 2005.

———. *Formal'naia shkola i sovremennoe russkoe literaturovedenie*. 1935. Edited by Tomash Glants. Moscow: Iazyki slavianskikh kul'tur, 2011.

———. "Grammatical Parallelism and Its Russian Facet." *Language* 42, no. 2 (April–June, 1966): 399–429.

———. *Language in Literature*. Edited by Krystyna Pomorska and Stephen Rudy. Cambridge, MA: Belknap Press of Harvard University Press, 1987.

———. "Moskovskii lingvisticheskii kruzhok." Edited and with an introduction by Maksim Shapir. *Philologica* 3, no. 5/7 (1996): 361–80.

———. *My Futurist Years*. Edited by Bengt Jangfeldt and Stephen Rudy. Translated by Stephen Rudy. New York: Marsilio, 1997.

———, ed. *N. S. Trubetzkoy's Letters and Notes*. The Hague: Mouton, 1975.

———. *O cheshskom stikhe preimushchestvenno v sopostavlenii s russkim.* 1923. Providence, RI: Brown University Press, 1969.

———. "Petr Bogatyrev (29.I.93–18.VIII.71): Expert in Transfiguration." In *Sound, Sign and Meaning: Quinquagenary of the Prague Linguistic Circle,* edited by L. Matejka, 29–39. Ann Arbor: University of Michigan Press, 1976.

———. "Principles of Historical Phonology." In *A Reader in Historical and Comparative Linguistics,* edited by Allan Keiler, 121–38. New York: Holt, Rinehart and Winston, 1971.

———. *Remarks on the Phonological Evolution of Russian in Comparison with the Other Slavic Languages.* 1929. Translated by Ronald F. Feldstein. Cambridge, MA: MIT Press, 2018.

———. Review of "Opyt dialektologicheskoi karty russkogo iazyka v Evrope," by N. N. Durnovo, N. N. Sokolov, and D. N. Ushakov. *Etnograficheskoe obozrenie* 1–2 (1916): 102–7.

———. "Romantické všeslovanství—nová slavistika." *Čin* 1, no. 1 (October 31, 1929): 10–12.

———. *Selected Writings.* 9 vols. Edited by Stephen Rudy et al. The Hague: Mouton, 1962–2014.

———. "Vliv revoluce na ruský jazyk (Poznámky ke knize André Mazona, Lexique de la guerre et de la révolution ne Russie)." *Nové Atheneum* 2 (1920–21): 110–14, 200–212, 250–55, 310–18.

Jakobson, Roman, and Petr Bogatyrev. "K probleme razmezhevaniia fol'kloristiki i literaturovedeniia." 1931. In Jakobson, *Selected Writings,* 4:16–18.

———. *Slavianskaia filologiia v Rossii za gody voiny i revoliutsii.* Berlin: OPOIaZ, 1923.

Jakobson, Roman, C. Gunnar, M. Fant, and Morris Halle. *Preliminaries to Speech Analysis: The Distinctive Features and Their Correlates.* Cambridge, MA: MIT Press, 1967.

Jakobson, Roman, and Krystyna Pomorska. *Dialogues.* Cambridge, MA: MIT Press, 1983.

Jameson, Fredric. *The Prison-House of Language: A Critical Account of Structuralism and Russian Formalism.* Princeton, NJ: Princeton University Press, 1972.

Jangfeldt, Bengt. *Mayakovsky: A Biography.* Translated by Harry D. Watson. Chicago: University of Chicago Press, 2014.

Jason, Heda. "Precursors of Propp: Formalist Theories of Narrative in Early Russian Ethnopoetics." *PTL: A Journal for Descriptive Poetics and Theory of Literature* 3 (1977): 471–516.

Joseph, John E. "The Unconscious and the Social in Saussure." *Historiographia Linguistica* 27, nos. 2/3 (2000): 307–34.

Kalinin, Ilya [Il'ya]. "Formal'naia teoriia siuzheta: Strukturalistskaia fabula for-

malizma." *Novoe literaturnoe obozrenie*, no. 128 (April 2014). https://www
.nlobooks.ru/magazines/novoe_literaturnoe_obozrenie/128_nlo_4_2014
/article/11024/.

———. "History as the Art of Articulation." *Social Sciences* 37, no. 1 (2006): 43–66.

———. "How Lenin's Language Was Made: Russian Formalists on the Material of History and Technique of Ideology." In *Words, Bodies, Memory: A Festschrift in Honor of Irina Sandomirskaia*, edited by Lars Kleberg, Tora Lane, and Marcia Sá Cavalcante Schuback, 335–46. Stockholm: Elanders, 2019.

———. "Istoriia literatury kak Familienroman (russkii formalizm mezhdu Edipom i Gamletom)." *Novoe literaturnoe obozrenie* 4 (2006): 64–83.

———. "Ot poniatiia 'sdelannost'' k tekhnologii 'literaturnogo remesla' Viktor Shklovskii i sotsialisticheskii formalizm." *Translit: Literaturno-kriticheskii al'manakh*, no. 6/7 (2010): 15–30.

———. "Viktor Shklovskii kak priem." In *Formal'nyi metod: Antologiia russkogo modernizma*. Vol. 1, *Sistemy*, edited by Serguei Oushakine [Sergei Ushakin], 63–106. Moscow: Kabinetnyi uchenyi, 2016.

———. "Viktor Shklovskii versus Roman Jakobson: Voina iazykov." In *Vestnik Sankt-Peterburgskogo universiteta*, series 9, no. 3 (2016): 55–63.

Kalmar, Ivan. "The Völkerpsychologie of Lazarus and Steinthal and the Modern Concept of Culture." *Journal of the History of Ideas* 48, no. 4 (October–December 1987): 671–90.

Kazanskii, Boris. "Ideia istoricheskoi poetiki." In *Poetika: Sbornik statei*, 1:6–23. Vremennik Otdela slovesnykh iskusstv. Leningrad: Gosudarstvennyi institut istorii iskusstv; Akademia, 1926.

Khlebnikov, Velimir. *Sobranie sochinenii v shesti tomakh*. Vol. 6, part 1, *Stat'i (Nabroski), uchenye trudy vozzvaniia, otkrytye pis'ma, vystupleniia 1904–1922*. Edited by P. B. Duganov. Moscow: IMLI RAN, Nasledie, 2005.

Khmel'nitskaia, Tamara. "Emkost' slova." In *Vospominaniia o Iu. N. Tynianove: Portrety i vstrechi*, edited by V. A. Kaverin, 121–137. Moscow: Sovetskii pisatel', 1983.

"Khronika: Otchet' o deiatel'nosti Etnograficheskogo Otdela i ego Komissii za 1915/16 god." *Etnograficheskoe obozrenie* 3–4 (1915): 145–51.

Kim, Alan. "Johann Friedrich Herbart." In Zalta, *Stanford Encyclopedia of Philosophy* (Winter 2015). https://plato.stanford.edu/archives/win2015/entries /johann-herbart/.

Kiparsky, Paul. "From Paleogrammarians to Neogrammarians." In *Studies in the History of Linguistics: Traditions and Paradigms*, edited by Dell Hymes, 331–45. Bloomington: Indiana University Press, 1974.

Kliger, Ilya. "On 'Genre Memory' in Bakhtin." In Kliger and Maslov, *Persistent Forms*, 227–48.

Kliger, Ilya, and Boris Maslov. "Introducing Historical Poetics." In Kliger and Maslov, *Persistent Forms*, 3–36.

———, eds. *Persistent Forms: Explorations in Historical Poetics*. New York: Fordham University Press, 2015.

Koerner, E. F. K. "Jan Baudouin de Courtenay: His Place in the History of Linguistic Science." *Canadian Slavonic Papers/Revue Canadienne des Slavistes* 14, no. 4 (Winter 1972): 663–83.

Kolesnikoff, Nina. "Russian Formalism." In *Encyclopedia of Contemporary Literary Theory: Approaches, Scholars, Terms*, edited by Irene Makaryk, 53–59. Toronto: University of Toronto Press, 1993.

Korsh, Fedor. *Vvedenie v nauku o slavianskom stikhoslozhenii: O russkom narodnom stikhoslozhenii*. 1901. Moscow: LIBROKOM, 2012.

Kotkin, Stephen. *Stalin*. Vol. 1, *Paradoxes of Power, 1878–1928*. New York: Penguin, 2015.

"Kratkii ocherk deiatel'nosti Postoiannoi Komissii po Dialektologii Russkogo Iazyka za 12 let (ianvar' 1914 g.–ianvar' 1926 g.)." *Trudy Komissii po Dialektologii Russkogo Iazyka* 9 (1927): 1–12.

Krohn, Kaarle. *Folklore Methodology [Die folkloristische Arbeitsmethode]*. 1926. Austin: University of Texas Press, 1971.

Kruszewski, Mikolaj. *Writings in General Linguistics: On Sound Alternation (1881) and Outline of Linguistic Science (1883)*. Vol. 11 of *Amsterdam Classics in Linguistics: 1800–1925*. Philadelphia: John Benjamins, 1995.

Kuhn, Thomas. *The Structure of Scientific Revolutions*. 1962. Chicago: University of Chicago Press, 1996.

Lawton, Anna, ed. *Words in Revolution: Russian Futurist Manifestoes, 1912–1928*. Translated by Anna Lawton and Herbert Eagle. Washington, DC: New Academia, 2005.

Lemon, Lee T., and Marion J. Reis. Introduction to *Russian Formalist Criticism: Four Essays*, edited by Lee Lemon and Marion Reis, ix–xvii. Lincoln: University of Nebraska Press, 1965.

Leshchak, Milan, and Svetozar Shvedlik. "Razgovor na proshchanie." In *Petr Grigor'evich Bogatyrev: Vospominaniia. Dokumenty. Stat'i*, edited by L. P. Solntseva, 41–49. St. Petersburg: ALETEII, 2002.

Levchenko, Jan. *Drugaia nauka: Russkie formalisty v poiskakh biografii*. Moscow: Izdatel'skii dom Vysshei shkoly ekonomiki, 2012.

———. *Istoriia i fiktsiia v tekstakh V. Shklovskogo i B. Eikhenbauma v 1920-e gg.* Tartu: Tartu University Press, 2003.

Levine, Caroline. *Forms: Whole, Rhythm, Hierarchy, Network*. Princeton, NJ: Princeton University Press, 2015.

Levinson, Marjorie. "What Is New Formalism?" *PMLA* 122, no. 2 (2007): 558–69.

Lévi-Strauss, Claude. Preface to *Six Lectures on Sound and Meaning*, by Roman

Jakobson, xi–xxvi. Translated by John Mepham. Cambridge, MA: MIT Press, 1978.

———. *The Savage Mind*. Translated by George Weidenfeld. Chicago: University of Chicago Press, 1966.

———. *Structural Anthropology*. 1945. Translated by Claire Jacobson and Brooke Grundfest. New York: Basic Books, 1963.

Lévi-Strauss, Claude, Roman Jakobson, C. F. Voegelin, and Thomas A. Sebok. *Results of the Conference of Anthropologists and Linguists*. Baltimore, MD: Waverly, 1953.

Livshits, Benedikt. *Polutoraglazyi strelets: Vospominaniia*. 1933. Moscow: Khudozhestvennaia literatura, 1991.

Lord, Albert. *The Singer of Tales*. Cambridge, MA: Harvard University Press, 1981.

Lotman, Yuri. *The Structure of the Artistic Text*. Translated by Ronald Vroon. Ann Arbor: University of Michigan Press, 1977.

Mallarmé, Stéphane. *Divagations*. Translated by Barbara Johnson. Cambridge, MA: Harvard University Press, 2007.

Mally, Lynn. *Culture of the Future: The Proletkult Movement in Revolutionary Russia*. Berkeley: University of California Press, 1990.

———. "Egalitarian and Elitist Visions of Cultural Transformation." In *Culture et révolution*, edited by Marc Ferro and Sheila Fitzpatrick, 137–46. Paris: Éditions de l'École des Hautes Études en Sciences Sociales, 1989.

Mandelbaum, Eric. "Associationist Theories of Thought." In Zalta, *Stanford Encyclopedia of Philosophy* (Fall 2020). https://plato.stanford.edu/archives/fall2020/entries/associationist-thought/.

Mandelker, Amy. "Russian Formalism and the Objective Analysis of Sound in Poetry." *Slavic and East European Journal* 27, no. 3 (Autumn 1983): 327–38.

Marcuse, Herbert. *Eros and Civilization: A Philosophical Inquiry into Freud*. 1956. London: Routledge, 1998.

Maslov, Boris. "Comparative Literature and Revolution, or the Many Arts of (Mis)Reading Alexander Veselovsky." *Compar(a)ison: An International Journal of Comparative Literature* 2 (2008 [2013]): 101–29.

———. "Lyric Universality." In *Cambridge Companion to World Literature*, edited by B. Etherington and J. Zimbler, 133–48. Cambridge: Cambridge University Press, 2018.

———. "Metapragmatics, Toposforschung, Marxist Stylistics: Three Extensions of Veselovsky's Historical Poetics." In Kliger and Maslov, *Persistent Forms*, 129–55.

———. "Oppozitsiia 'Vostok-Zapad' v istorii sravnitel'noi poetiki." *Arbor Mundi/Mirovoe drevo: International Journal of Theory and History of World Culture* 19 (2012): 72–94.

Matejka, Ladislav. "The Sociological Concerns of the Moscow Linguistic Circle." In *Language, Poetry and Poetics: The Generation of the 1890s; Jakobson, Trubetzkoy, Majakovskij*, edited by Krystyna Pomorska et al., 307–12. Berlin: Mouton de Gruyter, 1987.

Matejka, Ladislav, and Krystyna Pomorska, eds. *Readings in Russian Poetics: Formalist and Structuralist Views*. Cambridge, MA: MIT Press, 1971.

Maurer, Karl. "Kollektivnoe Tvorchestvo—Kollektives Schaffen." *Poetica: Zeitschrift für Sprach- und Literaturwissenschaft* 1 (1967): 98–108.

Mayakovsky [Maiakovskii], Vladimir. *Selected Poems*. Translated by James H. McGavran III. Evanston: Northwestern University Press, 2013.

———. "150 000 000. Poema." 1921. In *Polnoe sobranie sochinenii v 13 tomakh*, 2:113–64. Moscow: Khudozhestvennaia literatura, 1956.

———. "V. V. Khlebnikov." 1922. In *Polnoe sobranie sochinenii v 13 tomakh*, 12:23–28. Moscow: Khudozhestvennaia literatura, 1959.

Mayakovsky [Maiakovskii], Vladimir, and Osip Brik. "Nasha slovesnaia rabota." *LEF*, no. 1 (March 1923): 40–41.

Medvedev, P. N. *Formalizm i formalisty*. 1934. Ann Arbor, MI: University Microfilms International, 1981.

Meillet, Antoine. *The Comparative Method in Historical Linguistics*. 1922. Translated by Gordon Ford, Jr. Paris: Librairie Honoré Champion, 1967.

Merrill, Jessica. "The North American Reception of Russian Formalism." In *Literary Theory between East and West: Transcultural and Transdisciplinary Movements from Russian Formalism to Cultural Studies*, edited by Michał Mrugalski, Schamma Schahadat, Danuta Ulicka, and Irina Wutsdorff. Walter de Gruyter, forthcoming.

———. "The Role of Folklore Study in the Rise of Russian Formalist and Czech Structuralist Literary Theory." PhD diss., University of California, Berkeley, 2012.

Miller, Martin. *Freud and the Bolsheviks: Psychoanalysis in Imperial Russia and the Soviet Union*. New Haven, CT: Yale University Press, 1998.

Moretti, Franco. "Conjectures on World Literature." *New Left Review* 1 (January–February 2000): 54–68.

Morpurgo Davies, Anna. *Nineteenth-Century Linguistics*. Vol. 4 of *History of Linguistics*, edited by Giulio Lepschy. London: Longman, 1998.

Morris, William Edward, and Charlotte R. Brown. "David Hume." In Zalta, *Stanford Encyclopedia of Philosophy* (Spring 2021). https://plato.stanford.edu/archives/spr2021/entries/hume/.

Mueller-Vollmer, Kurt, ed. *The Hermeneutics Reader: Texts of the German Tradition from the Enlightenment to the Present*. New York: Continuum, 1994.

Mukařovský, Jan. *Aesthetic Function, Norm and Value as Social Facts*. Translated by Mark Suino. 1936. Ann Arbor: Michigan Slavic Contributions, 1970.

————. "Art as Semiotic Fact." 1936. In *Structure, Sign, and Function: Selected Essays*, edited and translated by John Burbank and Peter Steiner, 81–88. New Haven, CT: Yale University Press, 1978.

————. *Básnická sémantika: Univerzitní přednášky Praha—Bratislava*. Edited by Miroslav Procházka. Prague: Vydavatelství Karolinum, 1995.

————. "On Poetic Language." In *The Word and Verbal Art: Selected Essays*, edited and translated by John Burbank and Peter Steiner, 1–64. New Haven, CT: Yale University Press, 1977.

Naiman, Eric. "Shklovsky's Dog and Mulvey's Pleasure: The Secret Life of Defamiliarization." *Comparative Literature* 50, no. 4 (1998): 333–52.

Nekliudov, S. Iu. *Temy i variatsii*. Moscow: Indrik, 2016.

Nikolaev, Petr. *Akademicheskie shkoly v russkom literaturovedenii*. Moscow: Nauka, 1975.

Nöth, Winfried. *Handbook of Semiotics*. Bloomington: Indiana University Press, 1990.

Orlemanski, Julie. "Philology and the Turn Away from the Linguistic Turn." *Florilegium* 32 (2015): 157–81.

————. "Scales of Reading." *Exemplaria* 26, nos. 2–3 (2014): 215–33.

Oushakine [Ushakin], Serguei [Sergei]. "'Ne vzletevshie samolety mechty': O pokolenii formal'nogo metoda." In *Formal'nyi metod: Antologiia russkogo modernizma*. Vol. 1, *Sistemy*, edited by Serguei Oushakine, 9–60. Moscow: Kabinetnyi uchenyi, 2016.

Ovsianiko-Kulikovskii, D. N. "Lingvisticheskaia teoriia proiskhozhdeniia iskusstva i evoliutsii poezii." In *Voprosy teorii i psikhologii tvorchestva*, edited by B. A. Lezin, 1:21. 2nd ed. Kharkov: Mirnyi trud, 1911.

Parpulova, Lyubomira D., Charles E. Gribble, and James O. Bailey. "Obituary: Roman Jakobson (1896–1982)." *Journal of American Folklore* 97, no. 383 (1984): 57–60.

Pedersen, Holger. *The Discovery of Language: Linguistic Science in the Nineteenth Century*. Translated by John Spargo. Bloomington: Indiana University Press, 1959.

Percival, W. Keith. "Roman Jakobson and the Birth of Linguistic Structuralism." *Sign Systems Studies* 39, no. 1 (2011): 236–62.

Petrov, Petre. "Form." In *The Encyclopedia of Literary and Cultural Theory*. Vol. 1, *Literary Theory from 1900 to 1966: A–Z*, edited by Michael Ryan. Hoboken, NJ: Wiley, 2011. https://doi.org/10.1002/9781444337839.wbelctv1f003.

Pilshchikov, Igor. "Zasedanie moskovskogo lingvisticheskogo kruzhka 1 iuniia 1919 g. i zarozhdenie stikhovedcheskikh kontseptsii O. Brika, B. Tomashevskogo i R. Iakobsona." *Revue des Études Slaves* 88, nos. 1–2 (2017): 151–75. https://doi.org/10.4000/res.956.

Pilshchikov, Igor, and Andrei Ustinov. "Viktor Shklovskii v OPOIaZe i Moskovskom Lingvisticheskom Kruzhke (1919–1921 gg.)." *Wiener Slavistisches*

Jahrbuch, n.s., 6 (2018): 176–206. https://doi.org/10.13173/wienslavjahr.6 .2018.0176.

Pollock, Sheldon. "Future Philology? The Fate of a Soft Science in a Hard World." *Critical Inquiry* 35, no. 4 (Summer 2009): 931–61.

———. Introduction to *World Philology*, edited by Sheldon Pollock, Benjamin A. Elman, and Ku-ming Kevin Chang, 1–24. Cambridge, MA: Harvard University Press, 2015.

Pomerantseva, E. V. "Komissiia po narodnoi slovesnosti Obshchestva liubetelei estestvoznaniia antropologii i etnografii (1911–1926)." *Ocherki istorii russkoi etnografii folkloristiki i antropologii* 2 (1963): 197–206.

Pomorska, Krystyna. *Russian Formalism and Its Poetic Ambiance*. The Hague: Mouton, 1968.

Potebnia, Aleksandr. *Iz zapisok po teorii slovesnosti*. 1905. The Hague: Mouton, 1970.

Prague Linguistic Circle. "Theses Presented to the First Congress of Slavic Philologists in Prague, 1929." In Steiner, *Prague School*, 3–31.

Pratt, Mary Louise. *Toward a Speech Act Theory of Literary Discourse*. Bloomington: Indiana University Press, 1977.

Prins, Yopie. "What Is Historical Poetics?" *Modern Language Quarterly* 77, no. 1 (March 2016): 13–40.

Propp, Vladimir. *Morphology of the Folktale*. Translated by Laurence Scott. 2nd ed. Austin: University of Texas Press, 1968.

Pypin, A. N. *Istoriia russkoi etnografii*. St. Petersburg: Tip. M. M. Stasiulevicha, 1891.

Ram, Harsha. "Futurist Geographies: Uneven Modernities and the Struggle for Aesthetic Autonomy: Paris, Italy, Russia, 1909–1914." In *The Oxford Handbook of Global Modernisms*, edited by Mark Wollaeger and Matt Eatough, 313–40. New York: Oxford University Press, 2012.

Rancour-Laferriere, Daniel. "Why the Russian Formalists Had No Theory of the Literary Person." *Wiener Slawistischer Almanach* 31 (1992): 327–37.

Rasmussen, Mark David. "Introduction: New Formalisms?" In *Renaissance Literature and Its Formal Engagements*, edited by Mark Rasmussen, 1–14. New York: Palgrave, 2002.

Riffaterre, Michael. "Describing Poetic Structures: Two Approaches to Baudelaire's 'Les Chats.'" 1966. In *Reader-Response Criticism: From Formalism to Post-Structuralism*, edited by Jane Tompkins, 26–40. Baltimore, MD: Johns Hopkins University Press, 1980.

Robins, R. H. *A Short History of Linguistics*. 4th ed. London: Longman, 1997.

Rodowick, David. *Elegy for Theory*. Cambridge, MA: Harvard University Press, 2014.

Rogers, Everett. *Diffusion of Innovations*. New York: Free Press, 1962.

Rooney, Ellen. "Form and Contentment." *MLQ: Modern Language Quarterly* 61, no. 1 (March 2000): 17–40.

Rosenblatt, Allan, and James Thickstun. "A Study of the Concept of Psychic Energy." *International Journal of Psycho-Analysis* 51 (1970): 265–78.

Roth, Michael S. "Ebb Tide." Review of *Sublime Historical Experience*, by F. R. Ankersmit. *History and Theory* 46, no. 1 (February 2007): 66–73.

Sanders, Carol, ed. *The Cambridge Companion to Saussure*. Cambridge: Cambridge University Press, 2004.

———. "Structuralism." In *The Cambridge Encyclopedia of the Language Sciences*, edited by Patrick Colm Hogan, 811–13. Cambridge: Cambridge University Press, 2011.

Sandys, John Edwin. *A History of Classical Scholarship*. New York: Hafner, 1964.

Saussure, Ferdinand de. *Course in General Linguistics*. Translated by Roy Harris. LaSalle, IL: Open Court, 1986.

Saussy, Haun. *The Ethnography of Rhythm: Orality and Its Technologies*. New York: Fordham University Press, 2016.

Sayre, Robert, and Michael Löwy. "Figures of Romantic Anti-Capitalism." *New German Critique*, no. 32 (Spring–Summer 1984): 42–92.

Seifrid, Thomas. *The Word Made Self: Russian Writings on Language, 1860–1930*. Ithaca, NY: Cornell University Press, 2005.

Shakhmatov, Aleksei. *Ocherk sovremennogo russkogo literaturnogo iazyka*. 1913. 4th ed. Moscow: Gosudarstvennoe uchebno-pedagogicheskoe izdatel'stvo Narkomprosa RSFSR, 1941.

———. *Russkaia dialektologiia: Lektsii*. St. Petersburg: Fakul'tet filologii i iskusstv SPbGU, 2010.

Shannon, Claude E., and Warren Weaver. *The Mathematical Theory of Communication*. Urbana: University of Illinois Press, 1964.

Shapir, Maksim. "Iz istorii filologicheskoi nauki: Materialy po istorii lingvisticheskoi poetiki." *Izvestiia Akademii Nauk SSSR: Seriia literatury i iazyka* 50 (1991): 43–57.

Sheldon, Richard. "Viktor Borisovich Shklovsky: Literary Theory and Practice, 1914–1930." PhD diss., University of Michigan, 1966.

———. *Viktor Shklovsky: An International Bibliography of Works by and about Him*. Ann Arbor, MI: Ardis, 1977.

Sherwood, Richard. "Translation from *LEF* with an Introduction." *Screen* 12, no. 4 (Winter 1971): 25–58.

Shklovskii [Shklovsky], Viktor. "Aleksandr Veselovskii—Istorik i teoretik." *Oktiabr'* 12 (1947): 182.

———. "Art, as Device." Translated by Alexandra Berlina. *Poetics Today* 36, no. 3 (September 2015): 151–74.

————. *Gamburgskii schet: Stat'i—vospominaniia—esse (1914–1933)*. Edited by A. Iu. Galushkin and A. P. Chudakov. Moscow: Sovetskii pisatel', 1990.

————. "Izuchenie teorii poeticheskogo iazyka." *Zhizn' iskusstva*, no. 273 (October 21, 1919): 2.

————. *Knight's Move* [*Khod konia*]. 1923. Translated by Richard Sheldon. Champaign, IL: Dalkey Archive, 2005.

————. "K teorii komicheskogo." *Epopea* 3 (December 1922): 57–67.

————. "Lenin, kak dekanonizator." *LEF*, no. 1[5] (1924): 53–56.

————. *O teorii prozy*. Moscow: Federatsiia, 1929. Facsimile reprint, Ann Arbor, MI.: Ardis, 1985.

————. "Potebnia." In *Poetika: Sborniki po teorii poeticheskogo iazyka*. Vol. 3. Petrograd: OPOIaZ, 1919.

————. *A Sentimental Journey: Memoirs 1917–1922*. Translated by Richard Sheldon. Ithaca, NY: Cornell University Press, 1984.

————. "Siuzet u Dostoevskogo." *Letopis' Doma literatorov*, no. 4 (1921): 4–5.

————. *Third Factory*. 1926. Translated by Richard Sheldon. Ann Arbor, MI: Ardis, 1977.

————. *ZOO, or Letters Not about Love*. 1923. Translated by Richard Sheldon. Ithaca, NY: Cornell University Press, 1971.

Shklovskii, Vladimir. "Deklamatsiia Bloka." *Zhizn' iskusstva*, no. 18 (May 8, 1922): 2.

Shore, Daniel. *Cyberformalism: Histories of Linguistic Forms in the Digital Archive*. Baltimore, MD: Johns Hopkins University Press, 2018.

Silverstein, Michael. "Functions." *Journal of Linguistic Anthropology* 9, no. 1/2 (June 1999): 76–79.

Skalička, Vladimír. "Kodaňský strukturalismus a pražská škola." *Slovo a slovesnost* 10, no. 3 (1948): 135–42.

Sorokina, M. Iu. "Emigrant no. 1017: Roman Iakobson v moskovskikh arkhivakh." *Ezhegodnik Doma russkogo zarubezh'ia im. Aleksandra Solzhenitsyna* (2016): 73–92.

Sorokina, Svetlana. "Funktsional'no-struktural'nyi metod P. G. Bogatyreva." Introduction to Bogatyrev, *Funktsional'no-struktural'noe izuchenie fol'klora*, 5–72.

Speransky, Mikhail. *Russkaia ustnaia slovesnost'*. 1917. Reprint. The Hague: Mouton, 1969.

Steiner, Peter, ed. *The Prague School: Selected Writings, 1929–1946*. Austin: University of Texas Press, 1982.

————. "The Roots of Structuralist Esthetics." In Steiner, *Prague School*, 174–219.

————. *Russian Formalism: A Metapoetics*. Ithaca, NY: Cornell University Press, 1984.

———. "'Which Side Are You On, Boy?' Roman Iakobson v Prage mezhvoennogo perïoda." *Slovo.ru: Baltiiskii aktsent* 9, no. 1 (2018): 13–28. doi: 10.5922/2225-5346-2018-1-2.

Steiner, Peter, and Bronislava Volek. "Semiotics in Bohemia in the 19th and Early 20th Century." In *The Sign: Semiotics around the World*, edited by Richard Weld Bailey, Ladislav Matejka, and Peter Steiner, 206–26. Ann Arbor: Michigan Slavic Publications, 1978.

Stockwell, Peter. *Cognitive Poetics: An Introduction*. 2nd ed. London: Routledge, 2020.

Striedter, Jurij. *Literary Structure, Evolution, and Value: Russian Formalism and Czech Structuralism Reconsidered*. Cambridge, MA: Harvard University Press, 1989.

Svetlikova, Ilona. *Istoki russkogo formalizma: Traditsiia psikhologizma i formal'naia shkola*. Moscow: Novoe literaturnoe obozrenie, 2005.

Thompson, Ewa. "Formalism." In *Handbook of Russian Literature*, edited by Victor Terras, 151–54. New Haven, CT: Yale University Press, 1985.

Tihanov, Galin. *The Birth and Death of Literary Theory: Regimes of Relevance in Russia and Beyond*. Stanford, CA: Stanford University Press, 2019.

———. "The Politics of Estrangement: The Case of the Early Shklovsky." *Poetics Today* 26 (2005): 665–96.

———. "Why Did Modern Literary Theory Originate in Central and Eastern Europe? (And Why Is It Now Dead?)." *Common Knowledge* 10, no. 1 (2004): 61–81.

Timpanaro, Sebastiano. *The Genesis of Lachmann's Method*. Chicago: University of Chicago Press, 2005.

Todorov, Tzvetan. "Structuralism and Literature." In *Approaches to Poetics: Selected Papers from the English Institute*, edited by Seymour Chatman, 152–68. New York: Columbia University Press, 1973.

Toman, Jindřich. *Letters and Other Materials from the Moscow and Prague Linguistic Circles: 1912–1945*. Ann Arbor: Michigan Slavic Publications, 1994.

———. *The Magic of a Common Language: Jakobson, Mathesius, Trubetzkoy, and the Prague Linguistic Circle*. Cambridge, MA: MIT Press, 1995.

Tomashevskii, Boris. *Teoriia literatury: Poetika*. 1931. Moscow: Aspekt, 1996.

Toporkov, Andrei, ed. *Neizvestnye stranitsy russkoi fol'kloristiki*. Moscow: Indrik, 2015.

———. "Rannye stat'i V. B. Shklovskogo i uchebnik M. N. Speranskogo *Russkaia ustnaia slovesnost'*." *Izvestiia RAN: Seriia literatury i iazyka* 75, no. 2 (2016): 60–65.

———. "Russkie formalisty i izuchenie fol'klora: Folk'lornye temy na zasedaniiakh moskovskogo lingvisticheskogo kruzhka." In Toporkov, *Neizvestnye stranitsy*, 38–56.

————. *Teoriia mifa v russkoi filologicheskoi nauke XIX veka.* Moscow: Indrik, 1997.

Trotsky, Leon. *Literature and Revolution.* Ann Arbor: University of Michigan Press, 1960.

Trubetzkoy, N. S. *Principles of Phonology.* 1939. Translated by Christiane A. M. Baltaxe. Berkeley: University of California Press, 1969.

Turner, James. *Philology: The Forgotten Origins of the Modern Humanities.* Princeton, NJ: Princeton University Press, 2015.

Turner, Mark. *The Literary Mind: The Origins of Thought and Language.* New York: Oxford University Press, 1996.

Turner, R. Steven. "Historicism, *Kritik*, and the Prussian Professoriate." In *Philologie und Hermeneutik im 19. Jahrhundert II*, edited by Mayotte Bollack, Heinz Wismann, and Theodor Lindken, 450–77. Göttingen: Vandenhoeck & Ruprecht, 1983.

————. "The Prussian Universities and the Concept of Research." *Internationales Archiv für Sozialgeschichte der deutschen Literatur* 5 (1980): 68–93.

Tynianov, Yuri. "On Literary Evolution." In Matejka and Pomorska, *Readings in Russian Poetics*, 66–78.

————. *Permanent Evolution: Selected Essays on Literature, Theory and Film.* Translated and edited by Ainsley Morse and Philip Redko. Boston: Academic Studies, 2019.

————. *Poetika, Istoriia literatury, Kino.* Edited by E. A. Toddes, A. P. Chudakov, and M. O. Chudakova. Moscow: Nauka, 1977.

————. *The Problem of Verse Language.* Edited and translated by Michael Sosa and Brent Harvey. Ann Arbor, MI: Ardis, 1981.

Tynianov, Yuri, and Roman Jakobson. "Problems in the Study of Literature and Language." In Matejka and Pomorska, *Readings in Russian Poetics*, 79–81.

Ungar, Steven. "Saussure, Barthes and Structuralism." In Sanders, *Cambridge Companion to Saussure*, 157–73.

Van de Walle, Jürgen. "Roman Jakobson, Cybernetics and Information Theory: Critical Assessment." *Folia Linguistica Historica* 29 (2008): 87–124.

van Rees, C. J. "'Theory of Literature' Viewed as a Conception of Literature: On the Premises Underlying Wellek and Warren's Handbook." *Poetics* 13 (1984): 501–33.

Vassena, Raffaella. "K rekonstruktsii istorii i deiatel'nosti instituta zhivogo slova (1918–1924)." *Novoe literaturnoe obozrenie*, no. 4 (2007): 79–95.

Vatulescu, Cristina. "The Politics of Estrangement: Tracking Shklovsky's Device through Literary and Policing Practices." *Poetics Today* 27, no. 1 (Spring 2006): 35–66.

Velmezova, Ekaterina. "On the Early Stages of the Reception of the Saussurean Concept of *Semiology* in Russia." *Cahiers de l'ILSL*, no. 57 (2018): 165–78.

Verner, N., A. Bogdanov, V. Bazarov, A. Lunacharsky, and M. Gorky. *Ocherki filosofii kollektivizma*. St. Petersburg: Znanie, 1909.

Veselovsky [Veselovskii], Alexander [Aleksandr]. "From the Introduction to Historical Poetics: Questions and Answers." In Kliger and Maslov, *Persistent Forms*, 39–62.

———. *Istoricheskaia poetika*. Edited by V. M. Zhirmunskii. Leningrad: Khudozhestvennaia literatura, 1940.

———. *Izbrannoe: Istoricheskaia poetika*. Edited by I. O. Shaitanov. St. Petersburg: Universitetskaia kniga, 2011.

———. *Izbrannye stat'i*. Edited by M. P. Alekseev. Leningrad: Khudozhestvennaia literatura, 1939.

———. "On the Methods and Aims of Literary History as a Science." 1870. Translated by Harry Weber. *Yearbook of Comparative and General Literature* 16 (1967): 33–42.

Vinokur, Grigorii. *Filologicheskie issledovaniia: Lingvistika i poetika*. Edited by G. V. Stepanov and V. P. Neroznak. Moscow: Nauka, 1990.

———. "Moskovskii lingvisticheskii kruzhok." In *Nauchnye izvestiia: Akademicheskii tsentr Narkomprosa. Sbornik 2, Filosofiia, literatura, iskusstvo*, 289–90. Moscow: Gosudarstvennoe izdatel'stvo, 1922.

Voloshinov, Valentin. "Stilistika khudozhestvennoi rechi. Stat'ia tret'ia: Slovo i ego sotsial'naia funktsiia." *Literaturnaia ucheba* 5 (1930): 42–59.

Vysotskii, S. S. "Razvitie russkoi dialektologii v kontse XIX v. i v nachale XX v." In *Istoriia russkoi dialektologii*, edited by B. V. Gornung, 30–66. Moscow: Izd-vo Akademii nauk SSSR, 1961.

Wachtel, Andrew. *Remaining Relevant after Communism: The Role of the Writer in Eastern Europe*. Chicago: University of Chicago Press, 2006.

Wellek, René. *A History of Modern Criticism: 1750–1950*. Vol. 4, *The Later Nineteenth Century*. London: Jonathan Cape, 1966.

———. "The New Criticism: Pro and Contra." *Critical Inquiry* 4, no. 4 (Summer 1978): 611–24.

Wellek, René, and Austin Warren. *Theory of Literature*. 1949. New York: Harcourt, Brace, 1956.

Wolfram, Walt, and Natalie Schilling-Estes. "Dialectology and Linguistic Diffusion." In *The Handbook of Historical Linguistics*, edited by Brian Joseph and Richard Janda, 713–35. Malden, MA: Blackwell, 2003.

Wolfson, Susan J. "Reading for Form." *Modern Language Quarterly* 61 (2000): 1–16.

Wundt, Wilhelm. *Völkerpsychologie: Eine Untersuchung der Entwicklungsgesetze von Sprache, Mythus und Sitte*. Vol. 1, *Die Sprache*. Leipzig: Wilhelm Engelmann, 1904.

Zaidman, A. D. "Literaturnye studii 'Vsemirnoi literatury' i 'Doma iskusstv' (1919–1921 gody)." *Russkaia literatura* 1 (1973): 141–47.

Zalta, Edward N., ed. *The Stanford Encyclopedia of Philosophy.* Stanford, CA: Stanford University, Metaphysics Research Lab, 1997–. https://plato .stanford.edu/archives/.

Zhivov, Viktor. "Moskovsko-Tartuskaia semiotika: Ee dostizheniia i ee ogranicheniia." *Novoe literaturnoe obozrenie*, no. 98 (2009): 11–26.

Index

Page numbers in *italics* refer to figures.

Index

sion of information, 205–8, 210. *See also* language

Communist Party, 141–42

comparative historical method, 9–12, 14–15, 18, 25–26, 39, 42, 45–46

comparative philology: German origins of, 39–40, 42–43, 47, 54–55; vs. "great man" approach, 54–57, 69, 71; and historical poetics, 14–16; rationale for, 11–12, 68–69; and Romantic philosophy of language, 12–14, 16, 39; and rules or "laws," 10–12, 18; in Russian university system, 44–46, 50; and *slovesnost'* ("verbal art"), 5, 16–19

comparative poetics: and folkloristic orientation of, 67–68, 222; vs. "great man" approach, 54–57, 69, 71, 104; vs. hermeneutics, 74–75, 102, 221–22; vs. individual perception/production, 19, 29–32; outcome of, 102–4; tools of, 49–50

Conference of Anthropologists and Linguists, 209–10

consciousness: collective, 173–74, 185–87, 190, 197–99, 203; individual, 167, 173, 186, 203–4; linguistic, 175, 179; national, 45, 110; and representations, 23, 200–202; social, 267n33

conservatism, 30, 117, 147, 169, 173–74, 219

Constitutional Democratic (Kadet) Party, 32

contiguity, 23, 30, 61, 111–13, 117–20, 125, 206

conventionality (*uslovnost'*), 96, 144, 155

Copenhagen structuralism, 212–15

craftsmanship, 96–98, 100–104, 107–8

creativity: avant-garde ideology of, 162, 164–66, 170–72; and language politics, 167–72, 176–77, 224; "mass," 82, 103, 106; of the proletariat, 80–83; socially engaged, 103–4, 106, 108–9; and technique, 98–100. *See also* collective creativity; freedom; individual creativity; novelty

Culler, Jonathan, 213–14

cultural centers model: and cities/locales, 158, 161, 172, 174; and discourse under Civil War, 175, 177–79; and gravitation of speakers, 156–59, 169, 172, 178; and Khlebnikov, 156–57, 162, 165–67, 171–73; and migrant workers (*otkhodnik*), 160–61, 168; and Nezval, 172–73; and Pushkin, 152, 156–57, 162, 171. *See also* dialectology

cybernetics, 205–6, 209–11, 214

Czech structuralism: and Gestalt psychology, 181–84, 196–97, 199, 202–3; vs. post–World War II structuralism, 3, 204, 208, 214–16; reception of, 35, 184, 220; and semiotics, 46, 186, 194–98, 203; and social understanding of language, 184–85, 198; waves of scholarship on, 6–8. *See also* Prague Linguistic Circle; structuralism

Dada, 86

Dal, Vladimir, 16, 65, 238n50

dance, 33, 88–89, 103, 139, 142

Davies, Anna Morpurgo, 11 quoted, 24

Davydov, I. I., 47

"deceleration" (*zaderzhanie*), 62, 67, 121–22, 126, 132–33, 138–39, 143, 258n120

declamation, 73, 81, 85–87, 90

deductive study, 183–84, 192, 204

defamiliarization (*ostranenie*): and associationism, 111, 119, 121–22, 139–40, 201; centrality of as concept, 5, 59, 125; and disassociation, 29–30, 93; erotic, 135–37; and innovation, 25–27; and narrative structure, 131–33, 145; non-linguistic, 151; and perception/consciousness, 138, 167

Depretto, Catherine, 63

Derrida, Jacques, 71, 209, 214

deterioration/devolution, 47–48

determinism, 30, 108, 138, 144, 234

Deumert, Ana, 13–14

device (*priem*): as agential, 71, 144; for audience engagement, 92–95, 108; baring of, 29, 99, 167; and error/false solution, 132–33, 136–37, 142–43; motifs as, 121–22, 127–29; need to study, 59, 62, 103–4; Oedipal myth as, 135–36, 138; and psychological parallelism, 114, 119–22, 138, 140, 142; repetition of, 121–22, 126, 129–30, 139; and stock characters, 178–79; tradition as reservoir of, 12, 27, 29–31, 70, 107, 154–55, 223–24. *See also* defamiliarization; psychological parallelism

Index

Fish, Stanley, 35
Fitzpatrick, Sheila, 105–6, 161
Fizer, John, 52
folk costume, 149, 196–98
folk festivals/rituals, 69, 87, 160, 195–97
folklore: as "art," 77–78, 178; and collecting
    expeditions, 55, 65, 68, 79, 87, 101, 135,
    160, 195, 256n93; as collective creativity,
    75–80, 82–83, 102–3; and devolution-
    ary premise, 47–48; and dialectology,
    148–49, 160; erotic, 135–37, 142–43,
    258n120; and function of rituals, 195–97;
    as "fund"/reservoir, 54–57, 67–68, 100–
    104, 106–7, 129; and hermeneutics, 74–
    75, 77–78, 99; and modernist works, 28,
    69, 79–81, 163–64; parallelism in, 113–
    17, 126, 131; poetic language of, 64–66,
    155; and Russian performer studies, 76–
    78, 96, 99; and spoken language, 43, 45–
    46, 56; and tradition (predanie), 15–16,
    56, 100–101; urban, 176, 178; and writ-
    ten literature, 16–17, 56, 70, 77–80, 83–
    84, 95–96, 132, 191, 222. See also Com-
    mission for Folklore Study
folk song, 55–56, 112, 127–28, 131, 178
folktales (skazki): collecting of, 45, 55–56,
    76, 87, 160; creativity and, 15–16, 46,
    82–83, 99–100, 102; vs. oral epics, 76–
    77, 100; Shklovsky's study of, 61, 67, 97,
    104, 126, 129, 131–32, 135
folk theater, 69, 78–79, 85, 87, 149
form: and cognitive principles, 8, 21–22; as
    creating its own content, 126; persistence
    of, 203–4; in philological paradigm, 221–
    23; "return to," 3, 217–24, 227; for struc-
    turalists, 180, 182
formulas/rumors, 15, 174, 178–79
Fortunatov, Filipp, 188
Foucault, Michel, 71
Frazier, James, 111, 196
freedom: and information, 205; lack of, 96,
    104, 143–45; and language, 14–15, 47,
    168; modernists on, 27–28; of motifs,
    129; and tradition, 100, 112
French structuralism: on authorship, 71,
    91; as "cousin" to Russian Formalism,
    7; vs. interwar structuralism, 204, 208,
    214–16, 234; and "meaning," 91, 208–
    15; perceived centrality of, 3, 180, 214.
    See also structuralism

Freud, Sigmund: and associationism, 23;
    and instincts, 120, 134, 136–39, 138,
    144, 204; and Oedipal myth, 135–36,
    138; and Shklovsky, 111, 134–40, 204
"function": aesthetic, 34, 150, 193, 198;
    communicative, 124–25, 194; of dis-
    tinctiveness, 206–8, 212; Formalists on,
    192–95, 200; as mathematical depen-
    dence, 214; poetic, 124–25, 127, 193; as
    popular meaning, 195–97; Prague school
    on, 194–200, 203, 214–15; Trubets-
    koi on, 192, 195, 199–200; Tynianov on,
    199–200
"fund," 100–102, 106–7, 184–85, 223–24
Futurism: and avant-garde ideology, 162,
    164–66, 170–72; "evenings" of, 84–85;
    and Formalists, 28, 69, 88–89, 95, 119,
    162–63; Russian vs. Italian, 156, 166;
    and transrational poetry, 27, 84, 88–89,
    162–63. See also Khlebnikov, Velimir

Geeraerts, Dirk, 228–29
Geoghegan, Bernard, 205–6, 209
Gestalt psychology, 181–84, 196–97, 199,
    202–3
gestures, 86–92
Gil'ferding, Alexander, 76
Ginzburg, Lydia, 34
Glants, Tomash, 149
glossematics, 213–14
glossolalia, 89
Gogol, Nikolai, 62–64, 90–92, 95, 126, 148
Gordlevsky, V. A., 148
Gorky, Maxim, 32, 46, 80–83, 103, 140,
    251n100
Gornfel'd, A. G., 49
Gornung, Boris, 149, 163–64, 170–71,
    259n13, 265n143
Graff, Gerald, 44
Graffi, Giorgio, 207, 233–34
grammatical structures, 9–10, 42–43, 123–
    25, 150, 185, 207–9, 212
gravitation, 126–27, 156–59, 169, 172, 178
"great man" approach, 54–57, 69, 71, 74,
    80, 104
Grimm, Jacob, 9–12, 11, 39, 42–46, 48
Grimm, Wilhelm (brother of Jacob), 45
Grot, Iakov, 51
grotesque, 91
Gumilev, Nikolai, 87

Index

politics, 19, 167–71, 176–77; legacy of,
4, 57–59, 64; and Lévi-Strauss, 209–12;
"Linguistics and Poetics," 173, 194; and
MDC, 156, 158–60, 187; at MIT, 162,
206, 211; and MLC leadership, 58, 66,
148–49; and MLC meetings/debates,
122, 124, 146, 150–57, 159, 164, 167–71,
178–79, 259n13; and move to Czechoslovakia, 63, 146, 149; "The Newest Russian Poetry," 28–30, 33–34, 59, 119, 152,
156–57, 165, 171, 187, 193; and PLC
founding, 188–90; on poetic language/
function, 36, 59, 61, 119, 122, 124–25,
127, 133, 145; "Problems in the Study
of Literature and Language," 26, 189–
91; and psychological parallelism, 111,
113, 119–20, 122–27, 133, 150; *Remarks
on the Phonological Evolution of Russian*, 187–89; on rhetoric, 91–92; and
Shklovsky, 67, 141, 151, 184; on "Sorrow-
Misfortune," 122–24; and structuralist
methodological revolution, 10, 189–92,
203, 214; and structuralist phonology,
26, 148–49, 159, 181–82, 187–88, 192,
200, 209; theoretical trajectory of, 5, 108,
152–54, 159, 172–74, 180, 184, 187–88,
194, 206–7; training of, 156, 160, 179,
239n72, 261n49; and Tynianov, 26, 33,
63, 110, 189–91
Jakovlev, Nikolai, 148, 179, 262n77
Jakubinsky, Lev, 36, 60, 85, 92–93, 151,
193–95, 200, 260n33
James, William, 23, 29, 88, 90, 117
Jameson, Fredric, 6–7, 181, 215
Jews, 178–79
jokes, 102, 129–32, 160, 177–78
Joseph, John, 185
Jousse, Marcel, 101

Kalinin, Ilya, 8, 99, 108, 135
Kant, Immanuel, 50, 68, 172, 217, 225–26
Karcevski, Serge (Sergei Kartsevskii), 187,
189
Kazansky, Boris, 57, 78
Kenigsberg, Maksim, 176, 259n13
Kerzhentsev, Platon, 82
Khlebnikov, Velimir: as cultural center,
156–57, 162, 165–67, 171–73; Jakobson
on, 28–30, 33–34, 152–53, 163, 171–72,
187; Tynianov on, 231

Khmelnitskaia, Tamara, 73
Khodasevich, Valentina, 141
Khodasevich, Vladislav, 87
Kim, Alan, 201–2
kinship, 7, 210–11, 218
Kiparsky, Paul, 11
Kiukhelbeker, Vilgelm, 63, 104
Kliger, Ilya, 8, 12, 32, 34, 230–31
Koffka, Kurt, 181, 196
koiné, 154–55, 158. *See also* tradition
Konovalov, D. G., 89
Korsh, Fedor, 148, 155, 261n49
Kotkin, Stephen, 86, 174
Krivopolenova, Maria, 122
Kruchenykh, Aleksei, 27–28, 33–34, 119
Krushevsky, Nikolai (Mikołaj Kruszewski),
23–24, 118
Kuhn, Thomas, 38
Kushner, Boris, 167–70, 176, 259n13,
265n143

Labov, William, 35
Lacan, Jacques, 209, 211, 214
Lachmann, Karl, 9, 40–41, 44, 51
language: as agential, 71, 168; and associationism, 21–24, 26, 30, 112–13, 118–19;
common/universal, 124–25, 169–72;
as creative act, 13–14, 19, 25; vs. dialect, 157–58; and dialogue, 72–73, 103,
107–8, 141–44, 153, 193–94; functions
of, 193–95; and individual experiences,
146–47, 153; as a machine, 207–8, 210,
212; of the masses, 86–87, 171; modernists on, 27–28, 84, 171–72; and nation,
13, 216; as object of study, 164–66; "oppositional," 177; and oral speech, 14, 17,
46–48, 56, 70, 72–73, 95, 192, 207, 222;
and rhetorical analysis, 91–92, 174; Romantic philosophy of, 5, 12–14, 16, 20–
21, 45–46, 168, 170; social construct of,
112, 153–54, 185, 214–15, 233–34; and
Völkerpsychologie, 49–51, 68, 87–89,
226. *See also* communication; Humboldt,
Wilhelm von; poetic language; Saussure,
Ferdinand de
language politics, 167–72, 176–77, 216, 224
langue (social side of language), 7, 153,
174, 184–86, 190–91, 193, 233–34; vs.
predanie, 223; under information theory,
206–8

Index

and language politics, 19, 167–72, 176–77, 224; and linguistic approach, 5, 36, 150–51, 191, 193; meetings of, 19, 29, 147–52, 156–57, 164, 174–79; membership of, 148–50, 163, 171, 187, 262n77, 263n101, 265n143; and OPOIAZ, 146, 149–51, 191; and political authorities, 150, 169–70, 175–76. *See also* dialectology; Russian Formalism

Moscow University, 9, 31, 45, 49, 58, 65–66, 148

motifs, 15, 29, 48, 77, 121, 127, 129, 132, 150, 172, 178

Mukařovský, Jan, 186, 189, 194–95, 197–200, 202–3, 214–15

mystery novels, 132, 135, 137–38

mythology, 9–10, 39, 43–46, 56–57, 82–83, 96, 211

Nagel, Ernest, 43

Narkompros, 69, 85, 97, 150, 170, 175–76

narod (folk), 16–17, 45–46, 54–57, 65, 74–76, 83, 164, 178. *See also* folklore

narrative: and principles of plot construction, 61, 126, 128–34, *131*, 136; Shklovsky's theory of, 97–99, 102, 120, 132, 138–39, 150. *See also* oral narratives

nationalism and national identity: Romanticism and, 13, 16–17, 44, 64–65, 69, 110, 216; in Russian university system, 44–46; and *slovesnost'*, 16–17, 65, 68–69

Nekliudov, Sergei, 75, 222

Neogrammarian linguistics, 153–54, 159–60, 167, 181, 184, 187–89, 264n102

neologisms, 28, 156, 165, 170–71, 177, 263n91

New Criticism, 3, 34, 217–23, 227

new formalism, 3, 217–23, 227

new historicism, 217–18

New Literary History, 35

Nezval, Vítězslav, 172–73

Nicholas I, 44

1905 Revolution, 32, 76

non-equivalence, 127, 129–31, 133, 145

novelty, 26–29, 118–19, 122, 140, 177

Novyi LEF, 190

October Revolution, 31, 75, 170, 174

Oedipal myth, 135–36, 138

Onchukov, Nikolai, 76–77, 82, 96, 135, 256n93

OPOIAZ (Society for the Study of Poetic Language): on authorship, 5, 19, 71, 73, 83, 103–4, 109, 224; fervor of, 20; and Institute of the Living Word, 85–87, 90, 148; membership of, 58, 63, 68, 85, 87, 171–72, 263n101, 265n143; and MLC, 146, 149–51, 191; and poetic language, 36, 94–95, 150–52; publications of, 19, 92–93, 116, 123, 147, 151, 174, 193, 256n93; and "sound gesture," 87–91

oral epics (*byliny*): about Ilya Muromets, 130–31, *131*, 138; vs. folktales, 76–77, 100; Mayakovsky's, 79–81; Serbian, 113; "Sorrow-Misfortune," 122–24; study of, 28, 45, 57, 67, 87, 122, 132

oral formulaic theory, 101

oral narratives (*skaz*), 28, 35, 73, 174

oral traditions, 15, 75, 84–86, 101–2, 154–55, 174, 178–79

orientation (*ustanovka*), 25, 29–30, 94–95

Orlemanski, Julie, 3, 227

Osthoff, Hermann, 159

ostranenie. *See* defamiliarization

Ovsianiko-Kulikovsky, Dmitry, 17–18

parallelism. *See* psychological parallelism

parole (speaking), 7, 190–91, 193, 233–34

Parry, Milman, 101

Paul, Hermann, 159

Paulhan, Jean, 101

peasantry: and avant-garde art, 164–65; and Bogatyrev on culture of, 195, 197–98; vs. intelligentsia, 70, 74, 77–78; and migrant work in cities, 160–61, 168; and Socialist Revolutionary Party, 105, 107

Perets, V. N., 135

performance: authorship as, 70–73, 108–9, 224; and poetry/literary readings, 84–87, 90, 122; in revolutionary movements, 86, 92–93; and Russian performer studies, 76–78, 96, 99; and "sound gesture," 87–91

Peterson, M. N., 176, 259n13

Petrograd State Institute of Art History, 140

Petrov, Petre, 222

305

Index

philological paradigm: and disciplinary
autonomy, 33–34; and function of language, 193–95; and history vs. perception of verbal art, 25–32, 51; and
language-extrinsic explanatory logic, 4,
34–36, 146–47, 185, 220–21; as model
for today, 225–32; motivating questions
of, 38, 51, 57, 59–61, 65; on poetic language, 51–54, 150; and Romantic philosophy of language, 12–16, 21; and structuralist revolution, 189–92; and theory of
verbal art, 5, 14, 17–19, 46, 121. *See also*
comparative historical method; comparative philology; *slovesnost'*
philology: classical, 39–44, 46–48, 51, 54–
55, 58, 78, 242n33; defined, 9, 38; vs. disciplinarity, 224–25, 229–30; and "history
of literature," 50–51; "return to," 224–
31. *See also* comparative philology
phonetics, 86–87, 159, 183–85, 187, 190,
193
phonograph, 86–87, 101
phonology: and binary features, 206–9,
211, 215; and dialectology, 158, 160; his-
torical/structuralist, 26, 148–49, 159,
181–82, 187–88, 192, 200, 209, 212; vs.
phonetics, 184–85, 187, 190; vs. semantics, 11–12
physiology, 86, 88–91, 139, 177
Piaget, Jean, 211
Piast, Vladimir, 87, 245n102
Pil'shchikov, Igor, 149, 235n4
PLC. *See* Prague Linguistic Circle (PLC)
plots: circular or stepped construction of,
61, 126, 128–34, *131*, 136–44; forward
momentum of, 134–35; improvisation
on, 102; and "pressure," 133–34, 136–
39, 143; and *siuzhet* vs. *fabula*, 67–68,
125–26; Veselovsky's study of, 16, 49, 57,
59, 67; worldwide recurrence of, 16, 38,
59, 64. *See also* device
poeticity, 25–27, 30, 36, 165, 167
poetic language: and association of images,
112–15, 117–18, 127, 150; autonomy of,
36, 150–52; vs. everyday/practical language, 27–28, 30–31, 34–36, 60–61,
93–95, 119, 151–52, 200–201; evolution of, 154–55, 157, 171–72; parallelism and, 122, 133, 144–45; and the ques-

tion of "What is poetry?," 38, 51–54, 57,
59–62, 65–66; and Shklovsky's "A1, A,"
61, 121, 131, 138; social importance of,
171–74; and sonic repetitions, 28, 58, 60;
as universal language, 124–25. *See also*
language
poetics: and cognition/psychology, 24–26,
228–30; conceptualized, 14, 18–19, 54,
62, 64; vs. hermeneutics, 73–75, 83–
84; and rhetorical analysis, 91–93, 174;
and "sound gesture," 87–91; and the
sound of words/language, 84–87, 89; and
"structure" of poem, 221. *See also* historical poetics
Polivanov, Evgeny, 87
Pollock, Sheldon, 9, 225
Pomorska, Krystyna, 78, 91, 162
populism, 76, 104–5, 107
portmanteaus, 170, 177
Porzhezinsky, Viktor, 259n12
positivism, 50, 76, 149, 153, 159, 173, 180,
184, 203, 225–26
post-structuralism, 3–5, 71, 73, 91, 209,
215, 227, 234
Potebnia, Alexander: on authorship, 75;
and folklore studies, 55–57, 112; legacy
of, 5, 9, 48; on poetic language/thought,
51–53, 59–61, 125, 127, 151, 228; Russian Formalists and, 19, 28, 37–39, 66,
69, 151, 154; on speech as creative act,
17–18, 47, 72; and *Völkerpsychologie*,
49–51, 226
Prague Linguistic Circle (PLC): and "function," 194–99, 214; and Gestalt psychol-
ogy/holism, 183–84, 196–97, 199, 202–
3; introduced, 4–5; membership of, 149,
189, 194; and semiotics, 46, 186, 194–97,
203; and structural functionalism, 188–
89, 194–99; "Theses" and manifestos of,
180, 188–92. *See also* Czech structuralism
Pratt, Mary Louise, 35–36, 220
pressure (*davlenie*), 133–34, 136–39,
143–45
Priestley, Joseph, 117
Prins, Yopie, 220, 223
print industry, 84–85, 147–48
proletariat, 65, 79–83, 99, 103–6, 164,
169–71

306

Index

Proletkult, 80–83, 85, 97, 102, 106, 157
pronunciation, *11*, 85, 87, 160–61, 173, 188
Propp, Vladimir, 16, 48, 127, 129
proverbs (*poslovitsy*), 28, 55, 65, 72, 75, 160
psychoanalytic theory, 111, 134–35, 211, 214
psychological parallelism: and art's effect on mind, 117–20; Brik and, 60, 113, 116–17, 119, 121; and circular or stepped plot construction, 61, 126, 128–34, *131*, 136–44; vs. formal parallelism, 114–17, 123, 126–28, 130, 138, 141–42, 223; vs. grammatical parallelism, 123–25, 150; Jakobson and, 113, 119, 122–25; and recurring devices, 120–22, 138, 145; Shklovsky and, 61, 119, 121–22, 126–29, 132, 136, 138–39, 142–43, 201; Tynianov and, 63–64, 120–22, 124, 200; Veselovsky and, 60, 112–17, 126–28, 138
psychologism: and drives/instincts, 120, 134, 136–39, 143–44; Gestalt, 181–84, 196–97, 199, 202–3; and Herbart's "representations," 23–24, 50, 120, 200–203; in humanities, 225–26; and origins of literary devices, 65, 140; and poetic vs. prosaic thinking, 51–54, 57, 150, 228–29; and pressure, 133–34, 136–39, 143; Russian Formalism and, 8, 21–26, 29–30, 36, 60–61, 110–11, 114–18, 223; vs. sociology, 86, 185–86; and speech activity, 193–94; *Völkerpsychologie*, 49–51, 68, 87–89, 226. *See also* associationism
puns, 69, 104, 116–18, 129, 137
Pushkin, Alexander: as cultural center, 152, 156–57, 162, 171; Formalists on, 63, 93, 121, 126, 200–201; mentioned as canonical author, 21, 28, 51, 64, 70, 94, 104, 165
Pypin, Aleksandr, 51

Quintilian, 91

Ragozin, S. I., 148
Rancour-Laferriere, Daniel, 71
Rask, Rasmus, 9–10, 42, 45, 47
Rasmussen, Mark, 222
reconstruction, 11, 39–41, 47–48, 90, 159, 195

Remizov, Aleksei, 69
repetition: absence of, 77; of devices, 120–22, 126, 129–30, 139; expectation of, 145; of formulas/rumors, 15, 174, 178–79; grammatical, 123–24; perception of, 124, 131, 133; triadic, 15, 61, 129, 131. *See also* sound repetitions
Repin, Ilya, 164
revolutionary period: and collective vs. individual, 19, 70, 75, 78–81; and language politics, 167–72, 176–77, 224; and modernization of culture, 80–83, 99, 160–61, 166; and oral speech, 72–73, 84–86, 92–93, 103, 174; and populism, 76, 104–5, 107; and Russian Formalism's fervor, 19–21, 31–32, 92–93, 109, 118–19, 146–47, 149–50, 164
rhetoric, 27, 33–34, 73, 85–86, 92, 174
rhymes, 28, 61, 115, 122, 156, 163–64, 201, 223–24
rhythm, 76, 90, 92, 100–101, 115–16, 120, 130, 141, 200
Ribot, Théodule, 117
Richert, Charles, 117
Rickert, Heinrich, 225
riddles (*zagadki*): circular construction of, 129–34, 137–38, 142–44; and disassociation, 116–18; erotic/"catch," 135–37, 142–44; research interest in, 28, 55, 67, 69, 104, 160
Riffaterre, Michael, 124
Rimbaud, Arthur, 166
Ritschl, Friedrich Wilhelm, 9, 44, 48
Robins, R. H., 11, 13, 159–60, 264n102
Rockefeller Foundation, 206, 209
Rodowick, David, 19
Rogers, Everett, 158
Romanticism: and anticapitalism, 108; and folklore/collectivity, 16, 39, 45–46, 56, 70, 76, 78, 82–84, 99, 103; language philosophies of, 5, 12–14, 16, 20–21, 45–46, 168, 170; and nation, 13, 16–17, 44, 64–65, 69, 110, 216
Rooney, Ellen, 218
Rosenblith, Walter, 206
Roth, Michael, 3–4
Rozanov, Vasily, 132
Rozhdestvensky, Vsevolod, 87
rumors, 174, 178–79

Index

85, 87, 92, 149, 151, 174, 245n102; on perception of art, 20–31, 88, 107–8, 131–32, 138, 140; "Plot Construction," 59, 61, 67, 104–5, 121–22, 126–27, 135; "Plot in Dostoevsky," 129–30, 133; on Potebnia and Veselovsky, 16, 37, 48, 59–60, 66–68; and psychological parallelism, 5, 113, 119–22, 126–29, 136, 138–39, 142; "Resurrection of the Word," 107, 162; *Sentimental Journey*, 67, 107, 111, 140; and "sound gesture," 87–90; on stepped or circular construction, 61, 126, 129–34, *131*, 136–39, 141–45; on technique, 98–100, 103, 107; *Theory of Prose*, 67, 97, 129, 132–33, 136–38, 140; *ZOO*, 19, 98, 100, 140–44, 179

Shpet, Gustav, 149, 265n143

Sievers, Edward, 87

Silverstein, Michael, 193

similarity. *See* associationism

siuzhet, 67–68, 125–27, 129

Skalička, Vladimír, 214–16

skaz. *See* oral narratives

Skoropadsky, Pavlo, 175

slovesnost' (verbal art): boundaries of, 59–60, 62; conceptualized, 16–18, 65, 226; encompassing oral and written forms, 70, 75, 84, 191–92; history vs. perception of, 25–32, 51; and living word, 14, 72–73; national basis of, 65, 68–69; theory of, 5, 14, 17–19, 46, 121; and "verbal mass," 29, 162, 166

slovo, 238n50

Socialist Revolutionary Party, 31, 59, 67, 95, 105–7, 141

social thought, 12, 32, 34, 112–14

Society for the Study of Poetic Language. *See* OPOIAZ

Society of Devotees of Natural Science, Anthropology, and Ethnography, 65, 148

Sokolov, Boris, 76, 78, 82, 96, 102

Sokolov, Yuri (brother of Boris), 76, 78, 82, 96, 102, 148, 178, 259n13

Sologub, Fedor, 87

Sophocles, 135–36

Sorokina, Marina, 175–76

Sorokina, Svetlana, 197

"Sorrow-Misfortune," 122–24

sound gesture (*zvukovoi zhest*), 87–91

"sounding verse," 85, 87

sound recording technologies, 84–87, 101

sound repetitions, 28, 58, 60–61, 101, 115–17, 120–22, 156, 223

sound shifts, 10–12, *11*, 24, 43, 159–60, 167

Speransky, Mikhail, 67, 96

Spielhagen, Friedrich, 110

Stammbaumtheorie, 47–48

State Academy for the Scientific Study of Art, 149

State Psychoanalytic Institute, 134

Steiner, Peter, 6–8, 27, 180, 203

Steinthal, Heymann (Chajim), 13, 23–24, 29, 49–51, 68, 88, 226

"stepped construction," 61, 126, 129–33, *131*, 138–39, 141–44

Sterne, Laurence, 62, 97–98, 126, 132

stock characters, 178–79

Stockwell, Peter, 228–29

St. Petersburg University, 31, 63, 66, 193

Striedter, Jurij, 6–7, 180, 239n77

Stroganov, S. G., 45

structural functionalism, 188–89, 194–99

structuralism: Copenhagen branch of, 212–15; emergence of, 5–6, 181, 189–92; and "function," 192, 194; information theory and, 206–8, 210, 212; interwar vs. post–World War II, 204, 208, 214–16; Jakobson and, 59, 153–54, 172–74, 189–92; and language-intrinsic explanatory logic, 4, 34–36, 159; and reductive views of Russian Formalism, 3, 5–7, 126, 231; and social construct of language, 153–54, 185, 198, 233–34; and systemic understanding of language, 23–24, 26, 33–34, 181, 183–86, 233–34; waning of, 4, 227. *See also* Czech structuralism; French structuralism

structure, conceptualized, 196

Štúr, Ľudovít, 13, 216

substantive analogy, 43, 46

superstructuralism, 186, 234

Sveshnikov, P. P., 148

Svetlikova, Ilona, 6, 8, 21–22, 29, 58, 60, 63, 111, 117, 120, 200–203

Symbolism, 27–28, 35, 37, 65, 87, 89

synonyms, 28, 123, 125–26, 156

syntax, 28, 123–24, 155–56, 165, 212

Index

systems: vs. associationism, 23–24, 26; as autonomous, 33–34; and cybernetics/information theory, 205–8, 210–11, 214; as dynamic, 200–203, 221–22; and "holism," 181–83, 196–99, 204, 215; kinship, 7, 210–11, 218; literary evolution and, 25–26, 110, 203; literature as, 64, 199–200, 202–3; phonemic/phonological, 159, 173–74, 183–84, 188, 192, 211; Saussurean, 181, 183–90, 192, 208, 233; semantic series, 119–21, 197–98, 200

tale studies, 76–78
tautology, 52, 61, 115, 125, 130, 145
technique (*tekhnika*), 98–100, 103, 107
telegraphs, 170
teleology, 3, 205
textual criticism, 40–41, 44, 47–48, 50–51
Thanatos, 139, 144
theater: Eisenstein on, 89–90, 119; folk, 69, 78–79, 85, 87, 149; modernist, 81, 84, 96–97; and technique, 99; workers', 80, 97. *See also* drama/dramatic forms; performance
Tihanov, Galin, 6, 8, 20–21, 64
Tikhonravov, Nikolai, 51
Todorov, Tzvetan, 74
Tolstoy, Leo, 27, 61–62, 93, 97, 104, 108, 132–33, 136
Toman, Jindřich, 155–56, 180, 184
Tomashevsky, Boris, 58, 62, 87, 126, 129, 259n13
Toporkov, Andrei, 45, 49, 67–68
tradition (*predanie*): and author as craftsman, 96–98, 100–104, 107–8; and innovation, 104, 160–61; Potebnia on, 56, 75, 112; as reservoir of devices, 12, 27, 29–31, 70, 154–55, 223; as set of limitations, 77–78; Veselovsky on, 15–16, 29, 54, 110, 112–13, 154–55
translation, 97, 134; machine, 207–8, 210, 212
Translators' Studio, 140
"transrational" poetry (*zaum*), 27, 84, 88–89, 162–63
Trediakovsky, Vasily, 66
Tretiakov, Sergei, 89–91
Triolet, Elsa, 141–43
Trnka, Bohumil, 189
tropes, 27, 30, 92, 119, 152, 154

Trotsky, Leon, 105, 170–71, 177
Trubetskoi, Nikolai, 148–49, 165, 183–85, 188–89, 192, 195, 199–200
Trudgill, Peter, 158
Tulov, M. A., 47
Turner, James, 38, 46, 224–25
Turner, Mark, 228–29
Turner, R. Steven, 40
Tylor, Edward Burnett, 114
Tynianov, Yuri: and corpus studied, 62, 64–65, 104; and dynamic form, 25–26, 200–203, 221–22; era/politics of, 31–32, 34, 108; influences on, 48, 55, 63, 150; and Jakobson, 26, 33, 63, 110, 189–91; on Lenin's language, 92–93; on literary history (as living process), 73, 110, 190–91, 199–203, 231; "The Ode as an Oratorical Genre," 87, 92, 94–95; "On Literary Evolution," 25–26, 199–200; at OPOIAZ, 63, 85, 87, 92; *The Problem of Verse Language*, 63, 120–21, 200; "Problems in the Study of Literature and Language," 26, 189–91; and psychological parallelism, 63–64, 120–22, 124, 200; on speech orientation, 94–95; and structuralist terminology, 192, 199–200; verse theory of, 111, 120–21, 150

Ukraine, 55–56, 112, 175
UNESCO, 211
universal communicative model, 194
Ushakov, Dmitry, 176, 259n12, 259n15
utopian aspirations, 86–87, 106, 118, 124–25, 164–65
Uvarov, Sergei, 44

Van de Walle, Jürgen, 204–6, 209–10
vanguardism, 82, 104–7
Vasil'ev, N. V., 148, 259n15
Vassena, Rafaella, 86–87
Vengerov, Semen, 51, 63, 202–3
verbal art. *See slovesnost'*
Verner, Karl, 159
verse theory, 120–21, 150, 155
Veselovsky, Alexander: and comparative-historical method, 9–10, 54–57; and folklore studies, 55–57, 66, 129; and historical poetics, 8, 12, 14–16, 33, 57, 62, 204, 220, 229–30; on individual creativity, 49, 75, 110; legacy of, 5, 48,

310